STANDARD LOAN

Renew Books on PHONE-it: 01443 654456
Help Desk: 01443 482625
Media Services Reception: 01443 482610

Books are to be returned on or before the last date below

Securing Web Services with WS-Security

Demystifying WS-Security, WS-Policy, SAML, XML Signature, and XML Encryption

Jothy Rosenberg
David L. Remy

Sams Publishing, 800 East 96th Street, Indianapolis, Indiana 46240

Securing Web Services with WS-Security

International Standard Book Number: 0-672-32651-5

Library of Congress Catalog Card Number: 2003099324

Printed in the United States of America

First Printing: May 2004

07   06   05   4   3   2

Trademarks

All terms mentioned in this book that are known to be trademarks or service marks have been appropriately capitalized. Sams Publishing cannot attest to the accuracy of this information. Use of a term in this book should not be regarded as affecting the validity of any trademark or service mark.

Warning and Disclaimer

Every effort has been made to make this book as complete and as accurate as possible, but no warranty or fitness is implied. The information provided is on an "as is" basis. The authors and the publisher shall have neither liability nor responsibility to any person or entity with respect to any loss or damages arising from the information contained in this book.

Bulk Sales

Sams Publishing offers excellent discounts on this book when ordered in quantity for bulk purchases or special sales. For more information, please contact

U.S. Corporate and Government Sales
1-800-382-3419
corpsales@pearsontechgroup.com

For sales outside the U.S., please contact

International Sales
international@pearsoned.com

Associate Publisher
Michael Stephens

Acquisitions Editor
Todd Green

Development Editor
Sean Dixon

Managing Editor
Charlotte Clapp

Project Editor
Dan Knott

Copy Editor
Chuck Hutchinson

Indexer
Johnna Vanhoose Dinse

Proofreader
Jennifer Timpe

Technical Editor
Kunal Mittal
Pete Dapkus
Anne T. Manes
Shivaram Mysore

Publishing Coordinator
Cindy Teeters

Interior Designer
Gary Adair

Cover Designer
Alan Clements

Contents At a Glance

Table of Contents

About the Authors

Jonathan "Jothy" Rosenberg, Ph.D.
Founder, CTO, and CEO, Service Integrity

Dr. Jothy Rosenberg is a serial entrepreneur. He is a founder, Director, CTO, and CEO of Service Integrity, a company providing XML Web services monitoring and analysis products for end-to-end real-time enterprise visibility including security and compliance visibility or "early warning." Prior to Service Integrity, Jothy co-founded GeoTrust, the world's second largest certificate authority and a major innovator in enterprise-managed security solutions. As the company's COO and CTO, Jothy led the company's product development initiatives, developing patents on a series of ground-breaking security products and deploying a secure Web service integrating GeoTrust's reseller partners into the SSL provisioning process. Previous to GeoTrust, Jothy served as CEO and CTO of Factpoint, Inc., a pioneer in the area of content certification and content management. With his Service Integrity co-founders, he also co-founded Webspective, which was later sold to Inktomi.

Before these multiple ventures, Jothy held various executive positions at Borland International where he was General Manager of the Enterprise Tools Division and overall Development VP for Languages, including Delphi, C++, and JBuilder products. Jothy holds a B.A. in Mathematics from Kalamazoo College and a Ph.D. in Computer Science on VLSI Design algorithms from Duke University. He is also the author of *How Debuggers Work*. Jothy holds patents on debugger watchpoint mechanisms, content certification and site identity assurance, as well as a pending security compliance monitoring patent.

David L. Remy, CISSP
Director of Product Engineering for Security, Web Services and XML on WebLogic Workshop, BEA

David Remy works at BEA Systems, Inc., where he is a Director of Product Engineering responsible for security, Web services, and XML for BEA's WebLogic Workshop product line. Prior to working with BEA, David was founder and Chief Architect for GeoTrust, Inc., a security company and now the second largest certificate authority in the world. David has worked in the software industry for more than 16 years, holding such positions as Chief Technology Officer at Netstock, Director of Technology at Corbis, Director of Architecture at PEMCO Financial, Advisory Systems Engineer at IBM, and several other contracting and software development roles.

Acknowledgments

Jothy Rosenberg and Dave Remy started writing this book two years ago while working together as co-founders of GeoTrust. The project took a lot of twists and turns along the way, as did the careers of both authors. But it is finally finished, and the timing is great for a book about WS-Security and all its cousin specifications. We are grateful to have completed it and are excited about having it out in the hands of people it can help.

We would like to acknowledge Shivaram Mysore from Sun, one of the authors and drivers of the XKMS standard, for writing a significant portion of Chapter 9 for us on trust, key management, and the XKMS standard. We believe XKMS is critical for Web Services Security because key management is at the heart of what security is all about. It is also likely to give PKI a new lease on life. We thank Eve Maler, also from Sun and an SAML specialist extraordinaire, for her comments, especially on Chapter 6, and for introducing us to Shivaram to write the XKMS section.

Simeon Simeonov was "Mr. Networking" for us and introduced us to Eve Maler and the people at Sams Publishing who are publishing this book. Sams Publishing also published his book *Building Web Services with Java*. Sim had numerous valuable discussions with us about the technical material. Sim is brilliant, nice, supportive, and an accomplished author himself. He currently works at the venture capital firm Polaris Venture Partners.

We would like to acknowledge David Chappell, who initially got us started on this project and let us run with it for a year on our own. David has written several books on Web services and is the editor of a series for Addison-Wesley on related subjects. His feedback, although very critical in the early days, ultimately was just the kick in the pants we needed to focus on the right information for the right audience.

Todd Green, our editor at Sams, was great to work with. Todd had the vision to see that this was the right book on the topic at the right time, and he moved on it quickly. He has the necessary combination of hard pushing to make deadlines and positive encouragement so that we stayed energized. He and his team focused us on the audience that most needs this book. Thanks also to Sean Dixon, Dan Knott, and the rest of the team at Sams Publishing who worked very hard and very fast to turn our ideas into the book you're holding.

A host of excellent reviewers helped review, discuss, and improve various sections of this book. We are grateful for their expert assistance. Reviewers included Shivaram Mysore, Anne Thomas Manes, Kunal Mittal, Anant Kadiyala, and Dave Spicer.

Jothy would like to thank his colleagues at Service Integrity who got excited about this book and encouraged him to "hurry up and get it out before it was too late." That includes Joe Maloney and Arthur Mateos. Jothy is honored to have a very strong technical team at Service Integrity that knows distributed computing, Web technologies, XML, and security inside and out. Jason DeBettencourt, Stanley Yamane, and Marco Lara have been together as an unstoppable development team for 10 years; they are like the three musketeers of management and monitoring tools for distributed computing. Jothy feels privileged to call them co-founders and friends. He has worked with them off and on since 1996. The person who got Jothy's career going in the right direction, who encouraged his first book on debuggers, who helped unite the team that now forms Service Integrity is Paul Gross. Paul is back together with the team and encouraging this book and our work at the company as a board member. Jothy also would like to recognize and thank JT Hardy and Jack Horton, formerly at GeoTrust and currently at AMS, who have a vision to change the world one big deal at a time. They are wonderfully supportive, fun to work with, and are great friends. The founding team at GeoTrust—Dave Chen, Charles Jennings, Dave Remy, and Karla Friede—were inspiring and exciting to work with. They had a vision that was a bit early but is now coming to fruition. Dave Remy and Jothy learned the practical and business side of security at GeoTrust and along the way built some very innovative technology. Later, Jothy and Dave were fortunate to work with and learn from very talented security experts including Mike Rowan and John Steenbruggen. Current investors in Service Integrity, David Orfao and David Barrett (known as The Davids) have a great vision for how to start and build companies and have been great supporters of Jothy and his co-founding team. Throughout it all, from before GeoTrust until today, Jothy's long-standing assistant who helps him in countless ways is Anne Cusack; she is indispensable to Jothy, and he deeply appreciates her.

Working with Anne Thomas Manes and Greg Shanton, who both agreed to write forewords for the book from different perspectives, was a pleasure. Anne knows the Web services industry inside out because she comes from a distributed computing background that includes DCE at Open Environment. She was also the editor of *The Distributed Computing Monitor* for Patricia Seybold Group. Later, she was Java Evangelist for Sun and the CTO of Systinet before going off and writing her own book called *Web Services—A Managers Guide*. She now works as an analyst at The Burton Group. Greg Shanton, the CTO of AMS's Enterprise Security Group, is an expert in Internet security. He holds several critical patents. Greg is a big picture guy who has a vision about changing the Internet for the better and making a huge impact with the Web services projects he is leading at AMS. We are honored and humbled to have them both agree to contribute to this book.

Finally, Jothy would like to thank Dave Remy for starting this project. Dave is the most modest, hard-working, driven, and technically solid person he has ever worked with. They became fast friends in the early days of GeoTrust, and their friendship has grown from there. Dave is such a good friend that he comes to San Francisco every summer with his daughter to cheer Jothy on at the finish line of the Alcatraz Shark Fest open water swim across San Francisco Bay. When Dave came up with the idea for this book, they both knew it would be hard, but Jothy knew it would be done right because of Dave's deep knowledge and his attention to detail. They have a partnership and a friendship that he hopes will last a lifetime. (When do you want to write that next book, Dave?)

For his part, Dave would like to thank in particular Paul Reed, author of several books for Addison-Wesley, who has been a great friend and resource throughout Dave's career. Paul originally put us in touch with a publisher with the idea of writing a security book. He would also like to thank his compatriots at BEA, including David Bau, Eric Vasilik, David Read, Brendan Maclean, Anurag Pareek (who wrote the WS-Security in WebLogic Workshop chapter), Peter Dapkus (who sits in on the WS-Security meetings for BEA, gave great advice, and wrote the underlying BEA WS-Security implementation), and Giridhar Rao (who wrote the WebLogic Workshop WS-Security implementation). He would also like to thank other instrumental people in his life for their inspiration and influence, including David Chen, Dr. Emily Cooper, Eric Rudder, Doug Rowan, Adam Bosworth, Byron Sebastian, Charles Jennings (author of *The Hundredth Window*), and of course, his parents. Finally, Dave wants to save the ultimate thanks for Jothy. He made this book happen; it would never have been finished but for Jothy's tremendous follow-through, indicative of the perseverance, determination, and never-give-up way of being that Jothy is famous for (which got him through 10 Alcatraz Shark Fest swims). For Dave, it is a privilege to be Jothy's friend—a hero among us.

Finally, Jothy and Dave both deeply appreciate the strong support and encouragement from their wives Carole and Beth, respectively, and children Brendan, Zac, Joanna, Lisa, and Laura. Not only did they provide strong support, but they also suspended disbelief that we could not possibly do this when both of us were starting new jobs; Dave was also moving from one city to another and Jothy was funding and starting a new company.

Newton, Massachusetts, and Seattle, Washington

April 2004

We Want to Hear from You!

As the reader of this book, *you* are our most important critic and commentator. We value your opinion and want to know what we're doing right, what we could do better, what areas you'd like to see us publish in, and any other words of wisdom you're willing to pass our way.

As an associate publisher for Sams Publishing, I welcome your comments. You can email or write me directly to let me know what you did or didn't like about this book—as well as what we can do to make our books better.

Please note that I cannot help you with technical problems related to the topic of this book. We do have a User Services group, however, where I will forward specific technical questions related to the book.

When you write, please be sure to include this book's title and author as well as your name, email address, and phone number. I will carefully review your comments and share them with the authors and editors who worked on the book.

Email: feedback@samspublishing.com
Mail: Michael Stephens
            Associate Publisher
            Sams Publishing
            800 East 96th Street
            Indianapolis, IN 46240 USA

For more information about this book or another Sams Publishing title, visit our Web site at www.samspublishing.com. Type the ISBN (excluding hyphens) or the title of a book in the Search field to find the page you're looking for.

Forewords

Securing Web Services to Deliver on Their Promise

Web services have the potential to be the next great paradigm that will once and for all change computing as we know it. The main promise of Web services is that business systems can be used by anyone, from anywhere, at any time—and, of course, on any type of system. Another promise is that integration between disparate systems that are either internal to an organization or housed externally by another vendor or partner will be simplified. While these and other expectations surrounding Web services are tremendous, the truth about their potential may be somewhat less than what has been promised.

Truth be told, Web services are just the next leg of the ongoing journey to deliver ubiquitous business computing services. The journey started many years ago with business-to-business exchanges through the use of electronic data interchange (EDI) technology, and we've only scratched the surface to understand the journey's path or ultimate destination. But hold on tight; it is sure to be a long and thrilling ride.

Rosenberg's and Remy's book, *Securing Web Services with WS-Security: Demystifying WS-Security, WS-Policy, XML Signature, XML Encryption, and SAML,* sheds light on new and innovative Web Services Security technologies. Most importantly, the authors clearly depict how to properly deploy these technologies to secure Web services.

By embracing and implementing the Web services model described in this book, organizations have the potential to do the following:

- Reduce cost by streamlining online transactions, automating more back-end processes, and increasing interoperability between disparate systems through standardization of protocols and data formats (XML);
- Ensure compliance, increase accountability, and reduce fraud via real-time transaction monitoring and security enforcement systems; and
- Strengthen security due to a focus on building better systems and securing the data from the inside out.

System integrators who enable their customers to successfully deploy and manage Web services will thrive in the years to come. To do this, traditional system integrators will need to refocus on building better quality systems and performing actual security integration at the application and data levels. This new breed of system integrators must be able to advise their clients on which business systems make sense to Web service-enable, and which do not.

So, will Web services make a difference to your business and to your customers? Yes, but like most over-hyped technologies, Web services will not live up to the excitement surrounding them. Web services are only part of the greater technology systems and solutions that organizations will adopt; a one-size–fits-all Web services approach does not exist for every business application or problem. The current Web services model is constantly maturing and evolving; for example, some speculate that Web services and grid computing will combine to form an even more powerful and distributed Web services model.

The great promise of Web services will never be realized unless they are proven to be reliable, available, and have the appropriate level of security. Rosenberg and Remy are among the first to accurately portray Web Services Security by addressing how to apply the correct amount and types of security solutions.

The security issues that apply to Web services are similar to those surrounding other technology solutions and systems. Business applications deployed as Web services need to incorporate security building blocks including authentication, authorization, confidentiality, availability and reliability, fraudulent transactions, nonrepudiation, compliance, and auditing and monitoring.

However, there is one big exception with Web Services Security: What the Web services model brings front and center is that organizations must focus on building more secure applications from the ground up while protecting their business data at all times in storage and transit. Gone are the days of saying core assets—the organization's data and systems—are secure because they are simply hiding behind the corporate firewall.

The new Web services model brings about unique security challenges because the applications themselves and business data traverse outside the once-trusted corporate enclaves. Business data stored in these new XML messaging formats travels across untrusted networks and is then manipulated by numerous distributed systems. The data next passes back through the corporate firewall to the automated back-office systems with the same XML document that has now potentially been compromised. Throughout the entire business transaction, different classes of users and systems need access to the data for inspection, approval, and treatment. If any part of this chain is compromised, the entire trust model breaks down, and the business application deployed as a Web service will fail.

To help counteract these security challenges, there has been a huge effort by a few innovative companies leading the way to develop Web Services Security standards by the traditional means of standards bodies. This concerted effort has been done in the same way the basic standards for Web services were created. The good news is that most of the security technologies that will be used to secure Web services have been deployed for years, are proven, and work. For example, cryptography is the backbone of Web Services Security; shared or symmetric key ciphers such as the United States' Advanced Encryption Standard (AES), Triple Data Encryption Standard (3DES), and other proven ciphers will be used to provide the confidentiality of XML messages; public key cryptography or asymmetric cryptography will be used for the integrity and digital signatures of the XML message; and trust models, such as Kerberos or Public Key Infrastructure (PKI), will be used to share the cryptographic keys and enable trusted credentials, also known as digital certificates, between users and different systems.

One of the biggest obstacles for Web Services Security will be the management of the various security technologies, which includes securing multicast message communication and integrating new data formats and protocols. New emerging technologies will enable us to hurdle these latest obstacles. These solutions provide innovative ways to monitor and perform analysis on XML transactions in real time—for example, cryptographic management systems that enable XML encryption and XKMS that supports secure multicast message communication. By utilizing the proven security technologies and emerging Web Services Security standards and technologies, an organization can have a comprehensive approach to Web Services Security.

While the security technologies needed to secure Web services are mature, companies looking to seriously deploy Web services will find that the best way to integrate these stovepipe solutions is through the use of common security frameworks that support the new emerging security standards discussed in this book. Properly implemented common security frameworks, or Security Service Oriented Architectures (SSOA), will aid in the deployment, management, and interoperability of Web Services Security.

Rosenberg and Remy have not only clearly defined Web Services Security, but they also have put together a great roadmap on how to properly deploy secure Web services at all levels. I hope you find this book as enlightening and informative as I did.

M. Greg Shanton
American Management Systems, Incorporated
Chief Technology Officer and Security Engineering Director, Enterprise Security Group

Building the Foundation for Agile Computing

This book comes at a very opportune time. As I write, the OASIS Web Services Security (WSS) Technical Committee has completed development of three WS-Security specifications and submitted them to the OASIS community for ratification. The specifications include the core security framework (SOAP Message Security) and two authentication token profiles (Username Token Profile and X.509 Certificate Token Profile).

The non-normative descriptions in the WS-Security specifications are pretty decent, but it's still dense reading. This book makes it quite a bit easier to comprehend all the facets of Web Services Security; plus, it aggregates information on all the underlying and associated security technologies that WS-Security relies on, such as SSL, PKI, XKMS, SAML, and a host of other acronyms. It's a reference book that I intend to keep handy.

In all my conversations with enterprise companies, security reigns as the number one concern in their plans to deploy Web services. And I can't blame them. Without a proper security infrastructure in place, Web services can expose sensitive corporate processes and information and leave a company open to risk and malfeasance—from both internal and external perpetrators.

Traditional network-layer and perimeter security tactics, such as SSL, proxy servers, and firewalls, aren't sufficient to protect IT systems anymore. In the past, businesses maintained a clean separation between the applications that support internal business processes and those that manage interactions with external customers, partners, and suppliers. The former systems, referred to as intranet applications, typically require less stringent security. The latter systems, or extranet applications, require more. With clear boundaries set in place, perimeter security works reasonably well.

More recently, though, the boundary between internal and external business processes has become blurred, and the artificial separation of the two has stymied innovation. Business processes don't stop at corporate boundaries. The concept that "enterprise application integration" is somehow different from "business-to-business integration" imposes constraints and restrictions on a business. Business applications should be able to seamlessly execute the appropriate tasks required to complete a business process, regardless of which business entity hosts the application code.

The challenge, though, is enabling this cross-domain integration to happen in a secure and reliable fashion. Perimeter security tactics won't cut it. Instead, businesses need to deploy application-level security frameworks. WS-Security provides the foundation for implementing a comprehensive application-level security framework that supports both internal and external integration requirements, and with it agile computing.

To effectively compete in today's economy, enterprises need an IT environment that supports real-time responsiveness and enables business processes to seamlessly cross logical and physical boundaries. Unfortunately, many enterprises find that their IT systems aren't quite as agile as they'd like. Changes to a business process can take months to implement, and the opportunity costs are staggering. Seamless, dynamic integration with customers, partners, and suppliers remains elusive.

The inertia of most IT systems stems from their application architecture. Most applications are designed as monolithic and autonomous systems. Each application implements a complete business process, and the specifics of the process are hard-coded in the application. Any modification to the business process requires a corresponding modification to the application code.

So the industry is turning to service-oriented architecture (SOA) as a way to increase agility. SOA defines a set of principles and practices for designing application functionality as shared, reusable services. Developers can compose and recompose these services into orchestrated applications that implement a variety of business processes. With the proper infrastructure in place, an SOA-based environment can allow IT systems to respond rapidly to changing business conditions.

The Web services framework (WSF) supports this infrastructure. The WSF provides an open, vendor-independent, language-neutral middleware framework that supports application integration based on ubiquitous Web protocols. Unlike any previous middleware framework, the WSF has gained universal endorsement from virtually every software vendor in the industry. Vendors are adding WSF support to their platforms, tools, applications, and infrastructure products. The WSF is rapidly becoming as ubiquitous as the Web.

The WSF takes the Web to the next level, supplying the technology necessary to support real-time responsiveness and cross-domain integration. And perhaps more important, the WSF supplies a foundation for implementing SOA, which is the real key to business agility. The industry has been aware of the value of SOA for more than 20 years, but until now, technology has not really supplied the tools and standards necessary to make it practical.

But the WSF is still young. I characterize it as an adolescent—strong, capable, and energetic—but it requires supervision. In particular, it requires a robust security framework. This security framework must support end-to-end security, and it must work in conjunction with identity management systems. WS-Security provides the foundation for this security framework.

Now, that's not to say that Web services can't be secured without WS-Security. A number of companies have deployed secure Web services using SSL. But the capabilities and extensibility of these Web services are very limited when relying on the transport level to enforce security. SSL provides point-to-point security rather than end-to-end security. As Web services deployments get more sophisticated, IT organizations will start to deploy intermediary nodes between consumer and service to perform functions, such as monitoring, auditing, content-based routing, version mismatch resolution, reliability, and orchestration. SSL-based protection can't provide a seamless security infrastructure for these multi-hop requirements. Beside, SSL imposes a heavy burden on IT developers to implement a security management framework that maps transport-level authentication mechanisms to the back-end applications' authentication and authorization systems.

As companies begin to deploy more and more Web services, per-application security management will rapidly become untenable. When companies use WS-Security, all this low-level security functionality can be implemented, managed, and enforced using a combination of the Web services infrastructure and identity management. Companies will soon discover that Web services and identity management are inextricably joined at the hip.

Without identity management, developers must still manage security on an application-by-application basis. WS-Security currently supports two types of authentication tokens: simple username tokens and X.509 certificates. And while WS-Security with these tokens offers much more flexibility and granularity than SSL does, it also places an onerous burden on the developer to implement application-specific authentication and authorization mechanisms for username token, or—even worse—complex PKI processing facilities in every application for X.509 certificate processing. (See Chapter 3, "The Foundations of Distributed Message-Level Security," for information on PKI.) Any way you look at it, it's a much better idea to use centrally managed identity management solutions that abstract away complexity.

For this reason I'm somewhat disappointed that the OASIS WSS technical committee has not yet completed the specification that describes how to pass SAML tokens with WS-Security. (See Chapter 6, "Portable Identity, Authentication, and Authorization," for information on SAML.) SAML—the Security Assertion Markup Language—provides a standard, vendor-neutral, interoperable, and portable way to represent identity, and it has been adopted as the standard identity format by most identity management vendors. SAML also supplies a critical piece of the foundation that will eventually support identity federation.

Federation is a more challenging task than simple integration. Federation hinges on the notion of bridging domains—areas of control that manage infrastructure issues such as identity, transactions, provisioning, and the like. To achieve federation, separate domains must establish trust relationships, common protocols, and governance structures that permit them to coordinate their activities. Therefore, federation requires some type of cross-domain interoperability framework within which autonomous entities honor each other's decisions and trust each other's assertions. The most basic part of federation, therefore, is a standard syntax and data format to represent identity and assertions—that is, SAML.

Fortunately, integration between WS-Security and SAML is just a matter of time. The next work items on the agenda for the OASIS WSS technical committee are to complete the token profile specifications for SAML assertions, XrML licenses, and Kerberos tickets. The committee plans to publish these three token profiles simultaneously.

Another encouraging development is that the Web Services Interoperability Organization (WS-I) has initiated a working group to create an interoperability profile for Web services security. The forthcoming WS-I Basic Security Profile (WS-I BSP) will provide guidelines for developers to aid in the creation of secure, interoperable Web services. The working group has published a draft requirements document called "WS-I Security Scenarios" that outlines the set of issues and use cases that the profile should address. The WS-I BSP will define an interoperability profile that supports transport-level (SSL) and application-level (WS-Security) security. It will include support for any tokens that have been standardized by the OASIS WSS technical committee, and periodic updates will maintain parity with new token profiles as they emerge.

So, the future looks bright for IT agility. The combination of Web services framework and identity management will enable real-time responsiveness and borderless application systems. WS-Security is the critical component that ties these two technologies together. Web services infrastructure vendors, such as Actional, BEA, DataPower, IBM, IONA, Microsoft, Oracle, SAP, Systinet, Westbridge, and others, already provide support for WS-Security within their products. And many also support SAML.

Developers need to be prepared to start using WS-Security and SAML. This book is a great place to start.

Anne Thomas Manes
VP & Research Director
Burton Group
March 7, 2004

Introduction

Who This Book Is For

Securing Web Services with WS-Security is written with the needs of Web service architects, developers, operators, and security administrators in mind. We believe it is equally accessible and important for IT managers, development managers, CIOs, CTOs, Directors of IT, Directors of Operations, security architects, and business analysts. If this list includes you, you are the person within your organization entrusted with understanding, building, deploying, and operating secure Web services. This task is daunting, but we will try to arm you with what you need to know about securing those Web services to protect your company and those assets that Web services are supposed to liberate and leverage. Our goal is to enable you to build and deploy secure Web services so that you and your organization can then begin to leverage the incredible business potential you can derive from Web services; but only if they can be trusted.

About This Book

This book is not a formal programming reference, but we have included numerous snippets of sample code and a significant case study in Chapter 10, "Building a Secure Web Service Using BEA's WebLogic Workshop," that walks you through securing Web services on the WebLogic J2EE platform. It is a solid introduction to the body of knowledge about identity and security issues and the standards and solutions you will need to successfully build and deploy secure Web services. With this book as the starting point, you should be able to navigate the myriad detailed standards, specifications, and proposed standards and put them in perspective in the specific areas you need to develop into your secure Web service applications.

Already, thousands of people are deploying Web services either for application integration, for building powerful portals, for trading partner integration, or just to promote effective re-use of a useful service. In fact, because virtually every application being contemplated includes a set of SOAP or XML interfaces, this is a critical book to provide overview and perspective for most, if not all, programmers. Web services, as we will show in detail, create a whole new set of security challenges that we did not have with corporate networks, Web applications, or previous forms of distributed computing. Corporations will not deploy a Web service without first having a thorough understanding of its security implications on the organization. If you proceed without understanding this point, you might as well start installing Trojan horses right away.

This book provides a basic understanding of what Web services are for and the simple concepts behind how this new incarnation of middleware functions. We will put Web services in context, but as a prerequisite, you should know, at an overview level, what the alphabet soup set of Web services standards is all about. Although we dive into these standards in some detail, we do so in the context of Web services being middleware that extends across trust domains, and we will help you appreciate the security issues this new construct brings to your development scenarios. In terms of security, if you already have an understanding of simple concepts such as what Secure Socket Layer (SSL) is and what public key cryptography is, that knowledge will be helpful because we build on these concepts. A working knowledge of XML syntax is also important; we use concrete examples of XML throughout the book.

The approach we take in this book is not to just dive into the standards and specifications. We want to provide a strong perspective on how they relate both to Web services and the tried-and-true principles of security. When we introduce Web services, we try to show how they are a natural extension of middleware for distributed computing. What did we learn about security then that applies now? What is different? And where are those security approaches not relevant? When talking about security, we want to make sure you understand not just what XML Signature is for, but also why it uses public key rather than shared key encryption and why hashing is important for signatures and why XML Signature is not appropriate to use for confidentiality of messages. This book will answer these and many more questions about what you need to think about when beginning to plan the security of your Web services. It will help guide how you should go about implementing your secure Web services so they deliver the right level of security for what is at risk and still remain usable and useful for the business purposes for which they are intended.

How This Book Is Organized

Securing Web Services with WS-Security is not a reference text, but you can treat certain chapters as reference tools. We recommend you read Chapters 2, "The Foundations of Web Services," 3, "The Foundations of Distributed Message-Level Security," 4, "Safeguarding the Identity and Integrity of XML Messages," and 5, "Ensuring Confidentiality of XML Messages" in sequence because they build a foundation on which later chapters are built. In general, you do not need to read subsequent chapters in any sequence. Later chapters on WS-Security, WS-Policy, Portable Identity (SAML), and other WS-* technologies all stand on their own. Chapter 10 includes a case study on how secure Web services are built and deployed on a commonly used application server platform. An appendix includes detailed reference material about cryptographic algorithms. We have included a glossary at the end of the book to act as a guide to terms that can be confusing and for which it is hard to find definitions.

The "straight-line" text of the book covers the critical information you need. We also include "color commentary," opinions, juicy industry tidbits, and useful but not critical extra information about the topics in the chapters in sidebars, which are designed to enable you to better understand why things are done in a certain way or avoid making bad choices when laying down a security policy or implementation. Sometimes, though, they are just our opinions and nothing more.

In the end, we hope this book provides you with deeper insights into how Web services are similar to as well as different from previous forms of distributed computing middleware security. From there, we hope the book provides you with a much better understanding of identity and security but also of the depth and complexity of the security issues when applied to self-describing messages sent between machines over insecure networks. The book is not designed to scare you, so throughout we provide guidance—based on our opinions—of what parts of the emerging standards you can use today and which you need to prepare to use later.

Because this book is, in part, based on a substantial body of standards specifications, we will point you to those specific standards and other resources for more detailed information. In general, most of these standards come from OASIS (`www.oasis-open.org`) or from the W3C (`www.w3c.org`). Both of these organizations have well-organized sites you should visit frequently so that you can remain current on information provided there.

The code for the case study presented in Chapter 10 is available from the Sams Web site. Go to `www.samspublishing.com` and type the book's ISBN (0672326515) into the search field to go to this book's Web page and download the code.

1

Basic Concepts of Web Services Security

WEB SERVICES ARE A TRANSFORMATIONAL TECHNOLOGY for integrating information sources from both inside and outside an enterprise. Web services are the newest incarnation of middleware for distributed computing. Unlike all previous forms of middleware, however, this is a simpler, standards-based, and more loosely coupled technology for connecting data, systems, and organizations. That is good news for architects and developers wanting to quickly become proficient in this technology and deploy real systems. It is also somewhat bad news for architects and developers because all middleware needs strong security practices, and Web services need it more than any middleware of the past. Why more? Because Web services create loosely coupled integrations. Because Web services are not just being used to integrate internal systems, but they are also integrating data sources from outside the organization. Because Web services are based on the passing of readable and self-describing business messages represented in XML. Because Web services are based on underlying Web technologies that already had their own set of security challenges.

It is true that Web services—like most new transformational information technologies introduced—have been overhyped, and it is true that fears of security problems have also been overblown, which has impeded the development and deployment of Web services. It is also true that the standards for Web services are either quite new or in some cases not even fully baked yet. This book is designed to take the mystery and fear out of how to build secure Web services and to shed light on these new standards and how to best use them. It is also designed to show you the richness and complexity of the security issues around Web services so that you, the designers, builders, and operators of Web services, can fully exploit all the capabilities of Web services to your best advantage but do so knowing full well what all the security challenges are and how to face them.

This chapter covers the basics of Web services and information security and the way Web services security builds on existing security technology. This sets the stage for a deeper understanding of the major standards for information security associated with Web services.

Web Services Basics: XML, SOAP, and WSDL

Four technologies form the basis of Web services: eXtensible Markup Language (XML); SOAP[1]; Web Services Description Language (WSDL); and Universal Description, Discovery, and Integration (UDDI)[2].

XML and XML Schema

XML was created as a structured self-describing way to represent data that is totally independent of application, protocol, vocabulary, operating system, or even programming language. Many call XML the lingua franca of business because it is being used so broadly across all industries to portably transmit business data. The use of XML presents a broad set of security challenges.

XML Schema is a way of describing the rules for a particular XML instance (also known as a document). XML can be used independently of XML Schema; however, in Web services and most business situations, the XML that you work with will be governed by an XML Schema (perhaps created by a development tool and put into your Web services WSDL file for you).

XML is the foundation of the Web services standards. All standards for describing, discovering, and invoking Web services are based on XML. SOAP and WSDL are described using XML Schema. The core security standards of XML Encryption, XML Signature, Security Assertion Markup Language (SAML), and WS-Security are XML-based and are also described by an XML Schema.

XML and HTML are both text-based formats that came from the same roots. XML was initially developed to overcome the limitations of HTML, which is good at describing how things should be displayed but is poor at describing what the data is that is being displayed. XML being text-based is very important to Web services; because it is human-readable, no tools are needed to parse and render the data, and simple text tools and editors are sufficient for its manipulation. XML documents are very wordy, and although you can easily become lost in the depth and richness of the tags, its markup format of tagged elements arranged in a hierarchical structure makes XML documents easy to comprehend. But there is a security price to pay for the open, text-based structure of XML. As you will see later, to provide data integrity—a guarantee that not one bit in the original document has been changed—with XML, you have to guarantee that

---

1. SOAP used to stand for Simple Object Access Protocol, but in the W3C SOAP 1.2 specification, SOAP is now just a name and is no longer an acronym. The reason for the change is that the W3C realized that SOAP is neither especially simple, nor is it related to objects in any way.
2. Most authors consider the base set of Web services standards to include UDDI as well as SOAP and WSDL. UDDI stands for Universal Description, Discovery, and Integration. Advertising Web services so that systems can automatically discover them sounds like a good idea, but we don't believe it is practical for the public Internet. Instead, we view UDDI as a powerful mechanism to be used inside larger organizations to promote reuse of shared services. So, although we do view it as a useful standard, we don't view it as part of the core set of things that define Web services.

not one character—even whitespace—of an XML message has been changed. Verifying data integrity is particularly challenging when using XML since differences in platforms and XML parsers can result in logically equivalent documents being physically different; consequently, a process of *canonicalization* is necessary to make a valid comparison with the originally signed document. This is just one example of the special considerations needed when considering Web Service Security.

SOAP

SOAP was created as a way to transport XML from one computer to another via a number of standard transport protocols. HTTP is the most common of those transports and is, of course, the most prevalent transport used by the Web itself.

SOAP itself is defined using XML, and it provides a simple, consistent, yet extensible mechanism that allows one application to send an XML message to another. SOAP is what makes application integration possible, because after XML defines the contents of a message, it is SOAP that moves the data from one place to another over the network. SOAP allows the sender and receiver of XML documents to support a common data transfer protocol. SOAP allows you to treat XML messages as requests for remote services. The SOAP model allows a clean separation between infrastructure processing and application processing of messages. Figure 1.1 shows the basic structure of a SOAP message.

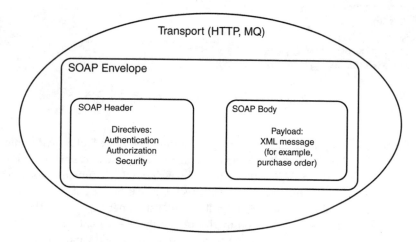

Figure 1.1   The basic structure of SOAP.

SOAP provides an envelope into which an XML message is placed. This envelope is just a container to hold XML data. The idea is for SOAP to create a uniform container that can then be carried by a variety of transports. SOAP prevents applications from caring about the transport; the applications see consistency in the SOAP envelope and its contents.

Inside the SOAP envelope are two parts: the *header* and the *body*.

- **SOAP header**—Contains information about the SOAP message (as opposed to the XML message contained in the SOAP body). This information is used to manage or secure the package. SOAP is designed to be extensible, and a major area for extension is the SOAP header. Chapter 7, "Building Security into SOAP," which describes WS-Security, provides more detail on SOAP header security extensions.

- **SOAP body**—Contains the message payload. This information is being sent from one application to another. It might be a full document such as a purchase order or contract, or it might be a description of remote-procedure call information, including the methods to call and parameters to those method calls.

The simple SOAP message in Listing 1.1 shows an envelope that contains both a SOAP header and a SOAP body.

Listing 1.1 **SOAP Envelope**

```
<?xml version="1.0" ?>
<env:Envelope xmlns:env="http://www.w3.org/2001/12/soap-envelope">
 <env:Header>
 <n:alertcontrol xmlns:n="http://example.org/alertcontrol">
  <n:priority>1</n:priority>
  <n:expires>2004-06-22T14:00:00-5:00</n:expires>
 </n:alertcontrol>
 </env:Header>
 <env:Body>
  <m:alert xmlns:m="http://example.org/alert">
   <m:msg>Pick up Bobby at school at 2PM</m:msg>
  </m:alert>
 </env:Body>
</env:Envelope>
```

To understand SOAP, you need to understand the different "styles" of SOAP bodies. RPC-style SOAP bodies tend to be simple parameters to facilitate calling a remote method. Document-style SOAP bodies tend to be rich XML documents. Document style, in our view, is more appropriate for B2B Web services because it is usually more optimal to have "chunky," coarse-grained calls across a slow network rather than the fine-grained type of RPC call that you might use locally or on a fast network. This is not just due to the network but also due to the cost of marshalling and unmarshalling the XML and performing security-related operations.

SOAP needs to be secured. The messages it carries must be kept secret from unintended recipients. The remote service being called must know who is calling it and know the caller is authorized to do so. SOAP is a packaging mechanism for XML messages and documents. Like any package, it needs to describe important information about its contents, such as who it is from, how a recipient can trust that it really is the sender, what the sender is allowed to do, and much more. These are identity- and trust-related issues; they are the core of SOAP security discussed in detail later in this book.

WSDL

WSDL is an XML language that defines the set of operations that a Web service provides and the structure of their related SOAP messages. That is, the WSDL defines what the input and output structure will be for a Web service, and that will define what you expect to see in the payload XML message. WSDL is how one service tells another which way to interact with it, where the service resides, what the service can do, and how to invoke it. WSDL directly supports developers and is absorbed at application development time into developer tools. WSDL's definitions of remote services are presented to programmer-like local objects that can be acted upon as if they were methods in classes, just like any of their other local objects.

When you publish a WSDL for one of your services, you are creating a contract for how other services may interact with you to utilize your service. WSDL is what you publish to describe your Web service and the rules for how to work with it. You might think that security would also be described in WSDL because this is part of the rules for working with a particular Web service; however, the security options (security policy) available are richer than what you typically see in WSDL, so the standards are evolving toward using WS-Policy to describe a Web services security policy and then *referring* to this policy from the WSDL. Chapter 8, "Communicating Security Policy," goes into more depth on WS Policy.

A WSDL file has a *what* section, a *how* section, and a *where* section. The *what* section specifies the input and output messages. The *how* section defines how the messages should be packaged in the SOAP envelope and how to transfer it. It also defines what information should be included in the SOAP header. The *where* section describes a specific Web service implementation and ways to find its endpoint.

UDDI

UDDI is typically the fourth leg of the stool used to define Web services. Although we view UDDI as a useful standard, we do not see its usefulness beyond internal promotion of reuse inside large organizations. Given that, we do not put it front and center as a part of our discussions of Web services security and will not treat it further in this book.

Before you dive into the security implications of each of these Web services standards, you need some context: What are Web services really for? The answer is, among other uses that undoubtedly will develop as this new paradigm matures, application integration, B2B business process integration, portals, and service-oriented architectures.

Application Integration

Application integration is critical to organizations large and small because *information integration* is so fundamentally important. When organizations integrate all their applications that deal with customers (CRM, ERP, accounting, billing), they are trying to create a single view of all the *information* about those customers. When they integrate all their trading partners into a single supply chain, they are attempting to create a holistic view of their entire supply chain and all the information that describes their trading processes. This kind of information integration is fundamental to the business process. Rarely does a business process (product development, product marketing, product manufacturing, product ordering, product fulfillment, customer relationships, partner relationships, financials, and so on) utilize one and only one source of information (an application). It is because business processes cross application boundaries and even enterprise boundaries that Web services are needed to create those bridges.

Application integration is hard because systems were not designed with the same data structures, protocols, or even the same vocabulary for describing the items they manipulate. Applications were built at different times by different vendors using different technologies. However, many of these different applications need to communicate to perform certain functions. This is where XML comes in. It makes information easy to interchange and therefore easier to integrate.

The glue used to communicate from one application to another has traditionally been called *middleware*. Middleware has never been pervasive and was always very expensive. Rarely has anyone ever tried to use middleware between enterprises because simply using it within a single enterprise's boundaries is hard enough. SOAP is a critical step in taking XML messages toward being Web services middleware. In one of its modes, SOAP makes XML into a request/response paradigm that is published via WSDL. Web services are becoming pervasive because they are middleware based on the Web, and the Web is pervasive.

B2B Business Process Integration

Business processes don't stop at your company's firewall. Just as internal application integration is partly motivated by the need to break down application barriers, interorganization business processes motivate B2B application integration. A driving need to integrate across organizations comes from management of supply chains and demand chains with trading partners. Traditional middleware could never be employed to solve this need because it never worked across the Internet.

The good news is that the Internet *is* pervasive. Most Internet communication occurs via text (for example, HTML is text, email is text), and virtually all applications have some form of text interface. XML is text-based and is designed to make business information transportable and self-describing. XML, plus the fact that all vendors support Web services, has moved us closer to solving the heterogeneous communication problems of different languages, different platforms, and different applications than any middleware technology of the past.

For these reasons, Web services technology is built on XML and Web technologies, which makes it the first middleware that can address the B2B business process integration challenge.

Portals

On the Internet and within intranets, portals are the entry point for customers into a site. Portals have been growing in utility and importance for some time as a way to aggregate information and applications into a single site that is accessible by browsers. Portals as major business models have been common for years. Amazon.com, Yahoo!, and Orbitz are all fundamentally portals. They pull information from their partners' repositories into a single site that consumers with browsers visit to buy books, music, and consumer goods; plan trips; and the like. Most of these major Web e-commerce companies built their portals long before Web services standards existed. They effectively built Web services to integrate all their information content using home-grown approaches. Companies trying to do what they have done now can do it much more cheaply and easily and remain much more interoperable by using the new Web services standards.

Companies are rapidly turning their corporate intranets into portals to provide a wide range of company-related information and services to employees, shareholders, and partners. One type of service they are providing employees is a unified benefits information resource. To make that a complete service, the 401k information from third-party providers must be integrated into the corporate portal. That is a perfect use for secured Web services that bring the employees' 401k account information into the corporate benefits portal by accessing the external services of the 401k provider.

Integrated customer information is so much the lifeblood of all companies that both customer relationship management (CRM) and customer information portals have represented large corporate investments for many years. Naturally, because Web services are less expensive and less complex than any previous form of middleware, they have been brought to bear on this common need.

Service-Oriented Architectures

In a service-oriented architecture (SOA), the interface is completely separated from the implementation. The software is provided strictly as a service that does not have to be downloaded and installed. SOA promotes reuse and sharing of services by numerous applications and even by different organizations. People describe an "SOA nirvana" when all systems are built as SOA and all applications are composite—built by stitching together several useful shared service components into powerful applications. Many people look to Web services to bring us to this SOA nirvana[3].

The idea of services as being a powerful computing paradigm is not new. A service is an application that can be consumed by software as opposed to a human at a browser. It is software that does work for other software. It is how RPC mechanisms work. This was the premise of the client/server computing revolution of the early '90s. In this model, the server provided the service.

The benefits of a service-oriented architecture are legion. The complexities of a software system are hidden behind its interface. A complex software system becomes a

---

3. In an SOA, UDDI will have a strong, meaningful role.

simpler black box defined only by its external interface. The service so constructed becomes a shared resource that can support many applications.

Web services combine the concept of software-as-a-service with the ubiquity and connectedness of the Web. This is what makes Web services so compelling and so exciting: They create a Web API. We are talking about building applications with a broadly accepted standard API based on Web technologies. Web services enable you to wrap legacy applications with this Web API and turn them into shared services. Now these applications can be integrated with other applications and with trading partners. Previously inaccessible information resident in these legacy applications can be brought out to portals and combined with other application information and all made accessible to any user with a browser. Any application can be modified to provide this type of Web API and therefore can be integrated with any other application, allowing you to use the entire Web for application-to-application integration. This, then, is the power of Web services.

Definition of Web Services

A good working definition of a Web service, then, is an application that provides a Web API. The API enables the software resource to act as a service. Being a Web API means that this service is accessible at an Internet URI. Further, an API supports application integration, so a Web API allows application-to-application integration using XML over Web protocols and infrastructure. All the security and trust issues of being part of the open Web infrastructure will concern us. All the information security and message security issues inherent in sending messages from one network point to another will concern us. All the authorization and authority security issues inherent in middleware that performs RPCs will concern us. Now, let's cover some security basics to build a foundation for our deeper discussions in later chapters.

Security Basics

The Web is an interconnected global information system that provides resources suitable for consumption directly by humans. In this model, security is critical for many of these resources (login-password authentication at restricted sites, SSL encryption of credit cards and other personally identifiable confidential information). It only makes sense, then, that application-to-application Web services need at least this much security as well.

In fact, because Web services expose critical and valuable XML-encoded business information, Web services security is a critically important concept to fully understand. For one thing, trade secret pilfering is already a large problem, and without security, Web services might even make this situation worse. The reason is that Web services can be thought of as allowing in strange, new users who might take your company's valuable business secrets out.

This section covers basic security concepts to establish the vocabulary that will be used throughout this book. Keeping communications secret is the heart of security. The science of keeping messages secret is called *cryptography*. Cryptography is also used to guarantee trust in a known *identity* across a network by "binding" that identity to a message that you can see, interpret, and trust. An identity asserting itself must be *authenticated* by a trust authority to a previously established identity known to the authority for the binding to be valid. After you know the identity, *authorization* allows you to specify what the individual with that identity is allowed to do. When you receive a secret message, you need to know that nothing in the message has been changed in any way since it was published, an attribute called *integrity*. When cryptography successfully keeps a message secret, it has satisfied the requirement for *confidentiality*. At times, you might want to know that someone who received confidential information cannot deny that she received it, an important security concept called *non-repudiation*.

Most of these core security concepts depend on encryption technologies, so before you look at any of them more closely, take a look at the fundamentals of encryption.

Shared Key and Public Key Technologies

We won't get very far in our security discussions without bumping into shared key and public key technologies. They, in turn, stem from cryptography. We will briefly introduce these concepts here so that we can apply them where needed throughout the rest of the book.

Cryptography

Cryptology is the branch of mathematics focused on designing algorithms to keep information (data) secret. Cryptography is the work of applying these algorithms to secure systems, protocols, applications, and messages[4].

The first and most important area of cryptography to discuss is *encryption*. Encryption is the basis for XML Encryption and also for XML Signature, which encrypts a digested form of a message. The message digest encrypted in a digital signature is created using another important cryptographic algorithm called a *hash function*, which is a special class of *one-way* function that creates a fixed-size (small) output that is unique for all input messages and that is not, in practice, reversible. In the Web services arena, you will find common uses for both shared key[5] and public key encryption.

A message that is completely readable and is in no way scrambled or disguised is called *plaintext*. Plaintext is unencrypted data. *Encryption* is the process of scrambling or disguising plaintext by applying a cryptographic algorithm to produce *ciphertext*. Ciphertext is encrypted data. *Decryption* reverses the encryption process and turns ciphertext back into its original plaintext form. These concepts are shown in Figure 1.2.

---

4. Recommended text on cryptography: *Applied Cryptography* by Bruce Schneier (John Wiley & Sons, 1996).

5. The terms *shared key*, *secret key*, and *symmetric key* are used interchangeably in various texts. To be consistent in this book, we choose to use the term *shared key* throughout, but occasionally context requires we also use the term *symmetric key*.

Figure 1.2   The relationships between plaintext and ciphertext, and the encryption and decryption processes that transform them.

The goal of encryption—and therein the way to achieve confidentiality—is to create ciphertext from plaintext that is undecipherable to anyone except the intended recipient. A special cryptographic algorithm that creates seemingly random permutations on the message, but which in fact are reversible under the right circumstances, performs the encryption process.

The algorithms for encryption and decryption require a key, which is a special numeric value that is required as a parameter for the algorithm to perform its task. The wrong key will get garbage out, not the correct output.

Shared key algorithms use the same key performing encryption and decryption *symmetrically* and are relatively fast. Public key encryption uses different but mathematically related (a *public* and *private* pair) keys performing encryption and decryption *asymmetrically* and is primarily used for secure shared key distribution and digital signatures.

Throughout this book, we will use the term *shared key* when we refer to symmetric encryption and *public key* when we refer to asymmetric encryption. We will use the term *subject* to refer to the holder of a key. A subject may be an individual or an entity (computer).

The magic is in the keys. But what is a key, and what does it have to do with encryption?

Keys

A *key* is a set of bits that acts as an input parameter to a crypto-algorithm. Think of the crypto-algorithm like the lock on your house door. That lock is standard, and so is your door. Lots of other people have doors and locks that are outwardly exactly the same as yours. But inside the lock on your door are some unique (or almost[6]) settings of tumblers that exactly match your and only your key.

Algorithms for encryption and decryption do not need to be and normally are not kept secret. It is the key that is kept secret. It is an important fundamental principle of cryptography that the algorithms be public, standard, and widely distributed and carefully scrutinized. This principle ensures that all the world's cryptographers fully shake out the algorithms for any security flaws.

The key is the variable that makes the algorithm result unique and secret. For some crypto-algorithms, the key may be a random number. For others, such as public key algorithms, it must be carefully chosen—a complex, time-consuming mathematical

---

6. "Almost unique" because, like door locks, there is not an absolute certainty that two keys are unique. But the chances of two keys being the same is infinitesimally small, just as is the chance that your key will happen to open a neighbor's door lock.

operation by itself. The key space needs to be large, so a large number of possible keys is available to prevent guessing attacks. Different algorithms require different key lengths for good security. Most keys today are typically 200 bits or larger.

Shared Key Cryptography

Shared key cryptography uses the same key to encrypt and decrypt the data. This requires that both communicating parties share the same key and, vitally important, keep it secret from the rest of the world. As shown in Figure 1.3, plaintext is encrypted into ciphertext by the sender using the shared secret key. The ciphertext is then decrypted by the receiver using the same shared secret key.

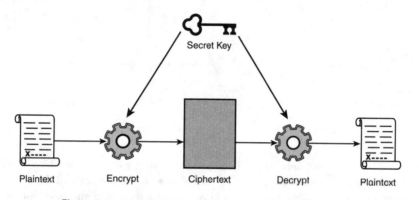

Figure 1.3   The shared key (symmetric) encryption process.

The advantage of shared key encryption/decryption is that the algorithms are fast and can operate on arbitrarily sized messages. The disadvantage is that this approach creates great difficulties managing a shared key that must be kept secret across a network between message sender and recipient. Within Web services security, you will run into shared key cryptography as the basis of Secure Socket Layer (SSL) security and as the foundation for XML Encryption. Much effort has been put into XML Encryption to take care of most of its details for you. But you will be exposed at the minimum to choices you will have to make about algorithms, key information, and the like, so it is important you gain a foundation in these concepts.

Public Key Cryptography

Public key cryptography uses a key pair called a private and public key. Whichever one is used to encrypt the data is not the one used to decrypt the data; only the other half of the pair can decrypt the data. Of vital importance is that the private keys are never shared. Only the public key can be, and it is widely distributed to others. We repeat that it is an absolute tenet of public key cryptography that each subject keeps his private key confidential, never sharing it with anyone.

Either key can be used to encrypt, but only the matching key from the pair can then be used to decrypt. In Figure 1.4, the sender uses the public key of the recipient to encrypt her plaintext message into ciphertext. The resulting ciphertext is sent to the recipient who uses her private key to decrypt the ciphertext back into the original plaintext message.

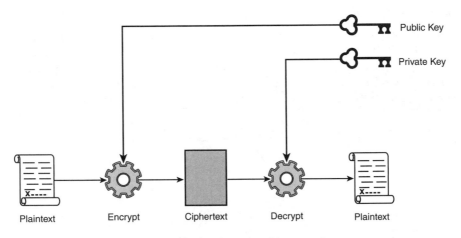

Figure 1.4 The public key (asymmetric) encryption process.

If you want to make sure only the recipient can read your message, use that person's public key to encrypt, and then he and only he using his private key can decrypt. If you want everyone who gets your message to know it came from you and only you, use your private key to encrypt and then the recipients can use your public key to decrypt. Because you keep your private key highly secure, the message could have been encrypted only by you.

Now that you have a basic understanding of encryption and digital signature, we can establish working definitions for critical security concepts that will be used throughout this book.

Security Concepts and Definitions

Authentication, authorization, integrity, confidentiality, and non-repudiation are critical concepts for your understanding of Web services security, so the following sections provide a bit more detail on each one.

Authentication

Authentication involves comparing provided identity information (a "challenge") to something already stored about this individual. Authentication is classically divided into three types: something you *know*, something you *have*, or something you *are*:

- **Something you know**—Pin, password, pass phrase, shared secret
- **Something you have**—Key, card, token
- **Something you are**—Biometrics such as fingerprint, retinal scan, voice print, palm print

Single-factor authentication (using just one of the preceding types) is the simplest but is not very strong. Stealing or guessing a password is easy, and the rightful individual has no way to refute this is the case. Furthermore, because a password is something you know, you can tell it to someone or she can guess it, and with no other factor checked, that person is into the system with nothing stopping her.

Two-factor authentication, also known as strong authentication, is much stronger and is considered the standard when authentication is for anything of high value. Either something you *have* or something you *are* is added to the something you *know* category of shared secret. Something you have is typically a card, token, or device of some sort. Something you are is a biometric such as a fingerprint, retinal scan, or voice print. Outside military applications, authentication stronger than two-factor is rarely found. To strengthen two-factor authentication, you must strengthen the process used to create the individual factors.

How rigorous the authentication needs to be and what types of factors should be used in the one-, two-, or more factors of authentication require that you think about the level of trust needed. What is it that you are trying to protect? If the Web service is one that integrates vendors into your supply chain, and they have no access to critical corporate or customer data, the level of authentication may be lower than for a Web service that integrates an employer to its 401k provider and represents an employee requesting fund reallocation.

Authorization

Authorization is the process of establishing what someone who has been authenticated is allowed to do. The entity receiving the request for service will be granting permissions for each identity to access certain items.

Most Web services coming in over the public network to an enterprise require authentication; it is not usually acceptable to provide services that you expect to be paid for without knowing who is using them. So fundamentally, authorization requires authentication. Additionally, Web services frequently expose vital business data to the requestor, who must be identified and not remain anonymous. Exceptions to this rule are free services that do not care who use them. If a service provides different levels of access depending on who is using it, that service also requires authorization to determine, based on identity, what services are accessible to whom.

One way that authorization is implemented is through a set of credentials that a subject identity carries and presents; those credentials are then mapped into access to certain restricted items. Alternatively, rights can be attached to restricted content, and these rights are mapped to identities and the permissions they will be granted to this content.

On the HTML-based Web, authorization has typically been very coarse grained and either gives access to entire sections of a Web site or denies access completely. With Web services, on the other hand, very fine-grained control specifying access to messages, parts of messages, or content carried by a message is possible. Unlike many security concepts, authorization is actually very easy to understand, but it turns out to be exceedingly complex technologically as well as socially. You will see why in Chapter 6, "Portable Identify, Authentication, and Authorization," which discusses standards such as SAML that are involved with this aspect of identity.

Integrity

Integrity is an assertion that no one has tampered with a message since it was initially created. This assures the sender and the receiver that every bit produced by the sender is received by the recipient in precisely unaltered form. In cryptographic terms, data integrity is accomplished by using digital signatures. Messages in which data integrity is required[7] must explicitly or implicitly include the identity and credentials of the sender to enable this kind of message-level security. Why? Because proving integrity means proving no bits have been changed in the message, which involves sending something with the message that no one in the middle could fraudulently create. That, in turn, requires signing that data with a key that only the sender could have had (more on this in Chapter 4, "Safeguarding the Identity and Integrity of XML Messages"). Message integrity- and identity-related issues (authentication and authorization) are often inter-related. Ironically, no matter how sophisticated your security technology becomes, the core security issue comes down to this: Do you know whom you are dealing with and do you trust those people?

Confidentiality

Confidentiality is keeping the message secret. This process requires encryption, which scrambles the message in such a way that only authorized identities can decrypt and see the data. To do this, you exchange a shared secret and an algorithm for encrypting and decrypting the message. You could imagine Bob and Alice agreeing that they were going to encrypt their messages to each other by adding some number to each letter in the alphabet (the algorithm) and that number would be 2 for the next five days (the key). Thus, the message from Bob to Alice would look scrambled to a reader, and even if you knew the algorithm, you would have to do some analysis (not much in this case) to figure out how to decode the message. In the real world, these algorithms are very challenging mathematical functions with keys that are very large numbers, and the time to do the analysis is technically infeasible even with modern computers.

   With typical contemporary encryption strategies, you provide the algorithm openly and rely on the strength of the key to keep the encryption secure. The trick is keeping the key secret. You could keep the key secret by giving it to the recipients in some way outside the message exchange, such as mailing it to them or phoning them. However, this approach doesn't scale up very well to large numbers of participants, so exchanging this key usually requires Public Key Infrastructure (PKI) technology, which is designed to manage and exchange keys. Chapter 3, "The Foundations of Distributed Message-Level Security," describes PKI in more detail, and Chapter 5, "Ensuring Confidentiality of XML Messages," goes into a lot of detail about encryption, specifically XML Encryption.

---

7. On the Web, for example, message integrity is not required and not possible. You request HTML documents from Web sites and assume you are getting what was sent; because the risks of a bit or a word or even the entire document having been modified is low, you don't worry about message integrity. When the message is a patient record, a purchase order, or a contract, as you expect Web services to carry, you care a lot about integrity.

Non-repudiation

As digital transactions are used in more and more legal contracts and as the acceptability of digital signatures becomes commonplace, the legal aspects of identity will become critical for Web services. First and foremost among those legal aspects of identity is non-repudiation.

Non-repudiation proves that one identity sent the data only to another identity. This then proves that this specific transaction was entered into by the recipient, and neither party can refute or deny that it occurred later. If the transaction is challenged legally, a contract that was supposedly executed must be shown to have been entered into by both parties. Each party must have seen the contract as signed, and their identities—confirmed traditionally by validating "wet" signatures on paper and notary witnesses—must have been confirmed at the time of signing. These are difficult, and as yet legally unchallenged, tenants to uphold in a digital and anonymous world, but that day is coming.

Non-repudiation depends on public key cryptography technology. You prove that one identity sent the data only to another identity because the sender used the recipient's public key, and it is only the recipient with his secret private key who can decrypt the data. To achieve legal non-repudiation, more is needed, such as a separate time-and-date-stamp notary to prove when the transaction occurred as well as independent verification of the participants' identities.

Web Services Security Basics

Building on the brief introduction to Web services and information security, you can now delve into Web services security basics. A basic tenet of Web services security is that no new security technologies were invented. Instead, you will build on established security technologies and purpose them to your message-level security needs.

XML Signature

XML Signature is foundational technology for the standard called WS-Security, covered in detail in Chapter 7, and for Web services security in general. XML Signature is built on top of mature digital signature technology. The purpose of digital signatures is to provide a mechanism for message integrity (no one has changed the message since it was created) and non-repudiation (you cannot refute that this message exchange occurred). XML Signature enables you to encode digital signatures into XML.

Electronic signatures were approved by Congress in June 2000. This approval gives legitimacy to electronic signatures and prevents the contesting of a signed contract solely because it is signed electronically. This event set the stage for digital signature standards. The genesis of XML Signature was a joint IETF/W3C working group called XML-DSig that was established to create a highly extensible signature syntax tightly integrated with existing XML technologies, but one that could also handle composite documents from diverse application domains as well. The XML-Signature Syntax and Processing W3C Recommendation defines the XML Signature syntax and associated processing rules. Its ancestors include PKCS#7 Signature and S/MIME. PKCS#7 is part of Public Key Cryptography Standards (PKCS) created by RSA Data Security. With this standard, someone could sign XML, but not in a way consistent with standardized XML format. And it was not possible to sign just part of an XML document as it is with XML Signature. Secure Multipurpose Internet Mail Extensions (S/MIME) already provided a way to bind a digital signature to an email message in a way that allowed the recipient to verify both integrity and non-repudiation of the signer.

XML Signature is a core foundation for Web services security. It was the first XML security standard to reach recommendation status. It is core to WS-Security, XKMS, and other Web services security standards you will be learning much more about. It will be core to your being able to provide integrity and non-repudiation, and you will also find it to be invaluable in the process of transporting shared secret keys that are needed by XML Encryption.

XML Signature is the topic of Chapter 4.

XML Encryption

Like XML Signature, XML Encryption is built on top of mature cryptographic technology—in this case, shared key encryption technology. Core requirements for XML Encryption are that it must be able to encrypt an arbitrarily sized XML message, and it must do so efficiently. Those two factors led its creators to choose shared key (symmetric) encryption as the foundation for XML Encryption. Encryption provides for message confidentiality (the message will be secret from all but the intended recipient). The reason XML Encryption is needed over and above transport-level encryption such as SSL is that you need to maintain confidentiality of messages in the face of the message taking multiple hops on its way to its destination. This will be common when shared services are utilized. You also need confidentiality when the XML message is stored even after it reaches its final destination. This requirement is called *persistent confidentiality*.

Like XML Signature, XML Encryption applies standard algorithms to data and then stores that encrypted result in XML. And as with XML Signature, you can apply encryption selectively only to portions of a document.

XML Encryption builds on and shares several concepts with XML Signature. Like XML Signature, it is a W3C Recommendation. It is a vitally important second foundation to Web services security because it is the way you will achieve confidentiality in your XML messages. Remember, the key benefit XML Encryption brings over any other encryption strategy is that it allows confidentiality to be satisfied across more than just the context of a single SOAP request.

XML Encryption is the topic of Chapter 5.

SAML

The purpose of SAML is to allow trust assertions to be specified in XML. Assertions apply to an individual or an entity and are "attached" to a message and go where it goes, leading to the simple description of SAML as enabling "portable trust." SAML assertions take the form of authentications, authorizations, or attributes of entities. Assertions can be claims, statements, or declarations. Assertions are accepted as true only in the context of the integrity and authenticity of the entity making the assertions. At this point, the situation becomes really complicated: Everything you are counting on depends on third parties; you have to trust them to trust the individual on whose behalf claims and assertions are being made.

SAML defines a set of Web APIs (that is, Web services) to be used to obtain these assertions from trust services that make authorization and authentication decisions about individuals and entities. After the SAML authority has made its assertions, SAML also provides a way to exchange this information with other systems. As you will see, WS-Security is enabled to use SAML as one of its *security tokens* applied to a SOAP message. You will also look at a large project called Project Liberty that is setting out to use SAML (and actually extend it) assertions across multiple security domains, allowing single sign-on to a *circle of trust* established between business partners.

SAML came from a blending of the two early standards efforts around portable trust called S2ML and AuthML. SAML is developed through the Organization for the Advancement of Structured Information Standards (OASIS) XML-based Security Services Technical Committee (SSTC). SAML 1.0 was approved as a standard in November 2002, version 1.1 was approved as an OASIS standard in August 2003, and a working group is already discussing v2.0.

SAML is the topic of Chapter 6.

WS-Security

XML Signature and XML Encryption are about XML security. So what is WS-Security about? It is about SOAP security.

WS-Security is an overarching conceptual model that abstracts different security technologies into "claims" and "tokens." Ways to package security tokens into SOAP messages are the nuts and bolts of WS-Security. The broader context of WS-Security is a set of additional road-map specifications built on these concepts and solidified into XML specifications. They involve how to apply for a security token, how tokens are linked to identity, how they are linked to a Web service, and more.

Microsoft initially released WS-Security in October 2001. In April 2002, IBM and VeriSign joined Microsoft in releasing their joint document called "Security in a Web Services World." This initial security framework was submitted to OASIS in June 2002. OASIS formed the Web Services Security (WSS) technical committee in September 2002 to standardize this specification. Most platform and tools vendors will have shipped support for the initial WS-Security draft specification by early 2004. The WS-Security specification reached "committee draft" status in January 2004.

WS-Security provides a mechanism that allows you to digitally sign (using XML Signature) all or part of a SOAP message and pass the signature in the SOAP header. It provides a mechanism that allows you to encrypt (using XML Encryption) all or part of a SOAP message. It also provides a way to pass information in a SOAP header about the encryption keys needed to decrypt the message or verify the digital signature. And it allows trust assertions about the SOAP message to be passed in the SOAP header as well. A variety of bindings for security tokens have been defined. All these tokens will be explained in detail later.

WS-Security is the topic of Chapter 7.

Trust Issues

WS-Policy allows organizations exposing Web services to specify the specific requirements of their Web services for such issues as privacy or security. WS-Policy is a high-level specification providing the basic constructs needed to compose a particular policy language (such as WS-SecurityPolicy). Closely related to WS-Policy is WS-PolicyAssertions, which provides some basic policy assertions that would apply to any type of policy (for example, the Language assertion), and WS-PolicyAttachment, which gives guidance on how to attach a policy to a resource (for example, a WSDL). WS-SecurityPolicy is a specific type of policy using the WS-Policy framework that answers certain security requirement and configuration questions for a Web service, such as What encryption algorithms are supported? What parameters must be encrypted? What types of security tokens are understood?

The WS-Policy family is the topic of Chapter 8.

Other WS-Security–Related Specs

WS-Security is a broad description of a framework indicating how to secure Web services. To complete the picture begun with the discussions of WS-Security and how it can be used to secure SOAP messages and continued with the policy framework described by WS-Policy and its constituents, we need to fill in the other technologies related to and used by WS-Security. They include more policy-related specifications such as WS-Privacy; the WS-Trust API to trust services; topics related to federation such as WS-Federation, WS-Authorization, and WS-SecureConversation; and a suite of supporting standards not directly in the WS-★ family. Those other important standards include The XML Key Management Specification (XKMS), eXtensible Access Control Markup Language (XACML), and eXtensible Rights Markup Language (XrML).

Coverage of other WS-Security–related specifications and technologies appears in Chapter 9, "Trust, Access Control, and Rights for Web Services."

Summary

This chapter asked the question "What are Web services, and why do they need security?" The answer is that Web services are the latest evolution of middleware that creates a loosely coupled RPC mechanism for application and information integration.

This chapter provided a brief introduction to XML, SOAP, and WSDL. The XML language is not only the way Web services messages are formatted, but it is also the language in which all other Web services standards are defined. XML is not new, and there are mature standards for securing XML messages. SOAP is the packaging mechanism for transporting XML messages over networking protocols and for treating XML as an RPC mechanism. WSDL separates the interface for a Web service from its implementation.

There are many types of application integration, and this chapter briefly covered the most common types and described why they need security. Internal application integration is most commonly used to integrate information from different sources within an organization to create more useful and more powerful composite applications. These types of integration need security from prying internal eyes and to comply with internal as well as external business practice policy regulations. B2B business process integration allows organizations to integrate with their supply chain or demand chain. Knowing for sure who is using what information is critical because these types of integration involve business-critical information exchange. Portals are used internally and externally as a way to aggregate information and applications into a single browser-accessible Web site. Users of portals must be authenticated to prove they are part of the group allowed access to the information. Service-oriented architecture is an approach more and more in favor as organizations try to leverage their information-processing assets maximally. SOA allows reuse of useful components and rapid construction of new applications. In SOA, messages move from point to point to point and need to maintain integrity and confidentiality all throughout their journey.

To fulfill all the security requirements Web services will place on you, this chapter asked the question "What are the core concepts of security that you need to know?" The answer starts with cryptography, a branch of mathematics focused on keeping secrets. The crypto-algorithms used to make messages secret are called encryption. The key to keeping secrets is in the keys to these algorithms. In shared key encryption, both sender and receiver share the same key for encryption and decryption of the message. In public key encryption, a matched pair of keys is used, one for encryption and its mate, and only its mate, for decryption. When you know what basic encryption is, the other critical concepts to understand and embrace are authentication (who is it?), authorization (what are they allowed to do?), integrity (is their message unaltered since they sent it?), confidentiality (was the message indecipherable by anyone intercepting it?), and non-repudiation (can you prove the message was indeed sent?).

Finally, this chapter introduced the Web services security basics that build on the security concepts just described. XML Signature provides integrity and non-repudiation for XML messages. XML Encryption provides confidentiality for XML messages. SAML assures the identity of a subject is made trustable and portable so that it can be attached to XML messages. WS-Security makes the entire SOAP system secure. And associated with WS-Security are also a host of other standards that help address a variety of trust issues brought on by Web services.

2

The Foundations of Web Services

THIS CHAPTER PRESENTS THE FOUNDATIONS of Web services. Before you can delve into the security of Web services, you need to make sure you have a solid understanding of how Web services work and, most importantly, what issues make Web services both critically dependent on good security and also so challenging for good security practices.

The Gestalt of Web Services

ge·stalt or **Ge·stalt** (g-shtält)

n. a configuration or pattern of elements so unified as a whole that it cannot be described merely as a sum of its parts.[1]

We say *gestalt* of Web services because we are going to show that, although most presentations of Web services describe the piece-part standards and technologies that taken together equal Web services, we believe that approach does not do justice to the unified concept of Web services. Instead, we believe it is much more instructive to look back at how distributed computing and middleware systems have evolved, how Web services relate to those previous generations of distributed computing, how Web services are similar or different from their ancestors, and what all of this means for Web services security. First, you need to understand the business problems that have driven the need for Web-based middleware.

Application Integration

Application integration occurs when you allow different software systems to share or aggregate information. For most of the history of computing, application integration has happened between applications that reside within corporate boundaries, but increasingly in a networked and integrated world, integrations reach outside organization boundaries. The fact is, applications do not work in a vacuum, and most need to communicate and be integrated with other applications to be effective.

---

1. Cognitive Science Laboratory's WordNet, Princeton University.
http://www.cogsci.princeton.edu/~wn/

Enterprise Application Integration

There is still a huge need for internal applications to share or aggregate information, and this creates a large backlog of need for integrating applications. One common example of the need for internal application integration comes from the way companies organize data about their customers. Some of that data might be in a customer relationship management (CRM) system, but that is not where the billing history with those same customers resides. When those customers are part of the company supply chain, that aspect of the relationship with them might be in a totally separate system. In some cases, a large enterprise acquires a smaller one and then finds itself with two different vendors' CRM systems. Acquisitions are a common cause of the need to integrate internal applications. Most major enterprise IT initiatives, such as enterprise resource planning (ERP), CRM, sales force automation, supply chain management, and more, are application integration initiatives.

B2C and B2B Application Integration

Organizations are discovering that there is potentially much higher value when they integrate applications between themselves and others. You can find numerous cases of business-to-consumer (B2C) integration that creates a holistic and better experience for consumers from a variety of disparate sources and applications. Amazon, Orbitz, and Yahoo! are all B2C application integration examples. Business-to-business (B2B) application integrations are increasingly important and common. Frequently, they integrate some sort of trading partner community. B2C and B2B integrations are helped by the fact that, for several years now, most companies have been building more and more of their capabilities with a Web face and are therefore prepared to deal with a networked world.

Countless businesses, each with its unique core competencies and value-add products and services, have been building more and more of their capabilities with a Web interface since the creation of the Web. Sometimes the motivation has been to provide higher value to Web-facing applications by directly integrating a business partner's services as features of the host business's application (as opposed to having users click away and start using the partner's Web site!). Increasingly, there is a huge demand for making applications out of multiple, distinct Web delivery points. But there are well-established standards for how you communicate on the Web, so these standards should be leveraged as you strive to make unified Web-based distributed applications. In some cases, the protocols you needed to accomplish this did not exist, so the past few years have seen a frenetic effort—which continues apace—to nail down the remaining standards. Consistent with the Web, these protocols and standards are ostensibly vendor neutral, eliminating the mutual assured destruction of past distributed computing efforts.

Note

We say "ostensibly vendor neutral" because some large vendors are influencing the standards processes to such an extent as to call vendor neutrality into question. Although this sounds bad on the surface, in practice if all other vendors fall into line, the desired result is achieved: All vendors agree to and build to a unified standard. The big vendors feel there is so much at stake and the standards committee process can be so lengthy that they are short-circuiting the process by building out standards themselves and then presenting them to a standards group like OASIS for discussion, recommendation, and finalization.

A number of other business issues are driving the need to integrate applications and information. Let's explore them now, starting with the need to automate and streamline business processes.

Automating Business Processes

Business processes—even the simplest ones such as requesting vacation time off—do not neatly stay within only one application. For an employee vacation request, at least the HR systems and the corporate financial systems need to communicate to approve and accrue for employee paid time off. Different applications assist in different parts of a business process. In the case of processing an order, one application handles ERP, one handles inventory, one handles billing, one handles customer information, and so on. When processes cross application boundaries, information needs to be shared; otherwise, the humans involved will either do a poorer or, at best, a less efficient job. Frequently, humans compensate for unintegrated applications, and you will find manual translation of information between one system and another, even in the operationally best companies. This outcome is unacceptable in today's business environment. Efficient information exchange, transparency of actual transactions, and data integration are fundamental and critical to the business process. So too are repeatability, auditability, and accountability, all of which require secure automated and monitored middleware systems.

Information Aggregation Portals

A portal is an integrated and personalized Web-based interface to information, applications, and collaborative services. Access to most portals is limited to corporate employees (an *intracompany* portal) or corporate employees and certain qualified vendors, contractors, customers, and other parties within the extended enterprise (an *intercompany* portal). Portals are also used on the Web to provide a single site for consumers to see a variety of related information, goods, or services.

The trend toward portals as a way to provide an information aggregation point accessible ultimately via a browser is testament to the importance of integration. Portals are used to deliver more products and services to employees, partners, or consumers by aggregating information from numerous sources into a single browser interface. Examples of consumer portals are numerous, including CNN, CBS Marketwatch, a portal site for parents of college-age children, and many more. Increasingly, portals are also used to deliver a single point of access to employees or business partners about a company and its internal operations, such as an employee benefits portal or a partner activities portal. Portals are used to create a simple interface on a collection of features previously encapsulated in a proprietary application or applications that would have required a client download but now provide the same functionality through a browser. The ubiquity of the browser and the "thinness" of a browser-based client make this paradigm a convenient way to offer application services to the end user.

All these examples have some security challenges. Orbitz's business partners, such as Delta Airlines, Marriott Hotels, and Avis Rent-a-Car, want to respond to Orbitz's requests for product availability but do not want to provide that information to someone other than Orbitz, who they are sure will pay them for it. Company intranet portals are incredibly powerful and useful resources for the people authorized to use them but could be damaging to the company or its employees if accessed by unauthorized people. Even internally accessed applications now surfacing their functionality through browser interfaces must have stringent controls over information security. Because all these types of portals are being developed using Web services, these and other security requirements will have to be addressed by Web services security.

The Importance of Universal Application Connectivity

The need for a universal way of connecting applications has been a driving force in the industry for 20 years. It has led to *middleware*. Middleware is *plumbing* software that connects computers and applications together. The goal for middleware is to make it easy for applications (and the users who use them) to access remote resources. Technologies such as Distributed Computing Environment (DCE) were used to integrate back-end legacy systems to newer, lighter user interfaces like Windows. This need is strong on the Web because e-business forces companies to expose their business processes over the Web. Those business processes have traditionally been codified into "back-end" systems.

Virtually every application requires integration. Business process automation and workflow rely on integration. Portals require integration. Knowledge management requires integration. Business intelligence requires integration. Universal application connectivity is all about better decision making. It is about better customer services, better product initiatives, and even better homeland security.

The ultimate goal many hold for Web services is service-oriented architecture (SOA). This is the essence of universal application connectivity. SOA makes every application act as a service hub using the Web as middleware. Web services and SOA provide a significant boon to application integration by making the interface to every SOA-adapted application standard, published, discoverable, and self-describing.

The Evolution of Distributed Computing

Distributed computing is an approach to computer-to-computer communication. It has remained a goal ever since time-sharing on mainframes reached its limitations. Either one computer was not really enough to complete the job, or islands of computing were found to be ineffective when business processes were seen to cross application boundaries. Distributed computing is also an approach to higher reliability and availability because it removes single points of failure for applications. The means of communication between the distributed systems—frequently euphemistically referred to as *plumbing*—is called middleware.

Middleware

The Distributed Computing Environment was an early '90s effort to standardize various competing remote procedure call (RPC) technologies. DCE was driven by the Open Group—a consortium of otherwise competing companies originally called Open Software Foundation (OSF). DCE's goal was distributed applications across heterogeneous systems. This was part of the late-80s to early-90s focus on "open" systems. If you recall, this was right in the middle of the client/server computing paradigm. At the time, everyone had lots of high-productivity, relatively new client machines that ran nice windowing operating systems. But they also had lots of fast, expensive, business-critical backend systems that they needed to utilize and even try to leverage more. This situation seems not to have changed much even today.

DCE was wildly successful in achieving some of its goals. It was the first attempt to operate independently of the operating system and networking technology. It succeeded at this effort. DCE was implemented as a set of software services that reside on top of the operating system. It was middleware that *used* lower-level operating system and network resources, as shown in Figure 2.1.

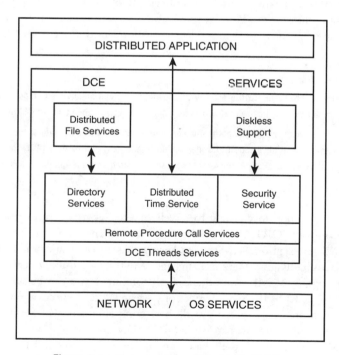

Figure 2.1   Components and services in DCE.

DCE broke ground on major distributed applications and formed part of the knowledge base from which Web services evolved. Barclay's—a huge bank—processed live transactions from 2,000 distributed locations using DCE. Charles Schwab handled 25,000 real-time stock transactions per day from a large DCE deployment. 3M deployed distributed clients to 87,000 employees worldwide for DCE-based access to mainframes and legacy applications—before the conversion to the company's intranet.

At about the same time, Common Object Request Broker Architecture (CORBA) was a huge middleware project led by the Object Management Group; this group included more than 700 companies—everyone it seems except Microsoft, which had its own competing Distributed Component Object Model (DCOM). The underlying communications protocol used by CORBA was called the Internet Inter-ORB Protocol (IIOP). In October 1996, Marc Andreesen, Netscape's co-founder, unknowingly contributed to the hype when he said, "The next shift catalyzed by the Web will be the adoption of enterprise systems based on distributed objects and IIOP. IIOP will manage the communication between the object components that power the system. Users will be pointing and clicking at objects available on IIOP-enabled servers."[2] This did not happen with IIOP as he had envisioned, but it is precisely what is happening with Web services.

A major failing of CORBA was its complexity, which contributed to making it much less scalable than DCE. This failure occurred because of its attempt to be too pure to object-oriented philosophies. However, CORBA was very strong on security, and much of what is happening today in Web services security traces directly from CORBA security.

> **Note**
>
> The following quote, from the CORBA security specification introduction, gives a glimpse into how all the issues Web services security has to deal with were front and center in the minds of CORBA's developers:
>
> "CORBA security services specify the authentication, authorization, and encrypting of messages. The user has all the instruments at his disposal. The span ranges from access-control-lists (ACL) for groups of objects (without impact on the application program) to very sophisticated and fine-grained mechanisms for sensitive data.[3]"

We may never see—nor do we want to—Web services security reach a single specification of 430 pages, as CORBA's did. However, when the specifications for XML Signature, XML Encryption, WS-Security, Security Assertion Markup Language (SAML), Kerberos, eXtensible Rights Markup Language (XrML), eXtensible Access Control Markup Language (XACML),and others are all combined, you can be sure it is more than the 430 pages CORBA used. The lessons learned and the innovations applied in CORBA security are clearly present in all these components of Web services security.

At about this same time, over at Microsoft, DCOM took its Component Object Model (COM)—which was loosely based on DCE—and extended it to allow applications to be built from COM objects that resided in different networked machines. This model was platform-neutral as long as it was a Win32 platform. DCOM was transport-

---

2. The Netscape Web site. http://wp.netscape.com/columns/techvision/iiop.html

3. See the CORBA security specification at http://www.omg.org/docs/formal/02-03-11.pdf.

neutral but virtually always used TCP/IP. DCOM was too complex, too fine-grained, too proprietary, and it was not scalable. However, it provided critical learning that went directly into Microsoft's .NET Web services.

The Web: *The* Global Network for Information Exchange

The Web forms the most pervasive distributed computing infrastructure ever envisioned. There are approximately 46 million registered Internet domains[4]. There are 172 million Internet hosts[5]. More than 500,000 of the servers on the Internet have Secure Socket Layer (SSL) certificates to support Transport Layer Security[6]. There are in excess of 3 billion accessible Web page documents[7]. Across all corporations, for every computer supporting the company's presence on the Web, we postulate that there are, on average, at least 10 completely internal servers also using the same Web technologies. If this is true, it means that as Web services become pervasive on internal not just external servers, this new form of middleware could theoretically affect almost 2 billion servers.

The Web is based on text messages; traditionally, they have been HTML documents, but increasingly they are XML dialect documents. Virtually all applications can deal with text messages.

The Web is also based on resources and links. Hypertext represents the links. The Web has exploited hypertext to create an incredible collection of interconnected documents based on unique identifiers. Those identifiers are called *uniform resource identifiers (URIs)*. A URI is a compact, formatted, text-based name that uniquely identifies a resource. A *URL*, on the other hand, substitutes *locator* for *identifier* and is a URI that is bound to a physical network address.

You interact with these Web resources via a protocol such as HTTP, SMTP, and FTP for Web browsing, email, and file transfer, respectively. The first part of a URL can indicate the application protocol to use when interacting with the resource, as in `http://www.sams.com`.

Virtually every organization has invested in computing infrastructure (or pays fees to someone who has on its behalf) to support its participation in the Web. Middleware that leverages this enormous investment and enormous commitment to a set of ubiquitous international standards will have an immediate acceptance unlike anything in computing history. This is the main reason for Web services' rapid adoption.

Web services were defined to communicate using the Internet and the infrastructure created for the Web (links, resources, transport protocols, security, and firewalls). Not surprisingly, Web Services Security begins with the security developed for the Web. We will discuss SSL and other building blocks for Web Services Security later.

---

4. Netcraft Web server survey, January 2004, `www.netcraft.com`

5. The Internet Domain Survey, January 2003, `http://www.isc.org/ds/WWW-200301/`

6. Netcraft SSL survey, `http://www.netcraft.com`

7. Search Engine Showdown,
`http://www.searchengineshowdown.com/stats/sizeest.shtm`

Early Web Services Using HTTP POSTing as an API

You have the Web, you have a Web site and the servers to run it, and you have a Web-facing application that uses HTML forms displayed in your site visitor's browsers. You realize you need to have a human who is using a browser access not just that form but your business partner's application as well. This happens because your business partner wants to incorporate your Web application directly into one of its own. What do you do?

If the set of standards and technologies currently being called Web services did not yet exist to integrate your applications to theirs, you would do what thousands of developers at their companies did: You would directly co-opt the Web as middleware using HTTP POST technology.

From the formal W3C HTTP specification:

"POST is a standard method in HTTP used to request that the server accept the entity enclosed in the request as a new subordinate of the resource identified in the Request-URI."[8]

Listing 2.1 shows what the POST looks like for a simple HTML-based form posted on a Web site.

Listing 2.1 **An HTTP POST Header for a Simple HTML Form**

```
POST /companyForm HTTP/1.1
    Host: www.awl.com
    Content-Type: application/x-www-form-urlencoded/
    Content-Length: 63
    firstname=Jothy&lastname=Rosenberg&email=jothy@acm.org&sex=male
```

HTTP POST used in this way creates a Web API. It treats a Web form normally accessed interactively through a browser as a programmatic interface accessed by another application from a remote location. Effectively, this is an RPC. As an API, it is very brittle—one tiny change to a form and it breaks. However, compared to DCE's RPC mechanism, this is much further up the protocol stack, so it is firewall friendly and much easier to support in the IT infrastructure. Companies used POST as an API because they were desperate. The fact that so much of this was going on was a strong impetus to nailing down the Web services standards and putting them into use.

As you will see later, SOAP, one of the key Web services–enabling standards, uses the HTTP POST mechanism, which makes SOAP slide into IT environments so easily.

The Inevitability of Web Services

You may wonder why Web services are being developed now. The reason is that the entire software industry has finally decided that there is more value in firms and consumers easily sharing information than in keeping data locked away. This is what happens

---

8. RFC 2616: Hypertext Transfer Protocol: HTTP/1.1. `ftp://ftp.isi.edu/in-notes/rfc2616.txt`

in any maturing industry: making sure one vendor's product works with everybody else's product. That's right, standards. Think about the light bulb socket, two-by-four lumber, and standard-gauge rail beds; each of those standards led to an explosion of use. That is what we and many others believe we are witnessing now with Web services.

There is an inevitability about Web services. They are not just the newest fad that is being overhyped (although they *are* being overhyped). This is the natural evolution of the Web, of distributed computing, and of e-business needs. As e-business has progressed from islands of marketing information about products and services to islands of credit-card retail stations to portals, the Web has been evolving from an information-centric platform to an application-centric platform. This is not a replay of the CORBA fiasco. The unification and the shear number of vendors working on these services dwarf what was accomplished with CORBA, DCOM, and DCE combined. Every tool, every major language, every vendor, even every enterprise is jumping into Web services because each one sees them as an approach that will work.

As with all previous successful development paradigm technology shifts, real success comes only when the programmers adopt something, not when the business people alone see the benefits. Web services give developers tools that can locate and utilize all functions and interfaces for interesting applications within and between organizations. When you deliver innovation to developers that actually increases their productivity in a major way, you see rapid adoption—which is the only thing that can shift the entire computing industry to a new application development paradigm like Web services. The same thing happened with Unix, C++, client/server computing, Java, and XML, to name just a few radical developer productivity multipliers.

What we want to get from Web services is to have both "perfect" enterprise application integration and "perfect" distributed computing in the same package of standard protocols, tools, languages, and interfaces. That grandiose vision may be unrealistic. But developers will not be fooled by hype and will continue to push these standards and aim for these goals. Several standards are still incomplete or immature, especially in the security area—the focus of this book. The development and management tools are still quite immature as well. However, the pent-up demand that met Java's introduction—an unprecedented adoption rate that was 10 times the adoption rate of C++—seems to at least be matched by the demand for Web services.

How We Got Here

It may at times seem as though Web services either just suddenly appeared out of nowhere or, at a minimum, evolved from the basic standards upon which the browser-based Web was built. Neither is true.

Web services are a natural evolutionary result of decades of work on distributed computing and, as with those previous generations, were driven by a continuing application integration crisis. The need to integrate all applications remains and, if anything, grows stronger because the current "integration" is frequently a human who copies information from one application's screen to another.

Successive generations of middleware evolved through experimentation with each generation building on the strengths and lessons learned from those preceding. RPC mechanisms evolved in this fashion. So did message-oriented middleware. The vision of a service-oriented architecture appeared early but remained quite elusive.

Then came the explosion of the Web, which began in earnest in 1994 when TCP/IP connectivity landed on everyone's desktops and Tim Berners-Lee's HTTP and HTML combined with Marc Andreesen's Mosaic and Netscape browsers created a new meaning for the word *surfing*. The pervasiveness of the Web is what made clear how the next generation of middleware should be built. It should leverage all the technology, standards, and infrastructure that already existed in most organizations supporting the Web.

Client/server was a major paradigm shift in how applications should be constructed and had its biggest impact on companies that for the first time started connecting all employees into the network to access centralized application resources. But it didn't take long to start building frustration with fat clients. Getting them installed and configured for all the people who needed them, updating them when new updates were needed, and providing training and support, as each one had its own ideas about how user interfaces should work, became so prohibitively expensive and time-consuming that companies and users began to rebel. The alternative was browser-based applications. Sometimes these applications are called portals when they combine information from numerous sources or applications. Many, if not most, of the issues of fat clients had been solved, but new issues with thin clients created their own new frustrations. The lack of interactivity and slow response time were huge backward steps from the high productivity that users of fat clients were accustomed to. In effect, browser-based applications with their Submit buttons felt very much like the old "green screen" applications of mainframe days.

There were some interesting early attempts at what are now called Web services. The first was the invention of browser frames. With frames, a site visited by a browser could create a new frame in the user's browser and redirect just that portion of the screen to a new URL. The original site remained in control of the overall browser, its outermost frame, and its security. Sites wanted to retain their users (a concept called *stickiness*) while still "integrating" the other sites into the overall information presented to the browser's user. CGI was another example of struggling with existing capabilities to deliver what are expected now from Web services. CGI allowed a browser to initiate execution of any program if a script to do so was installed and accessible on the Web server.

The most telling of all examples of the need for Web services and the almost desperate attempts to simulate them was the extensive use of HTTP POST as an integration scheme. Site A that had a Web application humans normally accessed through browsers could be integrated into site B's Web application if site B could "screen scrape" all the interactions necessary to make site A think a browser was interacting with it. This result was accomplished by having site B send the same HTTP POSTs to site A that would have been sent by a browser directly accessing it.

Along came XML to solve the problem of how different applications, organizations, and databases reach agreement on the way data they want to interchange should be structured and defined. XML made business information transportable. This was a huge contrast to client/server applications that each defined the database schema and binary data being transported unto itself with no eye toward integration with other applications, much less other organizations. But business processes never had and never will stay isolated within only one application. Companies were driving cost and inefficiencies out of their business processes, and they were looking at their supply chains, where paper-based processes ruled.

As companies became the dominant force behind application development, their tolerance for lack of inter-operability between platforms and applications became dominant as well. This was one of the reasons for Java's unprecedented acceptance, growth, and displacement of C++ as the enterprise's application development language of choice. IT budget pressures also drove companies to demand better ways to deal with their application integration crises.

The drive for platform neutrality, language independence, and interoperability in the face of heterogeneity finally reached the major vendors. For the first time, IBM, Microsoft, and others who joined them drove a set of middleware standards that were common, consistent, and quickly supported in their respective tools and platforms. This started with the collaboration between Microsoft and IBM to drive SOAP. It is fair to say that, the moment SOAP was proposed as a standard from these two vendors, Web services were born.

Security Challenges

A Web service is middleware that uses the Web infrastructure. It integrates applications inside and outside the organization. It enables a service-oriented architecture. Distributed computing has always had a challenging set of security issues. In this section, we explore the security challenges brought on by Web services.

Identities

One of the greatest security challenges brought on by Web services revolves around identities. Web services transport potential unknown identities into your organization. These identities are not individuals directly connected to your computer; they are connected to someone else's computer, and that person is presenting these identities on their behalf. Their identities are essentially attached to the Web service messages. Say a 401k provider offers a Web service to employers, who then have the problem of authenticating an employee and passing the authenticated identity of that employee from the company intranet portal back through the Web service to the 401k provider. Who are these individuals really? What services are they requesting? Are they authorized to do so? These are the security questions that must be answered for the 401k scenario to play out.

Another big problem created by Web services is asset protection. It is a sad but true fact that the vast majority of corporate intellectual property compromises are perpetrated from inside the organization. Web services can potentially make this problem worse unless you secure them first. A critical question, then, is this: What proprietary information is leaving the organization at the request of these persons? After they are done, can it be proven that they did these things?

Web services security problems related to identities are such a critical issue that we discuss them in several places in this book. All of Chapter 6, "Portable Identity, Authentication, and Authorization," is about portable identities and the authentication and authorization of those identities. In addition, Chapter 7, "Building Security into SOAP," focuses on how the WS-Security standard represents an identity and attaches it to a SOAP message.

Messages

Web services, at their core, are messages being transported from one place to another. Securing these messages is a variant of classic information security. The messages themselves, or things they refer to, need to be secured. That means confidentiality and integrity—two core concepts of information security. Because these messages are sometimes legal documents, they may need to be signed, so you need non-repudiation to be able to prove that a transaction took place, who initiated it, and when. These security concepts will be explored in depth in Chapter 3, "The Foundations of Distributed Message-Level Security."

Service-Oriented Architectures

Service-oriented architectures provide software as a service that leads to composite applications being constructed from a collection of reusable service components. SOAs built with Web services result in multi-hop message flow, as one Web service calls another service to handle one piece of functionality before the result is passed on to yet another service in the chain. The information transported this way must be kept confidential from all the entities that touch it along its way. The essence of SOA is that, instead of having software systems deployed as functionality accessed through specialized client software, functionality is accessed by sending the SOA application a request to which it responds. Stated another way, an application's full functionality is accessible through a request-response paradigm. The target application provides a service. The communication to this service is expected to be a Web service. If the service is not free, authentication is needed to make sure only authorized users access the service. If the content is confidential, responses to service requests may need to be kept confidential in transit, or perhaps the authenticity of the information's source may need to be proved in some secure way. Figure 2.2 shows how many different applications used by different types of users might all access a shared service.

At this point, we are ready to delve into the core component standards that make up Web services. We will cover each of these topics generally to be complete, but in all cases we will show how the various standards interrelate to the other standards and make sure the security context of each standard is plain. First, we will build on the description of XML, which was briefly introduced in Chapter 1, "Basic Concepts of Web Services Security."

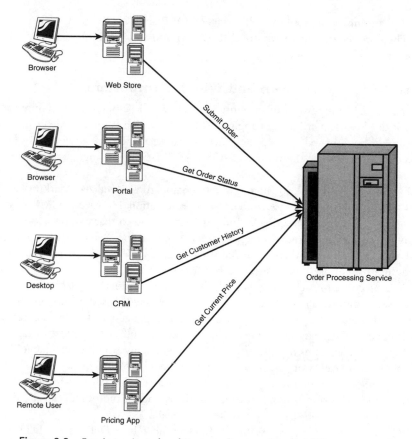

Figure 2.2   Service-oriented architecture diagram showing different types of
applications accessing a shared service.

XML: Meta-Language for Data-Oriented Interchange

The eXtensible Markup Language (XML) provides a standard text-based language that
all applications can understand. XML is completely platform neutral, is a universal data
format, and is self-describing. These points will become extremely critical to our Web
services security discussions. XML's text-based nature does make messages much bulkier,
but no special middleware is needed to process them. Security is much easier to monitor
with text-based messages than with proprietary binary formats. This point is critical
because security requires monitoring to provide assurance it is working as well as an
audit trail for later *discovery and defense* in case of challenge or incident.

XML is the heart and soul of Web services. SOAP and WSDL are described using XML. The core security standards of XML Encryption and XML Signature are also XML-based.

Where XML Came From and Why It's Important

XML is essential to the world of structured data. It was developed to overcome the limitations of the Hypertext Markup Language (HTML), which is good at describing how things should be displayed but is poor at describing what the data means that is being displayed. XML is already the most widely accepted data interchange format ever devised.

The granddaddy of markup languages is the Standard Generalized Markup Language (SGML). Its goal was to separate content from presentation. However, SGML was too large and too complex to describe Web documents. It had so many optional features that confounded simple sender-receiver agreements critical to the Web's early vision. So, HTML was the quick and dirty approach used to get the Web going with its rich text and graphics pages linked together using hypertext.

HTML succeeded in achieving its goals. It is a simple, human-readable format that uses one set of tags for all documents, and it is completely focused on documents. However, a fixed set of tags cannot *describe* data. Catalogs need a `<PRICE>` tag; repair manuals need a `<PARTNUM>` tag; drugs need `<ALLERGEN>` and `<SIDE-EFFECT>` tags. If you could apply these tags, this data description would suddenly become searchable. A non-extensible format could not add new tags and tell people (or machines) what they meant. No one except the browser manufacturers was able to add tags to HTML. In contrast, with XML, companies, consortia, standards bodies, and others can define their own document types with their own unique metadata.

HTML allows for little reuse. With XML, Document Type Definitions (DTDs)—now rapidly being replaced by XML Schema—allow communities to agree on schemas for types of data. This has been done in chemistry, music, math, insurance, pharmaceuticals, and hundreds of other industries. Individual companies even create schemas for internal use within their companies, as Merrill Lynch has done with its own X4ML.

XML addresses the engineering complexity of SGML and the fixed tag set of HTML. XML documents are completely legal SGML documents. XML is *not* an application of SGML, but it is a true subset of it. The most powerful attribute of SGML is the most powerful attribute of XML as well: It is extensible. Don't be fooled into thinking XML is not mature. The XML subset of SGML has already been in use for 15 years.

XML is technically a meta-language. It is used to define other languages. If you tell a computer about your language for insurance forms, software on that computer can parse the XML and extract the customer name and coverage amount correctly. Two different computers running different applications built in different languages by different teams can read the same XML, and both unambiguously have the same information content. This was not possible in HTML or any other format used to communicate between different applications or different organizations.

XML and Web Services

Data destined for a Web service can either be created in XML or converted into XML from its native format. This data may be taken from tables in a relational database or processed by a programming language such as Java or C# and then transformed into XML.

XML stores data within descriptive element tags like this:

```
<PartNo>54-2345</PartNo>
```

Here, `<PartNo>` is the descriptive element tag, and `54-2345` is the data it describes. XML tags are enclosed within angle brackets (< >) and have a start and an end. The end tag is marked by a leading slash (/). Elements can have one or more attributes using name/value pairs:

```
<Price Currency="USD">59.95</Price>
<TransportCode Type="Air" Carrier="United">452</TransportCode>
```

XML's tag structure is hierarchical. One tag may contain any number of tags within it as demonstrated in Listing 2.2.

Listing 2.2   XML's Hierarchical Tag Structure for a <ShipOrder> Construct

```xml
<?xml version="1.0"?>
<shipOrder>
  <shipTo>
    <name>Tove Svendson</name>
    <street>Ragnhildvei 2</street>
    <address>4000 Stavanger</address>
    <country>Norway</country>
  </shipTo>
  <items>
    <item>
      <title>Empire Burlesque</title>
      <quantity>1</quantity>
      <price>10.90</price>
    </item>
    <item>
      <title>Hide your heart</title>
      <quantity>1</quantity>
      <price>9.90</price>
    </item>
  </items>
</shipOrder>
```

XML Namespaces

To protect names in one XML document from being confused with the names in another document, XML namespaces provide a mechanism to keep these names separate and distinct. A namespace operates much the same way a package construct in C++ or Java keeps the names of local data or methods from colliding with names in other classes. Namespaces allow you to create your own element and attribute names without colliding with other element and attribute names that you might need to use in an xml instance. In other words, you could define a `CustomerNumber` element and so could a supplier that you are working with, and using namespaces have no collision when these two elements are used in the same XML document. Namespaces are often long and are abbreviated using a namespace prefix. Remember that a namespace prefix is just a shortcut to abbreviate a namespace within the context of a namespace declaration (the special `xmlns` attribute) so even though you will see common prefixes, such as `wsee` for the Web Services schema, these prefixes could really be anything as long as they are associated with the correct namespace.

Namespaces are critical in Web services because even if documents from different organizations are not being processed—where name collisions are common—a single Web service employs at least four related documents: the instance document carrying the data, the SOAP envelope defining the message format, the WSDL instance document describing the interface, and the WSDL schema validating the interface definition. This is the minimum number of documents involved with a Web services conversation; others are added depending on the service. Namespaces are uniform resource identifiers (URI) that look like this:

```
xmlns:myns="http://www.myorg.com/namespace/XML"
```

This name is prepended to elements in the XML document in which it resides. Technically, what you want is just a *uniform resource name (URN)*. A URN is just a name and does not point to anything and cannot be dereferenced. The only reason to use a URI as opposed to a URN is that the URI is a name with a DNS-registered hostname embedded in it that is guaranteed to be unique across the entire global Internet; therefore, it creates a unique prefix (that is, it's easier and more secure).

The Powerful, Enigmatic, and Confusing Uniform Resource Identifier (URI)

To be cool at a W3C meeting, you never use the term *URL* (unless you are very careful to use it exactly in the right context, in which case you can be extra cool). You almost always use the term *URI*. Dave was pretty embarrassed at his first W3C meeting and ran back to look at the IETF URI description (RFC 2396, at URI `http://www.ietf.org/rfc/rfc2396.txt`) because everyone was throwing around this term. Looking at this RFC would show you that the URI is much more significant than you may have imagined. Tim Berners-Lee (creator of the Web and chair of the W3C) intended URIs to be the "namer" of things in this universal space called the World Wide Web. The idea is that the URI should allow you to name *anything*. As a matter of fact, if something is not named, it really doesn't exist from the Web's perspective.

Conceptually, you can name anything—a person, a place, a concept, a device, you name it. Furthermore, after you name something, you can begin treating it like a Web page or Web service. For example, you can ask the Web for a phone number by typing a line similar to this:

```
person://www.bea.com/people/DavidLRemy#phoneNumber
```

When you think about it, this naming issue becomes hugely important when you consider that computers cannot make the contextual leaps people do when disambiguating names. Consequently, there needs to be a consistent global naming scheme that is

- Understandable by machines
- Globally unique

There are two schemes for URIs: uniform resource names (URNs) and uniform resource locators (URLs). Looking at the names for URNs and URLs, you might think that URNs *name* things and URLs *locate* things. Ah, if it were only so simple!

URNs are certainly about naming things. URNs have their own special syntax and, similar to domain names with URLs, the first part of the name must be registered with an authority, which for URNs is the IANA.

URLs are certainly known as *locators*. When you type a URL into your browser and press Enter, you are using it as a locator. Other, more sophisticated uses of URLs show up in XML Signature.

If you look at the progression of the XML Signature specification, you will find that URNs were used to name things in the early versions of the specification, but in the later versions an interesting change occurred. URLs began to appear as the way that things are named. For example, the algorithm attribute that appears in many of the elements is a *URL* that names something—in this case, an algorithm. For example, a SignatureMethod element for an RSA algorithm using SHA1 to hash looks like this:

```
http://www.w3.org/2000/09/xmldsig#rsa-sha1
```

This URL has the purpose of naming, but it has an interesting side effect as well: If you put it into your browser, you will see the portion of the XML Signature specification that discusses the RSA-SHA1 algorithm. This use of URLs as "namers" *and* "locators" is becoming a common strategy in modern specifications. Dave was curious why this was the case, so he emailed Joseph Reagle, the co-editor of the XML Signature specification (with Donald Eastlake), who came back with an insightful, useful answer that we will quote here:

> This is common practice at W3C because many of us feel that:
>
> 1. It is very useful to be able to dereference a URL (and perhaps get a schema or some other definition).
>
> 2. URLs are cheap, you don't have to worry about registration processes, nor cluttering a registry with early or test identifiers. Many folks that use URNs do this by "avoiding" registering their URNs at the start, and even at the end of their work. If you use URLs, everyone can define and experiment much more organically.
>
> 3. By using a URL one is explicitly recognizing that the answer to the question about URI stability is social/institutional. The W3C commits to maintaining persistent URLs as identifiers, and so should others.

Having URLs that at times are meant as locators and at other times are meant as namers might seem confusing at first. However, you will grow accustomed to this convention quickly and find that, in the end, whether it is your Web page or your Web service, the URL (okay, URI) system is a proven way of roping off your own namespace (you just register a domain) and then being responsible about organizing and persisting those names over time. Whether you are naming a location or a thing doesn't really matter.

Another fact to know about URIs is that they can be *absolute* or *relative*. An absolute URI is completely spelled out, including all parts of the URI, as follows:

```
http://www.mycompany.com/mySignatureExample
```

A relative URI contains a resource path and name that is meant to be resolved from the *BaseURI*. The BaseURI, if not made explicit, is the same directory as your current location. For example, the relative URI `myPicture.gif` would look for `myPicture.gif` in the same directory where the XML document is located. Using relative URIs can have the advantage of portability by allowing you to move around a set of resources without having to change references.

XML Schema

SGML includes a means of defining which particular elements and attributes are used to define meaning in an XML document. These are called Document Type Definitions. Confusingly, DTDs are specified in a different language than SGML itself. DTDs have other limitations as well. Until recently, XML also used DTDs to define the tags and their meanings used in documents. XML Schemas provide an alternative to DTDs to address these limitations.

XML Schemas are created to define and validate an XML document. They are specified in XML itself. Schemas describe data types and specify any required ordering of elements. If a need is found for additional types, a schema can be changed independently of the data. It is common practice that the xsd namespace prefix identifies an element as part of an XML Schema, as shown in Listing 2.3.

Listing 2.3 **An XML Schema for ShipOrder**

```
<xsd:schema xmlns:xsd="http://www.w3.org/1999/XMLSchema">

<xsd:element    name="shipOrder" type="order"/>

<xsd:complexType name="order">
    <xsd:element   name="shipTo"    type="shipAddress"/>
    <xsd:element   name="items"     type="cdItems"/>
</xsd:complexType>

<xsd:complexType name="shipAddress">
    <xsd:element   name="name"      type="xsd:string"/>
    <xsd:element   name="street"    type="xsd:string"/>
    <xsd:element   name="address"   type="xsd:string"/>
    <xsd:element   name="country"   type="xsd:string"/>
</xsd:complexType>

<xsd:complexType name="cdItems">
    <xsd:element   name="item"      type="cdItem"/>
</xsd:complexType>

<xsd:complexType name="cdItem">
    <xsd:element   name="title"     type="xsd:string"/>
    <xsd:element   name="quantity"  type="xsd:positiveInteger"/>
    <xsd:element   name="price"     type="xsd:decimal"/>
</xsd:complexType> </xsd:schema>
```

XML Schemas are critical for the automatic validation of XML instance documents, which are documents that purport to be valid *instances* of an XML document that conforms to a specified XML Schema or definition.

Simple types in XML Schemas are `string`, `integer`, `double`, `float`, `date`, and `time`. A type is specified as part of the element definition:

```
<xsd:element name="CustomerNumber" type="xsd:integer"/>
```

XML processors validate instance documents by processing the schema along with the document, matching elements in the document to the corresponding element definition in the schema, and checking the type specified to ensure a match. Complex types can be modeled as well using a special `ComplexTypes` construct.

XML Schemas are an important innovation for XML security. XML Schemas are more complex than DTDs, but they also provide for much tighter constraints on the XML document being defined. This is good when you're defining XML security because accuracy and consistency are essential. XML Schemas are critical tools for precisely defining Web Services Security technologies such as XML Signature, XML Encryption, and WS-Security.

XML Transformations

XML Transformations are the reason we say Web services are a loosely coupled form of middleware. Traditional middleware created tightly coupled and, therefore, brittle connections. This was true of DCE, RMI, CORBA, and DCOM. Changes made in any part of the system had to ripple through the entire system in harmony, or the whole system stopped working. With XML transformations, one part of the Web services system can be changed and made to perform necessary XML transformations dynamically at run-time to remain compatible with the as-yet-unchanged parts of the system.

The incredible power of XML over other data representations is that it is a data representation that all applications can understand: You can define and validate new document structures, and you can transform documents in transit. This is one reason why we say that XML is the "secret sauce" that makes Web services such a radically new and powerful form of middleware.

As you will see, XML transformations are an important part of XML security and therefore of Web Services Security. At the very least, you will be required to transform XML documents to completely consistent canonical forms before applying XML Signatures. First, though, let's explore four particularly important XML transformations that you will need to understand for later discussions. The four transformations described in the following sections are XPath, XSLT, XQuery, and XMLBeans.

XPath

The primary purpose of XPath is to refer to parts of an XML document. This transformation is called XPath because, at its simplest, it is a way to refer to part of an XML document in a similar manner to a file system path. For example, you can refer to the root node of an XML document by using the XPath expression /. You could refer to an XML node foo below the current node by using this XPath expression: ./foo. This is the basic idea of XPath. Like everything in XML, it seems to go from simple to complex reasonably quickly. We will not describe XPath in depth here, but we encourage you to become familiar with XPath for several reasons. First, when it is used in XML Signature, you must understand XPath to understand what is being signed. Second, it is used in many other specifications, such as XSLT, Xpointer, XML Encryption, and more. We highly recommend the XPath tutorial at ZVON:

http://www.zvon.org/xxl/XPathTutorial/General/examples.html

The tutorial not only takes you through the XPath syntax, but it also has an interactive lab where you can try different XPath statements.

XSLT

XSLT, which stands for Extensible Stylesheet Language Transformations, transforms an XML document into a different structure. A style sheet provides instructions on how to modify or restructure a document. In this way, you can change the names of element tags, reorder sequence, add and remove elements, and so on.

A typical scenario for XSLT might be to receive a purchase order and transform it to match the required internal structure. This means less error processing is required downstream. Another use is to merge multiple documents into one. Frequently, XSLT is used to perform outbound transformations from internal (or archaic) to industry standard formats. In the insurance industry, XSLT is used to translate internal forms into industry standard ACORD (an XML dialect) format.

XSLT can be used to transform an XML document into other types of documents. This capability is useful for creating HTML when XML is being displayed in a browser, creating a wireless-suitable presentation, emitting VoiceXML for a voice response system…you get the idea.

XQuery

XQuery is an emerging transformation language covering the same territory that XSLT does, but in a different, more query-focused way. You could argue that XSLT is more amenable to document-style transformation—for example, transforming an XML document into an HTML document—and that XQuery is better at data-style transformation, such as querying an XML document with the result being another XML document. (This is not altogether true, however; both XSLT and XQuery are perfectly capable of doing both.) As you will see in the following example, XQuery was influenced heavily by SQL and other query languages, so you would likely use XQuery when you want to query an XML document, or multiple documents joined together, like you would a database.

XQuery relies heavily on XPath. In fact, with XPath 2.0, the two technologies are tightly coupled—so much so that one of the many XQuery specifications is titled the XQuery 1.0 and XPath 2.0 Data Model (see the XQuery 1.0 and XPath 2.0 Data

Model at `http://www.w3.org/TR/xpath-datamodel/`). Quite often, an XQuery looks like an XPath statement surrounded by some outer XML, like this:

```
<books>
    { doc("http://bstore1.example.com/bib.xml")//author }
</books>
```

Notice the XPath statement within the braces after the XQuery function `doc("http://..")`; you probably guessed that this statement points to the XML document data you are querying. You can put any XPath statement you want in braces throughout an XML template. The result of the XQuery will be an XML document that looks like this:

```
<books>
  <author>Fred Jones</author>
  <author>James Thurber</author>
</books>
```

This example of XQuery is extremely simple, but this type of transformation is very valuable. Although this example does not show it, XQuery defines a full query structure similar to SQL, usually abbreviated FLWR (pronounced FLOWER), which stands for *For, Let, Where, Return*. This book does not go into great detail on XQuery, so suffice it to say that XQuery is extremely powerful and can become complex very quickly.

The specifications for XQuery are among the most voluminous, with complexity rivaling the XML Schema specification. Much of this complexity is related to striving to meet the challenge of both data-oriented and document-oriented use cases and also making sure that XQuery is as "correct," in a mathematical/logical sense, as possible. Dozens of XQuery implementations are on the market, and it is a foregone conclusion that XQuery will be an important technology for manipulating and querying XML in the future.

Note

At least a dozen formal W3C specifications are related to XQuery, and many more papers and presentations (but very few primers, unfortunately) are available. You can find a good online article introducing XQuery written by Howard Katz from FatDog software on IBM developerWorks at

`http://www-106.ibm.com/developerworks/xml/library/x-xquery.html`

XMLBeans

XMLBeans is a tool that allows developers to access the full power of XML in a Java-friendly way. It is an XML-Java binding tool. The idea is that you can take advantage of the richness and features of XML and XML Schema and have these features mapped as naturally as possible to the equivalent Java language and typing constructs. XMLBeans uses XML Schema to compile Java interfaces and classes that you can then use to access and modify XML instance data. Using XMLBeans is similar to using any other Java interface/class. When there is an XML element `<Foo>` in an XML document, XMLBeans will present a `getFoo` or `setFoo` method just as you would expect when working with Java. Although a major use of XMLBeans is to access XML instance data with strongly typed Java classes, there are also APIs that allow you access to the full XML infoset as well as allow you to reflect into the XML Schema itself through an XML Schema Object model.

> **Note**
>
> XMLBeans was submitted to Apache by BEA Systems in September 2003 and is currently in the Apache incubation process.[9]

XML's Role in Web Services Security

Everything in Web services is described and specified in XML. Good or bad, that is a fact. SOAP is an XML format. SAML—a way of expressing identity and what an identity is allowed to do—is an XML format. All the WS-Security specifications are XML formats. So, there is an overarching need for standards for expressing security data in XML format.

There has been no need to invent new cryptography technologies for XML or Web services. The XML security and Web services security standards developers have applied tried-and-true cryptography directly to XML. This is important because we need persistent message-level security, and by leveraging decades of well-tested cryptography, we are less likely to get it wrong. XML messages move from server to server and may make several hops in moving from source to destination; while doing so, these messages need to maintain their security the entire way. The Transport Layer Security (TLS but alternatively called SSL) works only point to point, so messages are decrypted as soon as a server receives them. This means the messages are in the clear on the server, and if they need to move on to another server, they need to be re-encrypted, a prohibitively expensive proposition. This need for keeping messages secret led to the development of XML Encryption, the topic of Chapter 5, "Ensuring Confidentiality of XML Messages."

Besides message-level confidentiality, there is a need for XML message integrity. Are the bits in the message that is received absolutely identical to the bits in the message that was sent? Additionally, who was the sender of the message? Not all messages require that these questions be answered, but when purchase orders, patient records, contracts, and thousands of other types of critical documents are being transported, it is essential that they are. These questions are answered by XML Signature, the topic of Chapter 4, "Safeguarding the Identity and Integrity of XML Messages."

9. See http://xml.apache.org/xmlbeans.

Web services will, more often than not, access critical data and services of organizations that do not want that data accessed by the wrong entities. They want the individuals, organizations, and machines accessing their information to be authorized to do so. They need to know for sure who it is (machine or individual), and they need to know what that machine or individual is trying to do. In security vernacular, these organizations need authentication and authorization. SAML is the XML specification for identity, authentication, and authorization. We will discuss SAML in Chapter 6. SAML is the basis of some very important projects such as The Liberty Alliance and Microsoft Passport, both of which we also discuss in Chapter 6.

When you know the authenticated identity of the Web service client, you need to specify in finely granular fashion the rights the client has to access specific content and services. There are currently two somewhat overlapping standards for this task; they are known as XACML and XrML. We cover both in Chapter 9, "Trust, Access Control, and Rights for Web Services."

As you build security into your Web services, the need for Public Key Infrastructure (PKI) will become readily apparent. You will need a way to prove the identity of sender, recipient, or both. Because you cannot assume people are always who they claim to be, you need trusted third parties whom you trust to vouch for the claims of people presenting their identities to you. This is the role of PKI, which is discussed in detail in Chapter 3. PKI for Web services is specified in XML format in an emerging standard called XML Key Management Specification (XKMS). We believe that Web services, with its strong need for keys that can be used to encrypt, decrypt, and sign data, will be the strongest impetus for PKI since SSL drove the need for server-based X.509 certificates. This being so, the XKMS standard, which specifies how keys are created, exchanged, and tested for validity within the context of Web services, will be an important part of the security foundation of Web services. XKMS is covered in detail in Chapter 9.

The standard framework for including XML-formatted security data into SOAP messages is WS-Security. WS-Security builds on all the XML security standards we have just mentioned, such as XML Signature, XML Encryption, SAML, XACML, and XrML. WS-Security does not invent any new security concepts or standards; it simply extends SOAP to include security data about the messages a particular SOAP envelope is carrying. WS-Security is the focus of Chapter 7.

A very useful way to look at the role of XML in Web Services Security is to examine the relationships among all the XML security frameworks that make up the overall Web services standards stack. This relationship is shown in Figure 2.3.

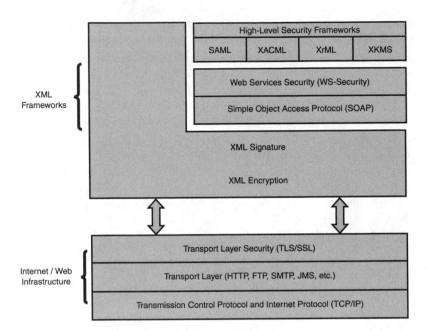

Figure 2.3   XML frameworks that define the core Web Services Security specification.

XML Versus ASN.1 Paradigm Shift: A Battle to the Death?

Security specifications pre-date Web services and XML by decades. So, for all this time, how have things cryptographic been described? The answer is with a binary format called ASN.1.

You may not have heard much about ASN.1 because it operates at the lowest levels of PKI implementations; however, you may have been exposed to it without even knowing. ASN.1 is a structured data language that allows well-defined data structures to be passed among differing applications and platforms. Sound a lot like XML? There *are* many similarities. The major difference is that ASN.1 is a binary encoding. This means that if you look at ASN.1, it will look like gibberish, whereas XML is a text-based encoding strategy. A benefit of ASN.1 is that it is more compact than a similarly defined XML document.

ASN.1 has been around much longer than XML (perhaps not if you count SGML, XML's precursor), and it provides rich, complex, data-typed semantics for describing data structures. Typically, an ASN.1 structure is created in text by a program and then compiled into an ASN.1 structure. When received, an ASN.1 structure must be decompiled (parsed) for that platform to get the fields within the file.

In the PKI world, many common structures are encoded in ASN.1. Examples of ASN.1 structures involving X.509 Certificates include PKCS#10 (certificate signing requests), PKCS#7 (public key bag typically containing a certificate and certificate chains), and PKCS#12 (flexible structure that is often used for carrying private/public key pairs). PKCS stands for Public Key Cryptography Standards proposed and maintained by RSA. Browsers, Web servers, VPNs, email systems, and many other applications support use of these types of structures. For example, if you get a personal digital certificate from a certificate authority such as VeriSign or GeoTrust, it will typically be installed into your browser directly from the PKCS#7 format. If you want to export the key pair generated on your machine, it will be exported in a PKCS#12 format.

Some XML proponents see ASN.1 becoming irrelevant because of XML. XML can generally model any ASN.1 structure, and the introduction of Encryption and Signature could allow many of the PKCS standard structures to be matched in an equivalent XML structure. A part of the reasoning here is that applications should not need to have two parsers, an ASN.1 parser and an XML parser. Due to the broad acceptance of XML, everyone will already have an XML parser available. From a practical perspective, ASN.1 parsers are specific to security type functions (although ASN.1 could have broader usage) and therefore are limited in scope. Consequently, wouldn't it be good if an ASN.1 parser were not required? This is considered particularly important for limited processing/memory devices such as cell phones, PDAs, and so forth. Other than basic X.509 support, other accepted ASN.1 structures have been left out of the XML security standards.

Our opinion is that there is a risk of throwing out a large investment in well-established cryptographic object representations. Certain ASN.1 structures have gained acceptance and are mature structures for keys, signed data, and digital certificates, for example. XML is flexible enough to support wrapped ASN.1 elements where it makes sense. XML Signature's KeyInfo element is an example of supporting X.509 as well as a similar XML-based structure. Web containers, VPNs, and email systems already have support for structures such as PKCS#7, 10, and 12, and it seems as though these structures should be usable in XML security scenarios.

Over time it is entirely possible, even probable, that XML structures will supplant the ASN.1 structures. However, this may take awhile, and it is important to the fast adoption of the current XML Security standards that co-existence with the most mature ASN.1 structures be supported.

SOAP: XML Messaging and Remote Application Access

SOAP is an XML-based packaging scheme to transport XML messages from one application to another. SOAP gives you a standard container that can send its XML payload over any transport protocol (such as HTTP). A great deal of directive information, especially security-related information, is placed in a SOAP header. We will focus on SOAP headers in more detail when we delve into WS-Security later.

SOAP envelopes can be routed through many intermediaries. SOAP intermediaries can process, save, or modify the SOAP messages they receive. Some SOAP intermediaries do security processing on the messages they receive.

SOAP supports RPC/encoded and Document/literal modes. RPC/encoded acts much like traditional RPC middleware. RPC communications tend to be synchronous and finer-grained, making them suitable for intra-organizational integrations where network speeds are high and latency is low. Document/literal supports a more loosely coupled approach. Document communications tend to be asynchronous and coarse-grained, making them suitable for inter-organization (for example, B2B) integrations.

The SOAP structure used for a particular Web service is described in the associated WSDL file.

Where SOAP Came From and Why It's Important

SOAP used to stand for Simple Object Access Protocol. With SOAP 1.1, the technical committee decided the term is no longer an acronym because SOAP is neither simple, nor does it deal with objects.

SOAP is what makes application integration (that is, distributed computing) possible. After XML defines the content of a message, it is SOAP that defines how the data moves from one place to another over the network. SOAP allows the sender and receiver of XML documents to support a common data transfer protocol. If the concept of sending and receiving messages over HTTP sounds familiar, it should: Web-based middleware is really not new; it has been around in primitive form as long as users have been appending extra commands to HTTP messages. SOAP formalizes this process and makes it work not only for XML documents, but also for executing remote procedures.

SOAP was developed in 1998 at Microsoft, with collaboration from UserLand and DevelopMentor. The goal, first espoused by Dave Winer of UserLand, was to establish a simple way for applications to exchange structured data over Web protocols. SOAP built on grass roots efforts spread throughout a community working on XML-RPC. XML-RPC continues to be used somewhat, but SOAP has gained such broad acceptance that it has quickly supplanted XML-RPC. A lot of RPC learning had gone on prior to SOAP, most recently with Java's Remote Method Invocation (RMI). SOAP is much simpler than RMI. Being based on XML makes SOAP extremely easy to work with, very late binding, and totally interoperable. It is not as simple as XML-RPC because it addresses some of XML-RPC's shortcomings. When SOAP was published as a specification on the Web in late 1999, it already had the backing of IBM in addition to Microsoft. But like XML, SOAP was open source from the beginning and still got the backing of the majors. It appears that with SOAP, distributed computing, for the first time, is free from industry giants and consortia going their own ways and creating competing standards.

SOAP is a derivative of XML as was XML-RPC. SOAP is what really defines Web services because it makes XML invoke a procedure remotely either directly via a remote procedure call or by using its Document/literal mode to transfer an XML document and change remote processing on that document. SOAP is in the same class of technology as Internet Inter-ORB Protocol (IIOP) for CORBA as well as RMI for Java. A big difference, however, is that SOAP is *text-based*. This has huge implications. It makes working with SOAP much easier, and it makes things developed with SOAP easier to debug. SOAP messages are firewall friendly. Processing text-based messages at every step in the communications path is extremely easy. This ease-of-use is in huge contrast to DCOM and CORBA, which had binary encodings and no metadata describing what was being passed. That SOAP is text-based also opens up interesting and powerful runtime monitoring, analysis, and compliance capabilities that tools are just now starting to fully exploit.

The most common way SOAP works is as an extension of HTTP that supports XML messaging. Just as HTTP GETs retrieve a Web page and HTTP POSTs submit form data to a Web server, SOAP uses those same mechanisms to send and receive XML messages. The Web server needs to understand SOAP, and it does so by having a SOAP processor that looks for these special types of POSTs. Technically, the SOAP specification supports expansion to other protocols (such as UDP, SMTP, JMS, and more), but the HTTP mapping is the only one that has formally been defined so far (up to and including SOAP v1.2).

As we have mentioned, there are two very different ways to view SOAP: Document/literal style and RPC/encoded style. With Document/literal style, an XML document is sent as the payload of the SOAP message. The client sends a message to the service, the service processes the message, and it sends back a response message. In essence, the client has no knowledge of how the service is implemented or how it processes the message (the XML document). This mode is particularly suitable for passing business documents asynchronously between loosely coupled services. When you are dealing with B2B integrations, this approach is best because it maximizes the effectiveness of lower-bandwidth, less-reliable connections and more accurately models real business-to-business communications and processes. It is correct to think of Document/literal-style Web services as batch processing. This mode is efficient, scalable, and because of its coarse granularity, it is reliable.

In contrast, RPC/encoded style provides RPCs transparently to the client, resulting in the translation of method calls into XML, sending them to the server, and returning the response message as the return value. This mode is most suitable for synchronous communication between tightly coupled services. Think of it as the online mode. In RPC mode, an important function of SOAP is a set of encoding rules that define a serialization mechanism. This creates a standard way of capturing programming language data elements such as integers, strings, and complex structures, in a language-neutral, interoperable format. Extending this concept, you can see how a remote procedure call can be expressed in XML and serialized by SOAP over HTTP. The RPC parameters are encoded as child elements of a common parent. The name of the procedure is attached to the parent indicating the operation to be performed remotely.

A SOAP request is most commonly sent as an HTTP POST with content type set to text/XML and a field called SOAPAction set to either an empty string or the name of the SOAP method. This way, the receiving Web server knows this is a SOAP message and acts accordingly. A SOAP message consists of an address and an envelope, which, in turn, is made up of some headers and a body; and the body consists of one or more elements. The structure of a SOAP message is shown in Figure 2.4.

SOAP Doesn't Really Access Objects

Although SOAP was originally named for the Simple Object Access Protocol, it isn't really accessing objects, but it does encapsulate data and operations on that data. So, we won't quibble that these are components or services, not objects. The point is that when you define a service, you are creating a collection of components and making the methods in those components available (remotely) through an interface that SOAP can affect. This object system is not sophisticated. It does not have garbage collection, it cannot access objects by reference, and it cannot batch together requests, all of which are capabilities that DCOM and

CORBA provided. However, neither of them was truly scalable, they were exceedingly complex, and for all intents and purposes, they are dead technologies.

SOAP is lightweight, highly interoperable, and easy to implement. It binds well to HTTP, and it supports RPC calls that map directly to HTTP requests and responses. SOAP even binds well to other protocols, so it becomes a powerful tool for enterprise application integration.

SOAP has supplanted XML-RPC, DCOM, and IIOP in one fell swoop. For all practical purposes, SOAP *is* Web services. There is even good news from SOAP on the battle of the behemoths. SOAP has, in fact, become the bridging protocol between J2EE and Microsoft .NET.

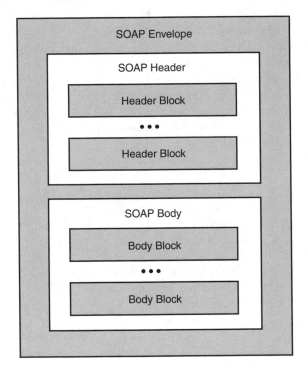

Figure 2.4 The structure of a SOAP message.

SOAP Envelope

The envelope is the top-level XML element in a SOAP message. You specify it using the ENV namespace prefix and the Envelope element:

```
<SOAP-ENV:Envelope
    xmlns:SOAP-ENV="http://www.w3.org/2001/12/soap-envelope">


. . .


</SOAP-ENV:Envelope>
```

A major function of the envelope is to define namespaces used by the SOAP message. Typical namespaces that are included are `xmlns:SOAP-ENV` (SOAP Envelope namespace), `xmlns:xsi` (XML Schema for Instances), and `xmlns:xsd` (XML Schema for DataTypes).

The envelope indicates the start and end of a message. It defines a complete package, thus making it unambiguous when the receiver is done receiving the message.

Headers are optional, but there can be more than one as well. If a header is present, it must be the first child of the envelope.

SOAP Header

SOAP headers are used for directive information. This is the place where SOAP security lives. System-level information used to manage and secure the message is placed here as well. SOAP runtimes and intermediaries process SOAP header directives.

Headers are intended to add new features and functionality. The intention for this incomplete and imprecise concept is to have it be used by specific applications that build on top of the basic protocol. These extensions need to be standardized. As an example, the WS-Security header, covered in detail in Chapter 7, will be located here. This is also the place where information about transactions, routing, payments, guaranteed delivery, and so forth will be placed. Any element in a SOAP processing chain can add or delete items from the header or choose to ignore items if they are unknown.

A sender can require that the receiver *understand* a header. This allows for graceful failure when a receiver receives a message too new for it to understand. Headers speak directly to the SOAP processors and can require that a processor reject the entire SOAP message if it does not understand the header. This security requirement is important. If a header contains critical security information that a SOAP processor does not understand, you may not want it to process this SOAP message at all because to do so would completely bypass the ignored header's security information.

SOAP Body

The SOAP body is the main payload of the message. The body contains the information that must be sent to the ultimate recipient. This is the place where the XML document for the application initiating the SOAP message resides. For an RPC, the body contains a single element that contains the method name, arguments, and a Web service target address. If a header is present, the body is its immediate sibling; otherwise, it is the first child of the envelope. The structure of a SOAP request is shown in Listing 2.4 and that of a SOAP response in Listing 2.5.

Listing 2.4   **The Structure of a SOAP Request**

```
<SOAP-ENV:Envelope
...
    <SOAP-ENV:Body>
        <m:GetOrderStatus
        xmlns:m="www.myservice.com/OrderEntry">
```

Listing 2.4 **Continued**

```
            <orderno>43564</orderno>
        </m:GetOrderStatus>
    </SOAP-ENV:Body>
</SOAP-ENV:Envelope>
```

Listing 2.5 **The Structure of a SOAP Response**

```
<SOAP-ENV:Envelope
...
    <SOAP-ENV:Body>
        <m:GetOrderStatusReply
        xmlns:m="www.myservice.com/OrderEntry">
            <orderstatus>Shipped June 18</orderstatus>
        </m:GetOrderStatusReply>
    </SOAP-ENV:Body>
</SOAP-ENV:Envelope>
```

The preceding are examples of RPC/encoded SOAP, the more tightly coupled Web services scheme. In RPC mode, there is always a request/response pair that models a function call/call return value pair.

This capability to invoke remote procedures when used in the RPC/encoded style is a major SOAP feature that plain XML over HTTP does not possess. For Web services that are building distributed applications over the Web, this capability of SOAP will be important. Included in an RPC mapping is a URI for the target SOAP node, a procedure name, an optional procedure signature, and the parameters to the procedure. (Throughout, you can substitute *method* for *procedure*.) RPC invocations are modeled as structs with an accessor for each parameter. The struct name is identical to the procedure name. The response struct uses a naming convention that easily identifies this as a response. The response is always a struct or a fault, but not both.

In Document/literal mode, the loosely coupled Web services scheme, the sender sends a message containing a document such as a purchase order. The receiver independently and transparently to the client determines how to process it.

When SOAP is used in the Document/literal style, its capability to transmit XML documents that are then processed by the recipient using either the Document Object Model (DOM) or Simple API for XML (SAX), both of which are XML parsing protocols, will be critical. For businesses, this mode will be a very powerful asynchronous paradigm; it can be used to turn critical business documents such as purchase orders into actionable objects with a defined set of operations that are performed on these documents as part of a standard business-process workflow.

SOAP Processing

Today's application servers all have SOAP processors built in. These SOAP processors are evolving to have support for Web services security standards built in as those standards stabilize. This enables sites to set up their Web services environments to automatically manage security. The SOAP header processor is called from the SOAP runtime system.

Alternatively, the Web services environment can route messages through an intermediary. SOAP intermediaries can process headers, but not the body. Intermediaries can add or remove headers. If the intermediary does not recognize a header, it must ignore that header and forward it on.

The security stage of SOAP processors is expected to authenticate identities, implement role-based security for authorizations, encrypt or decrypt the contents of a message, validate digital signatures, implement extended security conversations, and call out to external third-party authorities as needed.

SOAP v1.2 added attributes to indicate which SOAP nodes are responsible for processing which headers.

SOAP Attachments

Attachments are not part of the SOAP standard, but they are part of an accepted note by the W3C. Attachments are recognized as important and are accepted as part of e-business XML (ebXML) and RosettaNet.

Attachments are the way to send binary data or entire XML documents. Examples of binary data attachments include image files or large drawing documents. An example of an entire separately defined XML document placed as an attachment is an ACORD (an insurance industry XML dialect) document.

If the SOAP attachment approach were not available, all binary data would have to be Base-64 encoded and decoded because the XML body must be completely digestable plain text. This Base-64 encoding/decoding of binary data into ASCII form adds significant overhead. (Base-64 encoding is explained in detail in Appendix A.)

SOAP borrows from Multipurpose Internet Mail Extensions (MIME) to create SOAP attachments that mimic the way MIME allows email attachments. SOAP with attachments creates a MIME envelope with attachments that are linked from within the SOAP envelope. Processing of these attachments in the payload is directed to separate MIME part handlers in a fashion analogous to email attachment processing.

SOAP and Web Services Security

The defined SOAP transport currently binds just to HTTP. This has implications on SOAP being transparent through traditional firewalls and has some disconcerting security implications. The efforts to make sure that Web services "just work" with the existing Web servers, firewalls, and infrastructure also means that Web services can bring in new identities to organizations and take out critical business information if you are not careful. WSDL makes this situation worse because it advertises the Web services API to the outside world if you are not careful here as well.

The good security news is that SOAP binding to HTTP also means you can directly secure SOAP using SSL because all Web and application servers already know how to apply SSL to HTTP. This approach will suffice only for simple point-to-point Web services, but many do fit this description. Other SOAP transports that will quickly take hold include SMTP and JMS, as well as others over time.

For multi-hop Web services, for those that include identity, for those that require integrity of messages, and for many other reasons, SSL will not suffice for SOAP security, which is why SOAP headers were made extensible for security directives, as already mentioned. WS-Security secures SOAP through its security tokens in the SOAP header; these tokens attach identity to a SOAP message and provide for persistent security for the SOAP payload when used with XML Encryption and XML Signature. WS-Security and SOAP security are covered in detail in Chapter 7.

WSDL: Schema for XML/SOAP Objects and Interfaces

Web Services Description Language (WSDL) is typically produced by the development tools used to create the Web services. It describes what functionality the Web service provides, how it communicates, and where to find it. WSDL is divided into a *what* part, a *how* part, and a *where* part. The *what* part is the abstract interface much like Interface Description Languages (IDLs) of past generations of middleware. The *how* part maps the abstract interface onto a concrete set of communication protocols. The *how* part is called a binding. The *where* part defines a specific Web service implementation specified through a typical Web URL.

Where WSDL Came From and Why It's Important

WSDL is an XML language that describes a Web service. When we described a "contract" for service-oriented architectures earlier, the contract we were referring to was the WSDL file. It describes what functionality a Web service offers, how it communicates, and where to find it.

The earliest direct ancestor to WSDL is probably the Web Interface Definition Language (WIDL) from WebMethods. Like the IDLs from CORBA and COM, WIDL created a separate language-independent description of an interface to a service, but in XML format. A similar effort led to the Service Description Language (SDL) from Microsoft. And in another parallel effort, IBM had the Network Accessible Service Specification Language (NASSL). These efforts coalesced into WSDL, driven by Microsoft, IBM, and Ariba. This group submitted WSDL 1.1 to the W3C in March 2001, where it immediately gained the support of 22 other members. It remains officially categorized as a W3C note; however, it has languished a bit in the W3C but will continue to have broad-based support, solidifying its role as *the* de facto standard way to specify a Web service description.

We cannot overstate how important of a complement WSDL is to SOAP. Developers need WSDL to read SOAP interfaces directly into their programming tools.

Programming tools then present the WSDL-defined remote procedure calls as if they were local method calls in the programming language used by the tool. To the developer, calling one of these WSDL RPCs looks no different than calling a method on a local object. Operationally oriented monitoring and analysis systems also use the WSDL to understand the XML Schema that defines the XML messages such a tool is trying to observe.

This is an important point: Technically, WSDL creates a schema for XML/SOAP objects and interfaces. It's like a user's manual for XML/SOAP objects; like a resume for a Web service. Developers (or most often, their tools) read a WSDL document to understand what SOAP calls are required. Many development tools such as JBuilder, Visual Studio .NET, and WebLogic Workshop import the WSDL directly into the development tool to generate SOAP calls automatically from the description. Runtime tools operate the same way and use the WSDL to determine how to monitor, manage, and control Web services in production.

Services are described in a WSDL document as a collection of endpoints called *ports*. Ports perform specific operations on messages. Messages contain either document-oriented or procedure-oriented information as controlled by the binding style attribute. This information may be used to select an appropriate programming model: either RPC- or DOM-based.

If the operation style is RPC, each part is a parameter or a return value and appears inside a wrapper element within the body. The wrapper element is named identically to the operation name, and its namespace is the value of the namespace attribute. Each message part (parameter) appears under the wrapper, represented by an accessor named identically to the corresponding parameter of the call. Parts are arranged in the same order as the parameters of the call. If the operation style is document, there are no additional wrappers, and the message parts appear directly under the SOAP Body element.

The IDLs of past middleware systems such as DCE, CORBA, and DCOM correspond to the WSDL's *what* section (we describe all its elements next). Whereas WSDL portTypes are abstract (not yet bound), IDLs were specific and concrete. This made IDLs' tightly coupled connections very brittle. Additionally, IDLs had no information about how to communicate with their service. They supported only one type of communication protocol, and they provided no information about where to find a service. There was no corollary to WSDL's flexible URL that gives it the property of late binding.

> **Note**
>
> The late bindingness of WSDL is a very important feature. It enables you to have an intermediary "router" that can be a level of indirection between the client and the provider. The client always thinks it is connecting to the router or proxy. By incorporating good load-balancing strategies at this router level, you can build resilience and redundancy into the Web service, both of which enhance security.
>
> Typically, the router stores the WSDL of the provider. At the time of importing the WSDL, it actually modifies the WSDL URL so that the client always calls the URL of the router. The router maintains a table that maps to the "actual" provider address.

What this all means is that not only were middleware systems of the past tightly coupled and brittle, but consequently they were not suitable for cross-organizational boundary communication. This is the area in which Web services excel and what will propel them to become as pervasive as the Web itself. The dark side of this takes us back to our favorite topic: Web services security. When you cross organizational boundaries, security becomes orders of magnitude more important and more challenging.

The other dark aspect of late binding and loosely coupled distributed systems is that things can change somewhere in the system. From a security perspective, that puts a burden on you to be scrupulous about checking the security of all incoming messages. A change somewhere in the distributed system may have been malicious, and the incoming messages may be malformed. Not only do you need to implement strong security technology to combat this problem, but you also need to constantly monitor all your security provisions to make sure you can "see" whether a breach occurs.

WSDL Elements

A WSDL document contains three sections that provide operations, bindings, and services. The document begins with a `<definitions>` tag and establishes namespaces. The operations section, identified by `<message>` and `<portType>` tags, describes *what* operations are provided. The `<binding>` tag describes *how* the operations are invoked. Finally, the `<service>` tag describes *where* the services are located. This structure is shown in Figure 2.5.

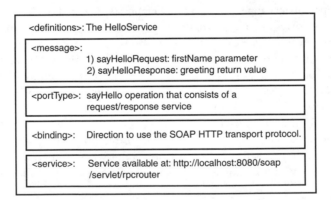

Figure 2.5   The layout of a WSDL file.

What follows in Listing 2.6 is a real WSDL for a simple add/subtract calculator service from the SalCentral Web site. We break up the example into sections to explain what each section is for.

The entire WSDL definition is bracketed by the `<definitions>` tag. Initially, the namespaces are defined for this specific WSDL, for the XML Schema used, for SOAP, and for WSDL.

Listing 2.6   **The WSDL Definitions Section for SimpleCalculator**

```
<definitions name="SimpleCalculator.csimplecalc"

targetNamespace="http://sal006.salnetwork.com:83/xmlone/SimpleCalculator/
    CSimpleCalc.xml"

xmlns:tns=http://"//sal006.salnetwork.com:83/xmlone/SimpleCalculator/
    CSimpleCalc.xml"
xmlns:xsd="http://www.w3.org/2001/XMLSchema"
xmlns:soap="http://schemas.xmlsoap.org/wsdl/soap/" xmlns="http://
    schemas.xmlsoap.org/wsdl/">
```

Next in Listing 2.7 is the operations section using `<message>` tags first and then `<portType>` tags. Messages are grouped in pairs, the first defining the request and the second defining the response. Next, port types identify to whom the message is sent and how. A port type is a collection of operations—in this case, Add and Subtract operations:

Listing 2.7   **The WSDL Operations Section for SimpleCalculator**

```
  <message name="AddRequest">
        <part name="X" type="xsd:long" />
        <part name="Y" type="xsd:long" />
</message>
  <message name="AddResponse">
        <part name="Return" type="xsd:long" />
</message>
  <message name="SubtractRequest">
        <part name="X" type="xsd:long" />
        <part name="Y" type="xsd:long" />
</message>
  <message name="SubtractResponse">
        <part name="Return" type="xsd:long" />
</message>
  <portType name="SimpleCalculator.csimplecalcPortType">
        <operation name="Add">
           <input message="tns:AddRequest" />
           <output message="tns:AddResponse" />
        </operation>
        <operation name="Subtract">
           <input message="tns:SubtractRequest" />
           <output message="tns:SubtractResponse" />
        </operation>
</portType>
```

The second major section of the WSDL file describes *how* the operations are performed by binding together a port, transport, and the operations earlier in the file as shown next in Listing 2.8:

Listing 2.8   **The WSDL Bindings Section for SimpleCalculator**

```
<binding name="SimpleCalculator.csimplecalcbinding"
type="tns:SimpleCalculator.csimplecalcPortType">
  <soap:binding style="rpc" transport="http://schemas.xmlsoap.org/soap/http" />
  <operation name="Add">
    <soap:operation soapAction="http://sal006.salnetwork.com:83/xmlone/
        SimpleCalculator/CSimpleCalc.xml#Add" />
    <input>
      <soap:body use="encoded"
namespace="http://sal006.salnetwork.com:83/xmlone/SimpleCalculator/
        CSimpleCalc.xml"
encodingStyle="http://schemas.xmlsoap.org/soap/encoding/" />
    </input>
    <output>
      <soap:body use="encoded"
namespace="http://sal006.salnetwork.com:83/xmlone/SimpleCalculator/
        CSimpleCalc.xml"
encodingStyle="http://schemas.xmlsoap.org/soap/encoding/" />
    </output>
  </operation>
  <operation name="Subtract">
    <soap:operation
soapAction="http://sal006.salnetwork.com:83/xmlone/SimpleCalculator/
        CSimpleCalc.xml#Subtract"/>
    <input>
      <soap:body use="encoded"
namespace="http://sal006.salnetwork.com:83/xmlone/SimpleCalculator/
        CSimpleCalc.xml"
encodingStyle="http://schemas.xmlsoap.org/soap/encoding/" />
    </input>
    <output>
      <soap:body use="encoded"
namespace="http://sal006.salnetwork.com:83/xmlone/SimpleCalculator/
        CSimpleCalc.xml"
encodingStyle="http://schemas.xmlsoap.org/soap/encoding/" />
    </output>
  </operation>
</binding>
```

The third and final section of the WSDL file describes *where* the service resides, giving a specific URL address. In many cases, a Web server running servlets will process an incoming Web service request. In the example in Listing 2.9, the Web server immediately turns this request over to a CGI script.

Listing 2.9   **The WSDL Section Defining Where the SimpleCalculator Service Resides**

```
<service name="SimpleCalculator.csimplecalcService">
  <port name="SimpleCalculator.csimplecalcPort"
binding="tns:SimpleCalculator.csimplecalcbinding">
    <soap:address
location="http://sal006.salnetwork.com:82/bin/simplecalc.cgi" />
  </port>
</service>
</definitions>
```

WSDL and SOAP

WSDL specifies the interface definition separately from the implementation definition in the service contract. That is, the *what* part is separate from the *how* and *where* parts.

WSDL defines the structure of the SOAP message. The linkage is strong and direct. The contents of the SOAP payload conform to the input and output messages defined in the WSDL *what* part. The *how* of the WSDL defines the way the messages will be packaged in the SOAP envelope, and it defines information that needs to be in the SOAP header. Finally, the binding between SOAP and its transport is defined in the *where* part of the WSDL.

WSDL Versus XML Schema

An XML Schema is an XML vocabulary for expressing data business rules. Data business rules are constraints. A sample constraint might be as follows: A location must be expressed as a latitude followed by a longitude followed by an uncertainty measure. Furthermore, latitude is a decimal real number between −90 and +90, and longitude is a decimal real number between −180 and +180. Finally, uncertainty must be a non-negative integer whose units are either feet or meters. This entire example can be expressed in an XML Schema.

An XML Schema defines a *contract* between a service provider and its clients. That sounds amazingly close to the definition of WSDL. Our definition of Web services could almost be met by using an XML Schema, but an XML Schema is not enough.

WSDL *contains* XML Schemas that describe the data so that both sender and receiver understand the data being exchanged. Beyond what XML Schemas can provide, WSDL also describes the operations and location of the service itself and the binding of the operations to the transport. WSDLs are typically generated by automated tools that start with application metadata that is transformed into XML Schemas and are then merged into the WSDL file.

WSDL and Web Services Security

WSDL can innocently be the biggest security hole in a Web services deployment. Here's why. The development tools place the automatically generated WSDL file in a standard location. If that structure is copied from the staging Web site structure directly into the production Web site structure, the WSDL is now on the exposed Internet in clear form. It is publicly advertising to the outside world the *what*, *how*, and *where* of your entire Web service. Anyone can read it and begin accessing your Web service. If you do not have additional security such as required authentication, outsiders are now happily pulling any and all information your Web service allows. The Web service might provide essentially direct access to your core enterprise applications or databases. This would be bad.

At the very least, organizations must protect the WSDL URL with SSL requiring client authentication. Then no people external to the organization can even read the WSDL file unless you specifically authorize them to do so. Your server will demand a client SSL certificate that identifies who is trying to access the WSDL, giving the server the power to deny anyone not recognized to it.

UDDI: Publishing and Discovering Web Services

Universal Description, Discovery, and Integration (UDDI) is an advertising and discovery service for Web services. UDDI was a collaborative effort of Ariba, CommerceOne, Accenture, Microsoft, IBM, and others. It has roots in Discovery of Web Services (DISCO) from Microsoft and Advertisement and Discovery of Services (ADS) from IBM. These efforts and similar ones elsewhere were coalesced into UDDI for a system of directories.

The purpose of UDDI is to register and publish Web services definitions. A UDDI repository manages information about service types and service providers and makes this information accessible through a well-defined protocol to potential Web service clients.

The UDDI specification is a format for registering a business, an API for SOAP access, and rules to operate a registry. Each service is given a unique identifier called a *tModel*. A tModel points to the specification that defines a resource.

You can search for a specific service in a registry through UDDI *white pages,* where basic identity and contact information is found. UDDI *yellow pages* categorize the business and services into taxonomies. Such categorization helps service consumers find a particular service that matches their requirements. The UDDI *green pages* provide binding details for a service. That is, they allow you to access the WSDL for the service.

UDDI can be used inside corporations as a single place to advertise and find any available services. This is the most useful role for UDDI in our view. Larger organizations that want to achieve all the benefits of reuse will find UDDI to be the best standard way to register and then search for those reusable services.

UDDI can also be used on the public Web to discover public Web services. This vision for UDDI will require the longest amount of time to take hold because Web services that are of significant value will not be free and open to any and all potential users. They will be subject to contracts, payments, liabilities—the sorts of things that contracts and lawyers are involved with. Ultimately, this model will require automated contract negotiation and a highly secure UDDI.

Security is critical in all UDDI registries. For example, who is authorized to publish, use, and update Web service descriptions? Business relationships require trust. Without a trust relationship, you will not enter into any transactions. The authentication and authorization of publishers and inquirers and their authority to access published services must be explicitly handled by UDDI, especially when it is used on the public Internet.

UDDI attempts to deal with these issues by leveraging strong security standards used throughout XML and Web services security. It uses XML Signature to establish the identity of publishers and subscribers. Published WSDL files are signed using XML Signature as well. UDDI uses SAML to establish authorization and to provide access control for UDDI registries. To control who can see or utilize an entry, UDDI uses XML Encryption of its elements to keep them confidential.

Is There Any Real Utility to UDDI?

Of all the standard Web services vocabulary terms discussed so far, UDDI has the least immediate utility. Its most legitimate purpose is to create a class browser for WSDL schemas. However, it was conceived and is still touted as the way to build distributed registries of Web services. The question is whether you need distributed registries of Web services. Will people have their systems go out on the World Wide Web and *discover* services and start using them automatically?

We all lived through the overblown hype of B2B. That is when the concepts for a UDDI global business repository were born. It is not clear whether UDDI will even become an accepted standard in the first place. Is the concept even useful? It will be hard to trust the information in such a repository. The need to go out to a repository to find a service that you want to use as a Web service in an application is questionable. The way information is categorized into white pages (business name, address, contact information, DUNS number), yellow pages (type of business, location, products, industry), and green pages (business services, business process definitions, their WSDL files) is not obviously useful. Because no authenticated identity protocol exists, if knowing whose service you are actually using is important, you cannot use UDDI. The standard is so extensible with so many options that it is impossible to predict the dialect you would happen upon.

Most people don't see this scenario happening. UDDI is more likely to be used in closed but large and distributed environments. The most likely use would be within a large enterprise that is promoting sharing across all development projects within the same company. When Web services provide an API that business partners will integrate into their applications, the interfaces do not need to be discovered; their location and much more will be specified in a negotiated contract.

When thought of as a public directory of Web services, UDDI leaves a lot to be desired, making it the least accepted of all the standards. If you need a service, as a developer, you go to places you know have services and find what you need, such as `salcentral.com` or `xmethods.com`.

As an internal—inside the firewall—directory of Web services, UDDI may excel. Using it may be the best way for an organization to actually achieve reuse of Web service components. Applications can be wrapped using XML integration technologies and registered with the internal UDDI. Now, when integrating internal applications, other departments can come along and discover applications that are ready to be integrated. If UDDI is to be successful, this is how we think it will happen.

UDDI is a critical enabling technology for the vision of a service-oriented architecture. The basic operations that define SOA are register, find, and bind. The process of tying

SOA back to Web services is as follows: The Web service provider publishes a contract in the form of WSDL. This contract is then registered with a service broker via UDDI. A Web service consumer queries the UDDI registry broker to find the desired service, which locates directions to the WSDL contract. These directions are then used to bind the client to the service using SOAP so that the client and service can now communicate. These steps are shown in Figure 2.6.

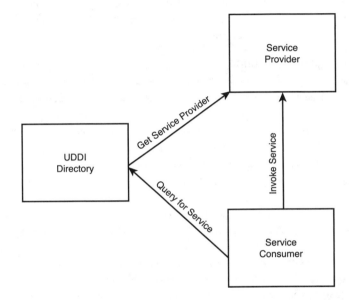

Figure 2.6   UDDI service discovery in service-oriented architectures.

SOA is talked about now more than in any previous generation of distributed computing because Web services deliver a much better SOA than any previous architecture could deliver. The reason is that the Web services model provides something much more flexible, much more pervasive, much lighter weight and supported from any language, working with any platform, and requiring no special homogeneous software installs.

SOA has enormous security implications by having services that are shared among numerous service consumers whose data must be kept confidential from other service consumers and who might have very different trust models. SOA also has security implications due to the fact that it will drive the use of multi-hop Web services that cannot be accomplished by simple point-to-point connections. SOA takes an "outside-in" approach. In traditional RPC-style interfaces, the interfaces were data-centric. In a true SOA, the interfaces are process-centric; that means the data structures and their handling are a black box to the client. This is even more true for document-style interfaces. All this means that, for SOA to work, Web services security must be built in at the message level. As you will see, that will be the emphasis in all the Web services security discussions throughout this book.

ebXML and RosettaNet: Alternative Technologies for Web Services

Two important initiatives can be considered competing with Web services: e-business XML (ebXML) and RosettaNet. We will describe them briefly in this section and then not cover them at all in the rest of the book.

The development of ebXML was driven out of a need to move EDI from being on expensive proprietary networks to leverage the benefits of XML and utilize the much cheaper public networks. The overriding goal for ebXML is to be a cheaper EDI on public networks and use the existing Web infrastructure.

ebXML is entirely document-centric as opposed to RPC-centric. It emphasizes B2B communications (like EDI does) as opposed to enterprise application integration. It assumes businesses can connect their IT systems over the Internet and then use ebXML standards and protocols to process orders, delivery schedules, receipts, invoices, and the like. ebXML tries to closely model business processes based on business documents being exchanged.

Because of its heritage in EDI and its B2B focus, ebXML has more built-in support for security and reliability than initial Web services had. It is based on SOAP with attachments but diverges from the de facto SOAP attachments standard for Web services. In addition to adding SOAP attachments, it also adds significant security and reliability capabilities. There is no analog to WSDL. There is also no endorsement from Microsoft and IBM. But OASIS—the same organization heavily involved in Web services standards such as SAML and UDDI—is the organization shepherding the ebXML standards.

RosettaNet was an early XML-based B2B integration approach. RosettaNet is a non-profit subsidiary of the Uniform Code Council. RosettaNet's origins are the semiconductor industry, where it was developed to support integrated supply chains. It has since been extended and adapted to support other industries.

RosettaNet's goal is to provide dynamic, flexible trading networks. It encompasses data dictionaries, an implementation framework, and XML-based business message schemas and process specifications to standardize e-business interactions. RosettaNet Partner Interface Processes (PIPs) are specialized system-to-system XML-based dialogs that define business processes between trading partners. Each PIP specification includes a business document with the vocabulary, and a business process with the choreography of the message dialog. RosettaNet and Web services are converging so that, over time, they will become indistinguishable.

The Web Services Security Specifications

In subsequent chapters, you will find detailed discussions of the core specifications and standards surrounding Web services security. We've dedicated entire chapters to XML Signature, XML Encryption, SAML, and WS-Security, respectively. Table 2.1 defines the core security specifications covered in this book.

Table 2.1 **The Web Services Specifications in This Book**

Specification	Description
XML Signature	XML Signature is the standard that defines how to guarantee XML message integrity. Additionally, this is the mechanism that provides for non-repudiation that the sender is the one who really sent a message and that the receiver is the one who really received it. This specification is the subject of Chapter 4.
XML Encryption	XML Encryption is the standard that defines how to guarantee XML message confidentiality. It prevents eavesdropping on any message being transported—even on an open, insecure network. This specification is the subject of Chapter 5.
SAML	The Security Assertion Markup Language is an XML-based framework for exchanging security information. This security information is expressed in the form of assertions about subjects, where a subject is an entity (either human or computer) that has an identity in some security domain. A typical example of a subject is a person, identified by his email address in a particular Internet DNS domain. This important OASIS standard is covered in Chapter 6.
XACML	The eXtensible Access Control Markup Language is a proposed OASIS standard for an XML specification to express policies for information access over the Internet. XACML is expected to address fine-grained control of authorized activities, the effect of characteristics of the access requestor, the protocol over which the request is made, authorization based on classes of activities, and content introspection. This OASIS activity is covered in Chapter 9.
XrML	The eXtensible Rights Markup Language fills the need for rights specification for digital media. The goals for an OASIS XrML standard are that it be capable of expressing simple and complex rights and that it be capable of describing rights for any type of digital content or service. This OASIS activity is covered in Chapter 9.
XKMS	The XML Key Management Specification is a W3C submission composed of protocols for distributing and registering public keys, suitable for use in conjunction with XML Signature and XML Encryption. XKMS is made up of two parts: the XML Key Information Service Specification (X-KISS) and the XML Key Registration Service Specification (X-KRSS). This specification is covered in Chapter 9.
WS-Security	This comprehensive security specification is built on and utilizes XML Signature and XML Encryption as fundamental components. This OASIS draft specification describes enhancements to the SOAP messaging to provide *quality of protection* through message integrity, message confidentiality, and single message authentication. These mechanisms can be used to accommodate a wide variety of security models and encryption technologies. This specification also provides a general-purpose mechanism for associating security tokens with messages. Chapter 7 is dedicated to this important standard.

Table 2.1   **Continued**

Specification	Description
WS-Policy	WS-Policy provides a general-purpose model and syntax to describe and communicate the policies of a Web service. It defines a base set of constructs that can be used and extended by other Web services specifications to describe a broad range of service requirements, preferences, and capabilities. The goal is a common language for describing the rules for interacting with a Web service, or what a client requires of a Web service, regardless of whether the domain is security, privacy, transactions, or any other category. WS-Policy is not very far along yet in the standards process, but we felt an early understanding of it so important that we created an entire chapter on the topic—Chapter 8.

Summary

This chapter established a base of knowledge we call the *gestalt* of Web services: an understanding of how the Web services standards and technologies form a configuration or pattern of elements that is so unified as a whole that it cannot be described merely as a sum of its parts. Those "parts" are the standards normally used to "define" Web services. Importantly, this chapter also sought to motivate and explain the need for security and how we will approach solving that need.

This chapter began with a discussion of the genesis of Web services. That genesis sprang from business problems such as a need for application integration because business processes cross application and organization boundaries. The desire for portals has been driven by the business problem of presenting a wide variety of to-be-integrated information sources to the widest possible audience. The genesis for Web services also has come from the natural evolution of distributed computing over several decades of work. That work showed the need for cross-platform neutral standards, and the dramatic explosion of the Web put a fine point on how critical broadly accepted standards are for new computing paradigms to really take hold. Learning from those previous evolutionary steps led to establishing simple but strong Web services standards that, for the first time ever, were not only supported by competing vendors, but also were actually driven by them working in collaboration.

Next, we delved into the security challenges inherent in any middleware but exacerbated by both the linkage to Web technologies and by the goal of cross-organizational use of Web services. One big area of security concern revolves around portable identities that attach to and ride along with messages and requests for service. Another is the fundamental nature of message-based systems that require security be applied at the message level and not at the network perimeter level. If we are closer to the longstanding but elusive goal of SOA, it will mean new and even more demanding security challenges such as ways to deal with shared services accessed by different organizations with different trust models and access rights.

The next few sections were dedicated to brief descriptions of the basic standards that are used by Web services, with a particular emphasis on the ways in which each of these standards affects or is affected by security issues. First up was XML and its origins. How does XML interact with Web services? XML topics particularly relevant to XML security were addressed—for example, XML namespaces that keep simple names used in one conceptual area from interacting with those from another; XML Schemas that define how to understand an XML document; and XML Transformations that change an XML document, sometimes a required step before security can be applied to it.

Second, we covered SOAP and its origins. The structure of SOAP is important especially when you are thinking about ways to secure SOAP messages, so we described in detail what goes into the SOAP envelope, header, and body. How SOAP is processed is important because this is where security information resident in the header affects the message and application it is destined for. Attachments, while not part of the current SOAP standard, are used extensively, especially where confidentiality of that data is important.

Third, we covered WSDL and its origins. We described all the elements of a WSDL description. WSDL and SOAP are tightly intertwined. WSDL is not secure and does not have a lot to do directly with Web services security, but some of the WS-Security standards augment WSDL with security, reliability, control, and policy extensions.

We covered a few of the other Web services technologies at the end of this chapter. UDDI is one that has enormous security implications. ebXML and RosettaNet are initiatives that pre-date Web services and effectively are competing alternatives. They are not the focus of this book, so this discussion is short.

We closed this chapter with definitions of the Web services security–related specifications that we will be covering in detail later in the book.

Resources

Web Services: A Manager's Guide by Anne Thomas Manes (Addison-Wesley, 2003).

Web Services: A Technical Introduction by H. M. Deitel, P. J. Deitel, B. DuWaldt, and L. K. Trees (Prentice-Hall, 2003).

3

The Foundations of Distributed Message-Level Security

SECURITY IS ONE OF THE MOST vital topics in Web services development today and will be for the foreseeable future. The lack of maturity of standards and tools in this area is the reason most often cited for large organizations delaying their commitment to Web services. The most important security standards are ready now, though, and the tools are coming online. Importantly, these Web Services Security standards are really not groundbreaking; they are, in turn, just extensions of very well-established information security standards.

In Chapter 2, "The Foundations of Web Services," we introduced Web services as a new form of middleware for building and integrating distributed applications by sending XML messages between computing nodes. Making Web services secure means making those messages secure and keeping them secure wherever they go. This chapter builds on the preceding chapter by adding a solid foundation in the principles of distributed message-level security. Those principles depend on solid knowledge of shared key cryptography and public key cryptography. We begin by setting the information security context for Web services.

The Challenges of Information Security for Web Services

Securing distributed systems is hard. Securing exchanged information between those systems is harder. Securing Web services with their distributed, shared, and exposed information (XML messages) is much harder still. In the following sections, we address each of these challenges in order.

Security of Distributed Systems Is Hard

In distributed systems, you are not securing just one system, but many. In addition, you are securing the interconnections between the distributed systems. The goal of distributed systems is to make a collection of independent computers appear to their users as a single integrated system. When you can successfully integrate separate and distinct networked computers together, the integrated system can handle higher workloads, aggregate more functionality, and share data that previously was locked up and inaccessible. But the more access points there are, the more places an attacker has to attack. In other words, a distributed system has all the security issues of one system multiplied many times over.

These distributed system security issues include access control, identity management, authentication, password management, authorization, encryption of confidential information on each node, integrity of information passing between nodes, and more. This is the reason the CORBA security specification is 430 pages long.

Because Web services use the Web and enable and even encourage integration between systems across organizational boundaries using public networks, they are, in fact, much more distributed than CORBA or any previous form of middleware could contemplate. Web services, when used in remote procedure call mode, involve some of the same issues as CORBA object invocation security.

A service-oriented architecture—such as what can be achieved when Web services become pervasive—projects a vision of geographically distributed services, many of which are publicly available shared services incorporated into numerous applications. Knowing who is using these services, what these users are authorized to do, and how to protect all information at these nodes is a difficult security task.

Security of Exchanged Information (Messages) Is Harder

When security administrators think about securing their systems today, they typically think about securing their organization's "four walls." They think about perimeter security such as firewalls, intrusion detection, honeypots, and DMZs. None of these elements deal with the security of messages in transit. Security administrators focus most on access control security believing that, if they know for sure who has access to their network, they *implicitly* have secured their critical assets: their information. In fact, perimeter security schemes are really a proxy for information security, because all along, what people are really trying to protect is the information created, processed, or stored on the machines inside their perimeters.

Distributed applications send back and forth messages that are the command, control, and coordination that make the distributed applications function. This means you have the problems of computer and network security you always had, *plus* the problems of information security for critical command and control messages flowing through the distributed system. Transport-based security like SSL provides one type of protection for messages in transit—just server-to-server non-persistent confidentiality—but offers little or no control at the application level, which is the place where the messages have meaning.

Messages must remain intact from sender to receiver regardless of how many hops occur in between. Shared services create a many-hops scenario in which messages go through many service endpoints on the way to their destination. The receiver must know for sure who the sender was to establish trust, which is critical in all aspects of business. The sender must be able to control who is allowed to see her messages because vital (and confidential) information is contained in them. In the case of transmitted legal documents, being able to prove what transpired and repudiate any denials is critical. Messages need to remain persistently secure not just while in transit, but also when residing in permanent storage because the message might contain highly confidential information such as a credit card number, Social Security number, or business deal terms.

Security of Web Services Is Hardest

Web services add a new dimension to the challenges already faced with distributed systems. Critical security questions must be reliably answered. Who is the end user? How do you maintain security when routing messages through multiple servers? How do you maintain security when using shared services?

Web services are fundamentally about how to share the burden of—and derive the benefits from—computing across a distributed network of computers connected with Web infrastructure and standards. These messages—being XML—are text-based, readable, and self-describing. Security of Web services is about knowing whether the Web services are talking to the correct endpoints; the communications between all the disparate elements are kept confidential; the messages transported maintain their integrity at all times; and the entities for which these Web services are being invoked are known, trusted, and authorized to use the services and can be clearly identified to all other authorized services.

The good news is that Web Services Security builds on existing security standards; very little that is new is being proposed. In general, Web Services Security provides an XML-based abstraction layer for established security technologies that delivers confidentiality, integrity, non-repudiation, authentication, and authorization.

Why All the FUD about Web Services Security?

Some Web Services Security vendors, the analysts that cover these companies, and the media are spreading fear, uncertainty, and doubt (FUD) about how an organization must fully implement Web Services Security before deploying the first Web service. Because early Web service deployments tend to be simple, straightforward, internal, *behind the firewall*, point-to-point integrations, sophisticated Web Services Security technologies are not always necessary. In fact, the same security used by these companies for securing their Web sites—namely SSL—is usually sufficient.

For the vendors who are selling either a product or service that implements Web Services Security in some form, however, it is in their best interest to have the early Web services adopters firmly believe they cannot be successful without these vendors' products or services. This thinking is a huge stretch, to put it mildly.

When designing an information security strategy for a Web services deployment, you must think like an information security professional. Think in terms of confidentiality, integrity, and the other building block security principles. If your messages need legal non-repudiation, perhaps you need to employ more sophisticated technologies. But if all you need to do is keep messages confidential between point A and point B, maybe what you already know how to do so well (use SSL) is perfectly sufficient.

To build on your understanding of these information security building blocks, you need to understand how the discipline of cryptography is applied to distributed messages. The following sections cover the shared key technologies and then cover public key technologies.

Shared Key Technologies

Shared key technologies, including shared key encryption and Kerberos, will be your critical tool for guaranteeing information security principle number one: confidentiality of Web services messages. The following sections discuss the cryptography behind the algorithms, the mechanisms for managing keys, and the relationship between shared key technologies and public key technologies.

Shared Key Encryption

Other synonyms for shared key encryption are frequently used. This technology is sometimes referred to as *symmetric encryption* or *secret key encryption* because the same key is used to both encrypt and decrypt the message, and this key must be kept secret from all non-participating parties to keep the encrypted message secret. For clarity and simplicity, in this book we consistently use the term *shared key encryption* because sender and receiver share the same key, which is distinct from public key encryption where one key is made open and public to the entire world. Shared key encryption is the key technology to achieve the security principle of message confidentiality. Message confidentiality means that no one other than the intended recipient will be able to read a message because it is encrypted strongly enough that no one without the correct key can decrypt it by any other means. We reproduce the shared key encryption diagram from Chapter 1, "Basic Concepts of Web Services Security," here in Figure 3.1.

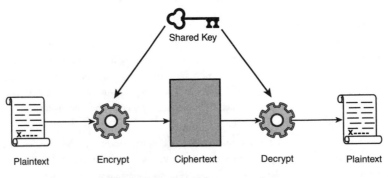

Figure 3.1   Shared key encryption.

The key to message confidentiality is *in the key*, so to speak. Because both sender and receiver must utilize the exact same key (it is *shared)*, this solitary key must somehow be separately and confidentially exchanged so that both parties have it—and no one else does—prior to message exchange. Under other circumstances, you might think you could send the key via U.S. Mail or read it over the phone, but neither of these approaches would be consistent with the goals of computer-to-computer Web services communication. For Web services, this exchange must be made over the same channel that the encrypted messages will flow. Cryptographers and security practitioners have determined that the best way to accomplish this is to encrypt the shared key using public key encryption before exchange. Public key encryption is described in the next section.

Only the shared key is secret, not the encryption algorithm itself. It is very important that the encryption algorithms themselves are public and well scrutinized. In the early days of information security, encryption algorithms were kept strictly secret and proprietary; however, after they were put into use, users found that they had dangerous flaws. Now the field of cryptography understands that the open study of algorithms enhances confidence in the algorithm's security due to the extensive testing and analysis by all the world's cryptographers. A proof of this point is how long the modern shared key encryption algorithms Advanced Encryption Standard (AES) and Triple Data Encryption Standard (3DES) have been in use, withstanding extensive testing with no flaws found.

Without going into extensive mathematical derivations to prove our points (see Appendix A for some details), we need you to take on faith the three most important factors you need to know about shared key encryption:

- Shared key encryption is much faster than public key encryption.
- Shared key encryption can operate on arbitrarily large plaintext messages, whereas public key encryption cannot.
- Shared key encryption utilizes public key encryption to manage distribution of the shared key securely to the recipient.

Shared key encryption uses cryptographic algorithms known as *block ciphers*. This means that the algorithms work by taking the starting plaintext message and first breaking it into fixed-size blocks before encrypting each block. Two strong encryption algorithms used throughout the software industry are part of the XML Encryption standard: the long-standing 3DES and the relatively new, but highly reviewed and analyzed AES.

DES involves many computationally fast and simple substitutions, permutations, XORs, and shifting on a data block at a time to produce ciphertext from an input plaintext message. The design of DES is so clever that decryption uses exactly the same algorithm as encryption. The only difference is that the order in which the key parts are used in the algorithm is exactly reversed.

DES is 25 years old and still going strong. Part of the reason for this is that DES was designed (and adapted over the years) to work really well in hardware. Numerous companies now include DES chips in their devices. Virtual private networks (VPNs) frequently use 3DES—the stronger version of DES described next—directly in the hardware to create secure IPSec tunnels. DES uses a 64-bit key: 56 effective bits, and 8 bits for parity. DES operates on an 8-byte fixed-block size. In the past decade, weaknesses found in DES have been addressed by 3DES.

Note
It is rumored that the NSA has machines costing under $50K that can brute-force crack DES with its 64-bit key in 15 minutes.

3DES saved DES from being abrogated to the cryptography scrap heap by responding to the fact that 2^{56} (72 quintillion) possible keys made plain DES susceptible to a brute-force attack, so the DES algorithm is run three times with a much longer key. 3DES uses a 192-bit key, of which the effective key length is 168 bits. The idea is to use DES three times: sequencing Encrypt-Decrypt-Encrypt with a different third of the 168-bit key used at each stage, as shown in Figure 3.2. This approach makes it relatively slow but very secure; on hardware, relatively slow is still plenty fast. Note that the middle step—Decrypt—does not actually decrypt the ciphertext created by the first step because a completely distinct key is used; it actually scrambles the message further.

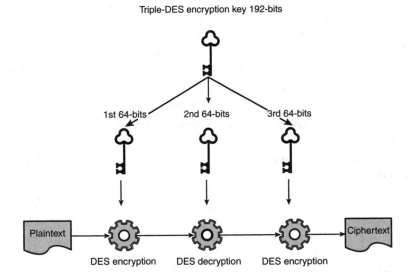

Triple-DES encryption key 192-bits

1st 64-bits   2nd 64-bits   3rd 64-bits

Plaintext   DES encryption   DES decryption   DES encryption   Ciphertext

Figure 3.2   How 3DES uses DES encryption three times in succession to be much more secure than DES alone.

AES is the newest shared key encryption standard. AES came out of a government-sponsored contest won by the cryptographers Joan Daemen and Vincent Rijmen (the algorithm was called Rijndael, pronounced "rain doll)." It also works well in hardware and can have keys up to 256 bits long, taking it out of the realm of ever being susceptible to a brute-force attack.

A critical concept for shared key encryption is padding. The blocks that are input to the cipher must be of a fixed size, so if the plaintext input is not already of the correct size, it must be padded. However, you cannot just add random data; to do so, you would need to communicate to the receiver the correct size of the data, which would be a dangerous clue to an attacker. You also cannot just add zeros because the message itself might have leading or trailing zeros. Consequently, padding must include sentinel information that identifies the padding and must not give an attacker any critical information that might compromise the message.

Kerberos

No discussion of shared key technologies would be complete without mention of Kerberos. Kerberos was originally part of MIT's project Athena. The goal set out for Kerberos was real-time authentication in an insecure (the client is not trusted) distributed environment. This technology predates the Web. Plus, it appears to be getting a new lease on life with Microsoft's adoption of it in the base Windows operating system security model. Kerberos is also one of the recognized security *tokens*—pieces of information used for authentication or authorization added to a SOAP header—in the emerging WS-Security standard, which is presented in Chapter 7, "Building Security into SOAP."

Kerberos is a trusted third-party authentication protocol. Users and services obtain an authentication token called a *ticket* that they use for identity and *shared keys* that they use for secure communications. A shared key known only to the server that encrypts tickets. The Kerberos model calls for a centralized authentication server. Kerberos performs centralized key management and administration. The server maintains all users' shared keys and generates session keys whenever two users want to communicate securely. It authenticates the identity of a user who requests access to secure network services. A client must have a valid password and ticket (which only the server can validate) to use any services.

The basic Kerberos authentication flow is as follows:

1. The client sends a request to the authentication server requesting "credentials" for a given application server. These credentials can be applied directly to an application server or to a ticket-granting server.

2. The authentication server responds with credentials encrypted with the client's key; it includes a ticket for the server and a session key.

3. If the ticket is for the ticket server, the client then requests a ticket for the application server from the ticket server.

4. The ticket server responds with the ticket.

5. The client transmits its ticket with the client identity and a session key copy encrypted using the server's key to the application server.

6. The session key is now shared between the client and application server, which authenticates the client and can be used to authenticate the server. It can also be used to encrypt further communication between the two parties.

Kerberos plays an important, but not leading, role in Web services security. Systems running Microsoft Windows frequently use the built-in Kerberos model, which is appropriate only for closed systems, but they still may want to connect to external organizations via Web services. Those external systems need to have their authentication scheme mapped into the Kerberos model for the two organizations to interact.

The WS-Security standard recognizes Kerberos tickets as one of the valid types of security tokens. A very important attribute and goal of WS-Security is to be able to bridge between different security models and trust domains—for example, one system that runs Kerberos connected to another that uses X.509 public key infrastructure.

Limitations of Shared Key Technologies

As we said earlier, shared key technologies fail to solve the problem of scalable key distribution. Shared key algorithms are fast and can handle infinitely large messages; however, both ends of the communication need access to the same key, and you need to get it to your recipient securely. Shared key cryptography also fails to solve the issue of repudiation. At times, you will need to be able to prove that a certain identity created and attests to sending a message (or document) and no one else could have. The sender must not be able to deny having sent this exact document at this moment in time. Shared key cryptography provides no help here.

Public Key Technologies

Public key technologies, including public key encryption and digital signature, will be your tools for delivering integrity, non-repudiation, and authentication to XML messages and more generally to Web services. The following sections begin with an explanation of the concepts behind public key encryption. We expand this description so that you can apply this knowledge to build the basis for digital signatures and then apply these concepts more specifically to digital signatures in XML. A discussion of public key technologies is not complete without a description of public key infrastructure and the issues of establishing trust, which are covered at the end of this section.

Public Key Encryption

Public key encryption is also referred to as *asymmetric encryption* because there is not just one key used in both directions, as with the symmetric form of encryption used in shared key algorithms. In public key encryption, there is a matched set of two keys; whichever one is used to encrypt requires the other be used to decrypt. In this book, we use the term *public key encryption* to help establish context and contrast it with shared key encryption.

The keys in public key encryption are non-matching, but they are mathematically related. One key (it does not matter which) is used for encryption; that key is useless for decryption. Only the matching key can be used for decryption. This concept provides the critical facility you need for secure key exchange to establish and transport a shared key.

The diagram from Chapter 1 that shows how basic public key encryption works is reproduced here in Figure 3.3.

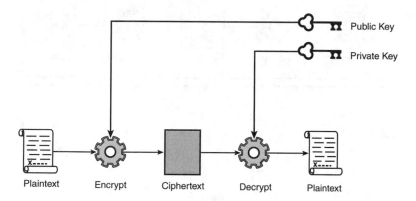

Figure 3.3 Public key encryption uses one key to encrypt the incoming plaintext, and only the other key can be used to successfully decrypt that ciphertext back into its original plaintext.

Although it is true that Kerberos provides a mechanism for distributing shared keys, Kerberos applies only to a closed environment where all principals requiring keys share direct access to trusted Key Distribution Centers (KDCs) and all principals share a key with that KDC. Thus, Kerberos does not provide Web services with a general mechanism for shared key distribution; public key systems without the restriction of working only in closed environments take that role. Public key systems work with paired keys, one of which (the private key) is kept strictly private and the other (the public key) is freely distributed; in particular, the public key is made broadly accessible to the other party in secure communications.

Parties requiring bidirectional, confidential communication must *each* generate a pair of keys (four keys in total). One of the keys, the *private* key, will never leave the possession of its respective creator. Each party to the communication passes his *public* key to the other party. The associated public key encryption algorithms are pure mathematical magic because whatever is encrypted with one half of the key pair can only be decrypted with its mate. Figure 3.4 shows how the key pairs are each used for one direction of the confidential message exchange.

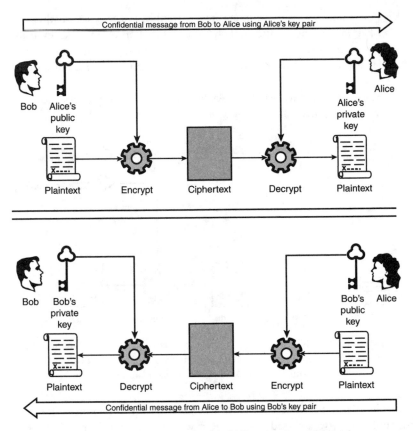

Figure 3.4 Two key pairs are involved in bidirectional, confidential message exchange. One pair is used for each direction. The sender always uses his private key for encryption, and the recipient always uses the sender's public key for decryption.

For Alice to send a confidential message to Bob, Alice must obtain Bob's public key. That's easy because anyone can have Bob's public key at no risk to Bob; it is just for encrypting data. Alice takes Bob's public key and provides it to the standard encryption algorithm to encrypt her message to Bob. Because of the nature of the public-private key pair and the fact that Alice and Bob agree on a public, standard encryption algorithm (like RSA), Bob can use his private key to decrypt Alice's message. Most importantly, *only* Bob—because no one will ever get her hands on Bob's private key—can decrypt Alice's message. Alice just sent Bob a confidential message. Any outsiders intercepting it will see useless scrambled data because they don't have Bob's private key.

We will describe digital signatures in a moment, but first we want you to notice something interesting about doing things just the reverse of Alice's confidential message. If Alice encrypts a message with her *private* key, which only Alice can possess, and if Alice makes sure Bob has her public key, Bob can see that Alice and only Alice could have encrypted that message. In fact, because Alice's public key is, in theory, accessible to the entire world, anyone can tell that Alice and only Alice encrypted that message. The identity of the sender was established. That is a principle of digital signatures.

The simple fact that in public key cryptography, whatever is encrypted with one half of the key pair can only be decrypted with its mate, combined with the strict rule that private keys remain private and only public keys can be distributed, leads to a very interesting and powerful matrix of how public key encryption interrelates to confidentiality and identity. This matrix is shown in Table 3.1.

Table 3.1   **The Matrix of Uses for Key Pairs in Public Key Cryptography Showing What Security Principle Applies and What Part of Web Services Security It Affects**

Public Key	Private Key	What This Means	WS Security Usage
Encrypt (with recipient's)	Decrypt (with recipient's)	Confidentiality (no one but intended recipient can read)	XML Encryption shared key exchange
Decrypt (with sender's)	Encrypt (with sender's)	Signature (identity) (it could only have come from sender)	XML Signature

Public key encryption is based on the mathematics of factoring large numbers into their prime factors. This problem is thought to be computationally intractable if the numbers are large enough. But a limitation of public key encryption is that it can be applied only to small messages. To achieve the goal of distributing shared keys, this is no problem; those keys are not larger than the message size limitation of public key algorithms. To achieve the goal of digital signatures on arbitrarily large messages, you can apply a neat trick to remain within this size limitation, as discussed next.

Limitations of Public Key Encryption

Even when implemented in hardware, shared key algorithms are many orders of magnitude faster than public key algorithms. For instance, in hardware, RSA is about 1,000 times slower than DES.

The first performance hit comes from key generation. You must find two multi-hundred-bit prime numbers that are near the same length. Then these two primes must be tested for primality. Primality testing is a very expensive operation requiring a series of steps that each has a certain probability of determining that the values are relatively prime. These steps must be run several times to make the probability high enough as to have an acceptably infinitesimal risk of being wrong.

The second reason that public key encryption is so much slower than shared key algorithms is that RSA encryption/decryption is based on the mathematics of modular exponentiation. This means you are taking each input value, raising it to a power (requiring a large number of multiplications), and then performing the modulo operation (the remainder after doing integer division). On the other hand, shared key ciphers are based on much faster logical operations on bit arrays. Public key algorithms are called asymmetric for a reason. Because the private key has a much larger exponent than the public key, private key operations take substantially longer than do public key operations. To establish identity and support non-repudiation (for example, in digital signatures) where the public key is used for encryption, decryption takes substantially longer than encryption. In integrity applications (also in digital signatures) where the private key is used for encryption, it is the other way around. This imbalance would be a problem when applied to large messages but is not an issue when applied only to small messages such as the 200-bit key being exchanged to enable shared key encryption or the 20-byte message digests used in digital signatures, which will be discussed shortly.

The third reason to be concerned about the computational complexity of public key encryption is the padding issue. The input to RSA encryption operations is interpreted as a number, so special padding is required to make the input totally consistent. The total length of the data must be a multiple of the modulus size, and the data must be numerically less than the modulus. A 1,024-bit RSA key has a 128-byte modulus. Therefore, data must be encrypted in blocks of 128 bytes. Each input number must be padded with zeros until its numerical value is less than that of the modulus. This padding places a critical restriction on the size of data that RSA can encrypt. This is why RSA is never used to encrypt the entire plaintext message but only encrypts the shared key being exchanged between communicating parties. Then, after the shared key is established safely between the parties, RSA (public key) encryption is no longer used, and instead AES (shared key) encryption is used on the plaintext message itself.

Digital Signature Basics

Digital signature is the tool you use to achieve the information security principle of integrity. Digital signature involves utilizing a one-way mathematical function called *hashing* followed by public key encryption. The basic idea is to use a hash function to create a *message digest* of fixed and short length and then to encrypt this short message digest. A message digest is a short representation (usually 20 bytes) of the full message. You need to do this because, as you have just seen, public key encryption is slow and is limited in the size of message it can encrypt. A hash is a one-way mathematical function that creates a unique fixed-size message digest from an arbitrary-size text message. One-way means that you can never take the hash value and re-create the original message. Hash functions are designed to be very fast and are good at never creating the same result value from two different messages (they avoid collisions). Uniqueness is critical to make sure an attacker can never just replace one message with another and have the message digest come out the same anyway; that would essentially ruin the goal of providing message integrity through digital signatures.

You know that public key encryption works only on small-size messages. You also know that if Alice encrypts a small message with her private key and sends the message to Bob, Bob can use Alice's public key to prove that the message could only have come from

Alice (as long as you are sure she protected her private key). This identification of the sender is one half of what digital signature is all about. The other half relates to obtaining the goal of verifying the integrity of the message. By *integrity*, we mean that you can tell whether the message has changed by even one bit since it was sent. The key to integrity in the digital signature design is the use of a hash function to create a message digest.

Hashing the Message to Create a Message Digest

A hash function creates a message digest that can be used as a proxy for the original message. You want this function to be very fast because, as you will see, you need to run this function on both the sending and verifying ends of a communication. Most importantly, you must be certain that it is impossible for two messages to create the same output hash value to achieve integrity; otherwise, you lose your goal of integrity. If it were possible for two messages to create the same message digest, it would mean that someone could substitute a new message for the original and fool the recipient into thinking the new fraudulent message is the correct one. For integrity's sake, it must also be impossible to reverse the function and take the small output value and regenerate the original message (that is, it must truly be a one-way function).

Functions that avoid duplicate values are exceedingly rare. The birthday paradox demonstrates this point. With any random 23 people in a room, the chance that two have the same birthday is 50%. Think of these people as representing 23 different plaintext messages. If a hash function applied to just 23 messages (or 2,300 or 23,000 messages) had a 50% chance of two of them resulting in the same message digest, you would not accept this type of hash function to deliver integrity.

Several one-way hash functions that have excellent collision avoidance properties have been designed and deployed, including MD4, MD5, and SHA1. Weaknesses have been found in the first two, and currently most security systems, and all the standards for Web services security, use SHA1. (Interestingly, SHA1 is a replacement for SHA which corrected a flaw in the original SHA algorithm.)[1]

> **Note**
>
> SHA1, which stands for Secure Hash Algorithm 1, refers to it being the first (implying there may be the need for variants in the future). NIST and the NSA designed the algorithm for use with the Digital Signature Algorithm (DSA).

> **SHA1**
>
> The SHA1 standard specifies a Secure Hash Algorithm, which is necessary to ensure the security of the Digital Signature Algorithm. When a message of any length $< 2^{64}$ bits is input, the SHA produces a 160-bit message digest output. The message digest is then input to the DSA, which computes the signature for the message. Signing the message digest rather than the message often improves the efficiency of the process because the message digest is usually much smaller than the message. The verifier of the signature should obtain the same message digest when the received version of the message is used as input to SHA.

1. http://www.rsasecurity.com/rsalabs/faq/3-6-5.html

> The SHA is called secure because it is designed to be computationally infeasible to recover a message corresponding to a given message digest or to find two different messages that produce the same message digest. Any change to a message in transit will, with a very high probability, result in a different message digest, and the signature will fail to verify. The SHA is based on principles similar to those used by Professor Ronald L. Rivest of MIT when designing the MD4 message digest algorithm, and is closely modeled after that algorithm.

SHA1 meets all the requirements for a secure one-way hash algorithm. In particular, it is not reversible. Guessing a 20-byte hash (160 bits) has a 1 in 2^{160} chance of coming up with the original message.

Note

By way of scaling how unlikely guessing a 1 in 2^{160} chance is:

- 2^{61} sec is the total lifetime of the universe.
- 2^{170} is the total number of atoms in the earth.

On a computer running 1 billion hashes per second (still beyond computing capacity today), brute-force guessing of a 20-byte hash would take 10^{22} billion years to accomplish, which is more than the lifetime of the universe.

If you hash the entire plaintext message and then protect the resulting message digest from being modified in any way, and if the sender and receiver use the exact same input message and hash algorithm, the recipient can check and verify the integrity of the message without going to the huge expense of trying to encrypt the entire message. So now let's discuss how to protect the message digest.

Public Key Encryption of the Message Digest

Protecting the message digest simply involves encrypting it with the private key of the sender and sending the original message along with the encrypted message digest to the recipient. Public key encryption of the message digest provides non-repudiation because only the subject identity with the private key that did the encryption could have initiated the message. Protecting the message digest by encrypting it such that no middleman attacker could have modified it provides message integrity.

Digital Signature Signing Process

You are now ready to put all this information together and create a digital signature. You will combine the hashing function (SHA1) used to convert the plaintext message into a fixed-size message digest with public key encryption (RSA or DSA) of that message digest to create a digital signature you can send to the selected recipient. The basic steps for creating a digital signature are as follows:

1. Hash the entire plaintext message, creating a 20-byte message digest.

2. Encrypt this message digest using the sender's private key.

3. Send the original message and the encrypted message digest along with the sender's public key to any desired recipients.

These steps are shown in Figure 3.5, where the hash algorithm being used is SHA1.

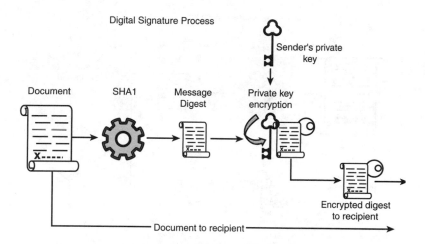

Figure 3.5 Digital signature signing process.

Digital Signature Verification Process

Signature verification is the process the message recipient goes through to determine the identity of the sender and to determine that the message arrived intact and unaltered. In other words, signature verification is necessary to achieve the security principles of message integrity and non-repudiation. The steps in signature verification are as follows:

1. The recipient receives the original plaintext message and the encrypted message digest from the sender.

2. Separately or at the same time, the recipient receives the sender's public key.

3. The original plaintext document is run through the same SHA1 hash algorithm originally performed by the signer. This algorithm is identical on all platforms, so the recipient has confidence that the exact same result will occur if the document has not been altered in any way.

4. The recipient uses the sender's public key to decrypt the message digest. If the decryption is successful and the recipient *trusts* the sender's public key to be valid, and the recipient also *trusts* that the sender has protected her private key, the recipient knows that it was the sender who sent this message.

5. The final step of the verification process is a bit-for-bit comparison of the message digest computed locally from the original document with the one just decrypted. If they match exactly, the signature is valid.

The verification process just outlined is shown in Figure 3.6.

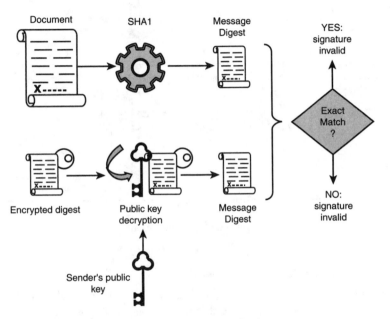

Figure 3.6 Digital signature verification process.

You now know for sure that the unique private key that matches this public key is the one that encrypted the message digest, which tells you the identity of the signer if you are certain she has protected her private key—all of which gives you non-repudiation. You also know that the message was sent unaltered, so you have integrity. What you still need, and will be discussed in a few moments, is assurance that you know the identity of the owner of the public key you just used.

RSA is the most commonly accepted digital signature algorithm used in Web services security, although officially DSA is also allowed.

Integrity Without Non-Repudiation

When non-repudiation is not a goal, a very different approach to verifying message integrity called Message Authentication Code (MAC) is used. This approach is like creating a cryptographic checksum of a message. The MAC's class of algorithms provides pure message integrity protection based on a secret shared key. To limit the size message MAC will operate on, Web Services Security combines pure MAC with a hash, so the acronym becomes HMAC. Figure 3.7 shows how an HMAC functions.

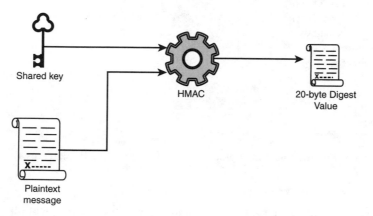

Figure 3.7   The Hashed Message Authentication Code (HMAC) algorithm.

Think of an HMAC as a key-dependent one-way hash function. Only someone with the identical key can verify the hash. You know that hashing is a very fast operation, so these types of functions are useful for guaranteeing message authenticity when secrecy and non-repudiation are not important but speed is. These algorithms are different from a straight hash because the hash value is encrypted and protected with a key. The algorithm is symmetric: The sender and recipient possess a shared key. You will see HMAC again in Chapter 4, "Safeguarding the Identity and Integrity of XML Messages," as part of the XML Signature discussion.

A Digital Signature Expressed in XML

Web services messages are XML-based. Message-level security in Web services requires that you apply digital signatures in an XML setting. Therefore, you need a digital signature expressed in XML. That is the simplest description of what the XML Signature standard is. XML Signature was designed to have a great deal of flexibility. An XML Signature can be placed inside an XML document, or it can refer to external elements that need to be signed. For example, an XML Signature could be applied just to a credit card number inside the XML document, or it could be applied to a complete personal medical history. It is also important to be able to sign external elements like online resources such as Web pages to prevent defacement. XML Signature supports that option as well.

The structure of an XML Signature is shown in Listing 3.1:

Listing 3.1   **The Structure of an XML Signature**

```
<Signature>
    <SignedInfo>
        (CanonicalizationMethod)
        (SignatureMethod)
```

Listing 3.1 **Continued**

```
        (<Reference (URI=)? >
            (Transforms)?
            (DigestMethod)
            (DigestValue)
        </Reference>)+
    <SignedInfo>
    (SignatureValue)
    (KeyInfo)?
    (Object)*
</Signature>
```

We expand on this structure and explore the full richness of XML Signature in Chapter 4.

Public Key Infrastructure

As you saw earlier, digital signature verification required that the recipient obtain the sender's public key. We were not specific about how that happened. This step is incredibly important to establishing trust between sender and recipient. The recipient needs to rely on the trust implied in the public key that it is really from the sender and that the sender has maintained custody and sanctity of his private key. This is the domain of Public Key Infrastructure (PKI). PKI emcompasses certificates, certificate authorities, and trust.

In all our discussions of public key encryption and its application to digital signatures, we oversimplified to the extreme when we said the public key is just sent to a recipient. In fact, the key alone is not enough. You need more than just the public key itself if the public key is from someone you don't know well. You need identity information associated with the public key. You also need a way to know whether someone you trust has verified this identity so that you can trust this entire transaction. Trust is what PKI is all about.

Digital Certificates Are Containers for Public Keys

A digital certificate is a data structure that contains identity information along with an individual's public key and is signed by a *certificate authority (CA)*. The official designation of standard digital certificates with which we will be dealing is X.509. By signing the certificate, the CA is vouching for the identity of the individual described in the certificate. This is so that relying parties (message recipients) can trust the public key contained in the certificate.

Bob, the relying party, must be certain that this is really Alice's key. He ensures that it is by checking the identity of the CA that signed this certificate (how he trusts the CA in the first place we will get to in a moment) and by verifying both the identity and integrity of the certificate through the CA's attached signature. A validity date included in X.509 certificates helps ensure against compromised (or out-of-date and invalid) keys.

The X.509 digital certificate trust model is a very general one. Each subject identity has a distinct name. The subject must be certified by the CA using some well-defined certification process it must describe and publish in a Certification Practice Statement (CPS). The CA assigns a unique *distinguished* name to each user and issues a signed certificate containing the name and the user's public key.

Version 3 of the X.509 standard specifies a certificate structure including certificate extensions. The v3 certificate extensions enable extra functionality. For example, they allow incorporating authorization information in the certificate, providing the possibility of defining special authorization certificates. However, there is no guarantee of uniformity in the use of extensions, which can lead to interoperability problems.

The most important fields in the X.509 structure include

- **Version**—Which version of the X.509 standard this certificate conforms to.

- **Serial number**—A unique identifier for this certificate. This number can be used for revoking certificates, as described later in this chapter.

- **Signature algorithm**—The algorithm used to produce the digital signature this certificate bears.

- **Issuer**—The name of the organization that issued this certificate.

- **Valid from** and **valid to**—The validity times of the certificate (that is, when the certificate begins being valid and when it will expire).

- **Subject**—The name of the principal whose public key is contained in this certificate.

- **Public key**—The public key of that principal.

- **Various other fields**—Some of which are referred to as extended attribute fields.

The issuing certificate authority always signs the certificate. Figure 3.8 shows how a digital certificate is represented by the Windows XP operating system.

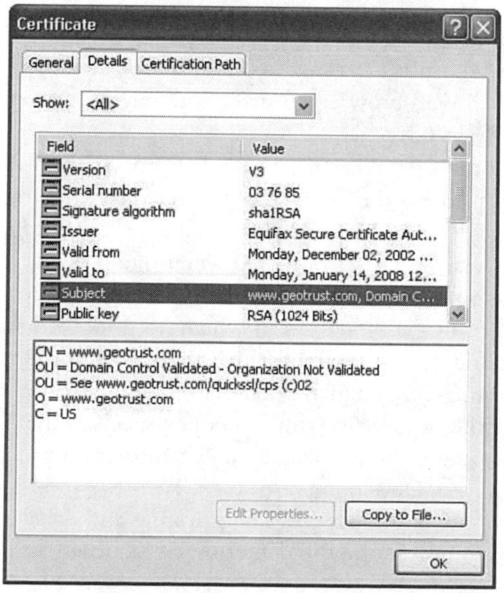

Figure 3.8 Certificate display screenshot from Windows XP.

Certificate Authorities Issue (and Sign) Digital Certificates

The CA signs the certificate with a standard digital signature using the private key of the CA. Like any digital signature, it allows anyone with the CA's matching public key to verify that this certificate was indeed signed by the CA and is not fraudulent. The signature is an encrypted hash (called the *thumbprint*) of the contents of the certificate, so standard signature verification guarantees integrity of the certificate data as well. That, in turn, allows you to believe the information contained in the certificate. Of course, what you are really after is trust in the validity of the Subject's (that is, the sender's/signer's) public key contained in the certificate.

So far, so good—if you trust the CA who signed this certificate.

The entire world may rely on such a signature, so you can be sure the CA goes to extraordinary lengths to protect its private key, including armed guards, copper-clad enclosures, and special hardware protecting the private key.

> **Note**
>
> Typical trusted CAs really do have armed guards protecting their buildings and areas called *man traps* that protect entry to the rooms in which the keys are contained. Two people must enter at once or not at all. The room contains a copper-clad enclosure that prevents stray electromagnetic radiation from emanating where it could be picked up by an intruder. Inside this copper-clad enclosure called a *tempest room* are the hardware devices that contain the keys. Changes in temperature or any attempts to move these devices cause them to self-destruct—yes, really self-destruct. To re-create a destroyed key requires five or more separate individuals taking their own special hardware card and combining them all under the observation of a trained auditor. The point is that these private keys are well protected.

The public key of the CA is typically very widely distributed. In fact, the public keys for SSL certificates—X.509 certificates issued to organizations for their Web sites—are found in all Web servers and all Web browsers to make sure relying parties can always verify certificates signed by those CAs.

The key to trusting the signed certificate is what process the CA used to verify the identity of the subject prior to the issuance of the certificate. It might be based on individuals being employees. It might require they produce a driver's license. Or it might be that they must correctly answer a set of shared secret questions drawn automatically from databases that know about all individuals, such as the telephone company, driver's license bureau, or credit bureau. In extreme cases in which no doubt is tolerable (national security, for example), a blood or DNA sample might have to be produced.

You can think of the CA as a digital notary. An individual's identity is based on the assurance (honesty) of the notary. A certificate policy specifies the levels of assurance the CA has to provide, and the CPS specifies the mechanisms and procedures to be used to achieve a level of assurance. Development of the CPS is the most time-consuming and essential component of establishing a CA. The planning and development of the certificate policies and procedures require the definition of requirements, such as key escrow, and processes, such as certificate revocation, which are covered later in this chapter.

A CA may be the guy down the hall, the HR department of your company, a local external company, a public CA, or the government.

Levels of Identity

One level of identity verification is never suitable for all situations. There is a need to declare different levels of identity "strength" so that some standardization can occur to benefit relying parties. A relying party is someone who is presented with a digital identity and must decide whether the process used to establish this identity is acceptable for his application. These strength levels are chosen based on

- Degree of confidence that the individual is who he says he is
- Risk of being wrong (release of information, completion of transaction, and so on)
- Severity of consequences of being wrong

Two different organizations are driving the push for standard levels of identity: the AICPA and the Federal Bridge Authority. Both deal with federated identity, but unlike the commercial federated identity projects Passport and Liberty Alliance, this application of federated identity is purely business-to-business or agency-to-agency in the government. One level of identity does not suffice in these situations because numerous different applications are involved with large variances in their assessment of the three criteria identified here.

The levels being proposed by the AICPA and Federal Bridge are similar in description, as shown in Table 3.2.

Table 3.2   **Federal Bridge and Proposed AICPA Criteria for Identity Levels Used in CA Processes When Establishing Digital Identities**

Level	Description	Appropriate Usage
1	Rudimentary—Whatever the individual claims, such as an email address	For anonymous transactions
2	Basic—May be based on employment records or consumer credit card and address verification	For pseudonymous transactions in which specific identity is not critical, but follow-up or delivery information is necessary
3	Medium—May use the consumer credit file and other databases that provide reliable shared secrets for identity verification	For identified transactions that require a person to be specifically identified
4	High—Person must be physically present	For verified transactions, the person must be identified, integrity of data and transaction event guaranteed, and evidence created to prove these were the parties to the transaction

CAs Must Be Trusted or Vouched For by a Trusted CA

If the CA that signed the certificate is not known to or not trusted by the relying party, that CA must itself be vouched for by a more trusted CA that satisfies the relying party. This *certificate chain* can continue indefinitely until eventually the chain reaches a trusted CA or it reaches a root certificate. In a root certificate, the issuer of the certificate is also the subject of that certificate (that is, the certificate is self-signed); it's a dead end. If the relying party does not trust the root CA, that party is out of luck and will have to reject the transaction being requested. If you are using a certificate issued by GeoTrust, you might have two certificates in a certificate chain, as shown in Figure 3.9.

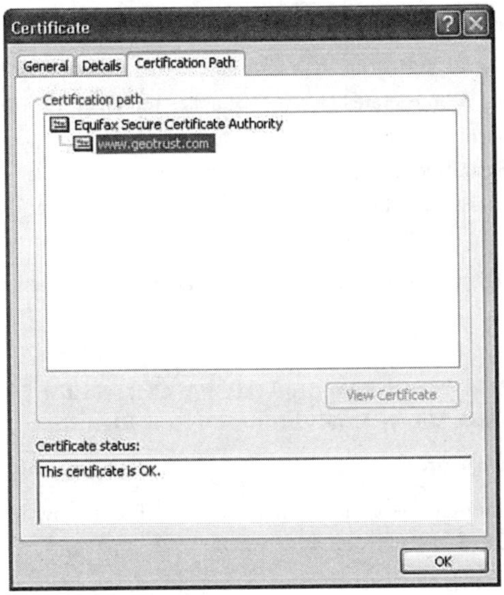

Figure 3.9 Screenshot showing a certification path. Certificate issued to www.geotrust.com is linked back to a certificate issued to (and by) Equifax Secure which is self-signed.

Two certificates are involved in this example. One certificate is issued directly to www.geotrust.com, who is the subject, and Equifax Secure is the issuer. The second certificate is the Equifax Secure root certificate, which is self-signed: The subject is Equifax, and the issuer is Equifax. Typically, you have a "trust store" or "trust list" in some database (it exists in Web servers, Web browsers, and in the operating system itself in many cases and for Web services will be placed in additional accessible places) containing the certificates of the certificate issuers that you are willing to trust. Through a process called *certificate path validation,* an attempt is made to create a "path" of valid, non-revoked certificates to one of the defined trusted certificate issuers in your trust list. This process can become quite complex; hence, one of the goals of the XML Key Management Specification (XKMS) discussed in Chapter 9, "Trust, Access Control, and Rights for Web Services," is to offload this complexity to a "trust engine" Web service that will handle this validation for other Web services.

> **Note**
>
> A reason for this complexity and for the long discussion about it here is that people believe that there will be hundreds and thousands of *registration authorities* eventually. Registration authorities are the organizations that establish and maintain the identities of individuals known to them. Company HR departments, universities, retailers, and hundreds of other types of organizations either already are or plan to become registration authorities. CAs are registration authorities themselves, or they can accept input from RAs and just be certificate issuers. Given this explosion in the number of RAs/CAs, it becomes quite clear why certification chains become complex and important in establishing trust.

If the relying party does not have the public key of the CA that signed the certificate presented, that party must acquire the key from someone else who vouches for that CA for the sub-CA below her. This means moving up the trust hierarchy to another CA that signed the certificate. This concept is shown in the diagram in Figure 3.10. Here, relying parties are end-entities (EE) that are presented with certificates from sub-CAs. Since the sub-CAs are not known or trusteed by the EEs, they require the certificate of the CA that signed the sub-CAs certificates. These CAs further up the trust hierarchy vouch for the sub-CA. These root CAs are the trust anchors for the EE allowing them to trust the certificates from the sub-CAs.

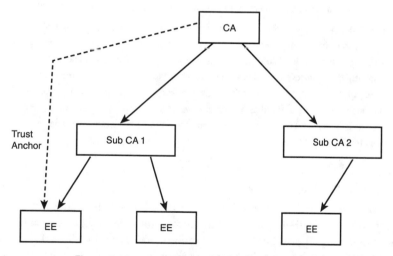

Figure 3.10 Certificate authority trust hierarchy.

> **Cross-Certification: Federated Trust**
>
> In the next few years, you will be seeing a lot more of cross-certification in contrast to the rooted chains of trust. In this trust model, another CA has performed the identification procedure on an individual who is otherwise a total stranger to your CA and all organizations yours serves. But the two CAs have agreed that their processes are in lock-step and agree to cross-certify each other's certificates. In other words, you will accept the other CA's certificates on faith. Figure 3.11 shows how the cross-certification model links together the sub-CAs and end entities (EEs) of two top-level CAs that have agreed to cross-certify each other.

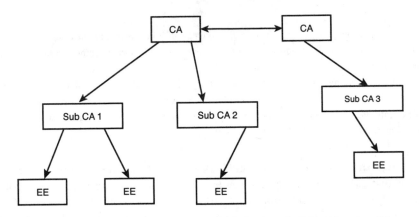

Figure 3.11   The cross-certification model links the sub-CAs and end entities (EEs) of two cross-certified top-level CAs.

Several organizations have implemented this model. The first was Identrus, now merged with Digital Signature Trust (DST). Several dozen banks have agreed to cross-certify based on standards and a root certificate from Identrus. If a Bank A customer is identified and issued a certificate, Bank B, being part of the same Identrus-rooted network, would accept the Bank A customer as if she were a Bank B customer.

The Federal Bridge program is a newer example of this model that is currently being deployed. Different departments within the federal government are agreeing to accept certificates from other departments. This has led to a strong push for levels of trust in certificates. A level from 1 to 4 would be based on how thorough the identification process was, as described earlier in Table 3.2. The AICPA—the organization that sets standards for all the audit firms—has recently decided to adopt this model and make it part of the standards to which it audits certificate authorities. The good news for Web services is that, because these levels would be specified as a standard X.509 extension, the Web services themselves can check and enforce compliance with a predetermined trust level.

Root CAs Are Trusted by Everyone

There are not many root CAs because, for their certificates to be understood by your tools, the public key for their self-signed certificates must already be accessible to those tools. For the most common kinds of certificates—those used for SSL—this has occurred by embedding the root keys for the root CAs right in the browser. In fact, the browsers typically have dozens of root keys and another batch of intermediate CA keys as well. Just a portion of the pre-installed roots on Windows XP are shown in Figure 3.12.

With Web services, it is not the browser having the keys that matters. It is the nodes or termination points of the Web service that matter, where signature validation or decryption must occur. As a Web service is deployed, a crucial step in that deployment is to make sure the appropriate public keys of all CAs whose certificates may be seen by that Web service are installed at all endpoint servers.

Figure 3.12   Pre-installed roots in Windows XP.

Controlling Trust in the Root CAs

You might be surprised to learn how the CA business started. How did companies such as VeriSign ensure their root keys were placed in browsers? Initially, they just made deals with Netscape and Microsoft. Netscape considered these deals much like a partnering "pay-to-play" program, so if you paid the fee, your key went in. Microsoft did not charge for the honor. But there was still very little scrutiny or process in choosing whose key went in.

The situation changed in 2001 when Microsoft decided that it could no longer use the ad hoc process. By this time, more than 300,000 active SSL certificates were in use, and consumers were committing serious money based on trust in these certificates. Microsoft realized it had a house of cards if it did not do something.

As mentioned previously, an organization called the AICPA establishes best practices for the accounting/auditing industry. Its members are accountants who do financial and other sorts of audits. The leadership of the AICPA comes from the big multinational accounting firms such as Ernst & Young, KPMG, Price Waterhouse Coopers, and Deloitte & Touche. The AICPA wanted to create new business for its members and so established best practices around the processes CAs must use to issue and manage digital certificates. With no other standard to rely on, Microsoft decided this approach was better than none and made an announcement in 2002 that the AICPA's WebTrust audit for CAs would be the new bar that CAs must get over to be allowed into the root store of the browser and of its application servers (including .NET servers used in Web services).

Key Escrow for Recovering Lost Private Keys

Key escrow is a very important and controversial aspect of PKI. This technology is about storage and retrieval of private keys to recover data in the absence of the private key owner. Key escrow goes against the very idea of a private key. The private key may ulti-mately be accessed by more than the owner of the key, which lessens the case for non-repudiation. Key escrow is often considered a necessary evil when critical information may be encrypted with this private key and loss of the key, death of its owner, or some sort of fraud means that information might be forever irretrievable. Requirements for key escrow/recovery systems may come from customer support or legal or policy requirements. International PKI implementations may require key escrow to comply with government and law enforcement restrictions.

The concept of a private key is crucial to the effectiveness of PKI because so many *downstream* PKI concepts depend heavily on the assumption that the private key is never compromised. And yet, humans are fallible and do indeed lose keys. If a critical private key is lost, there truly is no way to decrypt any data its matching public key encrypted. That data is lost forever—even to the CIA, NSA, or FBI. The risk of losing that data are too high for many reasons, which is what drives the need for a key recovery scheme. There are other reasons for a server-based key escrow scheme as well.

Key escrow may be an important consideration in Web service deployments. Critical information flowing through the Web services infrastructure may have been encrypted, and the governing organization, although it wants to maintain the confidentiality of this data, cannot afford to lose access to it forever. If the private keys used to encrypt it are lost, that is what would happen.

When an enterprise entrusts employees or agents with confidential data, this data is at risk of being forever lost if an employee loses her private key. Therefore, the employer may want a way to recover the private key in that eventuality. If the employee uses the key to encrypt email messages, and she violates company policy or if law enforcement subpoenas the email, key recovery is needed to decrypt the email. Finally, if an employee leaves the company, he may not cooperate with the return of the private key and that key may need to be recovered.

Certificate Revocation for Dealing with Public Keys Gone Bad

Key escrow is an optional feature of PKI, but certificate revocation is not. Revocation is an essential part of the certificate process to establish and maintain trust. Authentication of clients and servers requires a way to verify each certificate within the chain, as well as a way to determine whether a certificate is valid or revoked. A certificate could be revoked if a key is compromised or lost or as a result of modification of privileges, mis-use, or employment termination. It is essential, *especially for Web services,* that near real-time revocation of certificates be achieved.

Currently, two technologies are used for revocation: certificate revocation lists (CRLs) and online certificate status protocol (OCSP).

CRL Certificate Revocation Checking

The CRL is an up-to-date list of all certificates revoked; a CA must keep this list accessi-ble to relying parties. It goes without saying that the CA must make it easy for registra-tion authorities to revoke any given certificate (but prove that they have the right to do so). With CRLs, relying parties have the burden of checking this list each time a certificate is presented. Best practices call for a certificate deployment point (CDP) URL to be embedded in the certificate. A CDP is a pointer to the location of the CRL on the Internet, accessible programmatically by any relying party's applications.

CRLs are usually updated once per day because the process of generating them is non-trivial and time-consuming. When an organization is dealing with a compromised key or a rogue employee, once-per-day updates can mean a huge loss during the day compromise occurred, especially when interactions are automated with Web services. Currently, almost no one checks revocation lists. Although CRLs are created obediently by the sponsoring CAs and numerous tools can and do process them, there are so many unsolved problems with them that, in our view, CRLs on the Internet are a technological failure.

OCSP Certificate Revocation Checking

OCSP was an attempt to create a much finer-grained protocol for essentially real-time revocation checking. But as in CRLs, the trust information provided requires it be signed by the originating CA, which is an expensive operation to perform in real time. The best case on an unloaded system of moderate speed is 26ms response time for a single OCSP request in our tests. In our view, this makes standard OCSP so limited in scope that it will continue to be only a bit player in revocation solutions.

In our opinion, there is much promise in emerging techniques that are scalable and respond in microseconds and still conform to the OCSP standard without requiring time-consuming digital signatures on each request. One such approach is Silvio Micali's technique based on chains of hashed secret codes. Web services will require such a high-speed revocation system. For details, see the section on Silvio Michali's High-Speed Validation/Revocation in Appendix A.

Trust Services

What this discussion about CAs, trust chains, cross-certification, key escrow, and certificate revocation leads to is an overriding need for Web services that offer trust services to other Web services. The developer of a Web service does not want to be burdened with all the issues we have just outlined. Furthermore, companies will consider how these issues are handled as core corporate security policies and will want consistent, reliable, and centralized administration of these policies.

Having *trust services* available as Web services means developers can avoid writing key management and signature processes in every application. All the critical trust services will be encapsulated into a reusable service. Trust services must deal with the complexities of PKI, keys, signatures, encryption, and the like. Trust services are Web services that provide these and other security services for any application that needs them. Because they are just Web services themselves, they are accessed through SOAP messages. With this approach, special PKI client code does not need to be deployed any longer.

Key Management Services

The first trust service needed is one that manages the registration, distribution, and life cycle of public keys. Like any Web service, it needs to be a service that has a WSDL and is accessed via SOAP.

The W3C XML Key Management Specification (XKMS) specifies protocols for distributing and registering public keys suitable for use in conjunction with XML Signature and XML Encryption. See Chapter 9 for details on XKMS.

Digital Signature Services

The OASIS Digital Signature Services (DSS) is developing a set of services to help manage signature creation and validation. This will completely hide the PKI complexities of signature processing.

Single Sign-On Services

Single sign-on (SSO) services help facilitate authentication for Web services. Using SAML as the base standard (the subject of Chapter 6, "Portable Identity, Authentication, and Authorization"), a user can log in to the SSO service, provide one or two factor authentication challenges (user ID, password, and perhaps smart card or biometric), obtain a credential (or security token), and use that credential in SOAP headers on all subsequent Web services to provide necessary authentication information required by the Web services. Because Web services are not interactive (they are computer-to-computer), this approach is usually required when using Web services needing authentication. Single sign-on services are being developed by the Liberty Alliance and by Microsoft Passport.

Access Control Services

Sometimes referred to as Entitlement Services, Access Control Services (ACS) provide centralized access control policies. They support one of several evolving OASIS access control standards such as XACML and XrML. These standards are covered in Chapter 9.

Security in a Box

Because of its compute-intensive nature, application-level XML security is being built into hardware for acceleration. Such security will be required in high-volume applications. The box will be the termination point for encryption, signature, and transport security. These hardware accelerators will provide dramatic acceleration of time-consuming, compute-intensive cryptography tasks for Web services.

Billing and Metering Services

The last of the security-related Web services is billing and metering services. These services keep track of a user's service utilization and accrue billing information. They are vital to the business models that Web services will enable and encourage. You can't charge for the use of Web services if you cannot authenticate legitimate users and bill them for their usage.

"PKI's not dead. It's just resting!"

That controversial heading comes from a 2002 article by Peter Gutmann. Many had proclaimed PKI as dead because it was so hard to deploy and so few companies had deployed it successfully. It is true that PKI tried to be all things to all people and therefore sacrificed some utility.

One huge reason PKI has not "taken off" is that, because revocation is so difficult, it has never been implemented on broad networks such as the Internet. It is hard to know where to find revocation information. Revocation information cannot be issued often enough to be useful. Without effective revocation, PKI can never really be useful because trust in the privacy of private keys and the integrity and identity of public keys are absolutely fundamental to the whole notion of PKI.

Web services in general and XKMS in particular will bring back a new lease on life to PKI—but with some changes. CAs will have to provide a managed PKI service available as a high-performance, high-availability Web service. Locally meaningful identifier names will be used as opposed to the X.500-derived DN structure used in X.509 certificates.

Revocation is built into the XKMS protocol because you are establishing a direct relationship to the third-party trust provider (the CA) that issued the credential in the first place. Therefore, revocation is direct and explicit in the XKMS protocol.

Most importantly, Web services in general and the closed environments in which Web services will typically be used create application-specific PKIs, which always worked the best at solving the general problem with PKI.

(Based on an article by Peter Gutmann in *IEEE Security*, August 2002.)

SSL Transport Layer Security

Secure Socket Layer (SSL), also called Transport Layer Security (TLS), was invented by Netscape to provide for secure e-commerce transactions between a Web browser and a Web server[2]. SSL is arguably the most widely used implementation of PKI. It is important and relevant to a discussion of Web Services Security because it is so easy to use, it is already deployed in virtually every organization, and it is so effective for certain types of Web service deployments.

A Description of the SSL Protocol

SSL security is most commonly used for browser-to-server security in e-commerce transactions. Virtually all browsers support SSL. Likewise, virtually all Web servers—or more correctly, Web application containers, such as Microsoft Internet Information Server, BEA's WebLogic Server, IBM's WebSphere—do as well. Because most, if not all,

---

2. SSL was originally developed by Netscape. It is now also known as TLS and has been turned over to an IETF standards group (RFC2246: ftp://ftp.isi.edu/in-notes/rfc2246.txt). The IETF TLS working group's URL is http://www.ietf.org/html.charters/tls-charter.html.

of the current Web services containers (for example, Microsoft's .NET framework, BEA's WebLogic Workshop, IBM's WebSphere Studio Application Developer) are also Web application containers, you can use the existing built-in Transport Layer Security for Web services without modifying a thing.

SSL is effective at maintaining confidentiality of transactions. It implements shared key encryption between its endpoints after first transporting the shared key via public key cryptography. SSL will prove to be broadly useful for Web Services Security, especially in early implementations, because those early Web services require only simple point-to-point encryption and possibly the level of authentication SSL can provide. As Chapter 7 on WS-Security explains, SSL also will be useful as an added layer of transport security underneath the message-level security this book describes.

Four options are available when you are using SSL Transport Layer Security over HTTP (which you will see as HTTPS):

- **SSL/TLS (one-way)**—This is the same SSL that you use online when entering your credit card on a Web site. Using one-way SSL, you obtain two benefits:
  - Your client (browser) verifies the identity of the server.
  - You have an encrypted session between your client and the server.

> **Note**
>
> In one-way SSL, the idea that you are verifying the identity of the Web server's owner is technically valid but currently extremely weak in browser implementations. When you go into an SSL session with a Web site, the lock symbol in your browser lights up. Double-clicking on the lock opens a dialog box showing the server's certificate. You can view the identity of the company validated by the certificate authority by clicking on the Details tab and then the specific line item called `subject`. Look at the O= (for organization equals), and you will see the validated name of the company.
>
> This information is buried ridiculously deep, and for all intents and purposes, it has no value to an individual viewing a Web page. Many legitimate sites transfer control to another company when they get into a secure session, and the user never knows this transfer happens. You would be surprised if the real name of the company running the secure pages you encounter on the Web were to show up.

- **Basic authentication (basic auth)**—With basic authentication, the client sends a username and password for authentication. These credentials are sent in the clear, so it is common practice to combine basic auth with one-way SSL.
- **Digest authentication**—Digest authentication addresses the issue of the password being in the clear by using hashing technology (for example, MD5 or SHA1). Basically, it involves the server passing a *nonce* (just a number or string chosen by the server) down to the client, which the client then combines with the password and hashes using the algorithm specified by the server. The server then receives the hash and runs the same hash algorithm on the password and nonce that it has.

A couple of problems with digest authentication prevent it from being used often.

Note

Digest authentication between specific clients and servers may be viable. You can find an interesting article called "Web Services Security—HTTP Digest Authentication Without Active Directory" in Greg Reinacker's Weblog (http://www.rassoc.com/gregr/weblog/stories/2002/07/09/ webServicesSecurityHttpDigestAuthenticationWithoutActiveDirectory.html)

The main issue with digest authentication is that it is not supported in a standard way across Web servers and clients. The other issue is, for the server to participate, it must have access to a clear password, meaning the password must be stored in the clear. Many implementations store only a hashed password, making it impossible to participate in a digest protocol defined this way.

- **Client certificates (two-way or mutually authenticated SSL)**—This is one-way SSL, as discussed previously, with the addition that the *client* must also provide an X.509 certificate to authenticate itself with the server. The protocol involves challenge and response between the server and the client in which information is digitally signed to prove the possession of the private key. This, in turn, is to prove that the identity based on the public key contained in the certificate can be trusted. This option is powerful, but it adds a great deal of complexity, especially for Web applications with large numbers of consumer clients, because each client needs to be issued a certificate to gain access. In some Web services scenarios—such as business-to-business—this may not be quite so onerous because the number of *server clients* (a seemingly contradictory term but one that will be common in Web services where a server machine acts as a client because it is the service requestor) is typically small. However, one of the major complexities of using client certificates is that either

  - Your company needs to issue X.509 certificates to each client, meaning you need to get certificate management software and become a certificate authority.

  - You need to work with a certificate authority managed service. Also, unfortunately, configuring your Web server to accept client certificates is often not for the faint of heart, so you will need an experienced security systems administrator to be successful.

We will briefly explain how the SSL protocol works using an example in which the "client" is the Web service *requestor* and the "server" is the Web service *provider*. The steps outlined in Figure 3.13 are as follows:

1. The service requestor opens a connection to the service provider and sends a `ClientHello` message. This message lists the capabilities of the service requestor, including the version of SSL it is using and the cipher suites (cryptographic algorithms) it supports.

2. The service provider responds with a `ServerHello` message. The service provider returns the cipher suite it has chosen and a session ID that identifies this connection.

3. The service provider sends its certificate. This X.509 site certificate is signed by a certificate authority. The certificate contains the service provider's public key. It is assumed that the service requestor has access to the signing CA's public key perhaps because it is already installed in the trust store residing at the service requestor.

4. The service provider (optionally) sends the service requestor a request for its certificate. Client authentication will be necessary for almost all Web services, but if the Web service is a thin veneer directly to a human user, username/password authentication may be used instead.

5. The service requestor (optionally, if requested in step 4) sends its client certificate. It will have been signed by some trust authority to which the service provider will assign trust levels based on its policies in place. The service provider will also have to have direct access to the signing CA's public key. The service provider may or may not choose to trust that this is really the entity it claims to be, which will determine whether it agrees to provide the service being requested.

6. The service requestor sends a `ClientKeyExchange` message. The service requestor has created a shared key and is sending it to the service provider with this message. The full session key is not created directly because different shared key ciphers use different key lengths. The service requestor encrypts this shared key using the service provider's public key and sends it back to the service provider.

7. The service requestor (optionally, if requested in step 4) sends a `CertificateVerify` message. This is the authentication of the client step in client-authenticated, or two-way, SSL. The service requestor has to prove it knows the correct private key. The shared key from step 6 is signed using the service requestor's private key (which only it has and which it guarantees it has kept secret) and sent to the service provider, which verifies this using the service requestor's public key forwarded earlier embedded in the X.509 certificate.

8. Both service requestor and service provider send a `ChangeCipherSpec` message. It simply says both sides are ready to communicate in encrypted form using the shared secret session key.

9. Both service requestor and service provider send a `Finished` message. This is an MD5 and SHA hash of the entire conversation up to this point to confirm that the entire conversation was received by the other party intact and not tampered with en route. What is *finished* is just the handshake; the real communication of the confidential message is now about to begin.

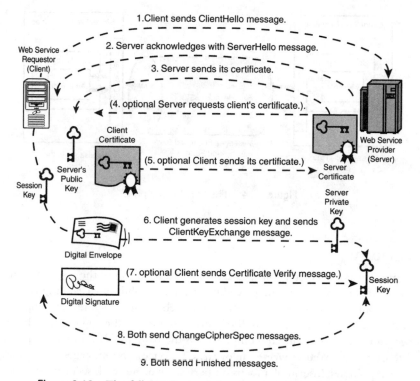

Figure 3.13   The full SSL Protocol showing two-way authentication.

When people talk about SSL Transport Layer Security, they sometimes use the term *secure pipe* as a metaphor. This means that after the SSL endpoints go through their protocol (either one-way or two-way SSL), a cryptographic pathway is created between the two endpoints (see Figure 3.14). Web services that are based on HTTP as the transport flow through this secure pipe, making all messages sent back and forth confidential. Remember, though, that the messages are encrypted just during transport. At the receiving endpoint, the messages are decrypted by the server. If the Web service uses multiple hops on its way to its real destination or if persistent confidentiality (encryption) is needed for the messages, SSL does not provide a solution. Hence, we still need to learn a lot more about message-level security applied to Web services messages.

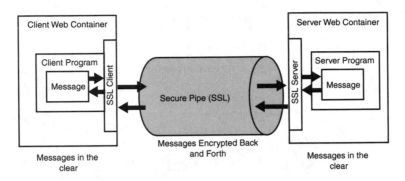

Figure 3.14   The SSL "secure pipe."

Summary

This chapter layers an information security foundation on top of the essential nature of the Web services established in the preceding chapter. A solid understanding of both is necessary to build secure Web services. Securing Web services requires securing the messages used to communicate between distributed systems and the applications that run on them. Web services add significant complexity to the basic problem of securing distributed systems because Web services employ shared services, and messages may follow multi-hop topologies. Instead of a focus on perimeter or network security, what is needed instead is persistent message-level security that delivers the core security principles of confidentiality, integrity, and non-repudiation to a distributed message-based architecture.

Shared key technologies are the key to confidentiality. Shared key is also referred to as symmetric key or secret key. In shared key encryption, the same key is used to encrypt and decrypt. This means the sender and recipient both need the same key but must find a way to share it and still keep it absolutely secret. Positive attributes of shared key encryption are that it is fast and can handle unlimited message size. However, getting the shared secret key to both ends of the conversation securely is very hard.

Kerberos is an alternative approach to shared keys that is useful only in a closed trust domain where all identities are known. Its importance to Web services security is that when services cross organizational boundaries and therefore cross trust domains, provisions have to be made to map between Kerberos and other trust environments.

Public key technologies are the key to integrity and non-repudiation. Public key encryption is also referred to as asymmetric encryption. Keys come in pairs, where one is used to encrypt and only its mate is used to decrypt messages. This technology is much slower than shared key encryption and is limited to small message sizes. However, it is of critical importance in key exchange to enable shared key encryption, and it is the basis for digital signatures. Public key encryption is used to securely establish secret shared keys in XML Encryption and is the core cryptographic technology used in XML Signature.

Public key encryption is at the heart of digital signatures. Hashing is also a critical security technology in digital signatures. A digital signature is an encrypted message digest of a hashed plaintext message sent along with the signer's public key and the original plaintext message. Signature verification involves using the sender's public key to decrypt the signed message digest and verifying that this exactly matches the locally computed message digest from the plaintext message also sent along. An XML Signature is a digital signature expressed in XML.

Trust issues are prevalent and fundamental to public key technologies. The private key must be kept secret and in the control of its owner without exception. The public key of an unknown identity must be vouched for by a trusted third party. Public keys need containers called digital certificates to transport them. Trusted third parties that issue digital certificates to identified individuals are called certificate authorities (CA). The infrastructure for dealing with CAs, certificates, and keys is called the Public Key Infrastructure (PKI). Numerous complex issues revolve around trusting the trusted third-party CAs. In a certification chain, one CA vouches for and signs the certificate of another CA. Root certificates are self-signed by a CA that is at the root of a certification chain and is so well known that its public keys are pre-installed in servers, browsers, and other repositories where applications can easily access them. A major issue for PKI in the past has been the lack of effective revocation in which the up-to-date validity of a certificate can be checked. This issue becomes even more critical for Web services.

Numerous Web services designed to deliver trust services are emerging. These services will include, but not be limited to, key management services, digital signature services, single sign-on services, access control services, hardware accelerators, and billing and metering.

Secure Socket Layer (SSL) is a mature, tried-and-true transport layer security. It works on HTTP, so it "just works" for Web services. All application servers support SSL. SSL supports two-way authentication, although its more common usage with browsers is one-way. SSL should always be considered first for Web services security because it is effective for message confidentiality in simple point-to-point Web services.

Resources

XML Security by Blake Dournaee (McGraw-Hill, 2002).

Web Services: A Technical Introduction by H. M. Deitel, P. J. Deitel, B. DuWaldt, and L. K. Trees (Prentice Hall, 2003).

Applied Cryptography, 2nd edition by Bruce Schneier (John Wiley, 1996).

4

Safeguarding the Identity and Integrity of XML Messages

Introduction To and Motivation for XML Signature

Chapter 2, "The Foundations of Web Services," and Chapter 3, "The Foundations of Distributed Message-Level Security," provided an overview of Web services (including XML) and security concepts. This chapter and the next bring two of the key security principles—confidentiality and integrity—into the world of XML. Confidentiality, in the world of XML, manifests itself as XML Encryption. Integrity manifests itself as XML Signature. XML Signature and XML Encryption are fundamental strategies for securing XML and are pillars of WS-Security. Because XML is one of the foundations of Web services, it follows that these two technologies are extremely important to understand and apply when you are implementing secure Web services.

A W3C Standard

XML Signature (as discussed in Chapter 3) is a joint standard of the IETF and the W3C for digitally signing all of an XML document, part of an XML document, or even an external object. Similarly, XML Encryption is a W3C standard, which followed XML Signature, for encrypting all of an XML document, part of an XML document, or an external object. Actually, you can sign or encrypt pretty much anything you can point to with a URL.

Critical Building Block for WS-Security

XML Signature and XML Encryption are fundamental to the next generation of emerging standards that use these two standards as building blocks. For example, WS-Security, the emerging OASIS standard for Web services security; XML Key Management Specification (XKMS), and Security Assertion Markup Language (SAML), among many others, all rely on XML Signature and/or XML Encryption.

Close Associations with Web Services Security

XML Signature and XML Encryption, two of the three major pillars of the WS-Security standard, are so predominant in current thinking about Web Services Security that some people mistake them as the *only* strategy for securing Web services. This is really not the case at all. When reading Chapter 3, you probably realized that Web Services Security must involve a broad spectrum of security technologies and strategies. Web services involve active use of XML messages across trust domains. Securing the message itself is critical, but it represents only one aspect of the whole Web Services Security picture.

That being said, we encourage you to pay special attention to the information in this chapter and, if you are interested in more detail, to pick up a book that treats this subject in more depth—for example, *Secure XML* by Donald Eastlake and Kitty Niles(Addison Wesley 2002).

The Goal of Ensuring Integrity (and Usually Identity) and Non-repudiation Persistently

XML Signature technology, like digital signature, is a tool for ensuring integrity and, usually, identity and non-repudiation. XML Signature takes the building block of digital signature as described in Chapter 3 and greatly expands upon it, taking advantage of the power and flexibility of XML as well as key Web technologies (such as URLs) to sign almost any type of resource, whether an XML document, a part of an XML document, or a non-XML object such as an image.

XML Signature and XML Encryption: Fundamental Web Services Security Technologies

You might think that Web Services Security in relationship to XML Encryption and XML Signature is about encrypting and digitally signing SOAP messages. This aspect of the application of these two technologies is certainly important, and this usage is well covered in this book; however, this probably will not be the most important usage for you, as a developer or administrator of Web services, at least in the near future. Web services containers or special Web services firewalls help manage this complexity by signing/encrypting or verifying/decrypting all or parts of the SOAP message based on policies you configure. It really does not make sense for Web services developers to have to worry about the blocking and tackling involved in securing the SOAP payload uniquely for every application and/or operation within a Web service. This operation will become part of the infrastructure. As a Web services developer, you should be able to focus on the SOAP payload itself, which is an XML document. Much of your direct use of XML Signature and XML Encryption will be for your applications themselves to take advantage of the power of these technologies to enrich the functionality of your systems.

The goal of this chapter is to inform you how XML Signature works while not burying you with too much detail. This standard is powerful and complex, so we focus on the parts that we think will be most applicable.

XML Signature Fundamentals

XML Signature combines the utility and power of digital signature technology with the power and flexibility of XML. An XML Signature is itself a piece of XML, and there is a corresponding XML Schema for how this XML will be structured. Within the XML Signature itself are references—URIs—to what is being digitally signed. These references are quite flexible as they can point to items within the same document or be external. Also, a single XML document can contain multiple XML Signatures. This flexibility and power make XML Signature technology somewhat complex when you consider the details. However, the basic concepts are not very difficult to understand, and the structure for an XML Signature, which is always rooted at the `Signature` element, provides a nice guide for understanding how XML Signatures work.

XML Signature Requirements

Understanding the formal requirements that were provided/gathered by the W3C Working Group can help you understand why certain parts of the standards turned out the way they did. The following are some of the key requirements that stand out (you can see the full requirements at `http://www.w3.org/TR/xmldsig-requirements`):

- XML Signatures apply to any resource addressable by a "locator" (uniform resource identifier), including non-XML content.

- XML Signatures must be able to apply to a part or the whole XML document.

- Multiple XML Signatures must be able to exist over the static content of a Web resource.

- The specification must permit the use of varied digital signature and message authentication codes, such as symmetric and asymmetric authentication schemes as well as dynamic agreement of keying material.

Other specified requirements affect the resulting standards as well, but considering these four demonstrates that XML Signatures are not just a simple application of digital signature technology on a piece of XML text. They are much more.

XML Signature Structure

In the following sections, we review the XML `Signature` element's basic structure and discuss its most significant aspects. We stay high level at first and then provide more detail further into the chapter.

Basic Structure

Before we delve deeply into the syntax of the `Signature` element, let's discuss it in concept first. At a very basic level, an XML Signature contains four major items, with the third and fourth being optional:

- A set of pointers (references) to things to be signed
- The actual signature
- (Optional) The key (or a way to look up the key) for verifying the signature
- (Optional) An `Object` tag that can contain miscellaneous items not included in the first three items

The syntax of the `Signature` element is shown in Listing 4.1.

Listing 4.1 **The Syntax of the `<Signature>` Element**

```
<Signature>
    <SignedInfo>
        (CanonicalizationMethod)
        (SignatureMethod)
        (<Reference (URI=)? >
            (Transforms)?
            (DigestMethod)
            (DigestValue)
        </Reference>)+
    </SignedInfo>
    (SignatureValue)
    (KeyInfo)?
    (Object)*
</Signature>
```

Listing 4.2 is a highly oversimplified XML Signature snippet to give you a feel for what an XML Signature might look like if it is cut down to its bare essence.

Listing 4.2 **A Highly Simplified XML Signature Snippet**

```
<Signature xmlns="http://www.w3.org/2000/09/xmldsig#">
  <SignedInfo>
    <Reference URI="http://www.foo.com/secureDocument.html" />
  </SignedInfo>
  <SignatureValue>...</SignatureValue>
  <KeyInfo>...
  </KeyInfo>
</Signature>
```

In this example, the three children of the `Signature` element are the `SignedInfo` element, the `SignatureValue` element, and the `KeyInfo` element. The `SignedInfo` element contains information about what is being signed, the `SignatureValue` element contains the actual signature bits, and the `KeyInfo` element contains information about the public key needed to validate this digital signature. Of course, this example is highly simplified; there is more detail to each of these elements, and there are more elements to discuss. However, these are the most significant three elements within a typical XML Signature.

Specifying the Items Being Signed

The set of pointers, represented by the `Reference` element, can point to an internal resource in the XML document, in which case they point to an XML node, or they can be external. If they are external, they can point to a binary or non-XML file (for example, an image or text document), or they can point to another XML document or even a node within another XML document. We discuss this usage in more depth in the section titled "The `Reference` Element." The content behind these references is what is being signed.

Understanding this reference concept is important because it can affect the meaning and usage of XML Signatures substantially. Most descriptions of XML Signature describe three classifications of XML Signatures: *Enveloping*, *Enveloped*, and *Detached*. Each reflects where the `Reference` element is pointing. Let's go through these three types of XML Signatures and then come back to that point.

Types of XML Signatures

As we mentioned previously, when reading about or discussing XML Signature, you will often hear about three different types of XML Signatures: *Enveloping, Enveloped,* and *Detached.* In the next three sections, we describe each of these signature types and show you how they work.

Enveloping Signatures

An *Enveloping Signature* wraps the item that is being signed, as shown in Figure 4.1. Later, we discuss specifically how this is done, but for now suffice it to say that the reference is to an XML element within the `Signature` element itself. The following simplified example in Listing 4.3 shows what an Enveloping Signature might look like (notice that the URI points to an item within the `Signature Object` element):

Listing 4.3   **A Simplified Enveloping Signature**

```
<Signature xmlns="http://www.w3.org/2000/09/xmldsig#">
  <SignedInfo>
    <Reference URI="#111" />
  </SignedInfo>
  <SignatureValue>...</SignatureValue>
  <KeyInfo>...</KeyInfo>
  <Object>
     <SignedItem id="111">Stuff to be signed</SignedItem>
  </Object>
</Signature>
```

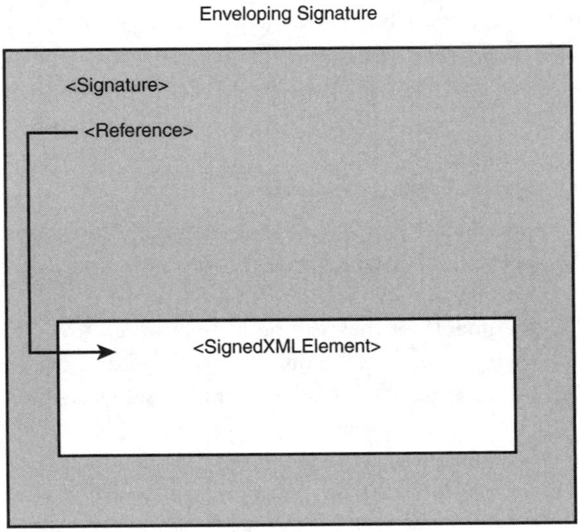

Enveloping Signature

Figure 4.1   Structure of an Enveloping Signature.

Enveloped Signatures

In an *Enveloped Signature*, the reference points to a *parent* XML element, as shown in Figure 4.2. The following simplified example in Listing 4.4 shows what an Enveloped Signature might look like (notice that the Reference is to an element that is a parent of the Signature):

Listing 4.4   **A Simplified Enveloped Signature**

```
<PurchaseOrder id="po1">
  <SKU>125356</SKU>
  <Quantity>17</Quantity>
  <Signature xmlns="http://www.w3.org/2000/09/xmldsig#">
    <SignedInfo>
      <Reference URI="#po1" />
    </SignedInfo>
    <SignatureValue>...</SignatureValue>
    <KeyInfo>...</KeyInfo>
  </Signature>
</PurchaseOrder>
```

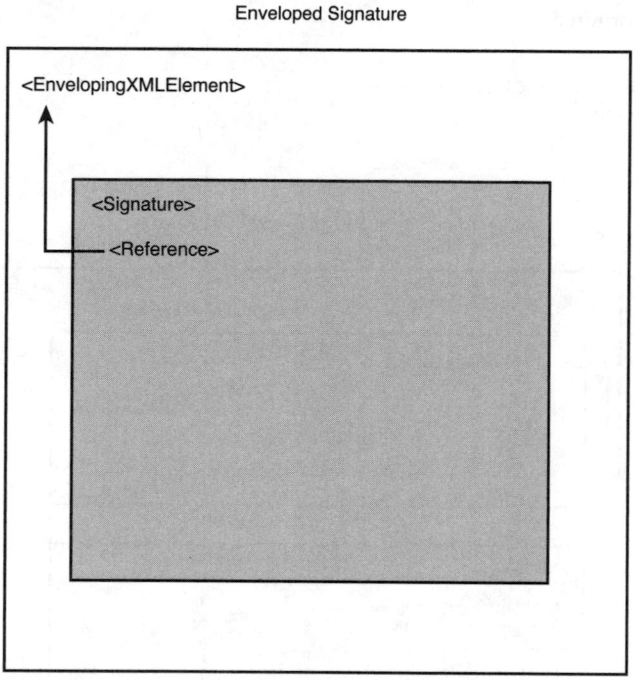

Enveloped Signature

Figure 4.2   Structure of an Enveloped Signature.

Detached Signatures

Finally, a *Detached Signature* points to an XML element or binary file outside the
Signature element's hierarchy. In other words, the item being pointed to is neither a
child *(Enveloping Signature)* nor a parent *(Enveloped Signature)* of the Signature element.
Therefore, a Detached Signature could point to an element within the same document,
as shown in Figure 4.3, or to a another resource completely outside the current XML
document, as shown in Figure 4.4. The following example in Listing 4.5 of a Detached
Signature points to another XML element within the same XML document but is not
an ancestor or child of the Signature:

Listing 4.5   **Structure of a Detached Signature**

```
<PurchaseOrderDocument>
  <PurchaseOrder id="po1">
    <SKU>12366</SKU>
    <Quantity>17</SKU>
  </PurchaseOrder>
  <Signature xmlns="http://www.w3.org/2000/09/xmldsig#">
  <SignedInfo>
    <Reference URI="#po1" />
```

Listing 4.5 **Continued**

```
  </SignedInfo>
  <SignatureValue>...</SignatureValue>
  <KeyInfo>...</KeyInfo>
</Signature>
```

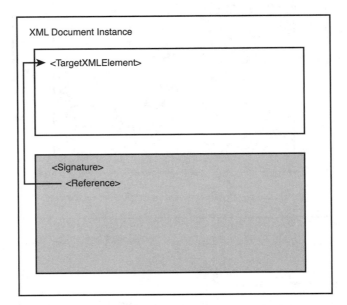

Detached Signature within same XML Document

Figure 4.3 Structure of a Detached Signature within the same XML document.

A Detached Signature can also point to an external resource such as another XML document, a node in another XML document, a text file, or generally any type of resource that can be referenced by a URI, as shown in Figure 4.4. The following simplified example in Listing 4.6 of a Detached Signature points to a JPEG file:

Listing 4.6 **A Detached Signature of an External JPEG File**

```
<Signature xmlns="http://www.w3.org/2000/09/xmldsig#">
  <SignedInfo>
    <Reference URI="http://www.foo.com/picture.jpg" />
  </SignedInfo>
  <SignatureValue>...</SignatureValue>
  <KeyInfo>...</KeyInfo>
</Signature>
```

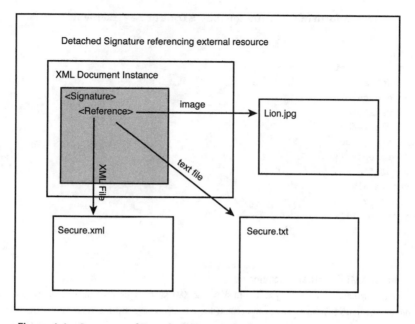

Figure 4.4   Structure of Detached Signature referencing an external resource.

Even though these are often called signature types, even in the XML Signature specification, they are really about references. It would be more accurate to describe them as *Enveloping Reference, Enveloped Reference,* and *Detached Reference.* Then the next statement becomes more understandable. An XML Signature can be enveloping, enveloped, and detached all at the same time! This means that the `Signature` element can contain more than one `Reference` element, and a `Reference` element can be enveloping, enveloped, or detached.

We wanted to give you the highest level overview of XML Signature and emphasize that XML Signature is mostly just one or more pointers (references) that can point to XML elements, internal or external to the Signature itself, or to an external resource. These pointers are dereferenced and grouped together; then they go through a signature process resulting in a signature. All of this—the pointers, the signature itself, and, optionally, the key information to validate the signature—goes into an XML `Signature` element.

Now let's go to the next level of detail and explore the different aspects of the `Signature` element.

The `Signature` Element Schema

Look at Listing 4.7 for an XML shorthand schema for the `Signature` element. It comes directly from the XML Signature specification[1] and, for convenience, is a repeat of the schema shown previously. Understanding this structure is key to understanding XML Signature.

Listing 4.7   **XML Shorthand Schema for the `<Signature>` Element**

```
<Signature ID?>
  <SignedInfo>
    <CanonicalizationMethod/>
    <SignatureMethod/>
    (<Reference URI? >
      (<Transforms>)?
      <DigestMethod>
      <DigestValue>
      </Reference>)+
  </SignedInfo>
  <SignatureValue>
  (<KeyInfo>)?
  (<Object ID?>)*
</Signature>
```

Reading an XML Shorthand Schema

A common shorthand for describing XML is to show the XML syntax with a set of "cardinality" indicators, the number of times that an element can occur. If there is always exactly one, there is no cardinality indicator. If there can be zero or one occurrence, the element or attribute is given a question mark (?) cardinality indicator. If the element or attribute can have one or more occurences, the element or attribute is given a plus sign (+) cardinality indicator. And finally, if the element or attribute can have zero or more occurences, the element or attribute is given an asterisk (*) cardinality indicator.

If an element has a cardinality indicator, it is usually wrapped in parentheses, and the cardinality indicator appears after the closing parenthesis. For example, in the XML Signature shorthand schema, the `KeyInfo` element is represented as (`<KeyInfo>`)?, which means that the `KeyInfo` can exist one or zero times. The `Object` element, shown as (`<Object ID?>`)*, can appear zero or more times, and its `ID` attribute can exist zero or one time within an `Object` attribute.

You need to familiarize yourself with this shorthand schema at a high level before you focus on each element. The more familiar you become with this schema, the better. A Signature must have at least a `SignedInfo` and a `SignatureValue`. A Signature can optionally have a `KeyInfo` or an `Object`. For now, just think of the `Object` as the place to put the thing that is being signed when you have an *Enveloping* reference.

At the next level, the `SignedInfo` must contain a `CanonicalizationMethod`, a `SignatureMethod`, and one or more `Reference` elements.

At a high level, canonicalization is a strategy for standardizing XML structures so that they compare the same across multiple platforms or different equivalent XML syntax. `CanonicalizationMethod` is a pointer to the actual algorithm used to do this. We discuss this in more detail in "The `CanonicalizationMethod` Element and Canonicalization" section later in this chapter.

---

1. XML Signature Specification, http://www.w3.org/TR/xmldsig-core

`SignatureMethod` is a pointer to the signature algorithm (one you will be familiar with from Chapter 3) used to calculate the digital signature.

The `Reference` elements are the pointers to what is being signed. The `Reference` element has a URI attribute, which is the actual pointer we alluded to earlier. We talk more about URIs later, but you need to understand now that the power and flexibility of URIs to point to just about any type of resource are critical to the power and flexibility of XML Signature. The `Reference` element can optionally contain one or more `Transform` elements—a powerful, necessary, but potentially dangerous, way of changing the document in some fashion before it is digested. Finally, the `Reference` element has a `DigestMethod` that contains the one-way hash algorithm (for example, SHA1) used to calculate the `DigestValue` for the Reference.

These elements are in `SignedInfo`, which is the XML block representing the information that will be signed.

The `SignatureValue` element is a digital signature of the `SignedInfo` block. This is an important point: What is signed is the `SignedInfo` block, not what was referenced in the `SignedInfo` block. In reality, both are signed at the same time because, if you remember from Chapter 3, with a digital signature you are encrypting/signing a digest. By digitally signing the `SignedInfo` block, which contains the digest of the references, you are not only signing the references, but you are also signing critical information about the signature itself, such as which signature algorithm was used, so that these items are also protected. This is required because it might be possible, by fiddling with the type of information that is in the `SignedInfo` element, to compromise a signature. The `SignatureValue` has no children; it just has the Base-64 encoded value of the binary signature data in it.

These two elements, `SignedInfo` and `SignatureValue`, are the guts of an XML Signature. Optionally, you can have a `KeyInfo` block that either contains the key to use for verifying the signature or has information necessary to look up such a key. `KeyInfo` has many children and is fairly complex. Also, under the `Signature` element, you can have an `Object` element. We discuss both `KeyInfo` and `Object` in more detail later in this chapter.

Now that we have quickly gone through most of the elements that comprise an XML Signature, let's look at a fuller but still simplified snippet of an XML Signature in Listing 4.8.

Listing 4.8   **A Fuller XML Signature Example**

```
<Signature xmlns="http://www.w3.org/2000/09/xmldsig#">
  <SignedInfo>
    <CanonicalizationMethod
      Algorithm="http://www.w3.org/TR/2000/WD-xml-c14n-20001011" />
    <SignatureMethod Algorithm="http://www.w3.org/2000/09/xmldsig#rsa-sha1" />
    <Reference URI="http://www.foo.com/securePage.html">
      <DigestMethod Algorithm="http://www.w3.org/2000/09/xmldsig#sha1" />
      <DigestValue>60NvZvtdTB+7UnlLp/H24p7h4bs=</DigestValue>
```

Listing 4.8   **Continued**

```
      </Reference>
    </SignedInfo>
    <SignatureValue>
      hTHQJyd3C6ww/OJz07P4bMOgjqBdznSUOsCh6P+0MpF69w2tln/PFLdx/EP4/VKX
    </SignatureValue>
    <KeyInfo>
      <KeyValue>
        <RSAKeyValue>
          <Modulus>
            uCiukpgOaOmrq1fPUTH3CAXxuFmPjsmS4jnTKxrv0w1JKcXtJ2M3akaV1d/karvJ
          </Modulus>
          <Exponent>
            AQBB
          </Exponent>
        </RSAKeyValue>
      </KeyValue>
      <X509Data>
        <X509SubjectName>
          CN=David Remy,O=BEA Systems Inc,ST=WA,C=US
        </X509SubjectName>
        <X509IssuerSerial>
          <X509IssuerName>
            CN=Test CA,O=GeoTrust Inc,ST=MA,C=US
          </X509IssuerName>
          <X509SerialNumber>167355</X509SerialNumber>
        </X509IssuerSerial>
        <X509Certificate>
          MIICeDCCAeGgAwIBAgIEOd3+iDANBgkqhkiG9w0BAQQFADBbMQswCQYDVQQGEwJJ
          . . .
          C/I/k9xGr7fneoIW
        </X509Certificate>
      </X509Data>
    </KeyInfo>
</Signature>
```

As you can see, this XML Signature signs the Web page
`http://www.foo.com/securePage.html`. Of course, you know this because you looked
at the `Reference` element child of the `Signature` element (bold in the preceding code
snippet). A lot of other information is also included in an XML Signature. As you will
see in the following sections, each piece of information plays a significant role.

XML Signature Processing

We have reviewed at a high level the XML `Signature` elements. Now let's review how
an XML Signature is created and then subsequently verified before we go into each

element in more detail. This process is actually relatively straightforward. The basic steps are described in the following sections. (Note that unless you are writing a signature processing engine, you won't be performing this process yourself. This description is provided mainly so that you understand what is going on under the covers.)

XML Signature Generation

XML Signature generation is broken down into two components: Reference generation and Signature generation.

Reference Generation

When generating an XML Signature, an XML Signature processing engine first creates all the References. This process involves iterating through all the data objects that are to be signed and calculating their digest value. This basic process is as follows:

1. Obtain the resource specified by the `Reference` URI or, if not specified, as determined by the application. Note that seeing XML Signatures that do not use that `Reference` element to refer to what is being signed is rare; however, the specification allows for the possibility that what is being signed is known from the context of the situation and therefore does not have to be specified.

   In the example earlier, the reference `http://www.foo.com/securePage.html` would be dereferenced.

2. Apply the Transforms.

   No Transforms were used in the earlier example. A simple Transform might be an XPath statement that causes the signature to apply only to a part of an XML document. We describe Transforms in more detail later in the chapter.

3. Calculate the Digest using the `DigestMethod` specified. This step results in the creation of the `DigestValue` element.

4. Create the `Reference` element, including all the sub-elements described previously.

At the end of Reference generation, the XML Signature processing engine will have everything necessary to generate the `Reference` element. In the simple example used earlier, this looks like Listing 4.9.

Listing 4.9   **The XML Signature** `<Reference>` **Element**

```
<Reference URI="http://www.foo.com/securePage.html">
  <DigestMethod Algorithm="http://www.w3.org/2000/09/xmldsig#sha1" />
  <DigestValue>60NvZvtdTB+7UnlLp/H24p7h4bs=</DigestValue>
</Reference>
```

Signature Generation

After all the `Reference` elements are created, the XML processing engine can create the `Signature` itself. To do this, it must gather all the information necessary to create the `SignedInfo` element, which is what is actually signed in an XML Signature. Here are the steps:

1. Create the `SignedInfo` element itself, including the `Reference` objects created in Reference generation and the `CanonicalizationMethod`, `SignatureMethod`, and `DigestMethod`. The information in `SignedInfo` is what is actually signed. Listing 4.10 shows the `SignedInfo` from the earlier example.

Listing 4.10 **The `<SignedInfo>` Element**

```
<SignedInfo>
  <CanonicalizationMethod
      Algorithm="http://www.w3.org/TR/2000/WD-xml-c14n-20001011" />
  <SignatureMethod Algorithm="http://www.w3.org/2000/09/xmldsig#rsa-sha1" />
  <Reference URI="http://www.foo.com/securePage.html">
    <DigestMethod Algorithm="http://www.w3.org/2000/09/xmldsig#sha1" />
    <DigestValue>60NvZvtdTB+7UnlLp/H24p7h4bs=</DigestValue>
  </Reference>
</SignedInfo>
```

2. Canonicalize `SignedInfo` using the `CanonicalizationMethod` specified. We talk in detail about canonicalization later, but suffice it to say that whenever XML is being signed, it needs to be "normalized" before creating the hash and actually signing the `SignedInfo` information.

3. Using the output from the canonicalization algorithm, create a hash of the `SignedInfo` element using the specified `DigestMethod`.

4. Calculate the `SignatureValue` using the algorithm specified in `SignatureMethod` against the hashed, canonicalized `SignedInfo` element that was calculated in step 3. Listing 4.11 shows the `SignatureValue` element from the earlier example:

Listing 4.11 **The `<SignatureValue>` Element**

```
<SignatureValue>
    hTHQJyd3C6ww/OJz07P4bMOgjqBdznSUOsCh6P+0MpF69w2tln/PFLdx/EP4/VKX
  </SignatureValue>
```

5. Bundle the `SignedInfo`, `SignatureValue`, `KeyInfo` (if supplied), and `Object` (if necessary) into the `Signature` element.

You now have an XML Signature. The key point to remember here is that the `SignedInfo` element is what is really being signed, not the direct resource(s) targeted by the Reference URI(s). Of course, because a digest of the target URI(s) is included in the

SignedInfo element, it is being indirectly signed along with the information about the signature in the SignedInfo element.

XML Signature Validation

The process to validate an XML Signature is similar, except that it occurs in reverse. It is composed of two major processes like Signature generation: Reference validation and Signature validation. The goal of Reference validation is to ensure that the resource being pointed to by each Reference has not been changed. The goal of Signature validation is to ensure that the entire SignedInfo block has not been changed. Only if both of these processes succeed is integrity confirmed for the entire Signature.

Reference Validation

For Reference validation, you need to validate that the resources pointed to by the Reference elements have not changed. The first step is to canonicalize the SignedInfo element based on the CanonicalizationMethod element. Then the following steps are completed for *each* Reference element in the SignedInfo.

1. Get the data that is pointed to in the Reference. This will either be from the URI attribute, or as we mentioned above, it may be supplied by the application calling the XML Signature processing engine.

2. Apply any Transforms to the data returned. For example, if the Reference URI points to an XML document, it is likely that a Canonicalization Transform will be specified in the Reference element.

3. Create a hash of the data using the DigestMethod specified in the Reference.

4. Compare the resulting hash with the DigestValue in the Reference. If there is any difference, the validation fails.

Signature Validation

If Reference validation is successful, the XML Processing engine can proceed to Signature validation. The objective of the Signature validation step is to confirm that SignedInfo has not been changed (integrity) and, as in any digital signature verification, that the appropriate key has signed this information (that is, non-repudiation). Here are the steps for Signature validation:

1. Obtain the key for verification from the KeyInfo block, or in some other manner. Note that it is critical to determine trust for this key—ensuring that it is certainly bound to the expected identity. You learn more about this topic in Chapter 9, "Trust, Access Control, and Rights for Web Services."

2. Using the output of the SignedInfo canonicalization, create a hash of the SignedInfo.

3. Using the verification key, decrypt the SignedInfo element. Compare the hash from step 2 to the result of this verification. If they do not match, Signature validation has failed.

The XML Signature Elements

So far, we have discussed the XML Signature element and its schema at a high level and reviewed the processing steps necessary to create and verify a Signature. In the process, we have glossed over a lot of the specifics; now let's discuss each element in more detail.

The SignedInfo Element

As we mentioned, the SignedInfo element contains all the information about what is digitally signed. As shown in Listing 4.12, the SignedInfo element contains three children elements—CanonicalizationMethod, SignatureMethod, and zero or more Reference elements.

Listing 4.12 **XML Shorthand Schema for the <SignedInfo> Element**

```
<SignedInfo>
    <CanonicalizationMethod/>
    <SignatureMethod/>
    (<Reference URI? >
        (<Transforms>)?
        <DigestMethod>
        <DigestValue>
    </Reference>)+
</SignedInfo>
```

We describe each of these three elements in turn, starting with CanonicalizationMethod.

The CanonicalizationMethod Element and Canonicalization

Canonicalization is quite a mouthful and is often abbreviated as *C14N* (14 letters bracketed by the *C* and the *N*). The concept behind canonicalization is straightforward, but you wouldn't know this to look at the amount of discussion and work it has engendered. The W3C has published multiple specifications on canonicalization and the subtle issues surrounding it. It continues to be a well-discussed subject (a recent google search on *canonicalization* located 35,500 hits). Let's look at this topic at its simplest level first and then determine where the more subtle issues arise.

As we discussed in Chapter 3, if even a single bit changes in a document that is being signed, the digest (hash) will not be the same, and Signature/Reference validation will fail. With XML, in particular, certain differences may exist between an XML document or XML fragment that has nothing to do with the underlying meaning of the XML but is introduced simply because of the operating system or a difference in the way an XML parser resolves the XML. For example, a file created on a Windows operating system or one created on a Unix operating system typically ends a line of text with different ASCII character sequences. Another example is that the whitespace outside the tags of an XML element might be handled slightly differently among different XML parsers. From an XML language definition standpoint, these whitespace differences mean nothing and are ignored.

> **Note**
>
> Normally, whitespace outside elements is ignored by XML parsers. The one exception to this rule is for elements that have been declared "mixed." Such elements can contain content as well as other elements.

As we mentioned, however, *any* difference between the resulting XML at signature time and the resulting XML that is resolved at validation time will result in the Signature validation failing. Canonicalization is the strategy used to deal with this issue.

Canonicalization *normalizes* the XML so that, regardless of inconsequential physical differences in the XML, two logically equivalent XML documents will become physically, bit-to-bit equivalent. This is a critical requirement for digital signatures to work.

The following simple scenario illustrates the issue. Say that Bob is creating an XML Signature over the XML structure in Listing 4.13.

Listing 4.13   **An XML Structure to be Signed**

```
<GroceryList>
    <GroceryStore>Safeway</GroceryStore>
    <Item Category="produce">Lettuce</Item>
    <Item Category="produce">Tomato</Item>
    <Item Category="meat">Bacon</Item>
</GroceryList>
```

Now, say that Bob created this XML document on a Windows platform. Hidden within Bob's hypothetical XML document is whitespace in the form of spaces, tabs, and end-of-line characters. His document actually looks like Listing 4.14 (hidden characters are bold and delimited by + in this example).

Listing 4.14   **The GroceryList XML Structure with Embedded Whitespace from Windows**

```
+t+<GroceryList>+c-r++l-f+
+t++t+<GroceryStore>Safeway</GroceryStore>+sp++c-r++l-f+
+t++t+<Item Category="produce">Lettuce</Item>+sp++c-r++l-f+
+t++t+<Item Category="produce">Tomato</Item>+c-r++l-f+
+t++t+<Item Category="meat">Bacon</Item>+c-r++l-f+
+t+</GroceryList>+c-r++l-f+
```

Note

In this and the following two examples, we had to refer to the hidden characters with abbreviations due to space considerations. Refer to the following legend to understand these abbreviations:

c-r	carriage-return
l-f	line-feed
sp	space
t	tab

Now say this document is emailed to Alice, who is running on a Unix platform and needs to validate this document. One difference between the Windows and Unix environments is the extra carriage return put in by Windows. As a convenience to Alice, when she opens her emails, the reader software converts the carriage returns and linefeeds to single linefeeds. So, now the XML document looks like Listing 4.15.

Listing 4.15   **The GroceryList XML Structure with Embedded Whitespace from Unix**

```
+t+<GroceryList>+l-f+
+t++t+<GroceryStore>Safeway</GroceryStore>+sp++l-f+
+tb++t+<Item Category="produce">Lettuce</Item>+sp++l-f+
+t++t+<Item Category="produce">Tomato</Item>+l-f+
+t++t+<Item Category="meat">Bacon</Item>+l-f+
+t+</GroceryList>+l-f+
```

Are these two XML documents different? Not semantically. But, from a classic digital signature perspective, *any* change to the underlying bits would break the signature. If Bob had digitally signed this XML using a traditional digital signing approach, the digital signature validation would fail verification (although the email reader could get around this problem by validating the signature *before* doing any convenience manipulation of the document). It is clear, however, that logically these two XML documents are identical, and they should compare equally. This is where canonicalization comes into play. There needs to be a common way to format XML regardless of platform so that, no matter what underlying physical changes have occurred, two semantically identical XML documents will be considered physically identical. This is not limited to physical changes, but also to certain syntactic changes where XML gives you options that do not change the underlying logical equivalence. We come back to this topic soon because this is the place where some of the difficulties of canonicalization lie.

Let's return to our simple Bob and Alice scenario with the concept of canonicalization. This time, before signing the XML document, Bob (or more accurately, the tool that he is using to create the XML Signature) *canonicalizes* the XML. Here are some simple rules for canonicalization for this example (note that these are not the canonicalization rules for XML Signature, just some simple rules for this example):

- Change carriage returns/linefeeds into single carriage returns.
- Strip any whitespace (tabs or spaces) that appears outside tags.

Applying these rules to the preceding XML document creates the structure in Listing 4.16.

Listing 4.16   **The GroceryList XML Structure After Canonicalization**

```
<GroceryList>+l-f+
<GroceryStore>Safeway</GroceryStore>+l-f+
<Item Category="produce">Lettuce</Item>+l-f+
<Item Category="produce">Tomato</Item>+l-f+
<Item Category="meat">Bacon</Item>+l-f+
</GroceryList>+l-f+
```

These examples might not be pretty to look at, but canonicalization is not for human consumption; it is to feed directly into the Digest algorithm. This canonicalized output is not *stored* anywhere. It is not in the `Signature` element, and the XML information being referenced is not changed.

The purpose of the `CanonicalizationMethod` element in the `SignedInfo` block is to provide the name of the canonicalization algorithm that Bob employed when digitally signing the XML. Alice's XML Signature processing engine will read the `CanonicalizationMethod` and apply the same canonicalization algorithm on the XML that might have been subtly changed by her operating system. Consequently, due to the canonicalization, the same XML will result, and the signature will be verified correctly.

The `CanonicalizationMethod` algorithm attribute is applied to the `SignedInfo` element. It is also a type of Transform that can be used as a `Transform` element with References that we will talk more about later.

The initial XML specification contains only one required canonicalization algorithm (`http://www.w3.org/TR/2001/REC-xml-c14n-20010315`). This version ignores comments, so, for example, you could put XML comments into a `SignedInfo` section and they would be ignored in the signature. There is also a recommended canonicalization algorithm that includes comments (`http://www.w3.org/TR/2001/REC-xml-c14n-20010315#WithComments`).

Canonicalization Actions from Canonical XML Version 1.0

Following is a list of the changes that occur to an XML document when it goes through a Canonical XML version 1.0 Transform (you can find the XML Canonicalization specification at `http://www.w3.org/TR/2001/REC-xml-c14n-20010315`):

- The document is encoded in UTF-8.
- Line breaks are normalized to #xA on input, before parsing.
- Attribute values are normalized, as if by a validating processor.
- Character and parsed entity references are replaced.
- CDATA sections are replaced with their character content.
- The XML declaration and Document Type Definition (DTD) are removed.

- Empty elements are converted to start-end tag pairs.

- Whitespace outside the document element and within start and end tags is normalized.

- All whitespace in character content is retained (excluding characters removed during linefeed normalization).

- Attribute value delimiters are set to quotation marks (double quotes).

- Special characters in attribute values and character content are replaced by character references.

- Superfluous namespace declarations are removed from each element.

- Default attributes are added to each element.

- Lexicographic order is imposed on the namespace declarations and attributes of each element.

Canonicalization Subtleties: Exclusive Canonicalization

Although the concept of standardizing the XML before digesting and before verifying is reasonably simple, complex subtleties arise in some specific situations. One of the subtleties became a significant issue as practical implementations of XML Signing were in the early stages of creation. It came up when applying XML Signing to fragments of XML within a larger XML document—which is the predominant scenario in Web services using SOAP. The issue was primarily related to namespaces. The XML Canonicalization 1.0 specification says that namespaces are to be propagated down to all its descendents. This makes sense because, in the context of the document, these namespaces are implicit, so making them explicit seems like a reasonable strategy. However, when you remove an XML fragment from the context of a document, as in the case of SOAP when you have an XML payload within the overall document, this can cause significant problems.

This issue resulted in the creation of a new canonicalization algorithm called Exclusive Canonicalization (`http://www.w3.org/TR/2002/REC-xml-exc-c14n-20020718/`). This canonicalization method strives to "exclude ancestor context" as much as is practical. It primarily does this by not propagating the ancestor namespaces down to the children nodes. This canonicalization approach turns out to be the most practical in most circumstances and the one that you should use.

The extensibility of the canonicalization method is a tribute to the XML Signature working group and is what made the advent of the Exclusive Canonicalization method possible. Custom canonicalization methods are also possible; however, you should be extremely careful about using one because the canonicalization algorithm modifies the XML to be signed and verified in a way that is difficult to see. It would not be difficult for a canonicalization algorithm to do something such as modify the XML to have all signatures verified correctly.

To summarize, canonicalization is an important concept that is straightforward but can quickly become complex. (Just search *canonicalization* on the Net, and you will see what we mean.) Most of the time in Web Services Security, you can use Exclusive Canonicalization and you will be fine. We describe canonicalization further when we discuss the `Transform` element because, as we mentioned earlier, the `CanonicalizationMethod` designates which Canonicalization Transform to use over the `SignedInfo` element.

The `SignatureMethod` Element

`SignatureMethod` names the algorithm that will be used for signing and verifying signatures. Two signature algorithms are required: DSAwithSHA1, which is an implementation of the Digital Signature Algorithm (DSA), and HMAC-SHA1. DSAwithSHA1 is a public key strategy (sign with a private key, decrypt with a public key), and HMAC-SHA1 is a shared key hashed message authentication code strategy. This is a little unusual. Digital signatures are typically meant to validate integrity (that the document has not changed) and identity (that a particular individual, device, or process signed the document). Validation of identity is associated with public key cryptography (for example, DSA or RSA), not shared key cryptography. A shared key approach is typically not associated with digital signatures; however, the XML working group wanted to allow for a situation in which the primary purpose for the signature was integrity, and HMAC-SHA1 is an excellent (and fast) way to accomplish this goal.

In addition to the DSA algorithm, RSAwithSHA1 is recommended (but not required). Remember that the DSA algorithm and, consequently, DSA keys can be used only for digital signatures. The RSA public key algorithms can be used for both digital signatures and encryption and are more commonly used than DSA. Most, if not all, XML Signature implementations support RSAwithSHA1.

The following is an example of a `SignatureMethod` element:

```
<SignatureMethod Algorithm="http://www.w3.org/2000/09/xmldsig#dsa-sha1" />
```

The `Reference` Element

While `SignedInfo` can be considered the meat of an XML Signature, in turn the `Reference` element can be considered the meat of `SignedInfo`.

> **Tip**
>
> When you are reading an XML Signature, which can often be remarkably long, the first place you usually look to get a feel for what is being signed is the `Reference` element(s). The URI attribute points to what is being signed.

As review, Listing 4.17 is the Reference XML fragment pulled from the `Signature` shorthand schema shown earlier.

Listing 4.17   **XML Shorthand Schema for the `<Reference>` Element.**

```
(<Reference URI? >
   (<Transforms>)?
 <DigestMethod>
 <DigestValue>
 </Reference>)+
```

The objective of the `Reference` element is to point to a resource to be included in the overall XML Signature. There must be at least one `Reference`, which stands to reason because you have to be signing something. To say that this element points to the resource is actually oversimplifying because it also can contain `Transform` elements that manipulate the resource that is being pointed to prior to its being digested. Arguably, most of the power and complexity of XML Signatures come from the `Reference` element. That power comes from the power of the uniform resource identifier.

See the sidebar titled "The Powerful, Enigmatic, and Confusing Uniform Resource Indentifier (URI)" in Chapter 2 for more information about what a URI is and how to use it. In XML Signature, URIs can show up in a variety of ways; see the sidebar here titled "URI/URL Variants in XML Signature" for a review of the different ways a URI can show up as a Reference URI in an XML Signature.

> **URI/URL Variants in XML Signature**
>
> For XML Signature and most of the XML security standards, you need to understand URIs well. The locator aspect of URIs when referring to XML is quite a bit more involved than the equivalent HTML usage. Let's review the locator type URI options in XML Signature:
>
> 1. Refers to an external XML document. This is straightforward and might look like `URI=http://www.mycompany.com/myDocument.xml`.
>
> 2. Refers to the current XML document root. It is common, especially with enveloping references to specify the root of the document that contains the `Signature` element. This looks like `URI=""`.
>
> 3. Uses the same document reference. If you are referring to an XML element in the same document, you can use a "same document reference," which looks like `URI="#PurchaseOrder"`.
>
> 4. Uses external document "bare fragment." This is similar to a same document reference, except that it is to a portion of an external XML document. It looks something like `URI="http://www.mycompany.com/myDocument.xml#PurchaseOrder"`.
>
> 5. Refers to a non-XML file (binary, text, and so on). This is similar to any URL you are already familiar with; it looks like `URI="http://www.mycompany.com/myPicture.gif"`.
>
> 6. Uses an internal URI with an XPointer argument (this type is recommended but not required, so all toolkits might not support it). It looks like `URI="#xpointer(/)"`, which refers to the root element. External URIs with XPointer arguments are not recommended.
>
> Another fact to know about URIs is that they can be absolute or relative. An absolute URI is completely spelled out, including all parts of the URI, such as `http://www.mycompany.com/mySignatureExample`. A relative URI contains a resource path and name that is meant to be resolved

from the BaseURI. The BaseURI, if not made explicit, is the same directory as your current location. For example the relative URI `myPicture.gif` would look for `myPicture.gif` in the same directory where the XML document is located. Using relative URIs can provide the advantage of portability by allowing you to move a set of resources around without having to change references.

The `Transform` Element

Transforms receive the results of dereferencing the Reference URI and alter the results in some way. A Transform algorithm can essentially change anything about the original XML document. Multiple Transforms can appear under a Reference working in a pipeline-type fashion, with the results of one Transform algorithm feeding into the next one. This is an extremely powerful capability but fraught with risk. We discuss this topic later, but the problem is probably obvious: After a Transform occurs, there is no way for a signer or validator to view what has been signed without going through the exact same Transforms in the exact same order. That being said, in some situations Transforms are necessary. You just need to be careful when you use them.

Actually, we already described one type of Transform when we discussed canonicalization algorithms. In the XML Signature specification, five Transforms are mentioned:

- Canonicalization
- Base-64
- XPath Filtering
- Enveloped Signature Transform
- XSLT Transform

XML Signature Transforms: Nodeset or Octets?

Remember that Transforms work in a pipeline fashion, taking in the input from the Reference URI or another Transform and outputting to either another Transform or to the final digest algorithm. This brings up a new wrinkle: The results of the Reference URI can be either an XML nodeset or octets (a true 8-bit byte). The digest algorithm needs octets. If only a Reference URI is included and no Transforms, the transformation from an XML nodeset to octets occurs automatically.

When Transforms are being used, however, you sometimes need to be aware of whether a particular Transform algorithm requires a nodeset or octets as input and whether the Transform algorithm outputs an XML nodeset or octets. The Reference URI is always the first input, and there is a basic rule as to whether it will result in an XML nodeset or octets. If it is a same document reference, it will result in an XML nodeset; if it is an external reference, even if the external document is XML, it will be octets. The final Transform must always output octets because that result is required for the digest algorithm. Your tool for converting from an XML nodeset to octets is canonicalization.

Don't sweat this issue too much; most of the conversions are handled for you. Just remember that the digest algorithm needs octets. Therefore, if, after applying one or more Transforms, you end up with an XML nodeset, you may need to add one more Transform, a Canonicalization Transform, to convert the XML nodeset to octets.

Canonicalization Transform

Any canonicalization algorithm that can be used in the `CanonicalizationMethod` can be used as a Transform. Canonicalization algorithms take XML nodesets as input and output octets.

Base-64 Transform

Base-64 is an algorithm for converting binary data into text, as discussed in Chapter 3. This algorithm maps the binary values to a subset of ASCII values that are human-readable text. See Appendix A for more detailed information on the Base-64 algorithm.

You would use the Base-64 Transform, for example, if the Reference URI were pointing to a GIF image like that in Listing 4.18.

Listing 4.18   **A `<Reference>` URI for a GIF Image Requiring Base-64 Transform**

```
<Reference URI="myPicture.gif">
   <Transform
              Algorithm=http://www.w3.org/2000/09/xmldsig#base64 />
   <DigestAlgorithm ... />
   <DigestValue ... />
</Reference>
```

The Base-64 Transform takes in octets and outputs octets.

XPath Filtering Transform

The XPath Filtering Transform allows you take advantage of the powerful XPath language[2]. See Chapter 2 for more information on XPath.

In addition to the `Algorithm` attribute, the XPath Filtering Transform adds a child called `XPath` to the `Transform` element. This is the place you put the XPath expression that will pull out the piece you want from the XML nodeset that was returned by the Reference URI or the previous Transform. An example of this is shown in Listing 4.19.

Listing 4.19   **The `<Transform>` Element Using Xpath Transform**

```
<Transform Algorithm="http://www.w3.org/TR/1999/REC-xpath-19991116">
   <XPath xmlns:dsig="&dsig;">
     not(ancestor-or-self::dsig:Signature)
   </XPath>
</Transform>
```

You commonly use the XPath Filtering Transform in XML Signatures when you want to sign just a fragment of an XML document. For example, it is not uncommon to want to create a `Signature` element that is a peer with the element you want to sign. Consider the following document shown in Listing 4.20:

2. XPath, XML Path Language (XPath) Version 1.0. W3C Recommendation. J. Clark and S. DeRose. October 1999. http://www.w3.org/TR/1999/REC-xpath-19991116

Listing 4.20   **An `<Order>` XML Structure Where `<Signature>` Needs to be a Peer With `<UserAgreement>`**

```
<Order>
    <CustomerInformation>
        <Name>David Remy</Name>
        <Address>123 Somewhere Street</Address>
        <City>West Linn</City>
        <State>OR</State>
        <Country>US</Country>
    </CustomerInformation>
    <LineItems>
        <LineItem Sku="1235">Lime green Umbrella</LineItem>
    </LineItems>
    <UserAgreement>
        I agree to be spammed, pay early and extra,
        and enjoy your popup adds.
    </UserAgreement>
    <Signature>-- Signature of UserAgreement here --</Signature>
</Order>
```

The requirement here is to create an XML Signature that is a peer (at the same level in the XML tree) of `UserAgreement`. You can accomplish this by using an XPath Filtering Transform like that used in Listing 4.21.

Listing 4.21   **Use of Xpath Filtering to Create an XML Signature at the Peer Level**

```
<Signature>
    <SignedInfo>
      <Reference URI="">
        <Transforms>
         <Transform
           Algorithm="http://www.w3.org/TR/1999/REC-xpath-
           19991116">
          <XPath>
           ancestor-or-self:UserAgreement[parent:Order]
          </XPath>
         </Transform>
        </Transforms>
        ...
      </Reference>
    </SignedInfo>
</Signature>
```

As you can see, the `Reference` element specifies the current document (`URI=""`), and the `Transform` element has XPath (`http://www.w3.org/TR/1999/REC-xpath-19991116`) as its algorithm and a child `XPath` element. This element contains the XPath expression ancestor-or-self:UserAgreement[parent:Order], which is a simple way of asking for the UserAgreement element and all its siblings. This particular XPath expression is somewhat brittle because it assumes the UserAgreement element is always a child of Order. XPath would allow a more elaborate expression to pick up a UserAgreement at any level in the document.

The XPath Filtering Transform takes in and outputs an XML nodeset.

Enveloped Signature Transform

The Enveloped Signature Transform is commonly used in XML Signature when the parent element is to be signed. The problem is that the Signature element would be within the information to be signed, so it must be removed before doing the validation. You actually can remove the Signature element by using the XPath Filter Transform described previously, so this Transform is primarily provided for convenience.

> **Note**
>
> The Enveloped Signature Transform is the only Transform (other than the canonicalization Transforms defined by CanonicalizationMethod) required by the XML Specification. The XPath Filter Transform is recommended, but it is not required. You will find in practice that most, if not all, current XML Signature toolkits support the XPath Filter Transform.

Using the Enveloped Signature Transform is the same as using the XPath Filter Transform with the following expression in Listing 4.22:

Listing 4.22 **The XPath Expression Equivalent to the Enveloped Signature Transform**

```
<XPath>
   count(ancestor-or-self::dsig:Signature |
   here()/ancestor::dsig:Signature[1]) >
   count(ancestor-or-self::dsig:Signature)
</XPath>
```

This XPath expression can a bit difficult to deal with, so having this Transform is convenient. If you are signing a parent element, you should use it. For example, say you want to sign the Order XML document in Listing 4.23 and want the Signature to be the last element within the Order:

Listing 4.23 **An <Order> Element Where <Signature> Needs to be the Last Element**

```
<Order>
    <LineItems>
        <LineItem sku="00001">Soap on a Rope</LineItem>
        <LineItem sku="00002">Cinnamon Shampoo</LineItem>
    </LineItems>
    <Signature> ... </Signature>
</Order>
```

To accomplish this, you must use the Enveloped Signature Transform (or XPath Filtering Transform). The `signature` element would then look something like Listing 4.24.

Listing 4.24   **The `<Signature>` Element After the Enveloped Signature Transform**

```
<Signature>
  <SignedInfo>
    <CanonicalizationMethod ... />
    <SignatureMethod ... />
    <Reference URI="">
      <Transforms>
        <Transform
          Algorithm="http://www.w3.org/2000/09/xmldsig#enveloped-signature"/>
      </Transforms>
      <DigestMethod ... />
      <DigestValue>...</DigestValue>
    </Reference>
  </SignedInfo>
  <SignatureValue>...</SignatureValue>
</Signature>
```

In this example, the Reference URI points to the document itself (`URI=""`), and the Transform algorithm is the Enveloped Signature Transform. If the target of the Signature is not the root of the document, you could use the "same document reference" type for the URI (for example, `URI="#someElementID"`) or an XPath Filtering Transform just prior to the Enveloped Signature Transform to reduce the resulting XML fragment to just the nodes you plan to sign.

Similar to the XPath Filtering Transform, the Enveloped Signature Transform takes in and outputs an XML nodeset. The only difference is that an Enveloped Signature Transform must be applied to a nodeset from within its parent document.

XSLT Transform

It is good practice to sign what the signer (a human being) actually sees, especially when the meaning of the signature represents the signer's intent. The visual aspects—even seemingly insignificant aspects such as a word being bold—can influence the meaning of a document. If an XML Stylesheet (XSL) is used, you have two choices for how to digitally sign it. One option is to have two Reference URIs: one pointing to the base XML document and the other to the XSL. Another is to use the XSLT Transform. The XSLT Transform simply applies the specific XSL expressions that are included under the `Stylesheet` element. To refer to an external stylesheet, you can use the `xsl:include` or `xsl:import` XSL expressions.

> **Note**
>
> The XSLT Transform requires octets as input, and the output is an octet stream. Also, because different XSLT processors do not necessarily return consistent results, it is a good idea to use a Canonicalization Transform after an XSLT Transform.

XPath Filter 2.0 Transform

The XPath Filter 1.0 Transform described in the preceding section allows for any type of XPath expression to be used. The underlying usage for XPath Filter 1.0 is often either to explicitly include some fragment of a document to be signed or to explicitly exclude some part of the document that could legitimately change without breaking the signature of the document. For example, say you want to have two signatures that are not co-signatures (one signature does not include the other). To do this, you would use an XPath statement to exclude the other signatures (and the Enveloped Signature Transform to exclude the current signature). These are "set" type functions that often require fairly complex XPath statements to accomplish. The XPath Filter 2.0 Transform adds the capability to shortcut these common types of XPath statements by specifying intersection, union, and subtraction. For example, to remove another signature, you would use the following XPath 2.0 filter:

```
<XPath Filter="subtract" xmlns="http://www.w3.org/2002/06/xmldsig-filter2">
    id("TheOtherSignature")
</XPath>
```

On the other hand, if the goal is to sign the other signature, such as when a counter-signature is desired, you might use the following:

```
<XPath Filter="intersect" xmlns="http://www.w3.org/2002/06/xmldsig-filter2">
    id("TheOtherSignature")
</XPath>
```

Using these intersect, subtract, and union set operations can be cleaner than using the equivalent XPath statements, and it is also possible for the Signature processor to work more efficiently. You can find an excellent example of the XPath Filter 2.0 Transform using the three set operators at the following location:

```
http://www.w3.org/TR/xmldsig-filter2/#sec-Examples
```

The Reference URI when using the XPath Filter 2.0 Transform must be an XML document. Often, it is the current document URI (URI="" without comments or URI="#xpointer[/]" with comments). This Transform takes in and returns an XML nodeset.

The DigestMethod Element

The DigestMethod element represents an identifier for the algorithm used to calculate the digest of the Reference URI plus all the Transforms.

> **Note**
>
> The digest algorithm itself must receive its information in the form of octets. Typically, if a conversion is needed from an XML nodeset to octets, it is handled automatically. However, in some cases, an additional Transform may be required to ensure that the input to the digest algorithm is in the form of octets or to ensure that the XML nodeset is canonicalized so that it has the highest likelihood of valid comparison on any platform.

The only required digest algorithm is SHA1, and it is designated by

```
Algorithm="http://www.w3.org/2000/09/xmldsig#sha1"
```

The `DigestValue` Element

The `DigestValue` element contains the Base-64 encoded value of the digest. The following `DigestValue` element is taken from the example we gave near the beginning of the chapter:

```
<DigestValue>60NvZvtdTB+7UnlLp/H24p7h4bs=</DigestValue>
```

The `SignatureValue` Element

At this point, the `SignatureValue` element must seem anti-climactic even though it represents the signature itself. The `SignatureValue` element is the Base-64 encoded resulting value of encrypting a digest of the `SignedInfo` element. The particular signature method used is defined within the `SignatureMethod` element itself (for example, RSA-SHA1). Here is an example of a `SignatureValue`:

```
<SignatureValue>
    hTHQJyd3C6ww/OJz07P4bMOgjqBdznSUOsCh6P+OMpF69w2tln/PFLdx/EP4/VKX
</SignatureValue>
```

So far, we have reviewed the core aspects of the XML `Signature`, `SignedInfo`, and `SignatureValue` elements. If you understand them well, you have a good basis for understanding and using XML Signatures. The next two elements, `Object` and `KeyInfo`, are optional, but in many circumstances, necessary and important elements.

The `Object` Element

We have not talked much about the `Object` element, but when we described Enveloping Signatures, we were discussing a function that the `Object` element facilitates. In the case of an Enveloping Signature, the Reference URI points to an element within the `Object` element. We further describe this use of the `Object` element later in the chapter.

The `Object` element is essentially an element in which you put miscellaneous items other than `SignedInfo`, `SignatureValue`, and `KeyInfo`. It is defined in a way that you can put anything you want into it; however, typically one of three things is included within an `Object` element:

- Something you want signed, such as an XML fragment or perhaps a Base-64 encoded binary object. This is to implement the *Enveloping Signature* concept mentioned previously.
- A `Manifest` element (described later).
- A `SignatureProperties` element (described later).

> **Tip**
>
> Remember that none of these items are inherently signed and therefore secured by the XML Signature. For these elements to be signed, they must be referred to by one of the Reference URIs in the `SignedInfo` section of the signature.

Listing 4.25 uses an `Object` element in the Enveloping Signature scenario.

Listing 4.25   **An `<Object>` Element Used in the Enveloping Signature Scenario**

```
<Signature>
    <SignedInfo>
    ...
    <Reference URI="#MyOrder"
        Type="http://www.w3.org/2000/09/xmldsig#Object">
        <DigestMethod
                Algorithm="http://www.w3.org/2000/09/xmldsig#sha1"/>
        <DigestValue>...</DigestValue>
    </Reference>
 </SignedInfo>
 ...
 <Object id="MyOrder">
        <Order>
            <LineItem sku="12348">Web Service Security Book</LineItem>
            <LineItem sku="2345">Life as a Geek Book</LineItem>
        <Order>
 </Object>
</Signature>
```

> **Note**
>
> In this example, the `Object` start and end tags would be included in the digest calculation for the Reference. If you do not want the `Object` tags to be included in the digest calculation, either
>
> - The Reference URI should point to the element below the `Object` tag that is to be signed.
>
> or
>
> - An XPath statement should exclude the `Object` tag.

First, notice that the Reference URI points to an ID (`MyOrder`) of an `Object` element. Also, notice that a `Type` parameter is included in the Reference to provide information about what the Reference is pointing to. We deferred mentioning this point when describing the `Reference` element.

The following three `Type` attributes are mentioned in the XML Signature specification; they all relate to items that can be contained within an `Object` element or the `Object` element itself:

- Object (Type="http://www.w3.org/2000/09/xmldsig#Object")—The reference is to an Object element.

- Manifest (Type="http://www.w3.org/2000/09/xmldsig#Manifest")—The reference is to a Manifest element (see the Manifest Element section next in this chapter for more information on the Manifest element).

- SignatureProperties (Type="http://www.w3.org/2000/09/xmldsig#SignatureProperties")—The reference is to a SignatureProperties element (see the Signature Properties section later in this chapter for more information on SignatureProperties).

The Object element, when used in an Enveloped Signature scenario like this, can also have attributes for MimeType and Encoding. For example, if the enveloped item is a GIF image, your Object tag might look like this:

```
<Object id="MyGif" MimeType="image/gif" Encoding="base64">
... a string of base64 characters ...
</Object>
```

You can have as many Object elements as you want. You typically create a single Object tag for each use. So, for example, if you have a signed Object and you have SignatureProperties (which is always within an Object), you have two Object elements.

Now let's discuss the two optional children of the Object tag: Manifest and SignatureProperties.

The Manifest Element

In terms of ocean shipping, a *manifest* is the list of things that the ship has onboard. In that sense, all the References within SignedInfo are a type of manifest because they list what is included in the XML Signature. Similar to SignedInfo, the Manifest element contains a list of Reference elements (exactly like the Reference elements that are children of SignedInfo). The only difference is that the References referred to in SignedInfo *must* be validated for the signature to be considered valid. The meaning of a Manifest Reference not validating is left up to you, as the application developer. In other words, you typically have the opportunity to be notified if a problem occurs with validation of the Manifest Reference elements; therefore, you can determine how best to handle the situation.

You might find at least two major uses for the Manifest element:

- You may want to have more granular control over which References matter and which do not (contextually). For example, you might want it to be okay if two out of three References are valid. You would not be able to accomplish this with SignedInfo alone.

- For performance reasons, when doing multiple signatures over the same information, you could refer to a Manifest element. The Manifest element would be computed only once, and the References from multiple signatures could point to the one Manifest. This approach could be valuable when multiple signers are signing a contract.

Use of the `Manifest` element is similar to the `Object` example described earlier, except that the `Manifest` element exists at one level below `Object`, as shown in Listing 4.26.

Listing 4.26   **Use of the `<Manifest>` Element**

```
<Reference URI="#MyManifest"
Type="http://www.w3.org/2000/09/xmldsig#Manifest">
      <DigestMethod Algorithm="http://www.w3.org/2000/09/xmldsig#sha1"/>
      <DigestValue>. . .</DigestValue>
  </Reference>
  ...
  <Object>
      <Manifest Id="MyManifest">
          <Reference>
              ...
          </Reference>
           <Reference>
              ...
          </Reference>
      </Manifest>
  </Object>
```

As we mentioned previously, the `Reference` elements in `Manifest` are *exactly* like the `Reference` elements in `SignedInfo`, except that it is up to you to decide what to do if the validation on the `DigestValue` fails.

The `SignatureProperties` Element

The `SignatureProperties` element provides a place to put name value information about the signature itself. For example, you often need to know the time of the signature. This is a classic candidate for a signature property. Listing 4.27 shows this type of usage (it is a slightly edited version from an example in the XML Signature specification).

Listing 4.27   **Use of the `<SignatureProperties>` Element**

```
<Signature id="MySignature">
    <SignedInfo>
        ...
        <Reference URI="#AMadeUpTimeStamp"
        Type="http://www.w3.org/2000/09/xmldsig#SignatureProperties">
            <DigestMethod Algorithm="http://www.w3.org/2000/09/xmldsig#sha1"/>
            <DigestValue>. . .</DigestValue>
        </Reference>
    </SignedInfo>
    ...
    <Object>
        <SignatureProperties>
```

Listing 4.27   **Continued**

```
        <SignatureProperty Id="AMadeUpTimeStamp" Target="#MySignature">
            <timestamp xmlns="http://www.ietf.org/rfcXXXX.txt">
                <date>19990908</date>
                <time>14:34:34:34</time>
            </timestamp>
        </SignatureProperty>
      </SignatureProperties>
    </Object>
</Signature>
```

Notice that the `Reference` element points to a specific `SignatureProperty` within `SignatureProperties` and specifies a `SignatureProperties Type`. Also, notice that the `Target` points back to the `Signature` that this property is associated with.

That wraps up our discussion of the `Object` element. It is kind of a quirky element but important in many circumstances.

The `KeyInfo` Element

The `KeyInfo` element is perhaps the thorniest element in the XML Signature specification. Its purpose is to give you the key needed to validate the signature or give you information to allow you to look up the key. XML Signature goes out of its way to define a flexible structure for `KeyInfo` such that

- It can be omitted completely.
- It can provide the key in a raw form right in the XML.
- It can provide the key within a digital certificate.
- It can give you a variety of types of keys to support different cryptography standards.
- It can simply provide a name for you to use to look up the key.

As it always seems when discussing PKI and security, things become more difficult as we move closer to the issues of key management and trust.

Because the `KeyInfo` element allows such a wide variety of options for providing information about the key needed to validate the signature, it consists mostly of optional elements. Listing 4.28 is a shorthand schema for `KeyInfo`.

Listing 4.28   **The Shorthand XML Schema for** `<KeyInfo>`

```
(<KeyInfo (id=)?>
   (<KeyName>)?
   (<KeyValue>)?
   (<RetrievalMethod>)?
   (<X509Data>)?
   (<PGPData>)?
```

Listing 4.28   **Continued**

```
    (<SPKIData>)?
    (<MgmtData>)?
<KeyInfo>)?
```

As you can see, *everything* is optional. This is a clue about the unwieldy nature of this element. Obviously, the XML Signature working group wanted to support as many possible key standards as it could; however, most of the time, you will encounter one of these three scenarios:

- You will receive an X.509 certificate within the X509Data element. X.509 certificates, issued by a certificate authority, either private or public (such as VeriSign or GeoTrust), are the predominant container for public keys.

- You will receive one of the X509Data elements that uniquely identify an X.509 certificate in a directory. We discuss these elements briefly later in this section, but examples include X509IssuerSerial and SerialNumber, which together can uniquely identify a certificate. In this case, you use this information to look into a directory to locate the X.509 certificate yourself.

- You will receive no KeyInfo. In this case, it is expected that you know what the validation key (either public or secret key) should be. For example, if you are in a protocol situation, exchanging multiple messages in a sequence, you may already have knowledge of the key.

As we mentioned earlier, X.509 certificates are the predominant standard for containing public key certificates. Practically every type of security application contains support for them, including Web browsers, Web servers, VPNs, email, and so on. X.509 certificates are ASN.1 structures (see the sidebar "XML Versus ASN.1 Paradigm Shift: A Battle to the Death?" in Chapter 2), and there is a common thread across XML security standards to not force applications to have both ASN.1 and XML parsers. However, X.509 certificates (either directly included or specified via some identifier approach) have two distinct advantages over other methods of providing keys:

- Most applications, tools, libraries, and environments support X.509 processing.

- X.509 certificates are digitally signed by a certificate authority in a standard way that leads to trust decisions. We discuss trust issues in depth in Chapter 9, but suffice it to say here that "trusting" that the key really represents the identity you think it does is fundamental to digital signatures. X.509 certificates fit into a relatively mature (although at times overly complex) strategy for establishing that a key is legitimate.

In certain circumstances, you might receive something other than an X.509 certificate or pointer to an X.509 certificate. These situations are most likely to occur when you are working within a known trust domain. In this case, the raw public key may even be provided directly in the KeyInfo structure.

KeyInfo is discussed again in later chapters about XML Encryption (which also uses KeyInfo and adds a few elements) and XKMS. XKMS allows you to pass a KeyInfo element to a "trust engine" to determine whether, based on your own trust policies, you can trust the key located through this KeyInfo.

Now let's examine the possible KeyInfo sub-elements.

KeyName

The KeyName element is simply a name to identify the key. It could be some string agreed upon in advance, or it could represent a unique value used to look up the key in a directory. For example, KeyName could contain an email address or a Distinguished Name (DN) for a digital certificate.

KeyValue

The KeyValue element is the actual key itself embedded in the XML. The format of this element varies based on the type of key. The two types of keys mentioned in the XML specification are DSA and RSA. Each of these has its own elements as children of KeyValue, DSAKeyValue, and RSAKeyValue.

RetrievalMethod

The RetrievalMethod element is used to reference a key that is stored at a separate location. It contains a URI (like the Reference URI) pointing to the key with an optional Type for the type of key information being retrieved. Most of the major KeyInfo elements can be targeted by RetrievalMethod. The valid Type values for remote KeyInfo structures are as follows:

```
http://www.w3.org/2000/09/xmldsig#DSAKeyValue
http://www.w3.org/2000/09/xmldsig#RSAKeyValue
http://www.w3.org/2000/09/xmldsig#X509Data
http://www.w3.org/2000/09/xmldsig#PGPData
http://www.w3.org/2000/09/xmldsig#SPKIData
http://www.w3.org/2000/09/xmldsig#MgmtData
```

In addition to these, there is a Type value for a binary X.509 certificate:

```
http://www.w3.org/2000/09/xmldsig#rawX509Certificate
```

One use of the RetrievalMethod element is to save space in the XML document because KeyInfo values such as X.509 certificates can be large. If multiple signatures use the same key or perhaps part of a certificate chain, you can store the KeyInfo structure in a standalone element in the document with a unique ID attribute and then refer to it using the same document reference in each Signature element's KeyInfo RetrievalMethod URI attributes.

X509Data

The X509Data element is a commonly used KeyInfo element. The objective of the X509Data element is to provide either an identifier to look up an X.509 certificate or the X.509 certificate itself.

A certificate chain can also be contained in X509Data. The idea is that there would be a set, or chain, of related certificates under X509Data. A certificate chain typically means all the certificates necessary to get to a root certificate. See Chapter 3 for more information about certificate chains and root certificates.

PGPData

The PGPData element is similar to the X509Data element; it can either point you to a PGP key or contain actual key material. It is unlikely that you will use this element for XML Signatures, although it is possible and the specification allows for it. The child element PGPKeyID is a unique ID of the key, and PGPKeyPacket is a structure that can contain a PGP public and/or private key. PGPKeyID and PGPKeyPacket are defined in the OpenPGP standard[3]. The PGPData and SPKIData elements are written flexibly, so elements in a different namespace can add to these elements, or if a PGP XML standard is written, it could replace the PGPData element.

SPKIData

The Simple Public Key Infrastructure (SPKI) was an effort to improve and simplify PKI. It does not have much momentum right now, due to slow commercial acceptance, so you are unlikely to need to use it. The structure of SPKIData is similar to PGPData in the sense that it contains sub-elements to help locate or contain the public key, and it can be extended and replaced by external namespace elements when and if they are defined.

We've now concluded our discussion of KeyInfo and the rest of the XML Signature elements. We will now discuss strategies for actual usage of XML Signature

Security Strategies for XML Signature

XML Signature, just like any security strategy, is effective only if it is used correctly within the context and constraints of the situation. It is effective in certain areas but can be inappropriate in others. The following sections describe some security considerations when you are using XML Signatures.

Using Transforms

Perhaps the scariest aspect of XML Signatures, at least when you come from a traditional digital signature perspective, is the concept that you can change (transform) the information being signed in a hidden way (by an algorithmic process) before it is digitally signed. This capability seems to go against the assumptions about fundamental integrity on which digital signatures are based. However, as we discussed earlier when talking about Transforms, there are completely legitimate reasons for using a Transform algorithm, such as when you need to Base-64 encode a binary object or remove a signature when creating/validating an Enveloped Signature. The XML Signature working group

---

3. RFC2440: OpenPGP Message Format. J. Callas, L. Donnerhacke, H. Finney, and R. Thayer. November 1998. http://www.ietf.org/rfc/rfc2440.txt

was concerned enough about the security issues around Transforms to call out three specific principles to consider when using Transforms in XML Signatures.

Only What Is Signed Is Secure

The principle "only what is signed is secure" seems obvious, but the point is that when a Transform is involved, you must be extra diligent to understand what the Transform does and to understand that the discarded information is not digitally signed. For example, in a Web services scenario, if an XML Signature has signed the XML payload, only the XML payload is secured, not the SOAP envelope information.

Only What Is Seen Should Be Signed

If a user's judgment or consent is being conveyed by the signature, every practical effort should be made to sign what a user has seen. For example, if a contract being signed (showing intent) has been rendered to the signer as XML with an XSL stylesheet, both the XML and the XSL stylesheet should be signed. In general, implementers should adhere to the principle of What You See Is What You Sign (WYSIWYS).

"See" What Is Signed

The idea behind the principle "see what is signed" is that you should make sure you are working with (seeing) what was actually signed. Making presumptions about the signature is risky. You should run the actual Reference URI and Transforms and work with the output to be sure. For example, you may know that a signature is supposed to contain a certain field, such as an amount. If Transforms are involved (and they always are when you consider canonicalization of the SignedInfo element), you cannot be positive that that field's integrity has been validated unless you run the Reference URI/Transform algorithms and then access the field's contents from the result.

Knowing the Security Model

In the context of our discussion, the term *security model* means the set of assumptions and constraints associated with a particular security or cryptographic strategy. For example, XML Signature supports both public key signatures and keyed hashed authentication codes (such as HMAC).

We discussed the security model around public key signatures in Chapter 3. The main point here to remember is that public key signatures are associated with identity *and* integrity.

Keyed hashed authentication codes, such as HMAC, are shared key based. They tend to run much faster than public key signatures, but they are primarily associated with integrity, *not* identity.

XML Signatures can and will be extended over time to include other types of algorithms and techniques. If you choose one of these approaches, it is critical that you understand the underlying security model well.

Knowing Your Keys

Key management is a fundamental issue of cryptography whether it is public key or shared key oriented. It is critical (and challenging) that you protect the private keys that are used for signing and confirm that the keys you are using for validation are valid, not revoked, and represent the identity that you expect them to represent.

Signing Object Elements

XML Signature processing does not automatically sign `Object` elements within a `Signature` element. If you want an element signed, you must create a Reference and point specifically to the `Object` element. This point is obvious when you are creating an Enveloping Signature, but it may seem less obvious when you are adding a `SignatureProperties` or `Manifest` element. Most of the time, you will want these elements signed. For example, if you add a "Time of Signature" property to a `SignedProperties` element, you usually want to add a Reference to it; otherwise, why would you provide this information to the verifier and potentially have it tampered with?

Signing DTDs with Entity References

One of the key capabilities of DTDs is keeping entity references that are resolved for you at XML parse time. For example, say you have a DTD that contains the following entity references:

```
<!ENTITY companyname "CompanyA">
<!ENTITY companylocation "Chicago, IL">
```

Then you receive a signed XML document representing an order commitment for $1,000,000 that was signed by Company A like Listing 4.29.

Listing 4.29 **An** `<OrderCommittment>` **Document Signed by Company A**

```
<?xml version="1.0"?>
<!DOCTYPE ordercommittment SYSTEM "ordercommittment.dtd">
<OrderCommittment>
    <CompanyName>&companyname;</CompanyName>
    <CompanyLocation>&companylocation;</CompanyLocation>
    <CommittedItem type="cash" denom="USD">$1,000,000</CommittedItem>
    <CommittedDate>ASAP</CommittedDate>
    <Signature>
        <SignedInfo>
            <CanonicalizationMethod ... />
            <SignatureMethod ... />
            <Reference URI="">
                <Transforms>
                  <Transform
                   Algorithm="http://www.w3.org/2000/09/
```

Listing 4.29   **Continued**

```
                        xmldsig#enveloped-signature"/>
                </Transforms>
            <DigestMethod ... />
            <DigestValue>...</DigestValue>
          </Reference>
      </SignedInfo>
        <SignatureValue>...</SignatureValue>
      </Signature>
</OrderCommittment>
```

Notice that the signature is an Enveloped Signature that signs everything under the `OrderCommittment` element. Because the Reference URI is `""`, the entire document includes the `<?xml` and `<!DOCTYPE` lines; however, the DTD itself has not been signed. Notice that the DTD has a relative address. So, imagine that an attacker—say, from Company B—substituted a different DTD file into the same directory as the XML containing the following entity references:

```
<!ENTITY companyname "CompanyB">
<!ENTITY companylocation "Pendleton, NJ">
```

In this case, the signature is validated even though different values appear in the `CompanyName` and `CompanyLocation` elements of the XML document! And Company B will receive the $1,000,000 because of it. The point is: Signing DTDs is very important when entity references are being used.

Entity references are not a problem with XML Schemas because schemas do not have the same entity reference capability; however, a similar problem can occur with default values. It is a good idea to include a Reference to the XML Schema for the same reasons you would sign DTDs.

> **SOAP Security Extensions: An Initial Stab at Web Services Security**
>
> In February 2001, Microsoft and IBM submitted a W3C Note regarding the use digital signatures in SOAP messages (see `http://www.w3.org/TR/SOAP-dsig/`). This precursor to WS-Security defines a standard way to put an XML Signature into the header of a SOAP message. For example, a signed SOAP message would look like Listing 4.30 using this method.

Listing 4.30   **Early Use of Digital Signatures in SOAP**

```
<SOAP-ENV:Envelope
  xmlns:SOAP-ENV="...">
  <SOAP-ENV:Header>
    <SOAP-SEC:Signature xmlns:SOAP-SEC="..."
      SOAP-ENV:actor="some-URI"
      SOAP-ENV:mustUnderstand="1">
      <ds:Signature xmlns:ds="...">
        <ds:SignedInfo>
```

Listing 4.30 **Continued**

```
                <ds:CanonicalizationMethod
                  Algorithm="...">
                </ds:CanonicalizationMethod>
                <ds:SignatureMethod Algorithm="..."/>
                <ds:Reference URI="#Body">
                  <ds:Transforms>
                    <ds:Transform Algorithm="..."/>
                  </ds:Transforms>
                  <ds:DigestMethod Algorithm="..."/>
                        <ds:DigestValue>...=</ds:DigestValue>
                </ds:Reference>
              </ds:SignedInfo>
              <ds:SignatureValue>...</ds:SignatureValue>
            </ds:Signature>
          </SOAP-SEC:Signature>
       </SOAP-ENV:Header>
       <SOAP-ENV:Body
          xmlns:SOAP-SEC="..." SOAP-SEC:id="Body">
          <m:GetLastTradePrice xmlns:m="some-URI">
            <m:symbol>IBM</m:symbol>
          </m:GetLastTradePrice>
       </SOAP-ENV:Body>
    </SOAP-ENV:Envelope>
```

You will not see this standard in much use today; it never went past the W3C Note stage. However, it is used in some situations, and it had a significant influence on the later WS-Security standard.

Summary

XML Signature is the latest and greatest technology for you to use to ensure integrity and non-repudiation (to the extent possible). Its remarkable flexibility allows you to sign parts or all of XML documents as well as binary and remote objects.

Despite the depth and size of this chapter, the medium-level concepts behind XML Signature and the way it works are not difficult to understand. An XML Signature is represented by a `Signature` element. The core elements of an XML Signature are the `SignedInfo` and `SignatureValue` elements. The `SignedInfo` element contains the `CanonicalizationMethod`, the `SignatureMethod`, and one or more `Reference` elements. The `Reference` elements contain URIs (pointers) to resources to be signed, zero or more `Transform` elements, a `DigestMethod`, and a `DigestValue`. Transforms are algorithms that modify the resource being referenced in some way. The `SignedInfo` element and all its descendents are canonicalized and signed, using the specified algorithms, with the result put into the `SignatureValue` element.

In addition to `SignedInfo` and `SignatureValue`, a Signature can have two other optional elements: `Object` and `KeyInfo`. The `Object` element is a flexible element typically used to contain items to be signed and/or other information about the Signature. The `Object` element may contain a `SignatureProperties` element, which is a place to put properties about an XML Signature such as the time the Signature occurred. Also, an `Object` element could contain a `Manifest`, which is a set of `Reference` elements, formatted exactly like `SignedInfo`, with the only difference being the application is notified if a `Reference` from a `Manifest` fails validation; whereas if a `Reference` from `SignedInfo` fails validation, the entire signature fails. `KeyInfo` provides the key, or a pointer to the key, needed to validate the XML Signature.

The Reference URI is quite flexible and can point to resources in a variety of ways. There are three types of References, also known as XML Signature types: Enveloping Signatures, in which the `Signature` element wraps the item being signed; Enveloped Signatures, in which the `Signature` element is a descendent of the resource being signed; and Detached Signatures, in which the resource being pointed to is none of the above. Detached Signatures can have Reference URIs pointing to an XML element within the current document (but not to an ancestor node), to a binary file such as a GIF image, or to all or part of an external XML document.

We have spent extra time on helping you to understand XML Signature primarily because it is the first of the XML Security standards and is fundamental to the newer XML and Web Services Security standards. A good familiarity with XML Signature will help you understand the following standards, as well as provide you with a powerful tool for securing your Web services applications.

In the next chapter, we look at XML Signature's sibling standard: XML Encryption.

5

Ensuring Confidentiality of XML Messages

Introduction to and Motivation for XML Encryption

In Chapter 4, "Safeguarding the Identity and Integrity of XML Messages," we discussed XML Signature and its importance as a foundational XML security standard. In this chapter, we describe XML Encryption, which is designed to keep all or part of a SOAP message secret. Because XML Encryption followed XML Signature as a standard, the two are similar and share some of the same concepts, terminology, and XML elements. However, XML Encryption addresses different issues than XML Signature and, consequently, shows up in quite a different manner than XML Signature. We first discuss at a high level the relationship between XML Signature and XML Encryption as a way of leveraging what we discussed in the XML Signature chapter. Later in this chapter, in the section "Using XML Encryption and XML Signature Together," we discuss the issues with using these two technologies together, which is quite common, as you will see in Chapter 7, "Building Security into SOAP," when we discuss the WS-Security standard.

Relating XML Encryption and XML Signature

XML Signature (formerly known as Digital Signature, or *DSIG*), as we discussed in the preceding chapter, was the initial W3C XML security standard that really got XML security off the ground. The development of XML Encryption followed and overlapped XML Signature. There were many common members on the two W3C specification committees, including the co-editors of the specification, Donald Eastlake and Joseph Reagle. You will notice that both technologies share many of the same concepts and even structures (for example, they share the `KeyInfo` element to hold key information).

First, let's look at the similarities between XML Signature and XML Encryption. In XML Signature, you can sign all or part of an XML document either by having the Signature's `Reference` URI pointing internally or pointing to an external resource. Similarly, in XML Encryption, you can encrypt all or part of an XML document either internally or externally. Just as an XML Signature structure can exist multiple times in a document, an XML Encryption structure can exist in multiple places within a document with different keys or the same key. Probably the most obvious similarity between XML Signature and XML Encryption is that they share the `KeyInfo` element, which was defined originally in the XML Signature namespace.

Although the structure and some of the elements defined for XML Signature and XML Encryption are similar, their purpose and usage are quite different. Whereas you might use XML Signature to ensure that an XML document has not been tampered with (integrity) and was acknowledged by a known entity, XML Encryption has an entirely different purpose. XML Encryption allows hiding of all or part of an XML document (confidentiality) from anyone other than the private key holder. These technologies are complementary because, often, with secure XML and Web services you need to both encrypt a message to a recipient as well as sign the message to confirm your identity and verify that the message you sent is the message that was received.

A more structural contrast between XML Signature and XML Encryption is noticeable when you look at the XML that comprises the two standards. An XML Signature is represented by one `Signature` element that has one or more `References` to the items that are signed. The item being signed is often outside the Signature. In contrast, XML Encryption has the `EncryptedData` element, which typically surrounds the information that is encrypted. Most often, although there are exceptions, an XML Signature *points* to what is being signed, and an XML Encryption `EncryptedData` element *contains* what is being encrypted.

These differences will become more clear as you see examples and learn more about XML Encryption in this chapter. The main point is that XML Signature and XML Encryption are siblings, which, like the human variety, have common genes that result in similarities but also, due to their different purposes, have profound differences. In the section "Using XML Encryption and XML Signature Together," later in this chapter, we discuss the inter-relationship between the two, describe a common usage pattern, and explain the best strategies to make them work together and avoid the natural "sibling rivalry" that could occur.

Critical Building Block for WS-Security

Both XML Signature and XML Encryption co-exist as fundamental building blocks for WS-Security. As you will see in Chapter 7, WS-Security depends on these two technologies as two of its three pillars (the third being SAML). So, understanding both XML Signature and XML Encryption is essential to understanding WS-Security.

The Goal Is to Ensure Confidentiality of Messages from End to End with Different Recipients

The vision of XML Encryption is more grandiose than simply to encrypt the information for one end recipient. XML Encryption allows for different parts of a document to be encrypted with different keys and therefore to be seen by different recipients.

As we demonstrate in an extended example near the end of the chapter, you can imagine scenarios in which an XML document could have parts that are readable by one party but completely hidden to another.

Perhaps what makes XML Encryption unique among XML standards is that its goal is to make selected parts of XML unintelligible. An important principle of XML has been to "make the wire protocol transparent." XML Encryption now allows you to obfuscate selective parts of the document through encryption. This capability has implications on other XML standards that perhaps had not considered the encryption scenario. See the sidebar titled "XML Encryption and XML Schema" near the end of the chapter. There, we discuss one such implication.

Think Shared Key Cryptography When You Think of XML Encryption

Remember that, for all intents and purposes, encryption is *always* done with shared (symmetric) key algorithms. This point may surprise you because you may sometimes hear about a sender encrypting a message using your public key so that you can decrypt it with your private key. In practice, this statement is correct, but it is an oversimplification. Due to efficiency considerations and the size of public (asymmetric) keys, only small amounts of data can be encrypted or decrypted using public key algorithms. A document or message of arbitrary length is encrypted with a shared key. If public key technology is being used (as it often is), the shared key to be used to encrypt the document is encrypted by the sender using the recipient's public key and then transported to the recipient safely. XML Encryption handles this requirement using the `EncryptedKey` element to *wrap* a shared key. The approach of encrypting a shared key (often called a *session key*) with the recipient's public key is so important and so common that XML Encryption introduces a specific element to support this called EncryptedKey.

XML Encryption Will Become Part of the Infrastructure Like XML Signature

As we mentioned in the preceding chapter, XML Signature and XML Encryption will likely evolve to be an embedded part of the infrastructure rather than a technology you work with directly on a day-to-day basis. More likely, whether your role is as a developer or administrator, you will work at the policy level and declaratively describe the security that a particular Web service or XML document requires rather than work at the fine-grained level that we describe in this chapter. Still, like most things, having a strong understanding of the underlying XML Encryption technology will help you work better at whatever level you need when working with Web Services Security.

XML Encryption Fundamentals

Probably the best way to understand XML Encryption is to jump right into an example. Let's work through a simple XML Encryption scenario to highlight what can be done with XML Encryption. Then we will go through the different XML Encryption elements.

Let's start with a sample document that has some sensitive data in it, as shown in Listing 5.1.

Listing 5.1   **A Sample Document Containing Sensitive Data**

```
<Employee>
    <EmployeeID>512-34-4567</EmployeeID>
    <Manager>Fred Jones</Manager>
    <Salary>$50,000</Salary>
</Employee>
```

Because the Employee ID number is a Social Security number, you may want to encrypt it as shown in Listing 5.2.

Listing 5.2   **A Piece of Sensitive Data Encrypted**

```
<Employee>
    <EmployeeID><EncryptedData>#A.Ije@OJFdl</EncryptedData></EmployeeID>
    <Manager>Fred Jones</Manager
    <Salary>$50,000</Salary>
</Employee>
```

And you may feel that the salary element is so sensitive that you don't even want the tag `Salary` to show up. So, the encrypted document might look something like Listing 5.3.

Listing 5.3   **The Sample Document Encrypting Even a Tag**

```
<Employee>
    <EmployeeID><EncryptedData> A.Ije@OJFdl</EncryptedData></EmployeeID>
    <Manager>Fred Jones</Manager>
    <EncryptedData>J1!%dW2s23#D'?D2@</EncryptedData>
</Employee>
```

XML Encryption allows this type of encryption and much more. XML Encryption allows you to encrypt different sections of the XML document with different keys, thereby making different sections of the document available to different readers. In a Web services scenario, you could imagine that parts of the SOAP message might need to be available to a specific "waypoint" receiver of the message but not necessarily the "endpoint" receiver. For example, say a firewall requires a special SOAP header that contains a priority field. The SOAP message might look something like Listing 5.4.

Listing 5.4   **SOAP Message with Two Different Encrypted Data Segments**

```
<SOAP:Envelope>
    <SOAP:Header>
        <!--Firewall info -->
        <EncryptedData>binary data</EncryptedData>
    </SOAP:Header>
    <SOAP:Body>
        <EncryptedData>binary data</EncryptedData>
    </SOAP:Body>
</SOAP:Envelope>
```

One of the tenets of Web services security is that the document itself, the SOAP message, should be protected "end to end" and should not necessarily rely on transport security (SSL, TLS, IPSEC, and so on), which is considered "point to point." This point of view is discussed in more detail in Chapter 7, but for now, let's just say that there are trade-offs to using each approach, and there are arguments for even combining both message-based security and transport security.

This example provides a taste of XML Encryption, but even with this tidbit, you can see the available power and flexibility. In the rest of this chapter, we explore the different aspects of XML Encryption and, at the end of the chapter, we discuss the interaction between XML Signature and XML Encryption more fully.

XML Encryption Structure

In the following sections, we walk you through the structure of XML Encryption. We work with sample XML fragments to show how these document fragments would look in encrypted XML.

EncryptedData: The Core of XML Encryption

The core data element in XML Encryption is EncryptedData. An EncryptedData element either wraps data within the XML document that is being encrypted, or it points to something that is encrypted.

If the target of what is being encrypted is within the same document, the EncryptedData element *replaces* the unencrypted information. This replacement can either include the element tags or just what is within an element tag (including the element's children).

If the target is a reference, then, similar to the XML Signature Reference URI, it can refer to an external non-XML file, or it can refer to all or part of an XML document.

You can also include the key for decrypting the encrypted data right in the EncryptedData element using a KeyInfo element. But if you include the key for decrypting the data right there with the encrypted data itself, why did you encrypt the data in the first place? Couldn't an attacker just take the key and decrypt the data? Yes, that would be the case if you used a symmetric key. Typically, the reason for doing this is to encrypt a shared key using the public key of the recipient, thereby gaining the speed and scalability of shared key cryptography for encryption while still maintaining the key management and trust characteristics of public key cryptography. There are specific techniques for doing this, and we describe them in more detail when we discuss the EncryptedKey and KeyInfo elements.

You can have more than one EncryptedData element in a document, which can be associated with the same encryption key or different ones. Thus, different parts of a document could be hidden from different recipients, and they could potentially see completely different views of the same document.

EncryptedData Schema

Now let's look at the XML shorthand schema for the EncryptedData element. Listing 5.5 comes directly from the XML Encryption specification.

Listing 5.5 XML Shorthand Schema for `<EncryptedData>`

```
<EncryptedData Id? Type? MimeType? Encoding?>
    <EncryptionMethod/>?
    <ds:KeyInfo>
      <EncryptedKey>?
      <AgreementMethod>?
      <ds:KeyName>?
      <ds:RetrievalMethod>?
      <ds:*>?
    </ds:KeyInfo>?
    <CipherData>
      <CipherValue>?
      <CipherReference URI?>?
    </CipherData>
    <EncryptionProperties>?
 </EncryptedData>
```

See the sidebar titled "Reading an XML Shorthand Schema" in Chapter 4 for information on how to read this schema.

Before we run through the EncryptedData schema, let's examine how it will show up in XML documents. In many ways, EncryptedData is simpler than XML Signature because it is more self-contained. The Signature element is about a collection of pointers that represent what is being signed. On the other hand, EncryptedData represents a single resource being encrypted; it does not contain pointers to multiple items. However, much of the strategy that is used in XML Signature is applicable to XML Encryption. An EncryptedData element could encompass an entire document or other XML structure similar to an enveloping signature. Also, an EncryptedData element could contain a pointer (not multiple pointers, though) to a detached resource that is encrypted. The pointer, a CipherReference, works just like Reference in XML

Signature, including the possibility of Transforms but with no DigestMethod or DigestValue. Probably the most significant difference (and additional complexity) with XML Encryption is related to EncryptedKey, which is a way to include an encryption key (which, by the way, is almost always synonymous with shared key). We discuss this topic in depth soon.

Let's set aside the KeyInfo element for now. You already learned about KeyInfo in XML Signature, but XML Encryption adds a few twists that we will discuss in the "KeyInfo" section later in this chapter.

The core elements within EncryptedData are EncryptionMethod and CipherData. EncryptionMethod is a pointer to the algorithm used for the encryption. CipherData either wraps the encryption data itself (CipherValue) or contains a pointer to the encrypted information (CipherReference URI).

EncryptionProperties is a place to hold miscellaneous information about the encrypted data. It is similar to the SignatureProperties element discussed in the preceding chapter and in some scenarios is used along with XML Signatures.

EncryptedData has four optional attributes: Id, an optional identifier for the EncryptedData element; Type; MimeType; and Encoding. Type is an identifier for the type of plain text that is behind the EncryptedData element. There are two valid Type values: *element*, indicating that the entire element (including tags) has been encrypted, and *content*, which indicates that only the information within the element was encrypted (not including the outer tags). In the XML Encryption specification, Type is optional but, in practice, is always included and is critical for the decryption engine to restore the original document correctly. MimeType and Encoding are optionally used to further describe the encrypted item. For example, if the encrypted item is a Base-64 GIF image, you might see an Encoding of http://www.w3.org/2000/09/xmldsig#base64 and a MimeType of 'image/gif'.

It is important to note here that the EncryptedData structure is not secured from an integrity perspective. To secure the structure this way, you need to wrap the encrypted structure(s) in an XML Signature. This subject brings in new subtleties that we discuss near the end of the chapter.

Before we go through the different elements within EncryptedData, we need to examine the concept of EncryptedType.

EncryptedType

When you look at the schema in the preceding section, you see two elements— EncryptedData and EncryptedKey—that have something in common: They both encrypt something. EncryptedType is an abstraction of both of these elements that defines a common structure that both EncryptedData and EncryptedKey extend, similar to the concept of a super class in object-oriented programming languages. EncryptedType is defined in the governing schema for XML Encryption, but you will not see an instance of it in any document containing XML Encryption because it is an *abstract type* in the XML Encryption schema. The point here is that the EncryptedData and `EncryptedKey` elements are both `EncryptedType` elements through inheritance, and they share a common structure. When we discuss the elements within `EncryptedData`, we will also discuss the elements within `EncryptedKey`. We will discuss `EncryptedKey` further, describing why and when you use it. For now, you should keep in mind that much of what we discuss about `EncryptedData` applies to both elements.

EncryptionMethod

`EncryptionMethod` specifies the encryption algorithm used. In Chapter 3, "The Foundations of Distributed Message-Level Security," we described different encryption algorithms. This is the place where they are specified in XML Encryption. The following encryption algorithms are choices provided by the specification:

- **Triple-DES**—`http://www.w3.org/2001/04/xmlenc#tripledes-cbc` (required)
- **Advanced Encryption Standard (AES) 128-bit key**— `http://www.w3.org/2001/04/xmlenc#aes128-cbc` (required)
- **Advanced Encryption Standard 256-bit key**— `http://www.w3.org/2001/04/xmlenc#aes256-cbc` (required)
- **Advanced Encryption Standard 192-bit key**— `http://www.w3.org/2001/04/xmlenc#aes192-cbc` (optional)

As you can see, the key lengths are included in the names of these algorithms. This may not be true of all algorithms, and an optional `KeySize` child element may be required for some optional or future encryption algorigthms.

We discuss the `EncryptedKey` element and key transport further in the "`EncryptedKey`" section.

CipherData

The `CipherData` element either contains encrypted information (`CipherValue`) *or* a pointer (reference) to the resource being encrypted (`CipherReference`).

CipherValue

If `CipherValue` is used, the Base-64–encoded encrypted information is right there inline within the element. In Web services scenarios, you usually see the encrypted information embedded in the SOAP message, as in Listing 5.6.

Listing 5.6 **Example of How** `<CipherValue>` **Is Used**

```
<CipherData>
    <CipherValue>A23B45C56</CipherValue>
</CipherData>
```

CipherReference

If the encrypted information is located in a URI-addressable resource, the `CipherReference` element is used. This element uses a URI attribute almost exactly like the `Reference` URI in XML Signature. This includes a `Transforms` element, which contains a pipeline of `Transform` elements that must end with octets for the decryption algorithm to decode (just as the `Reference` URI and `Transforms` within XML Signature must end up with octets to feed the digest algorithm).

EncryptionProperties

The `EncryptionProperties` element has many similarities to the `SignatureProperties` element in XML Signature. Its purpose is to hold useful information about the encryption. The only difference is that `SignatureProperties` is a child of `Object`, whereas `EncryptionProperties` is directly descended from `EncryptedData`. There is so much similarity between the two that XML Encryption even adds a `Type`, for use with the XML Signature `Reference` element used to digitally sign `EncryptionProperties`. Listing 5.7 shows an example.

Listing 5.7   `<EncryptedData>` **with** `<EncryptionProperties>`

```
<MyDoc>
    <EncryptedData Id="EncryptedData1" xmlns:=http://www.w3.org/2001/04/xmlenc#>
        <CipherData>
            <CipherValue>. . .</CipherValue>
        </CipherData>
        <EncryptionProperties Id="EncryptedProperties1">
            <EncryptionProperty Target="EncryptedData1">
                <EncryptionDate>2003-02-28</EncryptionDate>
            </EncryptionProperty>
        </EncryptionProperties>
    </EncryptedData>
    <Signature>
        <SignedInfo>
            <Reference URI="EncryptionProperties1"
Type=http://www.w3.org/2001/04/xmlenc#EncryptionProperties>
                <DigestMethod . . ./>
                <DigestValue. . ./>
            </Reference>
        </SignedInfo>
    </Signature>
</MyDoc>
```

This document (MyDoc) consists of an `EncryptedData` item and a `Signature`. We declared one `EncryptionProperty` called `EncryptionDate`. Notice that the `Target` of the `EncryptionProperty` points to `EncryptedData1`. The `Signature` has one

`Reference` that points to the `EncryptionProperties` element, which contains the `EncryptionDate`. As a reminder, this `Signature` is a *Detached* Signature (because it neither *envelopes* nor is *enveloped* by the item being signed). As you can see, the `Type` associated with the reference indicates that what is being signed is an `EncryptionProperties` block (`http://www.w3.org/2001/04/xmlenc#EncryptionProperties`).

To underscore the important point made earlier, the *integrity* of an `EncryptedData` item is not ensured by the encryption mechanism. This is a little more obvious with `EncryptionProperties` because they are in the clear and could be modified by an intruder; therefore, the need for a digital signature might seem more obvious. It is true that if a `CipherValue` or `CipherReference` were manipulated, the results would not decrypt intelligibly (unless perhaps a non-chaining mode type cipher was used, in which case it might be possible to delete parts of the message and have other parts partially decrypt). However, changes due to data transfer errors or simply a nuisance attack can still cause problems, and because a computer often cannot know whether a decryption was successful by reading the message like a human can, automatically detecting this type of problem can be difficult. We talk more about this issue in the "Using XML Encryption and XML Signature Together" section later in this chapter, but, again, you should strongly consider signing things that you encrypt.

KeyInfo

In general, `KeyInfo` in XML Encryption has the same function as `KeyInfo` in XML Signature: to either directly provide you a key or to provide you a hint or pointer to find the key. The big difference is that `KeyInfo` in XML Signature was generally about providing you with a *public* key to verify the signature. In XML Encryption, `KeyInfo` is generally about providing you with an *encryption* key that is almost always a *shared* key. This difference is significant and explains why there are additions to the `KeyInfo` semantics introduced by XML Encryption. In XML Signature, you can put the key right into the signature without problem; a public key is public information. Obviously, it would be a bad idea to include the *encryption* key directly in the `KeyInfo` block because an attacker could just get the key and decrypt the cipher data (hence, the reason a shared key is often called a *secret key*). The obvious alternative approaches would be to either

- Leave out the key (assuming both sides already know the secret key).
- Provide a name or pointer to an encryption key (this approach is similar to the preceding item except a name or ID is associated with the key) with the knowledge that the recipient already possesses the key and can determine the correct key to use by the name or pointer provided.
- Encrypt the encryption key using public key technology so that only the holder of the private key would be able to decrypt the encryption key.

We are getting ahead of ourselves a little bit here, so let's review `KeyInfo` and then look specifically at `EncryptedKey`. `KeyInfo` is referenced from the XML Signature namespace and, when used in an XML Encryption context, can contain all the strategies described in the XML Signature chapter to either find a key or actually embed the key. As we just mentioned, embedding the encryption key without additional protection would be a bad idea, but using the naming or reference capabilities described in XML Signature `KeyInfo` is a completely legitimate strategy for referring to an encryption key because the encryption key is not included directly in the message. The most likely candidates for using this approach within an `EncryptedData KeyInfo` element would be

- `KeyName`—A unique name for the key that would be recognized by the receiver or looked up in a directory of some sort.

- `RetrievalMethod`—A URI that would point to a key for decrypting the data. This approach might be used, for example, to refer to a key elsewhere in the same document for another `EncryptedData` element that was encrypted under the same key.

XML Encryption extends the XML Signature `KeyInfo` with two new elements: `EncryptedKey` and `AgreementMethod`. `EncryptedKey` is required, so your XML Encryption processor must support it; `AgreementMethod` is optional. These elements are discussed next.

EncryptedKey

We have been giving hints along the way about `EncryptedKey`, so you may have already figured this out: `EncryptedKey` is simply another `EncryptedData` element that will hold an *encrypted* encryption key. It has the same syntax as `EncryptedData` because, as we mentioned earlier, they both come from the abstract type, `EncryptedType`. The implication is that `EncryptedKey` can be *recursive*, meaning an `EncryptedKey` could have its own `KeyInfo/EncryptedKey`, which in turn could have its own and so on.

The most obvious use for `EncryptedKey` is to encrypt the encryption key with the public key of a specific recipient and put it into the `KeyInfo/EncryptedKey` block. This process is often described as *digital enveloping* or a *key transport* strategy. The idea is to take advantage of the power of shared key technology (speed, more information can be encrypted) and the power of public key techology (primarily key management). The difficulty of using a pure shared key approach is the difficulty of communicating the secret shared key to the other party. Obviously, you cannot just include it in the clear within the XML. You could encrypt it, but if you encrypt it with another shared key, you have the same problem all over again. Ultimately, you will either

- Use a shared key strategy, which implies an agreement on the key that is not represented in the XML itself (a *shared secret* key). In this case, there is either no `KeyInfo` (the recipient knows the key) within the `EncryptedKey`, or there is some indicator of the key, such as `KeyName`, for the recipient to look up the key.

- Use a combined shared and public key strategy in which the shared symmetric key is encrypted using the public asymmetric key of the recipient. In this case, there might be no `KeyInfo` within the `EncryptedKey`, or any of the strategies for designating or providing a public key, as described in the "The `KeyInfo` Element" section in Chapter 4, could be used.

The simplified example in Listing 5.8 uses a public key to encrypt the shared key that is used to encrypt an `EncryptedData` block.

Listing 5.8   **A Public Key Used to Encrypt the Shared Key That Is Then Used to Encrypt the `<EncryptedData>` Block**

```
<EncryptedData>
    <EncryptionMethod Algorithm=http://www.w3.org/2001/04/xmlenc#aes128-cbc" />
    <ds:KeyInfo xmlns:ds="http://www.w3.org/2000/09/xmlsig#" />
        <EncryptedKey>
            <EncryptionMethod Algorithm=http://www.w3.org/2001/04/
xmlenc#rsa-1_5" />
            <ds:KeyInfo xmlns:ds=http://www.w3.org/2000/09/xmlsig# />
                <ds:X509Data>
                    <ds:X509SubjectName>
                        o=MyCompany,ou=Engineering,cn=Dave Remy
                    </ds:X509SubjectName>
                </ds:X509Data>
            <ds:/KeyInfo>
            <CipherData>
                <CipherValue>. . .</CipherValue>
            </CipherData>
        </EncryptedKey>
    </ds:KeyInfo>
    <CipherData>
        <CipherValue>. . .</CipherValue>
    </CipherData>
</EncryptedData>
```

This example shows XML Encryption with a shared key that is, in turn, encrypted using the recipient's public key. First, notice the two `KeyInfo` elements within this `EncryptedData`. The first `KeyInfo` is for the shared key that is used to decrypt the `CipherValue`, which is the child of `EncryptedData`. The second `KeyInfo`, which is a child of the `EncryptedKey`, designates the public key that was used to encrypt the shared key. To unwind this, the recipient would need to have access to the private key associated with the `SubjectName`—`o=MyCompany,ou=Engineering,cn=Dave Remy`—to decrypt the shared key that is encrypted in the `CipherValue` element (the first one). After the shared key is decrypted, it can then be used to decrypt the `CipherValue` that is the child of `EncryptedData`.

Considering that XML Encryption allows you to encrypt multiple elements (with or without tags) in an XML document, you could imagine that most or all of them might be encrypted using the same key. The `EncryptedKey` element has two elements to help facilitate this scenario: `ReferenceList`, which is discussed in the "`ReferenceList`" section, and `CarriedKeyName`, which is discussed in the "`CarriedKeyName`" section later.

AgreementMethod

`AgreementMethod`, whose support is optional in an XML Encryption engine, is another strategy for safely communicating a secret key. The `AgreementMethod` refers to a key agreement protocol that was used to generate the encryption key along with the key material necessary to repeat the encryption key generation on the recipient's side.

Normally, a key agreement protocol—for example, SSL—involves multiple synchronous steps that arrive at a session key (a limited-time-use shared encryption key); however, with XML Encryption, an asynchronous strategy is required. It is expected that the first step of the key agreement protocol—the generation of the public key agreement material—has already been done, and the public key agreement material of the recipient is available to the sender. The sender then uses the recipient's public key agreement material combined with the sender's private key material to generate the shared encryption key. The sender then includes her public key agreement material within the `AgreementMethod/OriginatorKeyInfo` element so that the recipient can then generate the same encryption key and use it to decrypt the encrypted data.

As mentioned earlier, this public key agreement material must be pregenerated and could also be signed by a certificate authority for trust reasons. Listing 5.9 shows an example from the XML Encryption specification of an `AgreementMethod` with agreement material that is wrapped in an X.509 certificate.

Listing 5.9   **The `<AgreementMethod>` Element**

```
<AgreementMethod
     Algorithm="http://www.w3.org/2001/04/xmlenc#dh"
     ds:xmlns="http://www.w3.org/2000/09/xmldsig#">
  <KA-Nonce>Zm9v</KA-Nonce>
  <ds:DigestMethod
   Algorithm="http://www.w3.org/2000/09/xmldsig#sha1"/>
  <OriginatorKeyInfo>
    <ds:X509Data><ds:X509Certificate>
      ...
    </ds:X509Certificate></ds:X509Data>
  </OriginatorKeyInfo>
  <RecipientKeyInfo>
     <ds:KeyValue>
       ...
     </ds:KeyValue>
  </RecipientKeyInfo>
</AgreementMethod>
```

We will not go into any more detail on `AgreementMethod` and the use of key agreement protocols for creating an encryption key. It appears that there is actually a good fit for a key agreement type approach for generating encryption keys in this manner with XML Encryption; however, we have not seen this approach used with any prevalence in XML security implementations in the real world and, consequently, in Web Services Security.

Perhaps the reason is that it is optional in the XML security specification or that these types of protocols have primarily been implemented in a synchronous fashion in the past.

ReferenceList

Imagine that you want to encrypt an XML document that contains multiple `EncryptedData` items that have all been encrypted with the same key. Listing 5.10 shows an example (leaving out the `KeyInfo` element for now) of this.

Listing 5.10   **Multiple** `<EncryptedData>` **Items Encrypted with the Same Key**

```
<Employee>
    <Name>Dave Remy</Name>
    <SocialSecurityNumber>
        <EncryptedData Type="http://www.w3.org/2000/09/xmldsig#content">
            <EncryptionMethod Algorithm=". . .">
            <CipherData><CipherValue>. . .</CipherValue></CipherData>
        </EncryptedData>
    </SocialSecurityNumber>
    <Salary>
        <EncryptedData Type="http://www.w3.org/2000/09/xmldsig#content">
            <EncryptionMethod Algorithm=". . .">
            <CipherData><CipherValue>. . .</CipherValue></CipherData>
        </EncryptedData>
    </Salary>
</Employee>
```

Listing 5.10 has just two `EncryptedData` elements, `SocialSecurityNumber` and `Salary`, but it would be easy to imagine many more within the same document. Such an example could add a lot of size and redundancy to the XML document if you had to add the same `KeyInfo` block for each of the encrypted data items. The `ReferenceList` element (along with `CarriedKeyName`, as you will see) is a strategy for dealing with this situation. Let's expand the previous example using `ReferenceList` in Listing 5.11.

Listing 5.11   **Expanded** `<Employee>` **Element Now Using the** `<ReferenceList>`
    Element for Dealing Efficiently with Multiple `<EncryptedData>`
    Elements

```
<Employee>
    <Name>Dave Remy</Name>
    <SocialSecurityNumber>
        <EncryptedData id="socsecnum" Type="http://www.w3.org/2000/09/
xmldsig#content">
            <EncryptionMethod Algorithm=". . ." />
            <CipherData><CipherValue>. . .</CipherValue></CipherData>
        </EncryptedData>
```

Listing 5.11 **Continued**

```
    </SocialSecurityNumber>
    <Salary>
        <EncryptedData id="salary" Type="http://www.w3.org/2000/09/
xmldsig#content">
            <EncryptionMethod Algorithm=". . .">
            <CipherData><CipherValue>. . .</CipherValue></CipherData>
        </EncryptedData>
    </Salary>
    <EncryptedKey>
        <EncryptionMethod Algorithm=". . ." />
        <CipherData>
            <CipherValue>. . .</CipherValue>
        </CipherData>
        <ReferenceList>
            <DataReference URI="#socsecnum" />
            <DataReference URI="#salary" />
        </ReferenceList>
    </EncryptedKey>
</Employee>
```

Notice that, rather than including a separate `KeyInfo/EncryptedKey` for each `EncryptedData`, we created a standalone `EncryptedKey` with a `ReferenceList` to each of the `EncryptedData` items that had been encrypted with the key.

`ReferenceList` can contain a list of `DataReference` elements and/or `KeyReference` elements. If a `KeyReference` is used, the target of the reference is an `EncryptedKey` rather than an `EncryptedData` element. This approach would be valuable when using a key that was used to encrypt a set of keys such as a *master encryption key*.

When we discuss WS–Security in Chapter 7, you will see that `ReferenceList` is a fundamental concept for referring to the parts of the message that are encrypted when XML Encryption is used in a SOAP header.

CarriedKeyName

`ReferenceList` provides a mechanism for referring to all the `EncryptedData` elements from a single `EncryptedKey` element; however, in every other circumstance we have talked about, the `EncryptedData` element has a reference to the key using `KeyInfo`. The `CarriedKeyName` element provides the `EncryptedKey` with a name, so the `KeyInfo` can point to it using `KeyName`. Listing 5.12 shows the preceding example with the addition of a `CarriedKeyName` element to identify the `EncryptedKey` structure.

Listing 5.12   Previous Example with `<CarriedKeyName>` **Added to Identify the**
`<EncryptedKey>` **Structure**

```
<Employee>
    <Name>Dave Remy</Name>
    <SocialSecurityNumber>
        <EncryptedData id="socsecnum" Type="http://www.w3.org/2000/09/
xmldsig#content">
            <KeyInfo>
                <KeyName>Jothy Rosenberg</KeyName>
            </KeyInfo>
            <EncryptionMethod Algorithm=". . ." />
            <CipherData><CipherValue>. . .</CipherValue></CipherData>
        </EncryptedData>
    </SocialSecurityNumber>
    <Salary>
        <EncryptedData id="salary" Type="http://www.w3.org/2000/09/
xmldsig#content">
            <EncryptionMethod Algorithm=". . .">
            <CipherData><CipherValue>. . .</CipherValue></CipherData>
        </EncryptedData>
    </Salary>
    <EncryptedKey>
        <EncryptionMethod Algorithm=". . ." />
        <CipherData>
            <CipherValue>. . .</CipherValue>
        </CipherData>
        <ReferenceList>
            <DataReference URI="#socsecnum" />
            <DataReference URI="#salary" />
        </ReferenceList>
        <CarriedKeyName>Jothy Rosenberg</CarriedKeyName>
    </EncryptedKey>
</Employee>
```

As you can see in this example, when you add a `CarriedKeyName` element to the
`EncryptedKey`, you can then refer to it using the `KeyInfo` `KeyName` element. The advantage here is that an XML Encryption processor (or a reader, for that matter) can navigate from either the `EncryptedData` element itself *or* from the `ReferenceList`.

Super Encryption

It is entirely possible for an `EncryptedData` element to encrypt other `EncryptedData` elements. This type of encryption, which can occur an unlimited number of times, is called *super encryption*. The only limitation here is that you have to encrypt the entire `EncryptedData` element; you cannot just encrypt one of its children. If you have a document with multiple encryptions in it, perhaps with multiple recipients involved, you might want to encrypt the entire document under one EncryptedData element. Doing this is fine. The receiving XML Encryption process repeatedly decrypts until no more EncryptedData elements are left to decrypt.

XML Encryption Processing

XML Encryption processing involves two different but obviously related processes: the encryption process and the decryption process. We describe each of them in turn.

Encryption Process

The steps in the encryption process are as described in the following sections.

1. Choose an Encryption Algorithm

Under the EncryptionMethod element, you choose one of the supported encryption algorithms, such as 3DES or AES.

2. Obtain an Encryption Key and Optionally Represent It

An encryption key can be obtained and then represented in a wide variety of ways. Often the encryption key is generated, because generating a shared symmetric key is generally a relatively efficient operation, but it can also be pre-generated and looked up in some registry or file that contains an existing key.

We discussed strategies for representing a key in the section on the KeyInfo element earlier. Such strategies can range from not including anything about the key at all (meaning that the encryption key is shared "out-of-band" and both parties know contextually what the key is); to including a key name as a pointer to the key, using some sort of key agreement protocol; or encrypting the encryption key using the public key of the message's receiver.

3. Serialize Message Data

Encryption algorithms expect octets (a stream of bytes), so the XML data to be encrypted must be converted to octets.

4. Encrypt the Data

Now that you have chosen the algorithm, the encryption key, and the raw data, you have everything you need to do the actual cryptographic encryption.

5. Specify the Data Type

Remember that the EncryptedDataType attribute specifies either *element* or *content* encryption. This element (which is optional but should probably always be included), along with the optional MimeType and Encoding, are then specified.

6. Build the Corresponding EncryptedData Structure

All the pieces necessary to construct the EncryptedData element have now been identified. They are then assembled into the EncryptedData structure described earlier in this chapter in the "EncryptedData" section.

Decryption Process

We just described the steps for encryption; next are the high-level steps for decryption.

1. Get Algorithm, Parameters, and `KeyInfo`

The encryption algorithm (and related parameters) and the `KeyInfo` element are optional because they may already be known to the receiver based on some agreement outside the message exchange. If they are not already known, any parameters specific to this encryption algorithm and `KeyInfo` elements should be included in the `EncryptedData` element's `EncryptionMethod`.

2. Locate the Key

If the key was agreed to outside the message exchange, locating the key is not necessary. Otherwise, the `KeyInfo` block must be used to find the key. As we have discussed in this chapter and the preceding chapter, you can include a key in various ways. If the `KeyInfo` contains a reference to an `EncryptedKey`, this decryption process must occur recursively until the encryption key is resolved.

3. Decrypt Data

Remember that the encrypted data (`CipherData`) can be in one of two forms: an inline `CipherValue` or a `CipherReference`. The decryption process varies by which `CipherData` child is present; however, the result of either of the following steps is the raw bytes needed to feed into the decryption algorithm:

- `CipherValue`—If the `CipherData` is represented as a `CipherValue`, the content of the `CipherValue` element is Base-64 decoded into bytes.

- `CipherReference`—If the `CipherData` is represented as a `CipherReference`, the URI is dereferenced, and any specified Transforms are applied.

4. Process XML Elements or XML Element Content

At this point, the decryption has occurred, and the UTF-8 encoded bytes are available. If the `EncryptedDataType` attribute has been specified (either `element` or `content`), the decrypted information is placed back into the original XML, replacing the `EncryptedData` structure. If the `EncryptedDataType` attribute is not specified, go to the next step.

5. Process Non–XML Element (Type Not Specified)

If the `EncrypteDataType` attribute is not specified, the result of the decryption is passed back to the application. The `EncryptedData`, `MimeType`, and `Encoding` are optional advisory information to help the application know how to deal with the data.

Using XML Encryption and XML Signature Together

As we have mentioned previously, there are times, probably most of the time actually, when XML Signature is an important partner to XML Encryption. The relationship between XML Signature and XML Encryption may be more subtle than you might have originally thought. Because parts of the `EncryptedData/EncryptedKey` elements are in the clear, they could be changed, making the decryption invalid. For example, Listing 5.13 shows what you might expect to see in an XML document containing XML Encryption.

Listing 5.13   **An Example of How** `<Signature>` **Enters into XML Encryption Situations to Protect the Integrity of Parts of the** `<EncryptedData>` **Elements**

```
<MyDocument>
    <EncryptedData id="encryptedData1">
        <EncryptionMethod Algorithm=". . ." />
        <CipherText>
            <CipherValue>. . .</CipherValue>
        </CipherText>
        <KeyInfo>
            <EncryptedKey>
                <EncryptionMethod Algorithm=". . ." />
                <CipherText>
                    <CipherValue>. . . </CipherValue>
                </CipherText>
                <KeyInfo>
                    <X509Data>
                        <X509Subject>O=HisCompany,OU=Technology,CN=Jothy
Roesenberg</X509Subject>
                    </X509Data>
                </KeyInfo>
            </EncryptedKey>
        </KeyInfo>
    </EncryptedData>
    <Signature>
        <SignedInfo>
            <CanonicalizationMethod Algorithm=". . ." />
            <SignatureMethod Algorithm=". . ." />
            <Reference URI="#encryptedData1">
                <DigestMethod Algorithm=". . ." />
                <DigestValue>. . .</DigestValue>
            </Reference>
        </SignedInfo>
        <SignatureValue>. . .</SignatureValue>
        <KeyInfo>
```

Listing 5.13 **Continued**

```
            <X509Data>
                <X509Subject>O=MyCompany,OU=Engineering,CN=David
Remy</X509Subject>
            </X509Data>
        </KeyInfo>
    </Signature>
</MyDocument>
```

The main point of this example is that the `Signature` points back up to the `EncryptedData` element with the ID `"encryptedData1"`. The objective here is to protect the `EncryptedData` information from an integrity and authenticity perspective. For example, based on your confidence that the public key is really associated with the sender and recipient (David Remy and Jothy Rosenberg in this example) and that the private key of each has not been compromised, you *might* be able to reasonably make the following statement about the document: This document was prepared by David Remy (or at least by an individual holding David Remy's private key) and can be read only by Jothy Rosenberg (or at least only by an individual holding Jothy Rosenberg's private key).

One criticism of this approach is that the `Signature` and `EncryptedData` elements are detached from each other, and it would be possible to remove the `Signature` without the recipient inherently knowing that the `Signature` had ever existed—perhaps even substituting his signature in place such that the document appears to be authentically originating from another creator/sender. In other words, you need to have a *policy* for requiring signatures in a certain manner accompanying `EncryptedData` elements; otherwise, the document is not self-protecting. We describe this subject in more detail later in this chapter. This argument leads you to consider placing the `Signature` within the `EncryptedData`. To accomplish this, you first sign the target information and *then* encrypt it. For example, consider the signed XML in Listing 5.14.

Listing 5.14 **Setting Up to Place the** `<Signature>` **Element Inside the** `<EncryptedData>` **Element, You Sign the** `<Customer>` **Element with an Enveloped Signature**

```
<Order>
    <LineItem sku="82394" quantity="1">
        <ProductName>Birdcage</ProductName>
    </LineItem>
    <Customer id="customer" custNum="A2345">
        <FirstName>Fred</FirstName>
        <MiddleInit>L</MiddleInit>
        <LastName>Jones</LastName>
        <CreditCard>
            <CreditCardType>VISA</CreditCardType>
            <CreditCardNumber>43343456343566</CreditCardNumber>
```

Listing 5.14   **Continued**

```
            <CreditCardExpiration>10/08</CreditCardExpiration>
        </CreditCard>
        <Signature>
            <SignedInfo>
                <CanonicalizationMethod Algorigthm=". . ." />
                <SignatureMethod Algorithm=". . ." />
                <Reference URI="#customer">
                    <Transform Algorithm=".../#envelopedSignature" />
                    <DigestMethod Algorithm=". . ." />
                    <DigestValue>. . .</DigestValue>
                </Reference>
            </SignedInfo>
            <SignatureValue>. . . </SignatureValue>
            <KeyInfo>
                <X509Data>
                    <X509SubjectName>O=MyCompany,OU=Engineering,CN=David
Remy</X509SubjectName>
                </X509Data>
            </KeyInfo>
        </Signature>
    </Customer>
</Order>
```

In this example, the Customer element has been signed with an *Enveloped Signature*. Now assume that you want the Customer element to be encrypted. The document would then look like Listing 5.15 after encryption.

Listing 5.15   **Protecting the** <Signature> **Element Inside the** <EncryptedData>
             Element, Making the <Signature> **Element Not Even Visible**

```
<Order>
    <LineItem sku="82394" quantity="1">
        <ProductName>Birdcage</ProductName>
    </LineItem>
    <EncryptedData id="encryptedData1">
        <EncryptionMethod Algorithm=". . ." />
        <CipherText>
            <CipherValue>. . . </CipherValue>
        <CipherText>
        <KeyInfo>
            <EncryptedKey>
                <EncryptionMethod Algorithm=". . ." />
                <CipherText>
                    <CipherValue>. . .</CipherValue>
                </CipherText>
```

Listing 5.15   **Continued**

```
            <KeyInfo>
                <X509Data>
                    <X509Subject>O=HisCompany,OU=Technology,CN=Jothy
                     Rosenberg</X509Subject>
                </X509Data>
            </KeyInfo>
          </EncryptedKey>
        </KeyInfo>
    </EncryptedData>
</Order>
```

This approach has a couple of advantages. First, the `Signature` element, which could contain sensitive data in some circumstances, is not visible at all. For example, you might use this approach if you don't want any reader of the document to know that you are the originator of the content and yet still allow the recipient to know and validate the originator. Second, the order of processing may be clearer. In this example, obviously, the decryption would occur, and *then* the signature verification would occur. In the first example in this section, the *order* of processing is not clear (we discuss how to surmount this issue in the next section "The Decryption Transform for XML Signature").

The problem with this approach is that the integrity of the `EncryptedData` and related elements are not guaranteed. It would still be possible for someone to mess around with these elements and break the encryption—or even to substitute an entire new `EncryptedData` block.

As you can see, there are trade-offs with both approaches, and you will have to make your implementation decision based on the context of your specific situation. In high-security situations, you might implement a multi-layered approach that includes signatures, encryption, and then signatures again. As you determine your *policy* solution for XML Signature and XML Encryption in each situation, the most significant *technical* issue becomes telling the signature and encryption processor the sequence to process the XML Encryption and XML Signature. Consider the first XML Encryption and Signature example shown in this section. How would a processor know whether to process the XML Encryption or the XML Signature first? If the `EncryptedData` element were processed first, the signature would break because what was signed was the `EncryptedData` element itself. This sequencing requirement brought about the need for a new Transform introduced into XML Signature.

The Decryption Transform for XML Signature

The XML Decryption Transform is an additional Transform for XML Signatures[1] that enables an XML Signature processing engine to recognize `EncryptedData` structures that were encrypted prior to the XML Signature being applied so that they are *not*

---

1. The Decryption Transform for XML Signature has its own specification at
`http://www.w3.org/TR/2002/PR-xmlenc-decrypt-20021003`.

decrypted when validating the signature. An example will help you to understand this concept. Let's use an example similar to the one that is used in the specification. Sam is purchasing an item from Sally's furniture store, and MoneyBags Bank is being passed account information that will be used to verify and debit the account. In this scenario, the requirement is that Sally must be unable to read Sam's account information, so she simply forwards it to the bank. To accomplish this, Sam (or more correctly, the program Sam is using to submit this order) will encrypt his account information to MoneyBags Bank and then sign and encrypt the entire XML document so that Sally will know that a) Sam is verified to be the one who sent the order, and b) the order has not been changed in transit. Sam's order for two canvas hammocks and a matching table looks like Listing 5.16.

Listing 5.16   **An Order with Payment Information That Needs to Be Protected**

```
<Order>
    <CustInfo>
        <Name>Sam Spade</Name>
        <Address>123 Anywhere Lane, James, MO 34586</Address>
    </CustInfo>
    <LineItems>
        <LineItem skuID="12345">
            <Name>Country Hammock</Name>
            <Quantity>2</Quantity>
            <Price>$50.00USD</Price>
        </LineItem>
        <LineItem skuID="12346">
            <Name>Country Hammock Table</Name>
            <Quantity>1</Quantity>
            <Price>$50.00USD</Price>
        </LineItem>
    </LineItems>
    <PaymentInfo>
        <Bank>MoneyBags Bank</Bank>
        <AccountNumber>13245459</AccountNumber>
        <Amount>$150.00USD</Amount>
    </PaymentInfo>
</Order>
```

Now, in Listing 5.17, Sam encrypts the sensitive bank account information using MoneyBag Bank's public key and using content-based encryption so that the attribute "MoneyBags" stays in the clear and Sally will know which bank to route it to.

Listing 5.17   <Order> **from Listing 5.16 with the Confidential Payment Information**
               Encrypted

```
<Order>
    <CustInfo>
        <Name>Sam Spade</Name>
        <Address>123 Anywhere Lane, James, MO 34586</Address>
    </CustInfo>
    <LineItems>
        <LineItem skuID="12345">
            <Name>Country Hammock</Name>
            <Quantity>2</Quantity>
            <Price>$50.00USD</Price>
        </LineItem>
        <LineItem skuID="12346">
            <Name>Country Hammock Table</Name>
            <Quantity>1</Quantity>
            <Price>$50.00USD</Price>
        </LineItem>
    </LineItems>
    <PaymentInfo bank="MoneyBags">
        <EncryptedData Type="http://www.w3.org/2000/09/xmldsig#content">
            <EncryptionMethod Algorithm="http://www.w3.org/2001/04/
xmlenc#aes128-cbc">
            <CipherData>
                <CipherValue>. . .</CipherValue>
            </CipherData>
        </EncryptedData>
    </PaymentInfo>
</Order>
```

Next, in Listing 5.18, Sam signs the entire message using an *Enveloped Signature* to
demonstrate to Sally that he stands behind what is being sent and to provide for message
integrity:

Listing 5.18   <Order> **from Listing 5.17 Now Signed with an Enveloped Signature for**
               Integrity

```
<Order>
    <CustInfo>
        <Name>Sam Spade</Name>
        <Address>123 Anywhere Lane, James, MO 34586</Address>
    </CustInfo>
    <LineItems>
        <LineItem skuID="12345">
            <Name>Country Hammock</Name>
            <Quantity>2</Quantity>
            <Price>$50.00USD</Price>
        </LineItem>
```

Listing 5.18   **Continued**

```
            <LineItem skuID="12346">
                <Name>Country Hammock Table</Name>
                <Quantity>1</Quantity>
                <Price>$50.00USD</Price>
            </LineItem>
        </LineItems>
        <PaymentInfo bank="MoneyBags">
            <EncryptedData id="payInfo" Type="http://www.w3.org/2000/09/
xmldsig#content">
                <EncryptionMethod Algorithm=" http://www.w3.org/2001/04/
xmlenc#aes128-cbc" />
                <CipherData>
                    <CipherValue>. . .</CipherValue>
                </CipherData>
                <KeyInfo>
                    <KeyName>MoneyBags, Inc.</Keyname>
                </KeyInfo>
            </EncryptedData>
        </PaymentInfo>
        <Signature>
            <SignedInfo>
                <CanonicalizationMethod Algorithm="http://www.w3.org/2001/10/
xml-exc-c14n#" />
                <SignatureMethod Algorithm="http://www.w3.org/2000/09/
xmldsig#rsa-sha1" />
                <Reference URI="">
                    <Transform=http://www.w3.org/2000/09/
xmldsig#enveloped-signature" />
                    <Transform="http://www.w3.org/2002/07/decrypt#XML">
                        <Except URI="#payInfo">
                    </Transform>
                </Reference>
            </SignedInfo>
            <SignatureValue>. . .</SignatureValue>
            <KeyInfo>
                <KeyName>Sam Spade</KeyName>
            </KeyInfo>
        </Signature>
    </Order>
```

As you can see in this example, Sam signed the whole Order (Reference URI="") with an Enveloped Signature but also added a *Decryption Transform*. This Decryption Transform has an Except element that points to the encrypted data "payInfo". It says to the Signature processor, "Decrypt everything *except* these URIs before validating the signature." Next, in Listing 5.19, Sam will encrypt the entire message, minus the outer Order element and the `Signature` (which is a little contrived for this example), to send to Sally:

Listing 5.19   `<Order>` **from Listing 5.18 Now with the Entire Message Except for**   `<Signature>` **Encrypted**

```
<Order>
    <EncryptedData id="myOrder" Type="http://www.w3.org/2000/09/
xmldsig#content">
        <EncryptionMethod Algorithm="http://www.w3.org/2001/04/
xmlenc#aes128-cbc">
        <CipherData>
            <CipherValue>. . .</CipherValue>
        </CipherData>
        <KeyInfo>
            <KeyName>MoneyBags, Inc.</Keyname>
        </KeyInfo>
    </EncryptedData>
    <Signature>
        <SignedInfo>
            <CanonicalizationMethod Algorithm="http://www.w3.org/2001/10/
xml-exc-c14n#" />
            <SignatureMethod Algorithm="http://www.w3.org/2000/09/
xmldsig#rsa-sha1" />
            <Reference URI="">
                <Transform=http://www.w3.org/2000/09/
xmldsig#enveloped-signature" />
                <Transform="http://www.w3.org/2002/07/decrypt#XML">
                    <Except URI="#payInfo">
                </Transform>
            </Reference>
        </SignedInfo>
        <SignatureValue>. . .</SignatureValue>
        <KeyInfo>
            <KeyName>Sam Spade</KeyName>
        </KeyInfo>
    </Signature>
</Order>
```

The preceding then is the final form of the message sent to Sally. For it to be processed correctly, the processor has to unwind it in the right order. The XML Security processor that Sally is using must be both XML Encryption and XML Signature aware. This processor first attempts to process the `Signature` element. The `Signature` references the `Order` element, and within the *Decryption Transform*, it references the `"payInfo"` element. Because it cannot locate the `#payInfo` element, it must assume that `#payInfo` is within the `#myOrder EncryptedData` element. Because there are no `Signature` elements with an Except `#myOrder` Transform, `#myOrder` is decrypted. This results in the intermediate XML structure shown earlier but repeated in Listing 5.20.

Listing 5.20   **Intermediate Step in Unwinding the** `<Order>` **After Initial Decryption but Before Signature Processing**

```
<Order>
    <CustInfo>
        <Name>Sam Spade</Name>
        <Address>123 Anywhere Lane, James, MO 34586</Address>
    </CustInfo>
    <LineItems>
        <LineItem skuID="12345">
            <Name>Country Hammock</Name>
            <Quantity>2</Quantity>
            <Price>$50.00USD</Price>
        </LineItem>
        <LineItem skuID="12346">
            <Name>Country Hammock Table</Name>
            <Quantity>1</Quantity>
            <Price>$50.00USD</Price>
        </LineItem>
    </LineItems>
    <PaymentInfo bank="MoneyBags">
        <EncryptedData id="payInfo" Type="http://www.w3.org/2000/09/
xmldsig#content">
            <EncryptionMethod Algorithm=" http://www.w3.org/2001/04/
xmlenc#aes128-cbc">
            <CipherData>
                <CipherValue>. . .</CipherValue>
            </CipherData>
            <KeyInfo>
                <KeyName>MoneyBags, Inc.</Keyname>
            </KeyInfo>
        </EncryptedData>
    </PaymentInfo>
    <Signature>
        <SignedInfo>
            <CanonicalizationMethod Algorithm="http://www.w3.org/2001/10/
xml-exc-c14n#" />
            <SignatureMethod Algorithm="http://www.w3.org/2000/09/
xmldsig#rsa-sha1" />
            <Reference URI="">
                <Transform=http://www.w3.org/2000/09/
xmldsig#enveloped-signature" />
                <Transform="http://www.w3.org/2002/07/decrypt#XML">
                    <Except URI="#payInfo">
                </Transform>
            </Reference>
        </SignedInfo>
        <SignatureValue>. . .</SignatureValue>
```

Listing 5.20   **Continued**

```
        <KeyInfo>
            <KeyName>Sam Spade</KeyName>
        </KeyInfo>
    </Signature>
</Order>
```

Now the Signature processing can be attempted again. This time the #payInfo is resolved, and there are no other EncryptedData elements. Note if there had been other EncryptedData elements, they would have been decrypted prior to signature validation. The Signature is validated correctly, and Sally extracts the information destined for MoneyBags Bank for payment validation, wraps it in a PaymentRequest, and signs the message with her private key, as shown in Listing 5.21.

Listing 5.21   <PaymentRequest> **Created from Signature Validation of the Payment Information Embedded in the Incoming** <Order>

```
<PaymentRequest>
    <PaymentInfo bank="MoneyBags">
        <EncryptedData id="payInfo" Type="http://www.w3.org/2000/09/
xmldsig#content">
            <EncryptionMethod Algorithm=" http://www.w3.org/2001/04/
xmlenc#aes128-cbc" />
            <CipherData>
                <CipherValue>. . .</CipherValue>
            </CipherData>
            <KeyInfo>
                <KeyName>MoneyBags, Inc.</Keyname>
            </KeyInfo>
        </EncryptedData>
    </PaymentInfo>
    <Signature>
        <SignedInfo>
            <CanonicalizationMethod Algorithm="http://www.w3.org/2001/10/
xml-exc-c14n#" />
            <SignatureMethod Algorithm="http://www.w3.org/2000/09/
xmldsig#rsa-sha1" />
            <Reference URI="">
                <Transform=http://www.w3.org/2000/09/
xmldsig#enveloped-signature" />
                <Transform="http://www.w3.org/2002/07/decrypt#XML">
                    <Except URI="#payInfo">
                </Transform>
            </Reference>
        </SignedInfo>
```

Listing 5.21   **Continued**

```
        <SignatureValue>. . .</SignatureValue>
        <KeyInfo>
            <KeyName>Sally Brown</KeyName>
        </KeyInfo>
    </Signature>
</PaymentRequest>
```

Notice that the Decryption Transform pointing to `#payInfo` is still there because it is not the decrypted payment information that Sally is signing. By signing this, Sally is attesting that she has received this encrypted data; she is saying nothing about the integrity of the internal plaintext. MoneyBags Bank will now receive this message, process it, and return a signed acknowledgement to Sally that payment was processed successfully. We will spare you the acknowledgement back to Sally and from Sally back to Sam, but, of course, the messages would be signed and possibly partially encrypted in a similar manner to the message shown previously.

As you can see from these examples, in practice XML Signature and XML Encryption become closely related when you consider documents that flow through a workflow or documents that are exchanged in a SOAP message.

XML Encryption and XML Signature Strategies

In our opinion, you will most often want to *encrypt* and then *sign* when working at the message security level (such as in WS-Security, discussed in Chapter 7), and *sign* and then *encrypt* when working with information that will be viewable by a person. The reasoning here is that when a person is viewing a piece of information, what is signed should be representative of what the person saw (as mentioned in Chapter 4), thus encryption before signing would violate this principle. However, with message-level integrity, the server attests to the integrity of the message bits themselves, and this concept is not violated by signing encrypted data.

You should strongly consider signing the `EncryptedData` elements even when your primary requirement is encryption. Although the additional XML Signature does not make the encryption any stronger, it increases the reliability and robustness of your encryption because you can be confident that the configuration parameters (for example, `EncryptionMethod`) and the encrypted content are what the sender intended to send.

In some scenarios, signing the encrypted data could leave a security hole in that the encryption is not tied directly to the signature (although the signature is tied to the encryption). This violates a design goal of having a "self-describing" security mechanism such that traversing a document, discovering security artifacts, and validating them should, in the end, if there are no validation errors, result in a secure XML document.

XML Encryption and XML Schema

As described in Chapter 2, "The Foundations of Web Services," XML Schemas are used to validate the structure and data types of elements in a document. Use of XML Encryption results in `EncryptedData` elements that fold in and hide sets of elements, which then makes the original underlying XML Schema no longer valid. The external structure just doesn't match the new XML structure after the `EncryptedData` elements have been introduced and the original elements hidden. Using current XML Schema technology, a new schema would be required for each possible persistent layer of decryption until the document is fully decrypted. For example, say you have a document in a workflow situation, and it is going to the Receiving department, the Purchasing department, and finally to the department that ordered an item. You encrypted part of the document for each of these three recipients. To achieve schema validation at each stage, you would have to create three different schemas that represent the decrypted state for each department.

Some people in the standards world argue that there needs to be a way to designate elements as encryptable in XML Schemas, therefore allowing the possibility of a single XML Schema across all the different states of encryption. This work is in progress, and it is not clear that this idea has momentum. Therefore, you might need a schema for each stage of decryption for now—or, more likely, go without XML Schema validation.

Summary

XML Encryption is a flexible, powerful technology for keeping all or parts of XML documents or even external files confidential. It builds on XML Signature, using important parts of the XML Signature grammar such as `KeyInfo` and the `Reference` structure. XML encryption allows the use of shared (secret) key technology alone or to combine public key and shared key, utilizing the power of both.

Arguably the most important element within XML Encryption is the `EncryptedType` abstract element; it shows up in an XML document as one of its two derived elements, `EncryptedData` and `EncryptedKey`, which have exactly the same structure. As the name implies, `EncryptedData` shows up whenever some piece of data is encrypted. When the target is XML, `EncryptedData` indicates whether the encryption is of the type `element`—the entire XML fragment is encrypted including the outer tags—or `content`—the outer tags are left intact and everything within the XML fragment has been encrypted.

As we continue our discussions about Web Services Security, you will see that XML Encryption and XML Signature are fundamental parts of the *message-level* security of an overall Web Services Security strategy. In addition, they are useful tools for you to have in your toolbox in a myriad of situations, from simply needing to validate the integrity of a piece of data to keeping important, sensitive data confidential even beyond the life of the transaction.

6

Portable Identity, Authentication, and Authorization

W EB SERVICES INCREASINGLY CROSS ORGANIZATIONAL boundaries. Yet previously there was no standard way to convey security attributes about individuals from one organization to another. How subjects (individuals or entities) are identified, how their digital credentials are created and maintained, and how permissions for access to resources are specified were not standardized, so sharing identity or security attributes outside one organization was extremely difficult. Increasingly, as inter-organizational integrations become commonplace, the need for federation of security attributes becomes more and more important. It is this desire to establish identity in one organization with one set of policies and procedures—a trust domain—to be able to assert rights to do things in a separate and distinct trust domain—be portable—that motivates this chapter about portable identity, authentication, and authorization. First, we need to establish common vocabulary covering all the security aspects of identity we will be considering.

Digital security has always revolved around identity. Many questions focus on identity. For example, who is accessing my network or my information? Who is this request from? Who vouches for this information being correct? Who sent me this confidential information? How do I know it is really the sender? All these security questions revolve around identity.

Identity refers to an individual or an entity—such as a machine—that might represent itself to an organization. We use the term *subject* to refer to an entity that is asserting its identity. Establishing identity is a critical prerequisite in determining the legitimate actions that a subject may perform. A subject's identity is initially established and verified in some trust domain by a third party, which results in the creation of *credentials*. When a subject identity established and verified in one trust domain wants to assert its identity and rights in another trust domain, this identity is said to be *portable*. Credentials are presented as *assertions* when the subject identity who possesses them wants to initiate some action such as a transaction. An assertion is a claim that may be challenged and proven before being believed. *Authentication* is an assertion that a subject is who she claims to be, and it is proven by verifying that the presented credentials are legitimately in the possession of the subject. *Authorization* is an assertion that the subject identity is allowed to perform a specific action, and it must be proven before the requested actions are allowed.

Web services use SOAP to connect machines and applications by moving messages between them and causing remote actions to be performed on a machine that may be part of a different organization, as in business-to-business (B2B) integrations. SOAP defines how software should interact for collaborative commerce. But these types of B2B interactions may involve numerous companies that are aggregating their services. Just as all participants must be authenticated in a closed system for any participants to establish trust, a collaborative commerce environment needs all participants authenticated in a compatible way across the entire virtual system spanning multiple trust domains.

When two entities with different trust models want to interact, SOAP has no standardized and interoperable way to communicate their security properties to establish trust. Because SOAP messages are sent from one trust domain to another, the identity of the requesting subject and its assertions must travel with the message (that is, be portable). In this way, the receiving trust domain can apply its trust model to the message and the identity on whose behalf the message was sent. Security Assertion Markup Language (SAML) is the XML standard created to enable portable identities and the assertions these identities want to make.

SAML's addition to the Web Services Security constellation is important for four key reasons:

1. SAML is a standard XML format suitable for but not tied to any transport. No particular API is mandated; all the normal XML tools apply to SAML.

2. SAML includes a standard message exchange protocol, so it clearly defines how you ask for the information needed.

3. SAML specifies the rules for how it is transported, making interoperability explicit at the specification level.

4. SAML is unlike other security approaches because of its expression of security in the form of assertions about subjects. Most other approaches depend on a central certificate authority to issue certificates used to guarantee secure communications. This is especially important for Web services in which secured data flows through several systems for a transaction to be completed.

Introduction to and Motivation for SAML

Identity is the basis for security: A system is secure if the identities of all users (good identities) are known and intruders (bad identities) are blocked. Information is secure if the sender is known to the receiver, the information is provably intact and unaltered, and all secret information is constantly kept confidential from all non-participants. The identity of valid users must move around when information moves from one trust domain to another. The fact that Web services will be used to cross trust domains makes portable trust an early requirement for Web Services Security.

SAML pre-dates Web services, but because SAML addressed precisely the Web services need for portable identity, the OASIS Web Services Security technical committee working on WS-Security applied SAML to Web services, and it became part of WS-Security. Later, we describe how SAML tokens are incorporated into the WS-Security SOAP extensions.

SAML 1.1 is an OASIS-approved standard. It is also the foundation for Project Liberty, which is an important manifestation of Web Services Security, based on a concept called *federated identity*. We discuss Project Liberty in some detail later in this chapter.

The Problems SAML Addresses

In the past, each organization acted as its own identification authority for its users. The organization knew who its users were, established identity information about them, issued them credentials—maybe just in the form of usernames and passwords—and managed the life cycle of those credentials up to the time the individuals left the organization and ceased to have valid identities with the organization. Rights and permissions for each individual were maintained within the organization's information infrastructure. Each organization had a well-defined set of policies and procedures for how users were identified, what information was retained, how credentials were created and maintained, and how permissions for information access were administered and enforced. In other words, each organization formed its own trust domain. There was very little need for these credentials to cross out of the organization's own trust domain to interact with another trust domain, and doing so would have been nearly impossible.

The first indication that this model was too restrictive came from the larger, more complex organizations with large numbers of users and large collections of applications, each requiring secured access by users. The default mode of operation was that each application required an authenticated login for each user each time access to a new application was required. This led to a strong desire for single sign-on capability because users, at best, were inconvenienced by multiple logins and, at worst, became a large, expensive help desk burden due to lost, expired, or compromised passwords.

The second indication that a single trust domain model of identity would not work—especially for Web services—is the strong push for federated identity. Suppose Web services are used to integrate ChosenRentals.com as the preferred rental car provider, ChosenAirline.com as the preferred air carrier, and ChosenHotels.com as the preferred hotel chain for Company.com so that employees of Company.com can directly book their travel and obtain the best rates from the chosen providers. A Company.com employee asserts his identity and his ability to make travel arrangements. Before Web services, this employee would have had to visit the Web sites of all these suppliers and deal with multiple logins and passwords. The sites would administer all the passwords for the Company.com employees and their other corporate customers. With Web services, SAML messages assert the identity and authorizations of this employee at all the supplier systems without his having to make multiple manual site visits or use multiple passwords.

This scenario is illustrated in Figure 6.1. Users are authenticated into Company.com. Company.com communicates via Web services to ChosenAirline.com,

ChosenHotels.com, and ChosenRentals.com for travel arrangements the user wants to make through Company.com's employee full-service portal. The user's identity must be passed through to each of the suppliers, so ChosenAirline.com, ChosenHotels.com, and ChosenRentals.com know this user is authorized to make travel arrangements charged to Company.com.

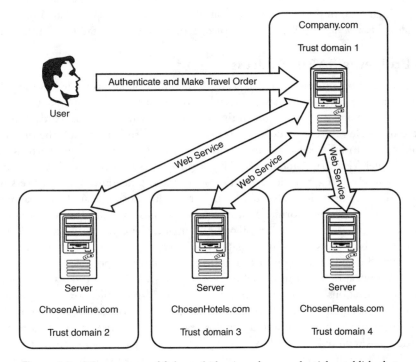

Figure 6.1   The concept of federated identity where credentials established at the initial site are passed to and trusted by subsequent sites, bypassing an additional authentication step and providing seamless access to resources.

It is impractical, if not impossible, for one organization to take on the responsibility for authenticating all incoming foreign individuals. A possible alternative is to have a central authentication registry for every partnership. This would be prohibitively costly. A better alternative is to provide a way to continue to allow individual organizations to retain their own authentication systems and still retain the loose coupling inherent in Web services that allows organizations to establish B2B integrations. The solution is cross-domain trust enabled by SAML and contractual agreements about how one entity will trust or not trust another entity whose members present their SAML assertions.

Web services are one expression of the growth of interorganizational distributed computing. Web services move messages with attached identities between organizations that do not utilize the same permissions structures. As Web services grow and more and more interorganizational services go online, the need for one organization to accept identities established by another organization will grow without bound. In a nutshell, Web services have all the problems that SAML was developed to solve, even though Web services came after SAML. This is the reason SAML has become so important to Web services security and WS-Security in particular.

Transporting Identity or "Portable Trust"

Chapter 7, "Building Security into SOAP," introduces WS-Security, which is essentially extensions to the SOAP envelope for transporting security assertions. SAML is now a major, standards-based method for describing those assertions. After you can specify identity information in XML, as SAML is designed to do, you can attach this to other XML messages, including SOAP. This kind of "portable trust" is critical for cross-domain trust and therefore for cross-domain (for example, B2B) Web services. These XML security encapsulations are what SAML calls assertions. Supporting these assertions is SAML's protocol for requesting authentication and authorization information to attach to identities. SAML's model is loosely coupled like Web services themselves and so has been easily adopted into the Web Services Security model.

The Concept of Trust Assertions

SAML defines three types of assertions: authentications, authorizations, and attributes. A *trust assertion* is defined in SAML as a claim, statement, or declaration of fact according to some assertion issuer (SAML authority), specifying

- **Authentication**—States that a particular authentication authority has authenticated the subject of the assertion, using a particular process at a particular time with a validity for a specific period of time.

- **Authorization**—States that a particular authority has granted or denied permission for the subject of the assertion to act on a particular resource within a specific period of time. An entity can be authorized to read, forward, delete, as well as perform other actions.

- **Attributes**—Provides qualifying information about either an authentication or authorization assertion.

The idea is to be able to pass these assertions around and have them mean something. So, for example, if you make an assertion that says you represent Entity A and that assertion is passed to another application that accepts it, you can see why repeated authentications can be avoided.

How SAML Works

SAML is fundamentally three XML-based mechanisms:

- **Assertions**—An XML schema and definition for security assertions. This makes SAML an XML framework that can be extended with new assertions.

- **Protocol**—An XML schema and definition for a request/response protocol. The requests are for policy decisions and enforcement from SAML authorities.
- **Bindings**—Rules on using assertions with standard transport and messaging frameworks. These rules are described as a set of bindings and protocols.

The relationship among these three aspects of SAML is shown in Figure 6.2.

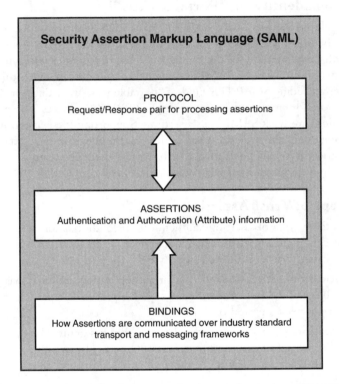

Figure 6.2   The relationship among the three underpinnings of SAML— bindings, assertions, and protocols.

SAML assertions are encoded in a common XML Schema, which includes basic information and the claims the requestor is making (for example, "I claim to be Jothy"). The basic information specifies a unique identifier used for the assertion name, date and time of issuance, and the time interval for which the assertion is valid, as shown in Listing 6.1.

Listing 6.1   **A Simple SAML Assertion**

```
<saml:Assertion>
  MajorVersion="1" MinorVersion="0"
  AssertionID="192.168.0.1.12345"
  Issuer="Company.com"
```

Listing 6.1   **Continued**

```
IssueInstant="2004-01-21T10:02:00Z">
<saml:Conditions>
  NotBefore="2004-01-21T10:02:00Z"
  NotAfter="2004-01-21T10:09:00Z" />
<saml:AuthenticationStatement>
  AuthenticationMethod="password"
  AuthenticationInstant="2004-01-21T10:02:00Z">
  <saml:Subject>
    <saml:NameIdentifier
      SecurityDomain="Company.com"
      Name="jothy" />
  </saml:Subject>
</saml:AuthenticationStatement>
</saml:Assertion>
```

Claims are made to an authority who returns another assertion (for example, "I vouch for the fact that this is Jothy"). An assertion may contain conditions and advice elements. For example, an assertion may be dependent on additional information from a validation service, and an assertion may be dependent on other assertions to be valid. Assertions may contain additional information as advice used to specify the assertions that were used to make a policy decision.

SAML assertions are submitted to authentication and authorization authorities through a request/response protocol exchange, as shown in Figure 6.3.

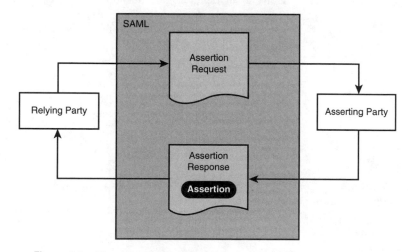

Figure 6.3   How the SAML protocol is applied to obtaining assertions.

SAML authorities are trusted third parties such as certificate authorities (CA) that provide SAML assertions on request. SAML assertions can be signed to link back to a trusted entity that vouches for the initial claim. They are always subject to the authenticity of the entity making the claim (just like a CA's signature on a digital certificate containing a public key vouches for the authenticity for the contained public key).

SAML assertions are bound to the transport and messaging frameworks used in a particular application. For example, SAML defines how assertions are passed around using HTTP, SMTP, or Java Message Services within a SOAP (that is, Web services) or ebXML messaging framework. Of course, we are most interested in SAML used in the SOAP messaging framework.

WS-Security, really just a security extension to SOAP, specifies SAML assertions as one of the types of security tokens it supports in the SOAP header.

SAML Assertions

The elements shown in Table 6.1 are common to all SAML assertions.

Table 6.1   **Elements Common to All SAML Assertions**

Element or Attribute	Element Description
Issuer	Issuer name
IssueInstant	Time stamp indicating time of issuance
AssertionID	Unique ID
Subject	Name plus security domain
SubjectConfirmation	Authentication protocol to authenticate a principal using `<ConfirmationMethod>` and any data in `<SubjectConfirmationData>`—for example, a public key
`<Conditions>`	Logical conditions that the assertion is subject to; also includes `<AudienceRestrictionCondition>`
`<Audience>`	The URI for the intended audience
`<Advice>`	Additional evidence relating to the assertion
`<ds:Signature>`	XML digital signature for authentication
MajorVersion	Assertion version info
MinorVersion	Assertion version info

A simple `<saml:Assertion>` issued by Smith Corporation with some conditions and advice is shown in Listing 6.2.

Listing 6.2   **A SAML Assertion with Conditions and Advice**

```
<saml:Assertion
  MajorVersion="1" MinorVersion="0"
  AssertionID="128.9.167.32.12345678"
  Issuer="Smith Corporation"
```

Listing 6.2   **Continued**

```
IssueInstant="2001-12-03T10:02:00Z">
<saml:Conditions
  NotBefore="2001-12-03T10:00:00Z"
  NotOnOrAfter="2001-12-03T10:05:00Z">
  <saml:AudienceRestrictionCondition>
    <saml:Audience>...URI...</saml:Audience>
  </saml:AudienceRestrictionCondition>
</saml:Conditions>
<saml:Advice>
  ...assertions and other elements go here...
</saml:Advice>
...statements go here...
</saml:Assertion>
```

Authentication Assertions

An authentication authority receives a subject's credentials. It processes those credentials according to its established policy. If the authentication process is successful, the authority asserts that subject S was identified and that the subject has authentically represented itself by method M at time T so that its digital identity can be trusted to represent its physical identity.

More specifically, if the authority determines that the presented credentials are valid, an `<AuthenticationStatement>` is created. This element contains the method, `<AuthenticationMethod>`, used for authentication, as well as the time, `<AuthenticationInstant>`, the authentication process occurred. The `<AuthenticationStatement>` element also optionally contains `<SubjectLocality>`, which specifies the DNS name and IP address of an authentication system, and `<AuthorityBinding>`, which indicates that additional information about the subject may be available.

The following authentication methods are supported:

Password	Authentication is performed via a password match (something the subject knew).
Kerberos ticket	Authentication is performed using the Kerberos protocol.
Secure Remote Password	Authentication is performed via a password not sent in the clear but protected via a shared key.
Hardware token	Authentication is performed via possession of a hardware token (something the subject had).
SSL client certificate	Authentication is performed via the transmission of a client certificate from the subject's machine according to the two-way SSL authentication protocol.

X.509 public key	Authentication is performed via the exchange of the public key contained in an X.509 certificate.
PGP public key	Authentication is performed via the PGP key using the PGP Web of Trust model.
SPKI public key	Authentication is performed according to the model established by the IETF's Simple PKI (SPKI) initiative.
XKMS public key	Authentication is performed via a key authenticated by means of an XKMS trust service.
XML digital signature	Authentication is performed via an XML digital signature.

Although SAML itself does not provide a revocation model, the fact that it can integrate digital certificates and digital signatures into its model provides a means to invalidate (revoke) an identity's validity before its lifetime expiration. Listing 6.3 shows a simple SAML `<AuthenticationStatement>` for someone named joeuser who was authenticated via a password:

Listing 6.3   **A `<saml:AuthenticationStatement>` for joeuser Using a Password for Authentication**

```
<saml:Assertion ...>
  <saml:AuthenticationStatement
    AuthenticationMethod="urn:oasis:names:tc:SAML: 1.0:am:password"
    AuthenticationInstant="2001-12-03T10:02:00Z">
    <saml:Subject>
      <saml:NameIdentifier
        Format="urn:oasis:names:tc:SAML:1.0:
assertion#emailAddress">joeuser@smithco.com
        <saml:SubjectConfirmation>
          <saml:ConfirmationMethod>
          ...specific to a profile or agreement...
          </saml:ConfirmationMethod>
        </saml:SubjectConfirmation>
    </saml:Subject>
  </saml:AuthenticationStatement>
</saml:Assertion>
```

Attribute Assertions

An attribute issuing authority receives credentials for subject S with the intent of attaching certain attributes to this subject's identity. This authority asserts that subject S is associated with attributes A, B, and C with values "a", "b", "c." This type of information is probably in some sort of repository of user attribute information such as an LDAP directory. Examples of typical attributes might include this individual's current account paid status and her credit limit. Listing 6.4 is an attribute assertion for an unspecified subject specifying their `PaidStatus` and `CreditLimit`.

Listing 6.4 A `<saml:AttributeStatement>` **Specifying** `PaidStatus` **and** `CreditLimit`

```
<saml:Assertion ...>
  <saml:AttributeStatement>
    <saml:Subject>...</saml:Subject>
    <saml:Attribute
      AttributeName="PaidStatus"
      AttributeNamespace="http://smithco.com">
      <saml:AttributeValue>
        PaidUp
      </saml:AttributeValue>
    </saml:Attribute>
    <saml:Attribute
      AttributeName="CreditLimit"
      AttributeNamespace="http://smithco.com">
      <saml:AttributeValue xsi:type="my:type">
        <my:amount currency="USD">500.00
        </my:amount>
      </saml:AttributeValue>
    </saml:Attribute>
  </saml:AttributeStatement>
</saml:Assertion>
```

Authorization Assertions

An authorization authority receives credentials for subject S along with a request for authorization. This authority asserts that subject S can be granted access of type A to resource R given evidence E. The subject could be human or a computer (Web service), and the requested resource could be another Web service. Listing 6.5 shows an authorization statement for an unspecified subject which authorizes (permits) the subject to access a resource specified by URL and to execute the accessed resource (it's a program) so specified.

Listing 6.5 A `<saml:AuthorizationStatement>` **Permitting Access to a Program a Subject May Execute**

```
<saml:Assertion ...>
  <saml:AuthorizationStatement
    Decision="Permit"
    Resource="http://jonesco.com/doit.cgi">
    <saml:Subject>...</saml:Subject>
    <saml:Action Namespace=
```

Listing 6.5   **Continued**

```
"urn:oasis:names:tc:SAML:1.0:action:rwedc">Execute
    </saml:Action>
  </saml:AuthorizationStatement>
</saml:Assertion>
```

SAML Producers and Consumers

SAML is concerned with access control for authenticated subjects based on a set of policies. The two critical actions that must be taken with respect to access control are making decisions based on a set of policies and enforcing those decisions. The SAML architecture provides for defined roles for these actions. A *Policy Decision Point (PDP)* makes decisions about access control based on one or more parameters. Simple types of access can be granted, or complex conditional access—such as a specific group on a specific day at a specific time—can be granted. If the PDP is external to the system, it needs to have access to an additional component called the *Policy Retrieval Point (PRP)* to retrieve policies for the decisions it is required to make.

A *Policy Enforcement Point (PEP)* is called in when an enforcement decision is required. A PEP makes a connection to the appropriate PDP for the decision. The policy function is evaluated with data supplied from the PEP to the PDP. These SAML architectural elements are shown in Figure 6.4. PDPs most likely communicate to back-end policy stores using the XACML access control/policy language. We cover XACML in Chapter 9, "Trust, Access Control, and Rights for Web Services."

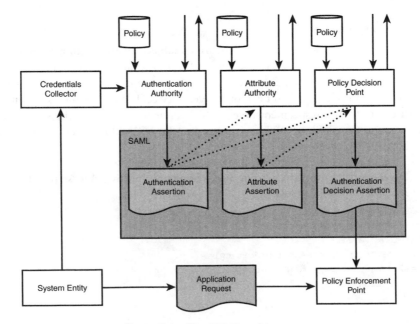

Figure 6.4   The SAML architecture.

SAML Protocol

SAML defines a request/response protocol to generate and exchange assertions. The SAML protocol is a completely separate schema (with a different namespace `urn:oasis:names:tc:SAML:1.0:protocol` usually prefixed with the namespace prefix `samlp`) from the assertions schema. A request contains a claim, and the response from the authority contains the resulting assertion. The queries are specifically targeted for authentication, attribute, and authorization. Requests contain the ID of the subject in question; that ID is included in the response to make sure the request and response are both talking about the same subject. An assumed trust relationship exists between the relying part and the asserting party. In other words, if you rely on the assertions presented to you, you need to trust the authority that vouches for the subject doing the asserting (making the claims).

The elements shown in Table 6.2 are common to all SAML requests.

Table 6.2   **Elements Common to All SAML Requests**

Element or Attribute	Element Description
RequestID	A unique identifier for the request; will be matched in the response with InResponseTo
IssueInstant	Time stamp indicating time of issuance of the request
<ds:Signature>	XML digital signature that authenticates the request
<RespondWith>	An element that specifies a type of response that is acceptable to the requestor
MajorVersion	Request version info
MinorVersion	Request version info

Authentication Request

An authentication request is like asking the question "What authentication assertions are available for this subject?" The response is in the form of an assertion containing an authentication statement. This response with an assertion is like a letter of introduction: "I would like to present to you my friend, whom I vouch for, Jothy."

The authentication authority receives a set of credentials about the subject from the credentials collector and processes them according to its policy. The assertion defines several authentication elements such as the identity of the issuer and the subject, the time the authentication was granted, and the lifetime for which it will be valid. The assertion clearly indicates that the subject was authenticated by a specific system at a specific time.

An <AuthenticationStatement> is generated after authentication is successful and contains the method used for authentication, the time it occurred, and the place it occurred. Listing 6.6 is a request for authentication that is signed using a digital signature to prove the source is valid. Authentication is requested for the Subject "jothy" from Company.com. The response will be an AuthenticationStatement.

Listing 6.6   **A** `<samlp:AuthenticationQuery>` **Requesting Authentication for Subject jothy from Company.com**

```
<samlp:Request
 MajorVersion="1" MinorVersion="0"
  RequestID="128.14.234.20.12345678"
  IssueInstant="2001-12-03T10:02:00Z">
   <samlp:RespondWith>saml:AuthenticationStatement</samlp:RespondWith>
   <ds:Signature>...</ds:Signature>
   <samlp:AuthenticationQuery>
     <saml:Subject>
       <saml:NameIdentifier
         SecurityDomain="Company.com"
         Name="jothy" />
     </saml:Subject>
   </samlp:AuthenticationQuery>
</samlp:Request>
```

Attribute Request

An attribute request is like asking for "all available attributes for this subject." The response is in the form of an assertion containing an attribute statement. The request can ask for information on specified attributes A, B, and C or, if not specific, on all available attributes. Only the attributes allowed for this subject are returned. The requestor may be denied access to some or all of this subject's attributes.

The attribute request is sent to an attribute authority along with a previously obtained authentication assertion. The attribute authority uses a policy to determine the privileges of the subject. The attribute assertion can be passed to a PDP for authorization.

The `<AttributeStatement>` contains `<Subject>`, `<Attribute>`, `<NameIdentifier>`, `<SubjectConfirmation>`, `<ConfirmationMethod>`, and `<SubjectConfirmationData>` elements. `<Attribute>` contains the attribute value `<AttributeValue>` element for the underlying assertion. Listing 6.7 is an `AttributeQuery` for an unspecified Subject requesting information about the attribute `"PaidStatus"` within a specific account specified via a URL for `AttributeNameSpace`.

Listing 6.7   **A** `<samlp:AttributeQuery>` **for a Subject's** `PaidStatus` **at a Specific Account**

```
<samlp:Request ... >
  <samlp:AttributeQuery>
    <saml:Subject>...</saml:Subject>
    <saml:AttributeDesignator
      AttributeName="PaidStatus"
      AttributeNamespace="http://smithco.com"/>
  </samlp:AttributeQuery>
</samlp:Request>
```

Authorization Request

An authorization request asks this question: "Is this subject allowed to access the requested resource in the specified manner, given this evidence?"

The response is an authorization assertion containing an authorization decision statement. This request is about whether a subject can access a specific resource, given an authentication assertion and an attribute assertion. This type of request directly involves the PDP and PEP for authorization decisions and enforcement, respectively. The resulting decision can be Permit, Deny, or Indeterminate.

The `<AuthorizationDecisionStatement>` specifies what decision was made with respect to the authorization request. The resulting `<AuthorizationDecisionStatement>` contains the URI of the resource that Subject is requesting access to, a decision of Permit or Deny, an action specifying what Subject is authorized to do, and the evidence on which the decision was based. Listing 6.8 is a request for authorization for "joeuser" at Company.com asking whether he is authorized to execute a resource (here, just a CGI script) to reserve a hotel room at the ChosenTravel.com resource.

Listing 6.8   **A `<samlp:AuthorizationDecisionQuery>` for joeuser to Gain Permission to Execute a Resource to Reserve a Hotel Room**

```
<samlp:Request ...>
  <samlp:AuthorizationDecisionQuery
Resource="http://ChosenTravel.com/reserve_hotel.cgi">
    <saml:Subject>
      <saml:NameIdentifier
        SecurityDomain="Company.com"
        Name="joeuser" />
    </saml:Subject>
    <saml:Actions Namespace="urn:oasis:names:tc:SAML: 1.0:action:rwedc">
      <saml:Action>Execute</saml:Action>
    </saml:Actions>
    <saml:Evidence>
    <saml:Assertion>...</saml:Assertion>
    </saml:Evidence>
  </samlp:AuthorizationDecisionQuery>
</samlp:Request>
```

SAML Protocol Response

SAML protocol responses are signed to identify the issuing authority and to guarantee the response remains unaltered. A response is one or more assertions with the status of the response.

Table 6.3 identifies elements common to all SAML responses.

Table 6.3 **Elements Common to All SAML Responses**

Element or Attribute	Element Description
ResponseID	A unique identifier for the response
InResponseTo	A reference to the RequestID request for which this is the response
IssueInstant	Time stamp indicating time of issuance of the request
<ds:Signature>	XML digital signature that authenticates the request
Recipient	The intended recipient for this response to prevent malicious forwarding of a response required in some SAML profiles
MajorVersion	Response version info
MinorVersion	Response version info

Listing 6.9 is a response to an authentication request that shows the issuer of the response as Company.com and specifies specific time-based validity conditions on the authentication:

Listing 6.9   **A `<samlp:Response>` to an Authentication Request**

```
<samlp:Response
 MajorVersion="1" MinorVersion="0"
  ResponseID="128.14.234.20.90123456"
  InResponseTo="128.14.234.20.12345678"
  IssueInstant="2001-12-03T10:02:00Z"
  Recipient="...URI...">
  <samlp:Status>
    <samlp:StatusCode Value="Success" />
    <samlp:StatusMessage> ... </samlp:StatusMessage>
  </samlp:Status>
  <saml:Assertion
    MajorVersion="1" MinorVersion="0"
    AssertionID="128.9.167.32.12345678"
    Issuer="Company.com">
    <saml:Conditions
      NotBefore="2001-12-03T10:00:00Z"
      NotAfter="2001-12-03T10:05:00Z" />
    <saml:AuthenticationStatement ...>...
    </saml:AuthenticationStatement>
  </saml:Assertion>
</samlp:Response>
```

SAML Bindings

SAML bindings are how SAML itself is made secure. SAML authorities are trusted Web services that an SAML system must consult. A binding is a way to transport SAML requests and responses to and from these authorities. A binding is the mapping of SAML request/response message exchanges into standard communication protocols. The SAML specification requires SOAP over HTTP as one binding. Other bindings will be specified over time. In the SOAP binding, the SAML information is contained inside the SOAP body. Later, when we discuss the WS-Security profile for SAML, we will see an alternate binding in which the SAML assertion sits in the SOAP header and the resource it refers to sits in the SOAP body.

SAML messages can be transported using SOAP without re-encoding from the "standard" SAML schema. An SAML requestor transmits an SAML `<Request>` element within the body of a SOAP message to an SAML responder. The SAML requestor includes only one SAML request per SOAP message. The SAML responder returns either a single `<Response>` element within the body of another SOAP message or a SOAP fault code.

With SOAP most commonly bound itself to HTTP, endpoint-to-endpoint authentication for SAML should be provided by SSL Transport Layer Security. Message integrity and confidentiality of the SAML payload are also provided by SSL. In other words, you need to use SSL when using SAML.

Listing 6.10 is an example of a SOAP request that asks for an assertion containing an authentication statement from an SAML authentication authority:

Listing 6.10   **A Full SOAP Request Sent to an SAML Authority Containing a `<samlp:AuthenticationQuery>` Showing SAML Transported via SOAP Bound to HTTP**

```
POST /SamlService HTTP/1.1
Host: www.example.com
Content-Type: text/xml
Content-Length: nnn
SOAPAction: http://www.oasis-open.org/committees/security
<SOAP-ENV:Envelope
  xmlns:SOAP-ENV="http://schemas.xmlsoap.org/soap/envelope/">
  <SOAP-ENV:Body>
    <samlp:Request xmlns:samlp:="..." xmlns:saml="..." xmlns:ds="...">
      <ds:Signature> ... </ds:Signature>
      <samlp:AuthenticationQuery>
        ...
      </samlp:AuthenticationQuery>
    </samlp:Request>
  </SOAP-ENV:Body>
</SOAP-ENV:Envelope>
```

Listing 6.11, which follows, is an example of the corresponding SOAP response, which supplies an assertion containing the authentication statement as requested.

Listing 6.11 **The SOAP Response to the Listing 6.10 SOAP Request with Contained** `<saml:AuthenticationStatement>` **Assertion**

```
HTTP/1.1 200 OK
Content-Type: text/xml
Content-Length: nnnn
<SOAP-ENV:Envelope
  xmlns:SOAP-ENV="http://schemas.xmlsoap.org/soap/envelope/">
  <SOAP-ENV:Body>
    <samlp:Response xmlns:samlp="..." xmlns:saml="..." xmlns:ds="...">
      <Status>
        <StatusCodevalue="samlp:Success"/>
      </Status>
      <ds:Signature> ... </ds:Signature>
      <saml:Assertion>
        <saml:AuthenticationStatement>
          ...
        </saml:AuthenticationStatement>
      </saml:Assertion>
    </samlp:Response>
  </SOAP-Env:Body>
</SOAP-ENV:Envelope>
```

SAML Profiles

SAML profiles describe how SAML assertions are embedded into and extracted from a framework or protocol. Browser profiles for SAML were specified first (SAML pre-dated Web services). Next, the profile for securing SOAP payloads was specified. WS-Security specifies an SAML profile as part of the WS-Security specification.

The SAML profile for SOAP is structured as shown in Figure 6.5.

Is SAML Too Complicated?

The promise of SAML is strong. SAML can deal with transactions as if they were secure documents. SAML is the key to having meaningful Web services connecting organizations. The possibility even arises that people will be able to send trusted personal checks via Web services or email. However, the cost in complexity is also very high.

SAML has three separate schemas and corresponding namespaces for its protocols, assertions, and bindings. Three very different but interrelated core concepts are the heart of SAML: authentications, attributes, and authorizations. Each of these three different concepts potentially involves a different trusted third-party authority that will involve establishing trust relationships as well as a trusted infrastructure between requestor and authority.

SAML is being applied to very different but critically important application areas, including single sign-on, authentication services, and directory services. These applications will pull the specification in many different directions, potentially with different requirements adding to complexity over time.

A complete SAML architecture involves Policy Decision Points and Policy Enforcement Points that interact with a comprehensive set of policies that all must interact with the authentication, attribute, and authorization authorities.

Although the SAML architecture is quite complex, it still pales in comparison to the added complexity when it relies on a Public Key Infrastructure (PKI) environment and digital certificates. The big stumbling block for pervasive deployment of PKI has been the difficulty in dealing with PKI client certificates issued to and maintained securely by individual humans. So, yes, SAML by itself is quite complex. The good news is that, in most cases, SAML does not require PKI, but when it does, it is exceedingly more complex.

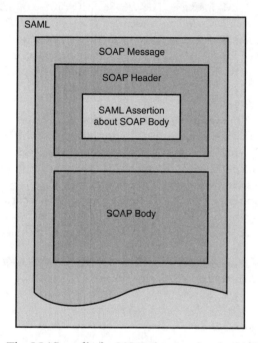

Figure 6.5   The SOAP profile for SAML showing that the SAML assertions contained in the SOAP header refer to the resource contained in the SOAP body of the same message.

Using SAML with WS-Security

SAML profiles are like documented processes that define patterns of SAML usage needed to secure a resource. Like Pretty Good Privacy (PGP), SAML is designed to work without a centralized certificate authority. This is why SAML is the basis for Liberty Alliance's federated identity system, which we describe in the next section.

Note that SAML assumes the resource owner trusts the SAML authorities and these authorities know the subject requesting an SAML security assertion. Transactions between two parties that do not know each other still need a trusted third party. In such cases, WS-Security needs to use XKMS instead of SAML.

The detailed introduction to WS-Security is still to come in the next chapter. Knowing that WS-Security is basically security extensions to SOAP is sufficient understanding to explore how SAML fits into WS-Security here.

The WS-Security SAML Profile

WS-Security defines an SAML profile (but confusingly calls it the WS-Security SAML binding) for securing SOAP messages. The WS-Security profile of SAML is based on a single interaction between a sender and a receiver. The sender is a Web service consumer who obtains one or more SAML assertions. Next, the sender adds the assertions to a SOAP message destined for the receiver (a Web service provider). The receiver processes the assertions present in the SOAP message. As with the SAML profile for SOAP, with the WS-Security SAML profile, the SAML assertion about the SOAP message is included as part of the SOAP header.

SAML is just one of the security tokens defined by WS-Security. A good way to think about WS-Security is that it is a specification that takes XML security (XML Encryption and XML Signature); links that with pre-existing security technologies that it calls tokens, such as X.509, Kerberos, and SAML; and binds it all to SOAP so that it can become part of a secure Web service interaction.

You attach SAML assertions to SOAP messages using WS-Security by placing assertion elements or references to assertions inside a <wsse:Security> header. Listing 6.12 illustrates a SOAP message containing an SAML assertion in a <wsse:Security> header.

Listing 6.12   **A SOAP Message with a** <wsse:Security> **Header Using a** <saml:Assertion> **Security Token**

```
<S:Envelope xmlns:S="...">
  <S:Header>
    <wsse:Security xmlns:wsse="...">
      <saml:Assertion
        MajorVersion="1"
        MinorVersion="0"
        AssertionID="SecurityToken-ef375268"
        Issuer="jothy"
        IssueInstant="2002-07-23T11:32:05.6228146-07:00"
        xmlns:saml="urn:oasis:names:tc:SAML:1.0:assertion">
      ...
    </saml:Assertion>
      ...
    </wsse:Security>
  </S:Header>
  <S:Body>
    ...
  </S:Body>
</S:Envelope>
```

Applying SAML: Project Liberty

The Liberty Alliance Project is developing a set of standards that allow you to use an SAML authentication assertion across multiple security domains. The Liberty federated identity infrastructure allows you to create a circle of trust with your affiliates. Although each member of this circle maintains and protects its own unique user information, a single federated identity credential can be used as proof of authentication with all members of the circle. Each member maps the federated identity credential into the private user identity known within that member's trust domain.

The Identity Problem

A *digital identity* is a name with a set of attributes. You can think of it as a credential. Attributes of this credential might be date of birth, email address, Social Security number, phone number, medical data, financial data, and so on. Each user has multiple identities. You have one for your laptop login; one for your online bank account; one for your ATM; one for your company intranet; one when you buy from Amazon.com, from Travelocity, from Avis, from Marriott, from Staples; and so on. In this case, each identity requires you to re-authenticate. This has led not only to a dramatic proliferation of passwords to remember, but also to a degradation in overall security as humans with limited memories use simpler passwords, use the same password at every location, and write them down in defense from this onslaught.

As long as each of these resources requiring authentication remains distinct with its own trust domain, this situation will persist. Worse, there is no possibility for merged services from these resources. For instance, buying a ticket directly from United.com, where you authenticate yourself and then to book a hotel directly from Marriott.com at your destination requires you to re-authenticate at Marriott.com because the company's trust domain and that of United.com have nothing to do with each other. This affects all these consumer services negatively. Portals are a stop-gap solution short of federation because they provide "one-stop shopping" for a variety of related resources. (Portals are most often constructed by using Web services to link all the back-end resources into a Web front end accessible to browser users.) Travel sites, company intranets, trading partners, employee benefits providers—all are hampered from delivering better service as long as the "islands of identity" problem persists.

One solution is a centralized identity provider. This is the model for Microsoft Passport. This model has met with a lot of resistance because it puts too much control in the hands of one provider. The alternative is an open federated model.

Federated Identity

Federated identity is really just *shared authentication*. It will open new relationships between partners on the Internet. Shared authentication allows one enterprise, which has an online relationship with a customer named Alice, and a means of authenticating Alice, to pass her identity over to another enterprise. The "receiving" enterprise does not have to re-authenticate Alice but can rely on the work done by the "sending" enterprise. The process by which these two entities establish this shared identity is called *identity federation*. Cross-domain authentication of humans is just part of what Liberty's federated identity is all about. Clearly, there is a need with Web services for cross-domain authentication of applications as well.

How Liberty Uses SAML

Travel providers all have dedicated sites with a different identity for you at each one. When you travel, you usually need a hotel and frequently a car at your destination. But if you started directly at the airline site because you wanted to use frequent flyer miles to buy the ticket (because airlines don't share that program with either the travel portals or their business partners), you are out of luck in reserving your hotel and car through that site. You have to go to the corresponding hotel or car sites and log in again. Web services between their back-end systems will link them together, and with Liberty enabled by SAML, your login at the airline site will be transported as a set of SAML assertions to the hotel and car rental sites, and you won't have to log in again. Liberty is designed to allow all the travel sites to create a circle of trust and to federate your identity between them as they send data about you back and forth over Web services. Banks, merchants, and many other federations that share users are ready to "flatten" out the Internet's hub-and-spokes model with Liberty and SAML.

Liberty explicitly uses SAML and even extends it to provide for an *authentication context* (described soon). Today, Liberty is used mostly in consumer-facing Web sites, but increasingly it will be used in Web services. The initial focus for the Liberty standards is to provide single sign-on (SSO) capability for Web services.

Account Linking

Privacy is a big concern for Liberty because it does not want to allow circle of trust partners to share your personal information with others. Identity federation provides for privacy through a concept known as *account linking*. As accounts are linked, each account owner needs a frame of reference for the user. If the account names were to be freely exchanged, privacy would be compromised. So Liberty defines opaque handles for each account that the others cannot see; only the user can resolve the handles.

Authentication Context

Liberty provides an enhanced single sign-on known as *authentication context*. It extends an SAML authentication assertion to include context. Context includes important questions relating to the identification step that initially established the subject's identity. That step results in stored shared secrets that later authentication uses in a challenge that must be met correctly for successful authentication. If the shared secret is "Fay" and the authentication challenge is "What is your mother's maiden name?" successful authentication will happen only if the SAML assertion included the correct answer to the challenge. But how strong was the identification when the user was initially identified and stored the maiden name as Fay? And when should re-identification be done? Answers to these questions are needed to know how trustworthy the identification is. Authentication is only as strong as

- The strength of the initial identification process
- The trustworthiness of the authentication authority and its processes

Liberty extends SAML authentication requests to allow for requesting a specific authentication type. And different levels of authentication are available. Authentication you need to buy a book, for example, is not the same as what you need to commit your company to a $100,000 contract.

Liberty's SAML Profiles

Liberty is building a suite of SAML profiles. Some of the profiles initially proposed include

- SSO and federation profiles, including one for wireless
- Name registration profiles
- Identity federation termination profiles
- Single logout profiles
- Identity provider introduction profiles

The Microsoft Passport Alternative Approach

Microsoft proposes Passport as an alternative approach for identity management. Consumers place all relevant personally identifiable information that might be useful when interacting with consumer-oriented Web sites into a centralized registry, which is managed. Sites that sign up to support Passport then accept login credentials from Passport as opposed to direct interaction with the consumer. Passport has not endorsed SAML nor made itself interoperable with SAML.

Microsoft Passport Versus Project Liberty

The Liberty Alliance has plans to support interoperability between its system and Microsoft's rival Passport system. However, Liberty Alliance officials doubt that Microsoft will seriously be interested in allowing its Passport users to log in to Web sites supporting the rival technology. Microsoft might be concerned about competition in this new area of technology. Although Microsoft claims to have 200 million Passport users, by Microsoft's own admission, this number is grossly inflated because every Hotmail user is automatically a Passport user, and almost none of them will ever visit a site that uses their Passport information because only a dozen or so sites actually exist.

The proponents of Liberty Alliance argue vociferously against the centralized control and proprietary nature of the Passport system. Meanwhile, Microsoft has modified its stance and announced that it will not be the only one controlling the user data repositories and that external organizations can also run Passport servers. This announcement makes the two rival systems look more and more alike. It remains to be seen how, if ever, they truly will become interoperable.

One big difference is that Liberty Alliance is a private consortium that operates like a standards body. Liberty Alliance publishes specifications—currently V1.1—and companies or groups develop implementations of that specification. There is even a group building an open source reference implementation callled PingIdentiity.

Summary

This chapter provided your introduction to SAML. SAML addresses the problem of transporting identity and in so doing creates the notion of *portable trust*. This concept is important because the Web, and Web services more particularly, connect organizations that do not have the same trust domains. Having different trust domains means that different users are known to each organization, and different rules and processes exist to establish who the users are and what they are allowed to do. Portable trust introduces the concept of trust assertions, which are claims that an identity—called a Subject—makes on its behalf and that someone must vouch for.

SAML is three XML-based mechanisms: assertions, a protocol, and a set of bindings. The three types of SAML assertions are authentication, attribute, and authorization. The SAML protocol is a request/response protocol that tracks the types of assertions. Together, an authentication request, attribute request, and authorization request elicit an SAML protocol response. For each type of assertion, there can be an independent third-party authority for policy decisions and enforcement.

Eventually, there will be multiple SAML bindings, but currently the specification requires the SOAP over HTTP binding. In this binding, the SAML information is contained in the SOAP body.

SAML profiles describe how SAML assertions are embedded into a protocol. A browser profile and a SOAP profile specify how to secure SAML when it is a SOAP payload. WS-Security specifies an SAML profile as well.

SAML is one of the tokens defined by WS-Security. In the WS-Security profile, SAML assertions are attached to SOAP messages by placing them inside a WS-Security SOAP header.

The Liberty Alliance's Project Liberty is a major application of SAML. SAML is being used in Project Liberty to provide *federated identity*. Within a federation of connected organizations, trust is established such that when one organization authenticates a subject, the other organizations within that federation do not require re-authentication. This means after authentication by one member, a subject can move freely around a federation using services from all members. This capability is important for B2B Web services to successfully connect organizations into trusted value chains doing real business with each other.

With SAML, as well as XML Encryption and XML Signature under your belt, you are now ready to apply these fundamental security building blocks to building secure Web services. You are now ready to dive into WS-Security, the subject of Chapter 7.

7

Building Security into SOAP

Introduction to and Motivation for WS-Security

This chapter describes arguably the most essential aspect of securing Web services: the WS-Security standard. We say *arguably* here because WS-Security should be considered *a* layer of an overall Web Service Security strategy—only one aspect, albeit a significant aspect, of an overall Web Services Security architecture. The WS-Security standard is a specification specifically created for using the security technologies you learned about in previous chapters in the context of a SOAP message. The WS-Security specification reached "approved status" status in April 2004. It is now a full-fledged OASIS open standard.

XML Signature and XML Encryption deal with XML security—securing the content of XML documents. So what is the purpose of WS-Security? It deals with SOAP security—securing the content of Web services messages. WS-Security is XML security in dynamic action, specifically designed to integrate into SOAP messages.

The good news is that you have already been exposed to much of the complexity of learning WS-Security in the previous chapters in this book. Most of the learning required to understand WS-Security is in understanding the underlying security technologies that WS-Security utilizes, not in understanding WS-Security itself. WS-Security defines practically no new security technology; instead, it focuses on applying existing security technologies such as X.509 certificates, SAML assertions, XML Signature, and XML Encryption to SOAP messages.

Problems and Goals

WS-Security is targeted at the problem of securing the Web service message itself, no matter where the SOAP message goes, no matter how long it lives. Contrast this with HTTP transport security (covered in Chapter 3, "The Foundations of Distributed Message-Level Security"), which is about creating a secure pipe between two servers through which messages travel.

Note

Web services are designed to work across any type of transport protocol, not just HTTP. For example, SOAP messages could be sent over email (SMTP) or even FTP. For the discussion in this chapter contrasting transport security and message-based security, we focus on HTTP transport security because it is the only transport binding specified for SOAP so far and is by far the most prevalent transport protocol used to carry SOAP messages today. In the case of non-HTTP transport technologies, other considerations may apply, but generally the contrast between transport-based security and message-based security remains consistent.

HTTP Transport Security Versus Message Security

It is helpful to understand the distinction between HTTP Transport Layer Security (shortened to *transport security* going forward) and SOAP message-level security (shortened to *message security* going forward). Understanding the trade-offs between these two options, their relative strengths and weaknesses, and their associated costs is important to engineering an effective security solution.

Transport security was covered in some detail in Chapter 3 when discussing the foundations of message-based security. Recall that the purpose of transport security is to create a secure pipe between two Web servers. Authentication occurs at the time the secure pipe is created, and confidentiality and integrity mechanisms are applied only while the message is in the secure pipe, as shown in Figure 7.1.

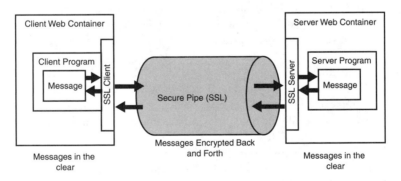

Figure 7.1   HTTP transport security.

Three of the transport security options described in Chapter 3—one-way SSL/TLS, basic authentication, and two-way SSL/TLS—are quite viable for securing Web services. In general, they are simpler to implement than their message-level security equivalents, and system administrators tend to have experience working with transport-level security. Table 7.1 presents a matrix of transport security pros and cons, and Table 7.2 presents a similar matrix showing message security pros and cons.

Table 7.1   **Transport Security for Web Services: Pros and Cons**

Pros	Cons
Mature: Tried and true	**Point to Point:** Messages are in the clear after reaching SSL endpoint
Support: Supported by most servers and clients	**Waypoint visibility:** Cannot have partial visibility into the message
Understood: Understood by most system administrators	**Granularity:** Cannot have different security for messages in and messages out
Simpler: Generally simpler than message-level security alternatives	**Transport dependent:** Applies only to HTTP

Table 7.2   **Message Security for Web Services: Pros and Cons**

Pros	Cons
Persistant: Allows the message to be self-protecting	**Immature:** standard, tools
Selective: Portions of the message can be secured to different parties	**Complex:** encompasses many other standards including XML Encryption, XML Signature, X.509 certificates, and many more
Flexible: Different security policy can be applied to request and response Transport independent	

Transport security works by establishing a secure pipe between two endpoints, whereas message security works by applying security technology to the message itself. The SOAP message request to a Web service has encryption, digital signatures, and authentication applied directly into the message (we show you how in this chapter). With transport security, the SOAP message is secure only when it is *in* the pipe. With message security, the message is (conceptually) secure wherever it goes. For example, if messages were logged automatically by the Web services container, under transport security the message could very well be in the clear; however, with message security the message would still be encrypted and/or signed and retain its security even in the log file.

As you might expect, WS-Security takes advantage of the flexibility of XML Encryption. Because XML Encryption allows you to sign all or part of an XML document, you have the flexibility to allow a specific recipient of a message to see only certain parts of the message. A common problem that has bothered application firewall vendors for years is that SSL packets are completely opaque to the firewall; these packets pass through the firewall to the Web container before they are decrypted. (Many application firewalls can be configured to act as the SSL endpoint to prevent this problem; however, the message either has to be sent in the clear from the firewall to the target server, or the firewall has to establish a new SSL session with that server.) Thus, creating certain types of firewall rules becomes impossible when an SSL session is involved. With Web services and emerging standards such as WS-Routing, which allows for many intermediate *way-points* to receive the message, you can imagine parts of the message encrypted in such a way that a waypoint (for example, a firewall) could read only the part of the message it needs to do its filtering. This is impossible with transport security, which works only endpoint-to-endpoint.

> **Note**
> SOAP Routing Protocol, or WS-Routing, is a SOAP-based, stateless protocol for exchanging one-way SOAP messages from an initial sender to the ultimate receiver, potentially via a set of intermediaries.

When you are thinking about message security, remember that each message can have its own security strategy. In the case of a simple synchronous Web service, there are two messages: one for the request and another for the response. It is entirely possible, and potentially reasonable, to have the request encrypted and the response in the clear (or any combination of authentication, encryption, and digital signature). This strategy would not be possible with transport security. With transport security, you have created a secure pipe, and every message—request and response—that passes through the pipe will be encrypted at one end and decrypted at the other end.

Of course, the extra power and flexibility of message security comes with a price: complexity. This price is partly due to the complexity of the underlying security technologies, such as XML Signature and XML Encryption; however, over time much of this complexity will be absorbed by your development and deployment environment, and you will simply declare rules for the way you want your specific Web service secured. Even when you have help from tools, the myriad possible options available make message-based security complex. For example:

- Do you want to require a username/password, a digital signature, and encryption?
- Do you want the encryption to be a certain algorithm or strength?
- Where will the client find the public key to encrypt with?
- On the response, do you want to encrypt the message back?
- Do you need to digitally sign it?

We could go on and on with these possible configuration and policy questions, but you get the idea. The bottom line is that deciding to use message security is like choosing to sit on a powerful, complex rocket engine with numerous knobs. It is sometimes said that the greatest security threat is complexity, and although the flexibility of WS-Security is a great strength, it is perhaps also its greatest weakness.

You can mix transport- and message-based security together. You need more of the WS-Security implementation details to understand this concept better, but one example is using username/password in WS-Security. One of the variations of username and password, UsernameToken, can have the password in the clear, similar to HTTP transport security's basic authentication. Using SSL to secure the transmission of the message is typically a good idea so that the password is not in the clear over the Internet. Of course, using `UsernameToken` with a clear-text password in the SOAP message defeats one of the major objectives of message security: How can the message be secure if the message contains a password sitting in the clear! But if you decided to take this approach, you would probably combine SSL/TLS from HTTP transport security with the `UsernameToken` from WS-Security. We discuss this and related issues later in this chapter in the section "Security Tokens in WS-Security."

Table 7.3 briefly summarizes the main differences between transport- and message-based security.

Table 7.3 **Message Security and Transport Security Comparison**

Transport Security	Message Security
Point-to-point	End-to-end
Mature, relatively straightforward to implement	New, relatively complex with many security options
Not granular, applies to entire payload and across session	Very granular, can apply to only part of payload and only request or response
Transport dependent	Same security can be applied across different transport technologies

The Origins of WS-Security

WS-Security is a standard originally proposed by Microsoft, IBM, and VeriSign in April 2002[1]. Prior to that, the only SOAP security standard was a W3C Note called "SOAP Security Extensions: Digital Signature"[2] (see Chapter 4, "Safeguarding the Identity and Integrity of XML Messages"). WS-Security supercedes that note and addresses authentication and encryption as well as digital signature. In late summer of 2002, WS-Security was sent to the OASIS standards body. In April 2004, it was established as an approved OASIS open standard. In terms of mind–share, WS-Security has had great success and is on the road to becoming the predominant method for securing Web services. What is frequently lacking in security technologies is the investment in making them easier for people to use. This is short-sighted because how good is a security technology if no one can put it to use? The involvement and interest shown by many high-visibility vendors on the WS-Security OASIS Technical Committee are promising, and emerging tools that will make WS-Security straightforward to use will continue to aid in its adoption.

1. You can view the original WS-Security note at `http://www-106.ibm.com/developerworks/webservices/library/ws-secure/?open&1=740,t=gr`.
2. "SOAP Security Extensions: Digital Signature," `http://www.w3.org/TR/SOAP-dsig/`

WS-Security Is Foundational

Microsoft and IBM are both strongly committed to WS-Security, and it is a base technology for their overall XML and Web services architecture. In April 2002, IBM and Microsoft published a joint whitepaper called "Security in a Web Services World: A Proposed Architecture and Roadmap,"[3] providing a far-reaching architectural vision of security that positions WS-Security as a foundational technology for a set of follow-on Web Services Security technologies.

From Figure 7.2, you can see how critical WS-Security is to a comprehensive Web Services Security framework. In the final two chapters of this book, we will review the other WS-★ security-related standards such as WS-Policy, WS-Trust, WS-Privacy, WS-SecureConversation, WS-Federation, and WS-Authorization.

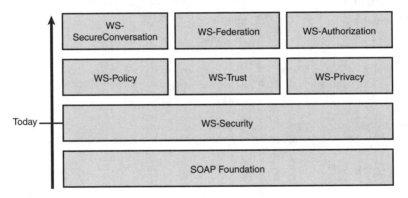

Figure 7.2   The Web Services Security stack.

Extending SOAP with Security

WS-Security defines a SOAP security header that provides a standard place for you to put security artifacts. The purpose of WS-Security is not to invent any new types of security, but instead to provide a common format for security in a SOAP message. Three major elements make up a SOAP security header: security tokens, XML Encryption, and/or XML Signatures. *Security tokens* are pieces of information used for authentication or authorization. Examples of security tokens are username/password and X.509 certificates. Many more token types are used, and we discuss them in detail later in this chapter. For XML Encryption, the security header may hold an `EncryptedKey` element containing a `ReferenceList` pointing to the specific parts of the message that have been encrypted. Similarly, if an XML Signature is within the security header, its `Reference` elements will point to the parts of the message that have been digitally signed.

3. "Security in a Web Services World: A Proposed Architecture and Roadmap," http://msdn. microsoft.com/webservices/understanding/gxa/default.aspx?pull=/library/ en-us/dnwssecur/html/securitywhitepaper.as

Listing 7.1 shows what the basic WS-Security header structure looks like within a SOAP envelope (we have removed namespaces throughout this chapter to simplify).

Listing 7.1   **Structure of a Basic WS-Security SOAP Header**

```
<S:Envelope>
    <S:Header>
        <wsse:Security>
  <!-- Security Token -->
            <wsse:UsernameToken>
                    ...
            </wsse:UsernameToken>
            <!-- XML Signature -->
            <ds:Signature>
                   ...
              <ds:Reference URI="#body">
                ...
            </ds:Signature>
            <!-- XML Encryption Reference List -->
                <xenc:ReferenceList>
                <xenc:DataReference URI="#body"/>
                </xenc:ReferenceList>
        </wsse:Security>
    </S:Header>
    <S:Body>
     <!-- XML Encrypted Body -->
     <xenc:EncryptedData Id="body" Type="content">
            ...
     </xenc:EncryptedData>
    </S:Body>
</S:Envelope>
```

As you can see, Listing 7.1 contains a security header, commonly referred to with the namespace prefix wsse, which has three children: UsernameToken, which is an example of a security token; Signature, which represents an XML Signature; and an XML Encryption ReferenceList. In general, you see the following structure for the security header:

1. **Security Tokens**—Zero, one, or more (but usually not more than one) security tokens. This example shows a UsernameToken.

2. **Signatures**—Zero, one, or more XML Signatures. Usually, if an XML Signature is included, at a minimum it signs all or part of the soap body.

3. **ReferenceList or EncryptedKey**—Zero, one, or more of these elements. As you learned about XML Encryption in Chapter 5, "Ensuring Confidentiality of XML Messages," the EncryptedData element can exist for each element encrypted. To consolidate these elements, you use a ReferenceList (from the XML Encryption

namespace) or an `EncryptedKey`, which contains a reference list, to reference all the different `EncryptedData` elements. This way, a WS-Security processor can read the security header and then decrypt all the data to which `EncryptedData` refers. Often, the soap body is encrypted, as shown in the previous example.

In the following sections, we look in turn at each of the security artifacts that can be included in a WS-Security SOAP header.

WS-Security Namespaces

The different XML listings in this chapter sometimes contain prefixes for which the associated namespace has not been declared. The following list provides a quick synopsis of the different namespaces we refer to here.

Prefix	Short for	Namespace
ds	Digital signature	`http://www.w3.org/2000/09/xmldsig#`
wsse	WS-Security extension	`http://www.docs.oasis-open.org/wss/2004/01/oasis-200401-wss-wssecurity-secext-1.0.xsd`
wsu	Web services utility	`http://www.docs.oasis-open.org/wss/2004/01/oasis-200401-wss-wssecurity-utility-1.0.xsd`
xenc	XML Encryption	`http://www.w3.org/2001/04/xmlenc#`

Security Tokens in WS-Security

Security tokens are security artifacts included in the message that are typically used for authentication or authorization purposes. Understanding tokens is relatively straightforward when you see examples such as username/password, an X.509 certificate, or an SAML assertion. Many different token types have been defined, and the WS-Security specification is extensible enough to enable new types of tokens as they emerge.

You might think that security tokens would look something like Listing 7.2.

Listing 7.2   **Assumed WS-Security Security Token Structure**

```
<wsse:SecurityToken>
  <username>fred</username>
  <password>password</password>
</wsse:SecurityToken>
```

This is not the case; no `SecurityToken` wrapper element is defined in the WS-Security XML Schema. The wrapper element for security tokens varies by the type of security token. Tokens are generally broken out into three types: `UsernameToken`, `BinaryToken`, and XML Token. `UsernameToken` and `BinaryToken` have a wrapping element to represent them; however, XML Tokens tend to have their own unique elements based on the type of token they represent. For example, an SAML token is represented by an

`Assertion` element. The following sections describe each of these types of security tokens in turn.

> **Note**
>
> XML Tokens were not specified in the WS-Security 1.0 specification; only `UsernameToken` and `BinarySecurityToken` were represented. A follow-on specification called WS-Security Profile for XML Tokens (`http://msdn.microsoft.com/webservices/default.aspx?pull=/library/en-us/dnglobspec/html/WS-Security-xml-tokens.asp`) came out in late August 2002. This strategy of breaking out different types of tokens into their own specification was continued in the OASIS committee, and all the different token types have been split into their own specification documents.

UsernameToken

No security mechanism would be complete without the old standby username/password option. We will try to forget that this mechanism is replete with problems—for example, simple, hackable passwords; or complex and therefore written-down passwords—and try to comment objectively. Security is often about making cost-benefit decisions, and in some situations, this is the appropriate security strategy. For example, you might consider using a username/password strategy if you have limited value or limited risk data and a user population unwilling or unable to use the more sophisticated authentication options such as X.509 client certificates.

A peculiar issue about putting username and password into a secured SOAP message is that one of the major objectives of using WS-Security is to have the message be self-protecting. Having a clear-text password persisted with the message defeats this purpose. You can employ strategies to move past this issue, but these strategies are not always available; therefore, additional vulnerabilities could be introduced if you are not careful. The following sections further explain what we mean.

UsernameToken **with Clear-Text Password**

Listing 7.3 shows the basic `UsernameToken` from the WS-Security specification.[4] This example shows a `Username` token with a WS-Security header.

Listing 7.3   **The Basic `<UsernameToken>` from the WS-Security Specification**

```
<S:Envelope>
    <S:Header>

        ...

        <wsse:Security>
            <wsse:UsernameToken>
                <wsse:Username>Zoe</wsse:Username>
                <wsse:Password>ILoveDogs</wsse:Password>
            </wsse:UsernameToken>
        </wsse:Security>
```

---

4. This example is from a February 2003 draft of the `UsernameToken` bindings document for WS-Security (`http://www.oasis-open.org/committees/wss/documents/WSS-Username-02-0223-merged.pdf`).

Listing 7.3   **Continued**

```
        </wsse:Security>
             . . .
      </S:Header>
      . . .
</S:Envelope>
```

You will notice, of course, that the password is right out in the clear. Ouch. That's not very secure. If you choose to use such an approach, you should at least consider running under SSL (or some other secure transport strategy) so that the message will be encrypted during transmission. This approach would be similar to combining HTTP basic authentication, which sends the username and password in the clear, with SSL. However, at least transport security does not represent itself as securing the message, and it is still hard to justify having the result of message security being applied and ending up with a clear-text password.

UsernameToken with PasswordDigest

WS-Security provides an alternative to the clear-text password approach. This approach, called PasswordDigest, is a viable alternative *as long as you already have the clear-text password on both sides of the exchange.* The process involves hashing some random information (more specifics on this topic in the next section, "Username PasswordDigest Algorithm") with the password and then sending it in the UsernameToken. The same process then occurs on the receiving end. The issue here is getting the password in clear text on both sides of the exchange.

In the Web application world, asking a user for a password is usually a straightforward process. The user is usually present to provide it, so you do not have to store it anywhere. If you have to store a password, it is common practice to store the password as a hashed value. When someone provides the password, you hash the password provided and compare the just-computed digest to the digest previously stored. Remember, hashes have the extremely valuable characteristic of being one way, so you cannot get from the stored digest back to the clear-text password. If, on the client *or* on the server side, the password has been stored as a hash value, the PasswordDigest option will not work for you because you need access to the password directly. Actually, in one situation, this is not completely true. If you know that both sides of the exchange have used the same hashing algorithm (SHA1, for instance), you can apply the algorithm described in the next section, substituting the digest itself for the password. In essence, the hash becomes the password.

Let's go through the details of the algorithm and then look at an example.

Username PasswordDigest *Algorithm*

To use the PasswordDigest type of UsernameToken, you hash together three items: a time stamp, a nonce, and the password itself:

- **Time stamp**—The time stamp is used to add entropy (randomness) to the resulting password digest, and it also helps the server side of the message exchange to enforce "freshness" constraints on the messages. In other words, the server can choose not to accept messages that have been sent more than *N* minutes before the current time. This raises the issue of clock *skew* between the client and server machines, so you will probably want to build some tolerance into the server to make up for this discrepancy. Enforcing freshness helps prevent an attacker from capturing and resending an old message (a replay attack).

Tip

You may want to pad the time frame by 10 minutes on either side to make up for potential differences in clocks on different machines. Time is an interesting subject in security, and we anticipate that reliable, synchronized time will become more and more important. Already most shops synchronize their servers to a universal common time. As servers become more interconnected via Web services, it will become more and more important for servers on the Internet to be synchronized to a common time. Consequently, several companies provide *trusted* time servers, synchronized to an atomic clock, that have been digitally signed by a trusted time authority. Such capabilities are critical for digital notary services, for example. When you think about how easily you can adjust the date and time on a particular computer, it is clear that globally synchronized, and perhaps "trusted," time will become critical in Web Services Security.

- **Nonce**—A nonce is just an arbitrary set of bytes that you create to help prevent replay attacks as well as add entropy to the resulting password digest. The client side generates the nonce, perhaps randomly, or perhaps by setting a counter. The trick is that the client should not send a duplicate nonce within the freshness period mentioned in the previous bullet. WS-Security recommends that the nonce be cached by the server for the duration of the freshness period and that any messages received with a duplicate nonce be rejected.

- **Password**—This item is just the clear-text password or shared secret. Note that it doesn't have to be a *password* in the common use of the word. It could be the hashed password, or it could be a pre-agreed-upon random set of octets. The type of password doesn't matter; in the end, it just must compare equally after the time stamp, nonce, and password have been concatenated and SHA1 hashed.

To summarize, as a client calling a Web service that requires a `UsernameToken` of type `PasswordDigest`, you (with help from your development tools most likely) will need to acquire a current time stamp, concatenate it to a unique nonce, and then concatenate them to the password. This combination then has the SHA1 algorithm applied, and you obtain the resulting digest password. You must then provide the information the server needs to repeat the process on the server side, which means the time stamp and nonce that were used are included in the `UsernameToken`. The `PasswordDigest` version of a `UsernameToken` looks like Listing 7.4.[5]

5. This example is from a February 2003 draft of the `UsernameToken` bindings document for WS-Security (http://www.oasis-open.org/committees/wss/documents/WSS-Username-02-0223-merged.pdf).

Listing 7.4   **The** `PasswordDigest` **Version of a** `UsernameToken`

```
<wsse:Security>
  <wsse:UsernameToken
    xmlns:wsse=" http://www.docs.oasis-open.org/wss/2004/01/oasis-200401-
wss-wssecurity-secext-1.0.xsd"
    xmlns:wsu=" http://www.docs.oasis-open.org/wss/2004/01/oasis-200401-
wss-wssecurity-utility-1.0.xsd">
    <wsse:Username>David Remy</wsse:Username>
    <wsse:PasswordType="wsse:PasswordDigest">
      D2A12DFE8D9F0C6BB82C89B091DF5C8A872F94DC
    </wsse:PasswordType>
    <wsse:Nonce>EFD89F06CCB28C89</wsse:Nonce>
    <wsu:Created>2001-10-13T09:00:00Z</wsu:Created>
  </wsse:UsernameToken>
</wsse:Security>
```

When the server receives this `UsernameToken`, it repeats the process that the client uses to create the password digest. As mentioned previously, it is recommended that the server help prevent a replay attack by checking for freshness of the time stamp, for example, and, if the message is fresh enough, checking for a unique nonce.

`UsernameToken PasswordDigest` *Summary*

If you can be confident that clients of your Web service will have access to a shared secret in the same form that you have it, password digest is a viable, secure technique for authentication that comes with some protection for replay and man-in-the-middle attacks. The digest approach is still password based and has the problems of keeping the passwords secret and difficult to guess, but, from an ease-of-use perspective, this option has significant appeal. (Even in security-sensitive organizations, passwords are still used as the most common authentication scheme today.)

BinarySecurityTokens

A `BinarySecurityToken` can contain one of a few classes of binary credentials. The two classes of `BinarySecurityTokens` designated in WS-Security are X.509 Version 3 certificates and Kerberos tickets. Listing 7.5 shows the template for a `BinarySecurityToken` element.

Listing 7.5   **The Template for a** `<BinarySecurityToken>` **Element**

```
<wsse:BinarySecurityToken wsu:Id=...
        EncodingType=...
        ValueType=...>
    ...Binary Data ...
<wsse:BinarySecurityToken/>
```

Because `BinarySecurityTokens` are binary, you must specify an encoding type to represent them in XML. For example, you define an encoding type of Base-64 by specifying the `EncodingType` value of `"wsse:Base64Binary"`. The `ValueType` specifies what type of `BinarySecurityToken` is being used. Three `ValueTypes` of `BinarySecurityTokens` are defined in the WS-Security specification: one is for X.509 Version 3 certificates, and the other two are related to Kerberos tickets. The following sections describe each of these types in turn.

X.509 V3 Certificate

As you have learned elsewhere in this book, an X.509 Version 3 certificate is a digital container for the public key part of a public/private (asymmetric) key pair. A certificate authority that attests to the identity related to the public key signs this digital container. An X.509 certificate is public information that can be freely distributed, which leads to the following question when using an X.509 certificate as an authentication token: How can a freely available public piece of information be used for authentication? Having access to an X.509 certificate by itself does nothing to authenticate the identity of the SOAP message's sender. The answer here is to require what is typically called *Proof of Possession*. In the case of an X.509 certificate, Proof of Possession means a digital signature, which in the case of WS-Security means an XML Signature. If your Web service requires an X.509 certificate in a `BinarySecurityToken`, you will almost certainly want an XML Signature along with it so that you can verify that the sender has access to the corresponding private key. Remember that public key technology relies on the security concept of "something you have," which is the private key. Digital signatures are the way you prove that you *have* the private key that was used to digitally sign a message. If the message's receiver is able to successfully verify the XML Signature with the public key in the X.509 certificate, and the receiver *trusts* the certificate authority that verified the identity associated with the private key that signed the X.509 certificate, an X.509 certificate becomes a strong authentication mechanism.

A `BinarySecurityToken` that contains an X.509 certificate contains a `ValueType` with the value of `"wsse:X509V3"` and, typically, an `EncodingType` of `"wsse:Base64Binary"`. Listing 7.6 shows an example of an X.509 certificate embedded in a `BinarySecurityToken`.

Listing 7.6   An X.509 Certificate Embedded in a `<BinarySecurityToken>`

```
<wsse:BinarySecurityToken Id="myX509Token"
        ValueType="wsse:X509v3"
        EncodingType="wsse:Base64Binary">
NIFEPzCCA9CrAwIBAgIQEmtJZc0 ... The rest of the X.509 base 64 data FExErTECA ...
</wsse:BinarySecurityToken>
```

We will further discuss including XML Signature in a `Security` header but now we need to make a point that relates to XML Signature and X.509 type `BinarySecurityTokens`. As you just learned, you will most likely have an XML

Signature whenever you have a `BinarySecurityToken` of `ValueType` `X509v3`. And, as you learned in Chapter 4, you can optionally specify the public key used to validate an XML Signature within a `KeyInfo` block. In a WS-Security implementation, it is recommended that the `KeyInfo` block point to a `BinarySecurityToken` instead of using one of the alternative methods of specifying the verification key. For example, with the `BinarySecurityToken` shown in Listing 7.6, the related XML Signature would have the `KeyInfo` block shown in Listing 7.7.

Listing 7.7   **The `<KeyInfo>`** **for the** `<BinarySecurityToken>` **of Listing 7.6**

```
<ds:KeyInfo>
    <wsse:SecurityTokenReference>
        <wsse:Reference URI="#myX509Token"/>
    </wsse:SecurityTokenReference>
</ds:KeyInfo>
```

Kerberos Tokens

As you read in Chapter 3, "The Foundations of Distributed Message-Level Security," Kerberos is a secret key technology–based network authentication protocol that involves a centralized Key Distribution Center (KDC). WS-Security makes it possible to pass a Kerberos ticket within a `BinarySecurityToken`. Two types of tickets are possible within Kerberos and, therefore, two `ValueType`s to represent them. When a Ticket Granting Ticket (TGT) is provided, the `ValueType` is `wsse:KerberosV5TGT`, and when a Service Ticket (ST) is present, the `ValueType` is `wsse:KerberosV5ST`. A TGT is independent of a particular service and is used more often for single sign-on purposes, whereas an ST is specific to a particular service. Listing 7.8 shows an example of a `BinarySecurityToken` containing a Kerberos ticket.

Listing 7.8   **A** `<BinarySecurityToken>` **Containing a Kerberos Ticket**

```
<wsse:BinarySecurityToken
    wsu:Id="myKerberosToken"
    ValueType="wsse:Kerberosv5TGT"
    EncodingType="wsse:Base64Binary">
MIIEZzCCA9CgAwIBAgIQEmtJZc0 ... The rest of the Kerberos base 64 data here ...
</wsse:BinarySecurityToken>
```

X.509 certificates and Kerberos tickets are the two binary security token types that currently have bindings specified within WS-Security. It is certainly possible that new binary type tokens will emerge; however, most of the movement of new token types has been in the area of XML Tokens, which we discuss next.

XML Tokens

In the original WS-Security specification, only `UsernameTokens` and `BinarySecurityTokens` were described. A follow-on specification for XML tokens was published soon after.[6] One distinguishing characteristic of XML tokens is that they are not grouped together under one wrapping element the way `BinarySecurityTokens` are. With XML security tokens, each type of token has its own wrapping top-level element. The following sections describe the XML-type tokens so you can get a feel for how they work.

SAML Tokens

As you learned in Chapter 6, "Portable Identity, Authentication, and Authorization," SAML is about representing identity, attributes, and/or authorization. In WS-Security, you can receive SAML assertion elements within the security header. Listing 7.9 shows the template for an SAML assertion.

Listing 7.9   **The Template for an SAML Assertion**

```
<saml:Assertion
    MajorVersion="1"
    MinorVersion="0"
    AssertionID="SecurityToken-ab12345"
    Issuer="yourIssuer"
    IssueInstant="2003-03-31T10:31:04.6118148-05:00"
    xmlns:saml="urn:oasis:names:tc:SAML:1.0:assertion">
...
</saml:Assertion>
```

SAML assertions have a problem similar to X.509 certificates. The relying party must be able to determine that the sender—or the identity being represented by the sender in the situation in which a third party is vouching for the sender—really has proof of that sender's identity. Thus, the relying party must confirm the *subject* of the assertion by one of two methods: `holder-of-key` or `sender-vouches`. With the `holder-of-key` method, the sender (requestor) includes an XML Signature that contains a `KeyInfo` block with a `SecurityTokenReference` pointing to the SAML assertion. In this case, the SAML assertion contains key material—for example, an X.509 certificate—for verification of the signature in its `ConfirmationMethod` element.

6. "WS-Security Profile for XML-Based Tokens," `http://msdn.microsoft.com/ webservices/default.aspx?pull=/library/en-us/dnglobspec/html/ WS-Security-xml-tokens.asp`

The other option for confirming the subject of the SAML assertion is `sender-vouches`. With `sender-vouches`, the sender of the message vouches for the assertion and will sign it. The major difference here is the target of the SAML assertions. With `holder-of-key`, the signature is typically created by the target of the SAML assertion; whereas with `sender-vouches`, the signature is created by a trusted third party that "vouches" for the SAML assertion.

Listing 7.10 shows an example of a full SOAP message with an SAML token using the `holder-of-key` subject confirmation strategy.

Listing 7.10   **A Full SOAP Message with an SAML Token Using the** `holder-of-key` `<ConfirmationMethod>`

```
<S:Envelope>
   <S:Header>
      <wsse:Security>
       <saml:Assertion
         xmlns:saml="urn:oasis:names:tc:SAML:1.0:assertion"
         MajorVersion="1" MinorVersion="0"
         AssertionID="myAssertion"
         Issuer="www.yourIssuer.com"
         IssueInstant="2003-03-31T12:58:21.132Z">
         <saml:Conditions
           NotBefore="2003-03-31T14:21:22.133Z"
           NotOnOrAfter="2003-03-31T16:02:11.123Z"/>
         <!-- An Authentication Assertion -->
         <saml:AuthenticationStatement
           AuthenticationMethod=
             "urn:oasis:names:tc:SAML:1.0:am:password"
           AuthenticationInstant="2003-03-31T14:21:22.000Z">
           <saml:Subject>
             <saml:NameIdentifier
               NameQualifier="www.company.com"
               Format="">
                 uid=fred,ou=company,ou=unit,o=company.com
             </saml:NameIdentifier>
             <saml:SubjectConfirmation>
               <saml:ConfirmationMethod>
                urn:oasis:names:tc:SAML:1.0:cm:holder-of-key
               </saml:ConfirmationMethod>
               <ds:KeyInfo>
                  <ds:KeyValue>. . .</ds:KeyValue>
               </ds:KeyInfo>
             </saml:SubjectConfirmation>
           </saml:Subject>
         </saml:AuthenticationStatement>
         <!-- An Attribute Assertion -->
             <saml:AttributeStatement>
```

Listing 7.10   Continued

```
                <saml:Attribute
                  AttributeName="E-mail"
                  AttributeNamespace=
                    "http://www.company.com/attributes">
                  <saml:AttributeValue>
                    fred@juno.com
                  </saml:AttributeValue>
                </saml:Attribute>
              </saml:AttributeStatement>
              <ds:Signature>...</ds:Signature>
            </saml:Assertion>
            <ds:Signature>
              <ds:SignedInfo>
                <ds:CanonicalizationMethod Algorithm=
                "http://www.w3.org/2001/10/xml-exc-c14n#"/>
                <ds:SignatureMethod Algorithm=
                  "http://www.w3.org/2000/09/xmldsig#hmac-sha1"/>
                </ds:Reference>
                <ds:Reference URI="#msgBody">
                  <ds:DigestMethod Algorithm=
                    "http://www.w3.org/2000/09/xmldsig#sha1"/>
                  <ds:DigestValue>
                    FxFtG0Ql3iPUr...
                  </ds:DigestValue>
                </ds:Reference>
              </ds:SignedInfo>
              <ds:SignatureValue>
                IKJwBVq81F32VjVRkF...
              </ds:SignatureValue>
              <ds:KeyInfo>
                <wsse:SecurityTokenReference>
                  <wsse:Keyidentifier ValueType="saml:Assertion"
                    myAssertion
                  </wsse:Keyidentifier >
                </wsse:SecurityTokenReference>
              </ds:KeyInfo>
            </ds:Signature>
        </wsse:Security>
      </S:Header>
      <S:Body wsu:Id="msgBody">
          <StatusRequest xmlns="http://www.mycompany.com/order">
            <OrderNumber>1234</OrderNumber>
          </StatusRequest>
      </S:Body>
  </S:Envelope>
```

Listing 7.10 includes an authentication assertion and an attribute assertion (asserting an email address for Fred). You will learn more about using XML Signatures to sign parts of a SOAP message later, but for now, notice that the XML Signature has as its `KeyInfo` a `SecurityTokenReference` that refers up to the SAML assertion. The SAML assertion wraps an `AuthenticationStatement` that specifies the `ConfirmationMethod` of `holder-of-key` (`urn:oasis:names:tc:SAML:1.0:cm:holder-of-key`) and contains its own `KeyInfo` that will contain the key material needed to validate the signature.

The concept of using SAML tokens with SOAP messages is powerful. Many of the scenarios outlined in the SAML specification are ideally suited to Web service scenarios. By including an SAML assertion in the security header of the message, you allow the message body to address the transaction and the security header to contain metadata to facilitate the transaction.

XrML Tokens

The eXtensible Rights Markup Language (XrML) is an XML syntax for Digital Rights Management (DRM), which is described in detail in Chapter 9, "Trust, Access Control, and Rights for Web Services." A binding for XrML is specified for WS-Security in which a `license` element can be included in the header. XrML has a similar problem to both X.509 certificates and SAML tokens with respect to confirming the claims a subject represented in the license. In XrML, you confirm these claims by including an XML Signature that points back to information in the license that provides the key material necessary to validate the XML Signature and therefore prove that the claim is legitimately bound to the message. Listing 7.11 shows an example of an XrML license in the security header of a SOAP message.

Listing 7.11   **An XrML License in the WS-Security Header of a SOAP Message**

```
<S:Envelope>
   <S:Header>
     <wsse:Security>
       <r:license licenseId="urn:foo:SecurityToken:ab12345">
         <r:grant>
           <r:keyHolder>
             <r:info>
               <ds:KeyValue>...</ds:KeyValue>
             </r:info>
           </r:keyHolder>
           <r:possessProperty/>
           <sx:commonName>John Doe</sx:commonName>
         </r:grant>
         <r:issuer>
           <ds:Signature>...</ds:Signature>
         </r:issuer>
       </r:license>
       <ds:Signature>
```

Listing 7.11   **Continued**

```
            <ds:SignedInfo>
              ...
              <ds:Reference URI="#msgBody">
                <ds:DigestMethod
          Algorithm="http://www.w3.org/2000/09/xmldsig#sha1" />
                <ds:DigestValue>...</ds:DigestValue>
              </ds:Reference>
            </ds:SignedInfo>
            <ds:SignatureValue>...</ds:SignatureValue>
            <ds:KeyInfo>
              <wsse:SecurityTokenReference>
                <wsse:Reference
                  URI="urn:foo:SecurityToken:ab12345"
                  ValueType="r:license" />
              </wsse:SecurityTokenReference>
            </ds:KeyInfo>
          </ds:Signature>
        </wsse:Security>
      </S:Header>
      <S:Body wsu:Id="msgBody">
          <PictureRequest xmlns="http://www.myCompany.com/pics">
            <Picture format="image/gif">
                AxElTrsRGGH...
            </Picture>
          </PictureRequest>
      </S:Body>
    </S:Envelope>
```

As you can see in Listing 7.11, similar to both the X.509 and SAML examples, an XML Signature references the SOAP message body. The KeyInfo contains a SecurityTokenReference, which in turn contains a Reference pointing up to the license security token identified by the licenseId that matches the URI.

XCBF Tokens

XML Common Biometric Format (XCBF) tokens are also specified as a type of security token that can be included in a WS-Security header. We do not describe these types of tokens in detail, but you can view the WS-Security XCBF binding specification at the OASIS Security TC site (http://www.oasis-open.org/committees/wss/documents/WSS-XCBF.pdf). The main point here is to show the flexibility of WS-Security to add new types of tokens by simply adding binding specifications.

Referencing Security Tokens

As you have seen in the examples just listed, one of the problems related to security tokens is how to reference them from other places. Whereas XML uses Key or Id as an identifier, the different types of security tokens can each have different strategies for unique identifiers. For example in XrML, licenseId is the most appropriate unique identifier. To address this issue, WS-Security introduces the SecurityTokenReference element as a standard way to refer to security tokens regardless of their format. Within a SecurityTokenReference, you can refer to a token in three ways: using direct elements, key identifiers, or key names.

A direct SecurityTokenReference simply points to the security token via a URI that optionally provides a hint, in a ValueType attribute, of what type of security token is being pointed to. A template for this approach is shown in Listing 7.12.

Listing 7.12 **The Template for a Direct** `<SecurityTokenReference>`

```
<wsse:SecurityTokenReference wsu:Id="...">
  <wsse:Reference URI="..." ValueType="..."/>
</wsse:SecurityTokenReference>
```

An example of a direct SecurityTokenReference is shown in Listing 7.13.

Listing 7.13 **An Example of a Direct** `<SecurityTokenReference>`

```
<wsse:SecurityTokenReference
  xmlns:wsse=" http://www.docs.oasis-open.org/wss/2004/01/oasis-200401-
wss-wssecurity-secext-1.0.xsd">
  <wsse:Reference
    URI="http://www.company.com/remy#X509token"
    ValueType="wsse:X509v3"/>
</wsse:SecurityTokenReference>
```

Alternatively, you can use a key identifier strategy in which you include an appropriate identifier of the key in the element. The key identifier approach allows for the use of a completely unique identifier based on the specific token type. Listing 7.14 shows a template for a `<KeyIdentifier>`-based SecurityTokenReference.

Listing 7.14 **Template for a** `<KeyIdentifier>`-**Based**
`<SecurityTokenReference>`

```
<wsse:SecurityTokenReference>
  <wsse:KeyIdentifier wsu:Id="..."
    ValueType="..."
    EncodingType="...">
    ... Value of Key Identifier here ...
  </wsse:KeyIdentifier>
</wsse:SecurityTokenReference>
```

An example of such a `<SecurityTokenReference>` is shown is Listing 7.15.

Listing 7.15   **An example of a** `<KeyIdentifier>`-**Based**
                `<SecurityTokenReference>`

```
<wsse:SecurityTokenReference>
  <wsse:KeyIdentifier
    ValueType="wsse:X509v3">
      uTHyQBrcgFu4xmo14mD/iYgyyIg=
  </wsse:KeyIdentifier>
</wsse:SecurityTokenReference>
```

You also can use a `ds:KeyName` element to refer to a security token by some arbitrary name of the key; however, the specification discourages this approach because the `KeyName` is not necessarily unique and could therefore match multiple security tokens.

    These three types of references refer to a security token that is outside the `SecurityTokenReference` itself. Another option is to embed the security token directly into the `SecurityTokenReference`, as shown in Listing 7.16.

Listing 7.16   **An Example of Embedding the Security Token Directly into the**
                `<SecurityTokenReference>`

```
<wsse:SecurityTokenReference>
  <wsse:Embedded>
   <wsse:BinarySecurityToken
     ValueType="wsse:X509v3"
     EncodingType="wsse:Base64Binary"
     wsu:Id="X509Token">
       MIIEZzCCA9CgAwIBAgIQEmtJZc0rqrKh5i...
   </wsse:BinarySecurityToken>
  </wsse:Embedded>
</wsse:SecurityTokenReference>
```

One common place you will see a `SecurityTokenReference` is a `KeyInfo` block within an XML Signature in the security header. It is also possible to have `SecurityTokenReference` elements directly in the security header.

    At this point, we've completed our coverage of security tokens in WS-Security. Over time, new types of security tokens will emerge and should fit into the flexible WS-Security specification. Already, the types of security tokens envisioned will provide powerful identification and authorization technology not only at the enterprise level, but also for the broader Internet.

Providing Confidentiality: XML Encryption in WS-Security

The next major feature of WS-Security to cover is using XML Encryption to hide selective information in SOAP messages. As you read in Chapter 5, "Ensuring Confidentiality of XML Messages," XML Encryption is a powerful, flexible technology for encrypting all or part of an XML document. Nearly everything discussed in Chapter 5 on XML Encryption is applicable to WS-Security, but there are few new features and considerations for weaving XML Encryption into a SOAP message.

Shared Key XML Encryption

Let's start our discussion of XML Encryption in WS-Security with a simple scenario: encrypting the body of a SOAP message using a shared (symmetric) key. In XML Encryption, you would represent this scenario by creating an `EncryptedData` block in the place where the clear-text element would have been. In WS-Security, in addition to the `EncryptedData` element, a `ReferenceList` in the security header will point to the parts of the message that have been encrypted. Listing 7.17 shows an example.

Listing 7.17   **Use of a `<ReferenceList>` in the Security Header Pointing to the Parts of the Message Encrypted with XML Encryption**

```
<S:Envelope>
  <S:Header>
    <wsse:Security>
      <xenc:ReferenceList>
        <xenc:DataReference URI="#body"/>
      </xenc:ReferenceList>
    </wsse:Security>
  </S:Header>
  <S:Body>
    <xenc:EncryptedData Id="body">
      <xenc:CipherData>
        <xenc:CipherValue>...</xenc:CipherValue>
      </xenc:CipherData>
    </xenc:EncryptedData>
  </S:Body>
</S:Envelope>
```

As you can see in Listing 7.17, the body of the SOAP message has been encrypted, and an `EncryptedData` element (with an `Id` of `"body"`) represents the SOAP body. The new feature here is the `ReferenceList` within the `Security` element. The `ReferenceList` contains `DataReference` elements for each item encrypted, which in this case is just the SOAP body.

As we have mentioned multiple times in this book, from a key management perspective, a shared key approach can cause serious difficulties because you need to communicate (share) the key with the receiver or receivers out-of-band so that they can decrypt the message. Consequently, you will often see the shared encryption key wrapped by another key, as discussed next.

Wrapped Key XML Encryption

Shared key encryption is very fast, scalable to any size message, and, consequently, is always used for encrypting the XML text of a message. Public key encryption has beneficial key management characteristics because a public key, typically wrapped in an X.509 certificate issued by a certificate authority, can be published publicly in a registry or even in the WSDL. The recipient's public key can then be used to encrypt the shared key, and the shared key can be used to encrypt the different parts of the message itself.

Let's go over that again but in a different order. First, the message itself, or perhaps multiple individual parts of the message, are encrypted using a generated arbitrary shared key. Second, this shared key is then encrypted using the recipient's public key. Because the recipient is the holder of the solitary matching and highly protected private key, theoretically, the recipient is the only one who can decrypt the shared key and then proceed to decrypt the rest of the message.

The technique is often called *key wrapping* or *digital enveloping* because the shared key is wrapped by the recipient's public key. Although we tend to emphasize using a public key for key wrapping, it is equally possible to use a shared key to wrap a shared key.

> **Tip**
>
> You might use a shared key to wrap other shared keys in a "master key" scenario. In this scenario, a single master shared key can be used to encrypt multiple other shared keys used to encrypt different parts of the document. With this approach, intended recipients can read only their parts of the document, but the holder of the master key can read the entire document.

When key wrapping is involved in WS-Security, an `EncryptedKey` element shows up in the security header. The `ReferenceList` in the `EncryptedKey` element points to the `EncryptedData` elements that use the underlying encrypted key. Listing 7.18 shows an example of a wrapped key in a security header.

Listing 7.18   A Wrapped Key in a Security Header for Use in XML Encryption

```
<S:Envelope>
  <S:Header>
    <wsse:Security>
      <xenc:EncryptedKey>
        <xenc:EncryptionMethod Algorithm="..."/>
        <ds:KeyInfo>
          <wsse:SecurityTokenReference>
            <wsse:KeyIdentifier EncodingType="wsse:Base64Binary"
```

Listing 7.18 **Continued**

```
                ValueType="wsse:X509v3">
              F2JfLa0GXSq...
           </wsse:KeyIdentifier>
         </wsse:SecurityTokenReference>
       </ds:KeyInfo>
       <xenc:CipherData>
         <xenc:CipherValue>...</xenc:CipherValue>
       </xenc:CipherData>
       <xenc:ReferenceList>
         <xenc:DataReference URI="#body"/>
       </xenc:ReferenceList>
     </xenc:EncryptedKey>
   </wsse:Security>
 </S:Header>
 <S:Body>
   <xenc:EncryptedData Id="body">
     <xenc:CipherData>
       <xenc:CipherValue>...</xenc:CipherValue>
     </xenc:CipherData>
   </xenc:EncryptedData>
 </S:Body>
</S:Envelope>
```

In Listing 7.18, you can see that the `EncryptedKey` uses a public key to encrypt a shared key, which is in turn used to encrypt the message body. The public key used to do the encryption is within a `SecurityTokenReference` using the embedded style in the `KeyInfo` block. The recipient uses this key to assist in locating the corresponding private key that will be required to decrypt the shared key that is encrypted within the `CipherValue`. The `ReferenceList`, which is used to list the `EncryptedData` elements that this key was used to encrypt, then points to the body of the SOAP message (`URI="body"`). This example is really no different from what was discussed in Chapter 5 except that the prescribed location of the `EncryptedKey` element is in the security header, not in the body.

Encrypting Attachments

We have not addressed attachments very much in this book, in large part because there is continued turmoil about how best to implement attachments, much less secure them. *SOAP with Attachments* (SwA) is a W3C Note and has never reached recommendation status. Microsoft has proposed an alternative based on Direct Internet Message Encapsulation (DIME). DIME[7] is meant to address issues that MIME has with speed and efficiency, especially for large attachments. Both of these approaches cause attachments

---

7. See the Microsoft DIME index page at `http://msdn.microsoft.com/library/` `default.asp?url=/library/en-us/dnglobspec/html/dimeindex.asp`.

to exist outside the XML Infoset, which makes it difficult for them to integrate well with the emerging WS-★ standards. Consequently, ongoing standards work is being done to have attachments become a full-fledged member of the XML Infoset. At this point, it is unclear whether a new approach to attachments will emerge or whether the existing approaches such as SwA or DIME will become de facto standards.

SwA, which is arguably the most prevalent attachments strategy, proposes MIME as an approach for handling attachments. With SwA using MIME, the overall message is broken up into parts, in which one part is the SOAP message and the other parts of the message are attachments that contain a MIME type such as text/plain, image/gif, and so on, as diagrammed in Figure 7.3.

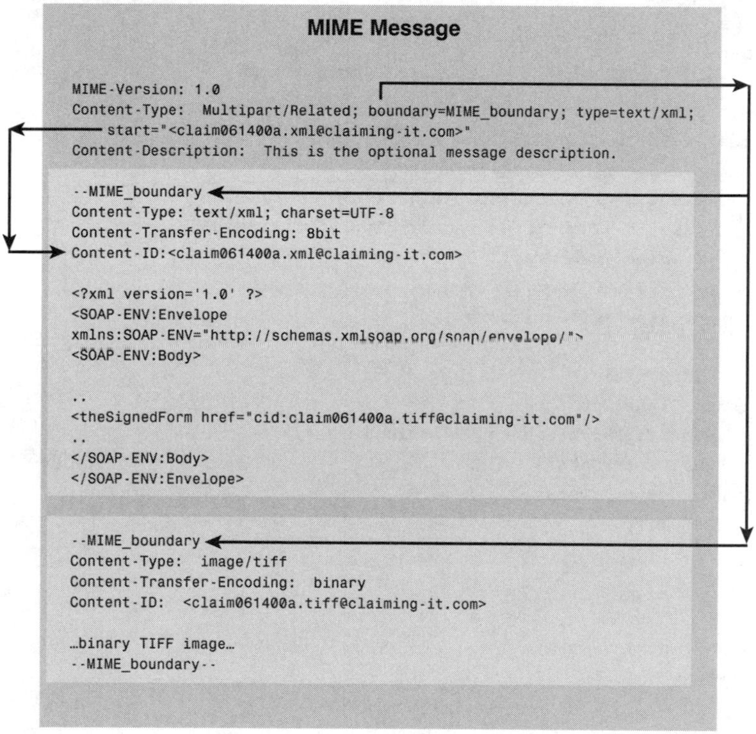

Figure 7.3 MIME message with attachment.

Obviously, when you have attachments, you may want to encrypt them along with or independent of the body of the message. To accomplish this, you use an `EncryptedData` element directly in the security header. This `EncryptedData` element will contain a `ReferenceList` pointing to the attachment that is encrypted. Listing 7.19 shows an example.

Listing 7.19   SOAP with Encrypted MIME Attachments

```
MIME-Version: 1.0
Content-Type: Multipart/Related; boundary=MIME_boundary; type=text/xml;
        start="<soapMessage>"
Content-Description: This is the optional message description.

--MIME_boundary
Content-Type: text/xml; charset=UTF-8
Content-Transfer-Encoding: 8bit
Content-ID: <soapMessage>

<?xml version='1.0' ?>
<S:Envelope
  <S:Header>
    <wsse:Security>
      <xenc:EncryptedData MimeType="image/tiff">
        <ds:KeyInfo>
          <wsse:SecurityTokenReference>
            <xenc:EncryptionMethod Algorithm="..."/>
            <wsse:KeyIdentifier EncodingType="wsse:Base64Binary"
              ValueType="wsse:X509v3">
                F2JfLa0GXSq...
            </wsse:KeyIdentifier>
          </wsse:SecurityTokenReference>
        </ds:KeyInfo>
        <xenc:CipherData>
          <xenc:CipherReference URI="cid:image"/>
        </xenc:CipherData>
      </xenc:EncryptedData>
    </wsse:Security>
  </S:Header>
  <S:Body>
  ...
  </S:Body>
</S:Envelope>

--MIME_boundary
Content-Type: image/tiff
Content-Transfer-Encoding: binary
Content-ID: <image>

...binary TIFF image...
--MIME_boundary--
```

In this example, a TIFF image, which is one of the message parts, is being encrypted. The attachment itself will have a MIME type of application/octet-stream, so the

MimeType on the EncryptedData element represents the original MIME type of the attachment before encryption. The CipherReference points to the attachment via the URI="cid:image" attribute.

WS-Security Encryption Summary

As you can see from the code listings, XML Encryption in WS-Security mostly just provides some extra rules about how to use XML Encryption within a SOAP message, although a few new uses are introduced with ReferenceList and EncryptedData in the security header. Notice that the main SOAP elements such as Envelope, Header, and Body are never encrypted because these elements are necessary for the SOAP infrastructure to work effectively.

Providing Integrity: XML Signature in WS-Security

Like XML Encryption, the XML Signature used in WS-Security is the same as discussed in Chapter 4. There are some special considerations for using XML Signature in a SOAP message, but mechanically it is just XML Signature put into the security header of a SOAP message.

XML Signature is used within WS-Security for two major reasons. One is to verify a security token credential such as an X.509 certificate or SAML assertion. Another is message *integrity*—verifying that the message (or important parts of it) has not been modified in transit.

XML Signature for Validating a Security Token

Let's examine the first reason for XML Signature using an X.509 certificate–based security token—to verify a security token credential. As we have mentioned previously, an X.509 certificate wraps metadata and a public key in an envelope that is digitally signed by a certificate authority. In addition to the public key, one of the most important pieces of metadata is the identity that is being represented by the certificate, which is attested to by the certificate authority. This identity is often the Subject or Common Name in the X.509 certificate but could also be a different attribute in the certificate, such as an attribute added for a partner identifier.

What makes the X.509 certificate valuable from an authentication perspective is the public key/private key relationship. If the presenter can prove that he has the private key that corresponds to the public key, then it is assumed that the presenter's identity is represented by the X.509 certificate. The presenter then proves *possession* of the corresponding private key by using a digital signature. If the presenter digitally signs a piece of known text with his private key, and you are able to validate the signature against this known text using the public key in the X.509 certificate, you can trust (to the extent you trust the certificate authority and to the extent you can trust that the private key has not been compromised) that the presenter has the identity represented.

XML Signature for Message Integrity

XML Signatures are also used to certify and maintain the integrity of the message itself. By signing the body of a message or some other part of a message, you can guarantee that the message arrives unaltered at the receiver's end as long as the receiver applies the signature validation process.

XML Signature in WS-Security Considerations

Chapter 4 described the different XML Signature models: Enveloped, Enveloping, and Detached Signatures. Because of the mutability of SOAP headers—an intermediary can add or make changes to messages—the Detached Signature model is the only one that makes sense for SOAP messages. This means that a WS-Security–signed message will always contain an explicit `Reference` element for what is being signed.

The possibility of legitimate changes in transit could conceivably cause problems with the XPath statements that are used in the Reference URI of the XML Signature. You must be careful when constructing XPath statements so that they remain valid at the point of signature validation.

The header can contain more than one XML Signature, and the signatures can potentially overlap. For example, imagine a scenario in which a message containing an order is traveling through intermediaries or processing stages within an enterprise. Say the message first goes to the order processing system that inserts a header containing the `order-id` and digitally signs it, putting an XML Signature into the security header that points to the `order-id` header. Then the message goes to the Shipping department, where someone inserts a `shipping-id` header and digitally signs both the `order-id` and `shipping-id`. When this message reaches the Billing department, these XML Signatures are validated prior to billing the customer.

WS-Security XML Signature Example

To illustrate this discussion of XML Signature in a SOAP message, Listing 7.20 shows a more complete example.

Listing 7.20   **A Complete Example of XML Signature in a SOAP Message**

```
<S:Envelope>
  <S:Header>
    <wsse:Security>
      <wsse:BinarySecurityToken
        ValueType="wsse:X509v3"
        EncodingType="wsse:Base64Binary"
        wsu:Id="X509Token">
        FIgEZzCRFlEgILBAgIQEmtJZcOrqrKh5i...
      </wsse:BinarySecurityToken>
      <ds:Signature>
        <ds:SignedInfo>
```

Listing 7.20 **Continued**

```
            <ds:CanonicalizationMethod
Algorithm=" http://www.w3.org/2001/10/xml-exc-c14n#" />
            <ds:SignatureMethod
Algorithm="http://www.w3.org/2000/09/xmldsig#rsa-sha1" />
            <ds:Reference URI="#body">
              <ds:Transforms>
                <ds:Transform
Algorithm=" http://www.w3.org/2001/10/xml-exc-c14n#" />
              </ds:Transforms>
              <ds:DigestMethod
Algorithm="http://www.w3.org/2000/09/xmldsig#sha1" />
              <ds:DigestValue>EULddytSo1...</ds:DigestValue>
            </ds:Reference>
          </ds:SignedInfo>
          <ds:SignatureValue>
            XLdER8=ErToEbll/vXcMZNNjPOV...
          </ds:SignatureValue>
          <ds:KeyInfo>
            <wsse:SecurityTokenReference>
              <wsse:Reference URI="#X509Token"/>
            </wsse:SecurityTokenReference>
          </ds:KeyInfo>
        </ds:Signature>
      </wsse:Security>
  </S:Header>
  <S:Body wsu:Id="body">
    <StatusRequest xmlns="http://www.myCompany.com/Order">
      <OrderNumber>1234</OrderNumber>
    </StatusRequest>
  </S:Body>
</S:Envelope>
```

As you can see, using XML Signature in SOAP is reasonably natural. Listing 7.20 signs the body of the SOAP message by assigning an Id of body to the Soap Body element and then uses that as a target of the Reference URI in the signature. Notice the use of a SecurityTokenReference pointing up to the X.509 certificate wrapped in a BinarySecurityToken.

Signing a Security Token Reference

In many circumstances, signing security tokens themselves is necessary. As we mentioned earlier, there is a standard way to refer to security tokens using a strategy represented by the SecurityTokenReference element. Because this dereferencing strategy is different from URIs, the WS-Security specification introduces a new XML Signature-referencing strategy called the *STR Dereference Transform*. The idea is that what is being signed does not include the `SecurityTokenReference` itself; it signs what the `SecurityTokenReference` *points* to. This makes sense: You care about keeping integrity on the security token itself, not the reference. Listing 7.21 shows an example of a digital signature applied to a security token that is represented by a `SecurityTokenReference`.

Listing 7.21   **A Signature Signing a Security Token to Maintain Its Integrity**

```
...
<!-- This is the security token to be signed -->
<wsse:BinarySecurityToken Id="myX509Token"
...
</wsse:BinarySecurityToken>
...
<!-- This the security token reference -->
<wsse:SecurityTokenReference wsu:Id="mySecurityToken">
  <wsse:Reference URI="#myX509Token"/>
</wsse:SecurityTokenReference>
...
<Signature xmlns="http://www.w3.org/2000/09/xmldsig#">
  <SignedInfo>
    ...
    <Reference URI="#mySecurityToken">
      <ds:Transforms>
        <ds:Transform Algorithm="...#STR-Transform">
          <wsse:TransformationParameters>
            <ds:CanonicalizationMethod
             Algorithm="http://www.w3.org/TR/2001/REC-xml-c14n-20010315" />
          </wsse:TransformationParameters>
        </ds:Transform>
      </Reference>
  </SignedInfo>
  <SignatureValue></SignatureValue>
</Signature>
...
```

As you can see in this example, the `Reference` element in the XML Signature points back to `#mySecurityToken`, which is a `SecurityTokenReference` (rather than a security token). The STR Dereference Transform that is associated with the Signature `Reference` will follow the `SecurityTokenReference` back to the security token itself and validate the signature against that rather than the `SecurityTokenReference`.

Message Time Stamps

In general the WS-Security standard does not define any new security mechanisms; it just provides a standard way of packaging existing mechanisms into a SOAP message.

Message time stamps are the exception to this in that WS-Security defines a specific structure for including a message time stamp in the security header. From a security perspective, you often need to know information about the *freshness* of a message. If a message is *stale*, depending on the context, it should possibly be ignored. WS-Security defines a mechanism, using the `Timestamp` header for the message's sender to add information such as when the message was created and when the message should expire. Listing 7.22 shows an example of a `Timestamp` header (note that the `wsu` prefix refers to the WS-Services Utility namespace).

Listing 7.22   **An Example of a `<Timestamp>` Header**

```
<S:Envelope>
  <S:Header>
    <wsu:Timestamp>
      <wsu:Created>2001-04-03T08:42:00Z</wsu:Created>
      <wsu:Expires>2001-04-04T09:00:00Z</wsu:Expires>
    </wsu:Timestamp>
    ...
  </S:Header>
  <S:Body>
    ...
  </S:Body>
</S:Envelope>
```

As you can see here, the message's sender has declared a `Created` time and an `Expires` time. You need to take into account that the `Expires` time was the time on the machine that sent the message; consequently, potential clock skew—a difference between the sender's clock and the receiver's clock—can exist.

Message time stamps are a useful addition to the security header and can be used for other purposes than just finding the time; for example, a `TimeStampTrace` element can be used as a target of an intermediary's signature to prove the claim of an X.509 certificate.

WS-Security and Web Services Performance

Just like SSL, WS-Security poses a performance penalty: in transmission time, memory, and CPU.

Message Size

As you may have noticed from the examples in this chapter, a message that has been secured with a WS-Security header can have a significant amount of security information embedded within it. In one of the examples with a message 39 lines long, the security header was 27 lines and the message body was only 5 lines! This example did not contain X.509 certificates or SAML assertions, which would have ballooned the size of the header even more. In high-volume situations, size could significantly affect transmission time, processing time, and memory consumption.

Message Processing

Although WS-Security itself can be Implemented in a streaming fashion, giving some improvement to the WS-Security processing itself, in general, WS-Security Signature and Encryption will hurt streaming Web services implementations. This stands to reason because the entire message must be read to create or validate the XML Signature(s) and to encrypt or decrypt through XML Encryption. This particularly hurts for large inbound messages because the optimizations of Web services engines for streaming are lost.

CPU Utilization

In general, security technologies such as digital signature and encryption are computationally intense. Shared key technology, used for bulk encryption, tends to be fast; however, public key technology tends to be slow. So, digital signature creation and validation, as well as shared key wrapping, could add significantly to the processing burden. Also, we have heard anecdotally that the XML Canonicalization process, similar to other XML processing operations, can be slow.

Although the significance of this will vary with the WS-Security and Web services engine you use, overall, you will likely find that WS-Security can significantly degrade your performance, particularly in high-volume or large-message-size situations.

The solution will probably be hardware accelerator devices that operate at or close to wire speed and that have specialized cryptographic hardware chips for fast encryption, decryption, and even hashing functions.

Summary

This discussion of WS-Security brings together all the concepts discussed in this book so far. The SOAP security header provides a location in the SOAP message for assembling the various security mechanisms available. Security tokens provide the mechanism for authentication and authorization technology in a very flexible manner. Security tokens mirror similar technologies outside WS-Security, such as username and password, X.509 certificates, and SAML assertions. XML Signatures fit into WS-Security in a natural way as *detached* XML Signatures, with the Signature element sitting in the security header and the Reference URI pointing to another part of the message, such as the SOAP body or another SOAP header. The effect on XML Encryption is greater because the EncryptedData element needs to be in the actual message part that is being encrypted. Consequently, the ReferenceList is used to point to the EncryptedData elements. However, this ReferenceList is really no different from the ReferenceList that is a child of EncryptedKey, so this concept is really not new.

The advent of security tokens with WS-Security is one of the more significant aspects of WS-Security for several reasons. One is the flexibility of the standard to add new security token types by adding new specification documents rather than having to amend the WS-Security specification itself. Thus, as new types of security tokens emerge, they can be brought in to the WS-Security world. The second reason is that they provide a more tailored mechanism than the standard KeyInfo structure provided from the XML Signature specification. The XML Signature KeyInfo structure has a predefined set of elements, most of which are optional but are constrained and appear to be mostly inspired by X.509 technology. Because a security token can have exactly the structure it needs to have, it can fully represent disparate authentication and authorization technologies. For security tokens to be fully supported, we needed to be able to point to them from a `KeyInfo` block; hence, the `SecurityTokenReference` rounds out the security token technology, allowing a generic way to point to the various security token types.

One issue of concern about WS-Security is that it does not define how to secure a SOAP message. For example, WS-Security does not specify what it means to have an encrypted message; it just tells you how to put encryption in the header. WS-Security is neutral about whether you should sign and encrypt the entire body, certain headers, or just a single character in the message. You should think of WS-Security as a set of tools that you can apply to your specific Web services scenario. The really hard work of determining your *security policy* is up to you, and with all the possible approaches that WS-Security provides, this task can be daunting.

As a developer, you will most likely be exposed to WS-Security functionality through development tools. Generally, these development tools create simplifying options to encrypt or sign a message, for instance. With BEA's Weblogic Workshop product, for example, when you designate that you want a SOAP request to be signed (perhaps because the Web service you are calling requires it), the entire message is signed by default. Also, related to this, interoperability organizations such as the Web Services Interoperability Organization (WSI, `http://www.ws-i.org/`) are defining standard profiles for WS-Security interactions so that applications secured with the various Web services development tools can successfully interoperate.

WS-Security has tremendous momentum, and the technology is available for every major Web services container such as Microsoft's Advanced Server, IBM's Websphere, and BEA's Weblogic Platform. As a developer or security administrator, you undoubtedly will need to have an understanding of this technology and the way it applies in your context.

WS-Security is not the end of the Web services–related security technology standards. Quite the contrary. When IBM and Microsoft laid out their Web Services Security roadmap, WS-Security was the base of the proposed architecture. WS-Policy, WS-Trust, WS-Privacy, WS-SecureConversation, WS-Federation, and WS-Authorization were all mentioned as follow-on standards to WS-Security in this roadmap. WS-Policy, which focuses on communicating the Web services security requirements, is the focus of Chapter 8, and Chapter 9 discusses the other WS-Security standards, often called the WS-* standards.

8

Communicating Security Policy

WS-Policy

At this point in the book, you have learned a great deal about what is required to secure a Web service using the many different available security options such as WS-Security, Security Assertion Markup Language (SAML), and so forth. Even if you did not read this chapter on WS-Policy, you could secure Web services using these technologies, and with some hard work and vigilance, you could successfully implement secure Web services.

Although you could implement secure Web services this way, and although many of the current Web services implementations will take just this approach, how will users of your Web service know the security requirements your Web service has? Similarly, if you want to use a Web service over the Internet or perhaps some far-away department of your company, how would you know what type of security to apply to your SOAP requests to interact with that Web service?

The emerging answers to these questions lie in the WS-Policy framework. The WS-Policy framework strives to provide a mechanism for exchanging requirements, not just security requirements (although WS-Policy was originally inspired by security policy issues), between a Web services client and a Web service provider. WS-Policy recognizes that the need to express a set of requirements for a Web service—a "policy"—exists across many domains, such as transactions, reliable messaging, privacy, security, and more we perhaps have not even thought of yet. Consequently, WS-Policy is actually a set of specifications providing generalized mechanisms for describing policy in a machine-readable way. The idea is that there ought to be a common language for describing the rules for interacting with a Web service, or what a client requires of a Web service, regardless of whether the domain is security, privacy, transactions, or any other category. Also, some of these rules, called *assertions* in WS-Policy, are common across all domains. For example, "I require SOAP version 1.1" could be a common rule whether in the security domain or in the privacy or reliable messaging domain.

WS-Policy and WSDL

At first, you might think that WS-Policy is just an extension of the Web Services Description Language (WSDL), and there have been early attempts at making it so; however, developers of WS-Policy have gone out of their way to make it a standalone concept that you can point to or include in various ways. Consequently, WS-Policy can be associated with a Web service in a variety of powerful ways. For example, you could choose to have specific parts of the WSDL, such as a specific operation or even a message for a Web service, point to a policy. Another possibility would be to have WS-Policy point to a set of Web services that it covers. This standalone nature of WS-Policy is also important because Web service clients do not have WSDLs, yet WS-Policy also applies to Web services clients. For example, you can easily imagine a situation in which a Web service's client expects sensitive information from a Web service and wants to require that encryption be used when the Web service responds to the request message. WS-Policy allows a Web services client to express this and not participate with any Web service that is unwilling or unable to participate in encryption.

At the time of this writing, the WS-Policy framework is still evolving, but the vision of WS-Policy is a powerful and important part of the evolution of Web services. Ultimately, the perfectly executed WS-Policy would involve policy negotiation between Web services, where multiple rounds of negotiation could occur. This capability would allow a mutually agreeable policy for both the Web service client and the Web service itself. This has been a long-standing vision, perhaps inspired by early visions of "agent" technology, which would allow for much more flexibility and dynamism between Web services. Although WSDL has been an extremely valuable standard and has been instrumental in the phenomenal growth of Web services, it has the problem of being a fairly static and limited instrument for describing a Web service. More and more technologies such as Web services message brokers are working to make WSDL more dynamic so that parts of the WSDL, such as the Web service's location URI, can dynamically change based on any number of factors, including message content. WS-Policy appears much more suited for these types of dynamic interactions and, perhaps, could become the description language for Web services (and Web services clients, a new thing) of the future.

WS-Policy and WS-SecurityPolicy

This chapter covers the WS-Policy framework in detail with emphasis, of course, on security policy. WS-Policy could change quite a bit by the time you read this chapter; however, the concepts and strategies used to describe policy will likely be stable, and these concepts will be the basis for the final WS-Policy specifications.

Let's start by discussing the need for a WS-Security policy and the ways you might use it at a high level. As you saw in the preceding chapter on WS-Security, you have numerous options when implementing WS-Security on your Web services. How could you express this information to a Web services client wanting to use your Web service?

What would you have to tell that Web services client? The following are some facts you might want to express:

- A security token of a specific type (for example, `UsernameToken`) is required.

- Encryption is required, and here is the public key you will need to encrypt a message destined for this Web service.

- A signature is required.

Having only three requirements doesn't seem so bad. It would be nice if the situation were this simple. In reality, multiple other issues must be addressed:

- How do you describe the part of the message that must be encrypted? XML Encryption is extremely flexible, and the WS-Security specification provides no guidelines for what constitutes an encrypted message. You must decide that based on your Web service's requirements.

- Similarly, how do you describe what must be signed? Does the whole body need to be signed, or just a part of the body or a specific header?

- What algorithms do the server and client support? If the server chooses a stronger algorithm, is it acceptable?

- A typical synchronous Web services call contains two independent SOAP messages: a request and a response. Naturally, when securing a Web service, most people think about what a client will be required to do with the incoming request for the Web service to accept that request. However, you also likely need to describe to the client what the Web service will do with the response SOAP message:

  - I will return this type of token.

  - I will encrypt the response message.

  - I will sign the response message.

- Finally, and this is the one of the largest issues, what message security does the client require? WSDL supports a one-way interaction in which the Web service publishes its requirements and the client of the Web service must adhere to them. However, in WS-Security scenarios, the client may want a say in the security requirements. For example, say that a Web service provides credit reports. As a client, you would likely want the Web service to sign and encrypt the contents of a message back to you. In this case, a mechanism must be in place for the client to communicate its minimum requirements.

The WS-Policy Framework

As you can see, there is a need for something more expressive than what exists with WSDL alone. In an effort to create a richer language for describing the constraints around WS-Security, as we discussed at the beginning of this chapter, another specification framework called WS-Policy has emerged. The WS-Policy framework describes policies about nearly anything related to Web services; however, it is particularly well suited to WS-Security. The WS-Policy framework consists of a set of specifications relating to policy:

- WS-Policy defines a framework for describing policy assertions.
- WS-PolicyAttachment describes how these policies are attached to a resource (for example, WSDL).
- WS-PolicyAssertions describes a common set of assertions that are applicable across different domains.

These three WS-Policy specifications set the stage for WS-SecurityPolicy, which provides a set of WS-Security–specific policies used to publish information about all aspects of WS-Security.

WS-Policy Details

WS-Policy is a generalized grammar for describing the capabilities, requirements, and characteristics of a Web service.[1] It is not specific to a particular problem domain such as security; however, security was the initial problem domain that provoked the creation of a higher-level WS-Policy grammar. Aside from security, WS-Policy can be used for reliable messaging, privacy, or quality-of-service characteristics. WS-Policy itself does not describe how a policy would be bound to a Web service; however, a separate specification called WS-PolicyAttachment[2] describes this use, and we will touch on this topic next.

To specify a policy in WS-Policy, you make assertions. A policy assertion describes some requirement that a Web service or client must adhere to. For example, the server might specify that a specific encryption algorithm must be used when encrypting messages bound for the service. Policy assertions are wrapped by a `Policy` element. Listing 8.1 shows an example of a `Policy` element from the WS-Policy specification.

Listing 8.1   **A Sample `<Policy>` Element**

```
<wsp:Policy xmlns:wsp="..." xmlns:wsse="...">
  <wsp:ExactlyOne>
    <wsp:All wsp:Preference="100"/>
      <wsse:SecurityToken TokenType="wsse:Kerberosv5TGT" />
      <wsse:Algorithm Type="wsse:AlgSignature"
        URI=" http://www.w3.org/2000/09/xmlenc#aes"/>
    </wsp:All>
    <wsp:All wsp:Preference="1"/>
      <wsse:SecurityToken TokenType="wsse:X509v3" />
```

1. See the WS-Policy specification at http://msdn.microsoft.com/webservices/default.aspx?pull=/library/en-us/dnglobspec/html/ws-policy.asp.
2. See the WS-Policy Attachment specification at http://msdn.microsoft.com/webservices/default.aspx?pull=/library/en-us/dnglobspec/html/ws-policyattachment.asp.

Listing 8.1 **Continued**

```
        <wsse:Algorithm Type="wsse:AlgEncryption"
                URI="http://www.w3.org/2001/04/xmlenc#3des-cbc"/>
        </wsp:All>
      </wsp:ExactlyOne>
</wsp:Policy>
```

Reading this policy is reasonably straightforward. The policy first has the `ExactlyOne` operator, which means that one of its direct child elements must be applicable. In this example, the `ExactlyOne` operator has two `All` operator children, so one of them must be applicable. An `All` operator means that all the assertions must be applicable. The first `All` specifies that the two assertions, a Kerberos token and an AES encryption algorithm, must be used. The second `All` specifies that an X.509 certificate and the 3DES encryption algorithm must be used. So this policy statement says you must have either a Kerberos v5 TGT token *and* use the AES algorithm to encrypt, *or* an X.509 token *and* use 3DES to encrypt.

Listing 8.2 shows a template of the usage syntax for a `Policy` statement.

Listing 8.2 **The Template for the `<Policy>` Structure**

```
<wsp:Policy wsu:Id="..."? Name="..."? TargetNamespace="..."? >
    <Assertion wsp:Usage="..." wsp:Preference="..."? /> *
    ...
    <wsse:Security>...</wsse:Security> ?
</wsp:Policy>
```

An `Assertion` is a placeholder for the element the assertion is about (such as `SecurityToken`). The two most interesting attributes here are `Usage` and `Preference`. `Usage` describes how the assertion is to be processed. It can have one of the following values:

- `wsp:Required`—The assertion must be applied to the subject. If the subject does not meet the criteria expressed in the assertion, a fault or error will occur.

- `wsp:Rejected`—The assertion is explicitly not supported and if present will cause failure.

- `wsp:Optional`—The assertion may be made of the subject, but it is not required to be applied.

- `wsp:Observed`—The assertion will be applied to all subjects, and requestors of the service are informed that the policy will be applied.

- `wsp:Ignored`—The assertion is processed but ignored. That is, it can be specified, but no action will be taken as a result of its being specified. Subjects and requestors are informed that the policy will be ignored.

Preference is an optional attribute for specifying a ranking of alternatives. The higher the Preference number, the more the party expressing the preference would like that particular option used.

As you saw in Listing 8.2, a Policy can have one or more operators within it. The three valid operators are as follows:

- wsp:All—All the child assertions must be satisfied.
- wsp:ExactlyOne—Exactly one of the child assertions must be satisfied.
- wsp:OneOrMore—One or more of the child assertions must be satisfied.

If no operator appears directly under the Policy element, all the child assertions must be satisfied, the same as the All operator specified previously.

The WS-Policy specification does not provide any specific types of assertions itself; it focuses on the syntax for declaring assertions. Specific sets of assertions are defined in other specifications for a specific domain (such as security). However, a set of general assertions is defined in the WS-PolicyAssertions specification.

WS-PolicyAssertions

The objective of WS-PolicyAssertions[3] is to define a set of common policy assertions that would be applicable across all Web services rather than just within a specific area such as security or reliable messaging. So far, only four of these general policy assertions are defined. The following short sections cover them with examples so that you can get a feel for how you might use policy assertions.

TextEncoding

The TextEncoding assertion allows a Web service to specify one or more character sets that it supports. For example,

```
<wsp:TextEncoding wsp:Usage="wsp:Required" Encoding="iso-8859-5"/>
```

Language

A Web service can allow multiple languages to be used in the message content. The Language assertion allows a Web service to denote supported and preferred languages, as shown in Listing 8.3.

Listing 8.3   The <Language> Assertion

```
<wsp:ExactlyOne>
  <wsp:Language wsp:Usage="wsp:Required"
                wsp:Preference="10"
                Language="da"/>
  <wsp:Language wsp:Usage="wsp:Required"
```

3. You can find the WS-PolicyAssertions specification at http://msdn.microsoft.com/webservices/default.aspx?pull=/library/en-us/dnglobspec/html/ws-policyassertions.asp.

Listing 8.3 **Continued**

```
                wsp:Preference="7"
                Language="en-gb"/>
    <wsp:Language wsp:Usage="wsp:Required"
                wsp:Preference="1"
                Language="en"/>
</wsp:ExactlyOne>
```

SpecVersion

As schemas and specifications evolve, they are revised, and Web services may support different versions of the same specification. For example, in some cases, the Web service is backward compatible; in other cases, it is not. Listing 8.4 shows an example of the SpecVersion assertion.

Listing 8.4 **The** <SpecVersion> **Assertion**

```
<wsp:SpecVersion wsp:Usage="wsp:Required"
    URI="http://schemas.xmlsoap.org/ws/2002/12/policy"/>
```

MessagePredicate

The MessagePredicate assertion allows a Web service to specify that a message must have a particular precondition defined by an XPath (or perhaps some other dialect, but XPath 1.0 is the default). For example, perhaps a Web service requires a particular header. Listing 8.5 shows an example of a MessagePredicate assertion requiring that a message contain a security header.

Listing 8.5 **The** <MessagePredicate> **Assertion**

```
<wsp:MessagePredicate wsp:Usage="wsp:Required">
    count(wsp:GetHeader(.)/wsse:Security) = 1
</wsp:MessagePredicate>
```

WS-PolicyAttachment

You have learned how a WS-Security policy can be put together using a set of assertions, but how do you now associate this policy with a particular Web service? The answer to this question is described in the WS-PolicyAttachment specification.[4] Two strategies are described for associating the policy. One strategy is to define the policy within the definition of the Web service—for example, in the WSDL or pointed to from

---

4. You can find the WS-PolicyAttachment specification at http://msdn.microsoft.com/
webservices/default.aspx?pull=/library/en-us/dnglobspec/html/
ws-policyattachment.asp.

the WSDL. Another strategy is for the policy to stand alone and for it to point back to the Web service or services that it is associated with.

Arbitrary Resource Attachment

The simplest policy attachment strategy to understand is the standalone approach, called *Arbitrary Resource Attachment*. This approach allows you to describe the policy and what resources it applies to separately from the definition of the resource itself. To accomplish this, you use the `PolicyAttachment` element with children of the `AppliesTo` element and a set of policy assertions. Using the `AppliesTo` element is a general way to describe resources that the policy applies to. Listing 8.6 shows an example from the specification that uses a domain expression pointing to a deployed WSDL endpoint.

Listing 8.6   **The `<PolicyAttachment>` Assertion**

```
<wsp:PolicyAttachment>
   <wsp:AppliesTo>
       <wsp:EndpointReference xmlns:fabrikam="...">
          <wsp:ServiceName Name="fabrikam:InventoryService"/>
          <wsp:PortType Name="fabrikam:InventoryPortType"/>
          <wsp:Address URI="http://www.fabrikam123.com/acct"/>
       </wsp:EndpointReference>
   </wsp:AppliesTo>
   <wsp:PolicyReference Ref="http://www.fabrikam123.com/acct-policy.xml"/>
</wsp:PolicyAttachment>
```

In this example, the policy applies to the `PortType` titled `InventoryPortType` in the Web Service called `InventoryService` located at `http://www.fabrikam123/acct`. You can find the policy assertions at `http://www.fabrikam123.com/acct-policy.xml`.

Specifying WS-Policy in WSDL

Specifying policy in WSDL is somewhat more complex than the standalone approach and requires some understanding of WSDL because you can attach the policy at different locations in the WSDL and therefore have different meanings to the policy. For example, if you want to specify WS-SecurityPolicy for a specific Web service operation, you add an attribute to the specific WSDL operation element you want the policy or policies to apply to. Let's go through the different aspects of attaching a policy to WSDL.

You first need to know that WS-PolicyAttachment defines two attributes that can be used within WSDL to contain a list of pointers to policies that apply. These two attributes are `PolicyURIs` and `PolicyRefs`; the only difference between the two is that the first points directly to a policy via URI, and the second makes use of QNames.

You can use one of these attributes within WSDL to point to one or more appropriate policies. The trick is to determine where in the WSDL to add these policy pointer attributes. To understand this concept, let's quickly review the structure of the `definitions` section in WSDL 1.1. Hierarchically, for an `operation` with a request and response, the part of the WSDL `definitions` section that we are interested in for this discussion is structured like Listing 8.7.

Listing 8.7   **A WSDL `<definitions>` Section to Be Modified with WS-Policy Attributes**

```
<wsdl:definitions .... >
    <message name=""> *
        <part name="" element=""? type=""?/> *
    </message>
    <wsdl:portType .... > *
        <wsdl:operation name=""
            parameterOrder=" ">
            <wsdl:input name=""? message=""/>
            <wsdl:output name=""? message=""/>
            <wsdl:fault name="" message=""/>*
        </wsdl:operation>
    </wsdl:portType >
</wsdl:definitions>
```

Policy that is attached higher in the hierarchy is inherited. So, for example, a policy attached to the `message` element would apply to each of the `part` elements. If the lower-level element has policy defined for it, the parent's attached policy is merged with the child's policy.

As you can see in the WSDL structure in Listing 8.7, two hierarchies are represented: the `message/part` hierarchy and the `portType/operation/(input | output | fault)` hierarchy. Listing 8.8 shows an example from the specification using the `PolicyRef` attribute on the `message` and `part` elements of the WSDL structure.

Listing 8.8   **A WSDL `<definitions>` Structure with `<PolicyRef>` Attributes on the `<message>` and `<part>` Elements**

```
<?xml version="1.0"?>
<wsdl:definitions name="Inventory"
    xmlms:wsdl="http://schemas.xmlsoap.org/wsdl"
    targetNamespace="http://example.com/inventory.wsdl"
    ...
    xmlns:ps="http://example.com/policies">
    <wsp:UsingPolicy wsdl:Required="true"/>
    <wsdl:message name="LookupResponse"
        wsp:PolicyRefs="ps:Q1">
      <wsdl:part name="key" type="xs:string"
                wsp:PolicyRefs="ps:Q2" />
      <wsdl:part name="value" type="xs:string"
                wsp:PolicyRefs="ps:Q3" />
      <wsdl:part name="hint" type="xs:string"  />
    </wsdl:message>
</wsdl:definitions>
```

In Listing 8.8, first notice that a `UsingPolicy` element must be defined in the WSDL definitions section and must be marked as a mandatory extension (`wsdl:required = "true"`) to make sure that consumers of this service have the capability to process policies. The message `LookupResponse` points to the policy with the qualified name `ps:Q1` (a policy in the namespace `http://example.com/policies` named `Q1`; see Listing 8.9). The first `part` element, `key`, points to the policy with the qualified name `ps:Q2`; and the second `part` element, `value`, points to the policy with the qualified name `ps:Q3`. The third `part` element does not point to any policy explicitly. Listing 8.9 shows the three fictitious policies that `ps:Q1`, `ps:Q2`, and `ps:Q3` refer to, respectively.

Listing 8.9   **Three Fictitious Policies Referred to from the WSDL in Listing 8.8**

```
<wsp:Policy xmlns:wsp="..." xmlns:wsu="..." xmlns:xxx="..."
    xml:base="http://www.fabrikam123.com/policies"
    wsu:Id="P1"
    Name="Q1"
    TargetNamespace="http://example.com/policies">
  <xxx:Sign wsp:Usage="wsp:Required" />
</wsp:Policy>
<wsp:Policy xmlns:wsp="..." xmlns:wsu="..." xmlns:xxx="..."
    xml:base="http://www.fabrikam123.com/policies"
    wsu:Id="P2"
    Name="Q2"
    TargetNamespace="http://www.fabrikam123.com/policies">
  <xxx:Encrypt wsp:Usage="wsp:Required" />
</wsp:Policy>
<wsp:Policy xmlns:wsp="..." xmlns:wsu="..." xmlns:xxx="..."
    xml:base="http://www.fabrikam123.com/policies"
    wsu:Id="P3"
    Name="Q3"
    TargetNamespace="http://www.fabrikam123.com/policies">
  <xxx:ExpeditedDelivery wsp:Usage="wsp:Required" />
</wsp:Policy>
```

In Listing 8.9, because the `Q1` policy is associated with the `LookupResponse message` from the WSDL, all three parts inherit the `Sign` policy (presumably meaning that the message must be digitally signed). The `key message part` from the WSDL explicitly points to the `Q2` policy, so it would also have the `Encrypt` policy. Therefore, the *effective policy* for the `key message part` would be that shown in Listing 8.10.

Listing 8.10   **The Effective Policy for the** `key message` **part of the Sample WSDL from Listing 8.8**

```
<wsp:Policy>
  <xxx:Sign wsp:Usage="wsp:Required" />
  <xxx:Encrypt wsp:Usage="wsp:Required" />
</wsp:Policy>
```

Similarly, the `value message part` from the WSDL in Listing 8.8 points to `Q2`, giving it the *effective policy* of `Sign` and `ExpeditedDelivery`. Because the `hint message part` from the same WSDL example does not point explicitly to a policy, it simply inherits from the `LookupResponse message` and has an *effective policy* of just `Sign`.

In Listing 8.10, we attached policies to the `message` and `parts` elements in WSDL, but we also could have attached policies to the `portType`, `operation`, `input`, `output`, or `fault` elements in WSDL. The same inheritance characteristics that were shown in the `message` example would apply.

WS-PolicyAttachment provides a tremendous amount of flexibility for assigning policies to different aspects of a Web service—from the `portType` (which would apply to all the operations in a Web service), to an `operation`, or even to a specific `input` (request) and `output` (response).

WS-SecurityPolicy

Now that you have learned about WS-Policy (a general approach for creating policy assertions across any type of problem domain), WS-PolicyAssertions (a small set of policy assertions that could apply in any situation), and finally WS-PolicyAttachments (specifying how to attach a policy to a particular resource), you can now learn specifically how you can build on them to create a specific policy that relates to WS-Security. The main purpose of WS-SecurityPolicy[5] is to provide six policy assertions that apply directly to WS-Security. The following sections describe each of these assertions in turn.

SecurityToken

The `SecurityToken` assertion specifies which security tokens are required and accepted by a Web service or Web service client. This could apply to messages in (requests) or out (response). Listing 8.11 shows the template for a `SecurityToken` assertion.

Listing 8.11   **The `<SecurityToken>` Assertion Template**

```
<SecurityToken wsp:Preference="..." wsp:Usage="..." >
  <TokenType>...</TokenType>
  <TokenIssuer>...</TokenIssuer>
  <Claims>...Token type-specific claims...</Claims>
  ...   (TokenType-specific details)
</SecurityToken>
```

---

5. The specification used for a resource for the WS-SecurityPolicy text is located at http://msdn.microsoft.com/webservices/default.aspx?pull=/library/en-us/dnglobspec/html/ws-securitypolicy.asp. Note that this is an initial draft dated December 18, 2002. Consequently, some of the details are sure to change as the specification evolves. However, examining this information should be useful because it reviews most of the material on WS-Security, and something very close to this will be required to express and publish WS-SecurityPolicy.

The `Preference` and `Usage` elements were described in the "WS-Policy Details" section and are on all the WS-SecurityPolicy assertions. `TokenType` describes the type of token that is required; following is a list of the valid `TokenTypes`:[6]

- `wsse:X509v3`—X.509 v3 certificate
- `wsse:Kerberosv5TGT`—Kerberos v5 Ticket Granting Ticket
- `wsse:Kerberosv5ST`—Kerberos v5 Service Ticket
- `wsse:UsernameToken`—Username token defined in WS-Security
- `wsse:SAMLAssertion`—SAML assertion
- `wsse:XrMLLicence`—XrML license

`TokenIssuer` is the name of a trusted issuer (or names of trusted issuers). The `Claims` element describes token type–specific information about a token. For example, if a particular X.509 extension is required for an `X509v3` token, you describe it as a child of the `Claims` element. WS-Security describes claims for three token types: Username, X509v3, and Kerberos. The following sections review what the Username and X509v3 claims can specify.

Username **Token Claims**

A `Username` policy assertion with the claims specified has the options shown in Listing 8.12.

Listing 8.12   **The Options for a** `Username` **Policy Assertion**

```
<SecurityToken wsp:Preference="..." wsp:Usage="..." wsu:id="...">
  <TokenType>wsse:UsernameToken</TokenType>
  <Claims>
    <SubjectName MatchType="...">...</SubjectName>
    <UsePassword wsp:Usage="..." Type="..."/>
  </Claims>
</SecurityToken>
```

The `SubjectName` element specifies the contents that match the contents of the `Username` element in a WS-Security `UsernameToken`. The `MatchType` attribute on the `SubjectName` describes what type of match should be done. The `MatchType` options are as follows:

- `wsse:Exact`—The values must be exactly the same.
- `wsse:Prefix` (default)—The specified value must be the prefix of the value in the certificate.
- `wsse:Regexp`—The specified value is a regular expression that matches the value in the token.

---

6. The valid `TokenTypes` were defined in the December 18, 2002, WS-SecurityPolicy specification located at `http://msdn.microsoft.com/webservices/default.aspx?pull=/library/en-us/dnglobspec/html/ws-securitypolicy.asp`.

The `UsePassword` element describes the policy related to the `UserName` password. The attribute `Usage` is the same as the WS-Policy `Usage` element (required, optional, and so on). The `Type` attribute specifies the type of password that is required. The options for password are as follows:

- `wsse:PasswordText` (default)—The `<Type>` attribute of this `<UserNameToken>` is `<wsse:PasswordText>` (in other words, a plaintext password is used).

- `wsse:PasswordDigest`—The `Type` attribute of this `<UsernameToken>` is `<wsse:PasswordDigest>` (in other words, a digested password is used).

X509v3 Token Claims

X.509 tokens have specific claims as well, referring to X.509 `Extensions` and/or the `SubjectName`, for example. Listing 8.13 shows a template for a `SecurityToken` with an X509v3 token type.

Listing 8.13   **The Template for a** `<SecurityToken>` **of Type** X509v3

```
<SecurityToken wsp:Preference="..." wsp:Usage="..." wsu:id="...">
  <TokenType>wsse:X509v3</TokenType>
  <TokenIssuer>...</TokenIssuer>
  <Claims>
      <SubjectName MatchType="...">...</SubjectName>
      <X509Extension OID="..." Critical="..." MatchType=",,,">
      ...
      </X509Extension>
  </Claims>
</SecurityToken>
```

If the `TokenIssuer` element is present, the distinguished name of the certificate issuer is either the actual issuing certificate authority, or the root certificate authority who vouches for the issuing certificate authority.

`SubjectName` is similar to `Username` in the "Username Token Claims" section and Listing 8.12. If present, the presented X.509 must have a subject name that matches based on the `MatchType` attribute value. The `MatchType` attribute values are the same as shown for `Username` token claims.

The `X509Extension` element describes the value that must be present in an X.509 token in an extension. We won't go into X.509 extensions here; suffice it to say, using such extensions is a way to add different types of descriptive data to an X.509 certificate. The value in the element must match the value of the extension based on the `MatchType`. The Object Identifier (OID) attribute is a string representation of the OID of the matched extension. The `Critical` attribute is a Boolean that, if true, indicates that the extension must be marked as critical; if false, must not be marked as critical; or if omitted, does not specify criteria for critical.

Integrity

`Integrity` assertions allow you to set policy that a SOAP message must be digitally signed, what specifically in the message needs to be signed, and how it is to be signed, such as what algorithms must be used. Listing 8.14 shows a template for an `Integrity` assertion.

Listing 8.14   **The Template for the** `<Integrity>` **Assertion**

```
<Integrity wsp:Preference="..." wsp:Usage="...">
        <Algorithm Type="..." URI="..." wsp:Preference="..."/>
        <TokenInfo>
            <SecurityToken>...</SecurityToken>
        </TokenInfo>
        <Claims>...</Claims>
        <MessageParts Dialect="..." Signer="...">
            ...
        </MessageParts>
<Integrity>
```

The `Preference` and `Usage` attributes of the `Integrity` element are the same as those discussed previously in the "WS-Policy Details" section.

The `Algorithm` element allows you to specify a specific algorithm that must be used in the signature. If no algorithms are specified, only the algorithms specified in XML Signature are supported. The `URI` attribute points to the specific algorithm URI from the XML Signature specification (for example, `http://www.w3.org/2000/09/xmldsig#dsa-sha1`). As you read in Chapter 4, "Safeguarding the Identity and Integrity of XML Messages," numerous algorithms are possible in an XML Signature, such as canonicalization and the various signature algorithms.

The `Type` attribute allows you to specify the type of algorithm. Following are the possible `Type` values:

- `wsse:AlgCanonicalization`—Canonicalization
- `wsse:AlgSignature`—Signature method
- `wsse:AlgTransform`—Transformation
- `wsse:AlgDigest`—Digest method

Multiple algorithms with the same type can be listed along with a preference such that the other party can choose from them. Also, you can include algorithm-specific elements within the `Algorithm` element; for example, you could put `HMACOutputLength` on an HMAC signature algorithm.

The `TokenInfo` element allows a list of required `SecurityToken` formats. `TokenInfo` has a child element, `SecurityToken`, which is the same `SecurityToken` mentioned in the "`SecurityToken`" section earlier in this chapter. Consequently, you can use the attributes and children of `SecurityToken` to constrain specific `SecurityTokens` that must appear with a signature. Also, you can use the `OneOrMore` operator specified in WS-Policy to show that one or more of a certain `SecurityToken` must be present.

The `Claims` element is also the same as the one described in the "`SecurityToken`" section earlier in this chapter.

The `MessageParts` element enables you to describe what part of the message must be signed. You do this by providing an expression whose syntax is determined by the `Dialect` attribute. The default dialect is XPath 1.0. The following two dialect types are predefined in the specification:

- `http://www.w3.org/TR/1999/REC-xpath-19991116`

  (Default) An XPath 1.0 location path that identifies the nodes to be protected. The XPath expression is evaluated against the `S:Envelope` element node to select which nodes are to be protected. Additionally, the expression *should* use the functions defined in Appendix I of the WS-PolicyAssertions specification (where appropriate).

- `http://schemas.xmlsoap.org/2002/12/wsse#part`

  A list of message parts to be protected that are identified using the set of predefined functions defined in Appendix II of the WS-PolicyAssertions specification. The functions are evaluated against the `S:Envelope` element node.

You can have multiple `MessageParts` elements in list format, and the concatenated set of `MessageParts` must be signed unless they are separated by the `Choice` operator from WS-Policy. The `Signer` attribute allows you to designate who must sign the message. In this version of the specification, only one type of `Signer` is predefined, `Sender` (`http://schemas.xmlsoap.org/2002/12/secext/originalSender`), meaning that the originator of the message, at a minimum, must sign the message.

Listing 8.15 shows an example of an `Integrity` assertion.

Listing 8.15 An Example of an `<Integrity>` Assertion

```
<wsse:Integrity wsp:Usage="wsp:Required">
        <wsse:Algorithm  Type="wsse:AlgCanonicalization"
         URI="http://www.w3.org/Signature/Drafts/xml-exc-c14n"/>
        <wsse:Algorithm Type="wsse:AlgSignature"
            URI=" http://www.w3.org/2000/09/xmldsig#rsa-sha1"/>
        <wsse:TokenInfo>
            <wsse:SecurityToken>
                <wsse:TokenType>wsse:X509v3</wsse:TokenType>
            </wsse:SecurityToken>
        </wsse:TokenInfo>
        <wsse:MessageParts
         Dialect="http://schemas.xmlsoap.org/2002/12/wsse#soap">
            S:Body some-URI:HeaderBlockElementName
        </wsse:MessageParts>
</wsse:Integrity>
```

The `Integrity` assertion in Listing 8.15 indicates that the message must be digitally signed, exclusive canonicalization must be used, the RSAwithSHA1 signature algorithm must be used, an X.509 `BinarySecurityToken` must be included, and the part of the message to be signed is the SOAP body and a header called `"some-URI:HeaderBlockElementName"`.

Confidentiality

A `Confidentiality` assertion allows a sender or receiver of Web services messages to require that some specific part of a SOAP message must be encrypted. For instance, it allows the sender (or receiver) of a message to specify that parts of a message must be encrypted with a certain algorithm.

Listing 8.16 shows the template for the `Confidentiality` assertion.

Listing 8.16   The Template for the `<Confidentiality>` **Assertion**

```
<Confidentiality wsp:Preference="..." wsp:Usage="...">
        <Algorithm Type="..." URI="..." wsp:Preference="..."/>
        <KeyInfo>
            <SecurityToken .../>
            <SecurityTokenReference .../>
            ...
        </KeyInfo>
        <MessageParts Dialect="...">
            ...
        </MessageParts>
</Confidentiality>
```

The `Confidentiality` element represents a policy assertion about encryption.

The `Algorithm` element is the same as described for the `Integrity` assertion except that it has only one valid `Type`, `wsse:AlgEncryption`, to specify encryption.

The `KeyInfo` element is similar to the `TokenInfo` element described previously for the `Integrity` assertion. (Why it is called something different is not clear; this discrepancy will likely be remedied in a future version of the specification.) This element contains one or more (if the `OneOrMore` operator from WS-Policy is used) `SecurityTokens`. The `SecurityTokenReference` is a reference to a `SecurityToken` that must be used for the encryption.

The `MessageParts` element in a `Confidentiality` assertion is the same as the `MessageParts` element defined in the "Integrity" section earlier in this chapter. Listing 8.17 provides a simple example of a `Confidentiality` assertion.

Listing 8.17   An Example of a `<Confidentiality>` **Assertion**

```
<wsse:Confidentiality wsp:Usage="wsp:Required">
        <wsse:Algorithm Type="wsse:AlgEncryption"
          URI="http://www.w3.org/2001/04/xmlenc#3des-cbc"/>
```

Listing 8.17   **Continued**

```
        <MessageParts
        Dialect="http://schemas.xmlsoap.org/2002/12/wsse#part">
            wsp:GetInfosetForNode(wsp:GetBody(.))
        </MessageParts>
</wsse:Confidentiality>
```

In this example, the body of the message must be encrypted using the 3DES algorithm.

Of course, you will often use digital signature and encryption together. Listing 8.18 shows `Confidentiality` and `Integrity` assertions used together.

Listing 8.18   **Typical Use of** `<Confidentiality>` **and** `<Integrity>` **Assertions Together**

```
<wsse:Confidentiality wsp:Usage="wsp:Required">
        <wsse:Algorithm Type="wsse:AlgEncryption"
            URI="http://www.w3.org/2001/04/xmlenc#3des-cbc"/>
        <MessageParts
        Dialect="http://schemas.xmlsoap.org/2002/12/wsse#part">
            wsp:GetInfosetForNode(wsp:GetBody(.))
        </MessageParts>
</wsse:Confidentiality>

<wsse:Integrity wsp:Usage="wsp:Required">
        <wsse:Algorithm  Type="wsse:AlgCanonicalization"
        URI="http://www.w3.org/Signature/Drafts/xml-exc-c14n"/>
        <wsse:Algorithm Type="wsse:AlgSignature"
            URI=" http://www.w3.org/2000/09/xmldsig#rsa-sha1"/>
        <wsse:SecurityToken>
            <wsse:TokenType>wsse:X509v3</wsse:TokenType>
        </wsse:SecurityToken>
        <MessageParts
        Dialect="http://schemas.xmlsoap.org/2002/12/wsse#soap">
            S:Body
        </MessageParts>
</wsse:Integrity>
```

This example requires that the SOAP body be encrypted before it is signed.

Visibility

The `Visibility` assertion allows an intermediary to require that a certain portion of the SOAP message be visible to it. *Visible* means either in the clear or encrypted in a way that the intermediary is able to decrypt. Remember that a SOAP message can pass through multiple intermediaries before arriving at its final destination. An example might be a firewall, but it also could be a business waypoint such as an audit or approval processor. When you use the Visibility assertion, these intermediaries can make sure that the portion of the message they need to view will be available.

Listing 8.19 shows the template for the Visibility assertion.

Listing 8.19   **The Template for the** `<Visibility>` **Assertion**

```
<Visibility wsp:Usage="...">
        <MessageParts Dialect="...">

          ...

        </MessageParts>
</Visibility>
```

The main element here is MessageParts, which is the same as used in Listings 8.14 and 8.16 in the Integrity and Confidentiality assertions. Listing 8.20 provides an example of a Visibility assertion.

Listing 8.20   **An Example of a** `<Visibility>` **Assertion**

```
<wsse:Visibility wsp:Usage="wsp:Required">
        <MessageParts>
           wsp:GetInfosetForNode(wsp:GetBody(.))
        </MessageParts>
 </wsse:Visibility>
```

SecurityHeader

The security header in WS-Security allows significant flexibility as to how it can show up in a SOAP header. The SecurityHeader assertion allows for constraints to be put on the security header.

Listing 8.21 shows the template for the SecurityHeader assertion.

Listing 8.21   **The Template for the** `<SecurityHeader>` **Assertion**

```
<SecurityHeader MustPrepend="..."
                MustManifestEncryption="..."
                wsp:Usage="..."/>
```

The SecurityHeader element, which is composed of three main attributes, also allows any elements to be added for extensibility purposes. The two new attributes are MustPrepend and MustManifestEncryption. If MustPrepend is true, the security header must be prepended to the message. If MustManifestEncryption is true, only the encryptions that are listed in the security header will be processed (by the WS-Security processor); all other encryptions will be ignored. This forces use of one of the encryption manifest strategies we discussed earlier in this chapter using either EncryptedData (if not using a wrapped key) or EncryptedKey.

MessageAge

As you might guess, the `MessageAge` assertion is related to the WS-Security `Timestamp` element, which has the sub-element `Created`, representing the date/time that the SOAP message originated. Using the `MessageAge` assertion, you can specify the acceptable time period before which a message will be declared "stale" and discarded.

Listing 8.22 shows the template for the `MessageAge` assertion.

Listing 8.22   **The Template for the** `<MessageAge>` **Assertion**

```
<wsse:MessageAge wsp:Usage="..."
    wsp:Preference="..."
    Age=.../>
```

In this example, `Usage` and `Preference` are the same attributes discussed in the "WS-Policy Details" section, and `Age` represents the maximum age timeout for the message expressed in seconds.

Listing 8.23 provides an example of the `MessageAge` assertion.

Listing 8.23   **An Example of a** `<MessageAge>` **Assertion**

```
<wsse:MessageAge
    wsse:Usage="wsp:Required"
    Age="3600"/>
```

Summary

As you can see, publishing your security policy for a Web service is not as simple as just putting some new attributes in WSDL. Four specifications, all in early stages, are needed to describe the requirements of a Web service:

- WS-Policy provides a framework for describing policy across many domains, such as security, reliable messaging, privacy, and so on.
- WS-PolicyAttachment provides strategies for binding WS-Policy–based documents to a particular resource such as WSDL.
- WS-PolicyAssertions describes a few common policy assertions that apply across the different policy areas.
- WS-SecurityPolicy describes policy assertions specific to security.

A Web service typically involves at least two parties, a sender (client) and receiver (server), as well as potential intermediaries. Each party may have its own security requirements. The receiver may not care that the message being received is encrypted but requires that sent messages be encrypted. For that same message, the sender may require that the sent information be encrypted. In other words, you, as a sender, may have different security requirements than the message's receiver. These differences may be resolvable. For example, if the receiver does not care whether the message is encrypted but the sender requires encryption, the receiver could go ahead and receive the message in encrypted format. In other cases, the differences may not be resolvable. Looking at WS-Security from this perspective leads to the possibility of negotiation between the sender and receiver for a mutually acceptable security policy. To negotiate like this, a protocol is required to determine the back-and-forth steps. This is not surprising when you consider that security protocols such as SSL have been around for a while. In the next chapter, we describe WS-SecureConversation, which takes this type of approach.

One of the compelling aspects of Web services has been their simple, request/response nature. It is unclear whether this simplicity will be abandoned to support a richer policy negotiation strategy that requires multi-step protocols. A simpler one-time exchange of policies seems more likely in which the sender consults the receiver's policy, found via WSDL, and determines the intersection between the receiver's and sender's requirements. At that point, a message that is secured based on the sender's requirements will be sent or otherwise rejected by the receiver.

9

Trust, Access Control, and Rights for Web Services

Security Assertion Markup Language (SAML) was the topic of Chapter 6, "Portable Identity, Authentication, and Authorization." WS-Security was presented in Chapter 7, "Building Security into SOAP." Then WS-Policy was the focus of Chapter 8, "Communicating Security Policy." They are the three pillars of WS-Security.

Several other important standards are derived from and complementary to WS-Security; they relate to such fundamental security topics as trust, access control, and rights. In this chapter, we review the family of WS-Security–related technologies. An important additional topic is the XML Key Management Specification (XKMS) for managing keys used in signatures, encryption, and SAML. We also cover two other WS-Security security related specifications not already covered: eXtensible Access Control Markup Language (XACML) and eXtensible Rights Markup Language (XrML). Let's begin with the WS-Security family.

The WS-* Family of Security Specifications

In April 2002, IBM and Microsoft published a joint whitepaper called "Security in a Web Services World: A Proposed Architecture and Roadmap."[1] This whitepaper describes a far-reaching, comprehensive vision of a set of security standards and technologies meant to create a unifying approach for dealing with security in a Web services world. The proposed architecture attempts to bring together for Web services what, to date, had been disparate worlds in security. Just as WS-Security allows security mechanisms such as Public Key Infrastructure (PKI) and Security Assertion Markup Language (SAML) to

---

1. IBM Corporation and Microsoft Corporation. "Security in a Web Services World: A Proposed Architecture and Roadmap." April 7, 2002.
http://msdn.microsoft.com/library/default.asp?url=/library/en-us/
dnwssecur/html/securitywhitepaper.asp

participate in Web Services Security, the Web Services Architecture Roadmap generalizes many of the security functions that previously existed in other domains and proposes a framework for meeting the security requirements of the Web services domain. It provides an evolutionary strategy for putting the different pieces of the security puzzle in place. The proponents of this framework, and the standards bodies they are working through, are accomplishing this by first rolling out foundational specifications such as WS-Security (which, in turn, was built on XML Signature, XML Encryption, SAML, and various other security token standards) and then following with other standards that rely on these foundational standards. Figure 9.1 repeats the diagram shown previously in Chapter 7; in this figure, you can see the related WS-Security standards as well as the dependencies.

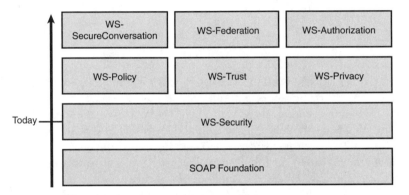

Figure 9.1   The WS-Security family of standards built on SOAP.

As a quick review, WS-Security describes SOAP extensions for securing messages. It is a general-purpose mechanism for associating security tokens with SOAP messages. WS-Security builds on and is fully compatible with established, mature security technologies such as SSL, IPsec, XML Signature, and XML Encryption. It is designed to address message integrity, message confidentiality, message authentication, and the encoding of security tokens that must travel with the messages they are securing.

WS-Security provides the foundations for the set of *composable* security building blocks in Figure 9.1 built on top of WS-Security. By *composable*, we mean that various building block standards can be combined to provide new and different security standards to solve specific security challenges. For example, WS-Privacy is composed from WS-Security plus WS-Trust and WS-Policy. These composable standards provide a "use only what you need" approach to securing Web services. The composable specifications still under development together with WS-Security are built on a core foundation of technologies such as SOAP, WSDL, XML Signature, XML Encryption, and SSL.

What is amazing is that, with this model, for the first time users have an approach that allows integration of Kerberos, X.509/PKI, and other security models. Building up from WS-Security are the following *composable* building blocks:

- **WS-Policy**—Defines how to express capabilities and constraints of security policy. (This topic was covered in Chapter 8 but is summarized here.)
- **WS-Trust**—Describes the model for establishing both direct and brokered trust relationships, including intermediaries.
- **WS-Privacy**—Enables users to state privacy preferences and Web services to state and implement privacy practices.
- **WS-SecureConversation**—Describes how to manage and authenticate message exchanges between parties, including exchanging security contexts and establishing and deriving session keys.
- **WS-Federation**—Describes how to manage and broker the trust relationships in a heterogeneous federated environment, including support for federated identities.
- **WS-Authorization**—Defines how Web services manage authorization data and policies.

> **Note**
>
> The purpose of describing all these "standards" here, even when some of them are as yet unpublished, is two-fold. First, we hope our introduction to these evolving specifications will help you avoid re-inventing the wheel on an area you need for your Web services to be successful. Second, our goal is to let you know that significant work is being done on these standards, and progress is rapid. Consequently, if these standards are important to you, you will be able to find some useful guidance by scouring the Web and the standards bodies' repositories.

WS-Security and the layers above it support what could be called the *triangle* of distributed message-based security that is composed of trust, interoperability, and integration. The triangle of WS-Security specifications is shown in Figure 9.2.

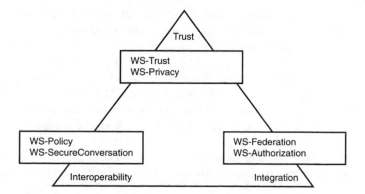

Figure 9.2   The WS-* Security triangle of trust, integration, and interoperability.

The first point of the security triangle is trust. Trust, of course, is fundamental to security. No trust, no security. In a Web services world, trust is very complex. Trust is represented in relationships; it can be explicitly established, or it may be presumed. Assertions are used to represent trust and trust relationships. WS-Trust is the WS-★ security standard building block focused on trust relationships. The other trust-related standard in this point of the security triangle is WS-Privacy. WS-Privacy specifies the rules that must be followed when an entity trusts a service with its self-descriptive (that is, personally identifiable) data.

The second point of the security triangle is interoperability. You can think of interoperability in terms of communication standards that allow distinct systems to cooperate. This capability is especially important when those communications are secured. Secure communications adhere to several different protocols, so interoperable secure communications must be able to map one protocol to another. Besides WS-Security itself, the two other WS-★ security family standards that relate to interoperability are WS-Policy and WS-SecureConversation.

The third point of the security triangle is integration. Web services' primary *raison d'e-tre* is for application and organizational integration. Integration involves one system that previously did not communicate with another extending its architecture to be able to do so. It means that existing services are reused for new purposes. This necessarily means that identities and the trust model under which they operate need to interoperate and do so across heterogeneous environments. An important issue this raises is federation. *Federation* is the agreement among a group of entities that they will share identities as well as the attributes of those identities with other members of their group. Two of the WS-★ family of standards relate to integration: WS-Federation and WS-Authorization.

WS-★ Security Specifications for Trust Relationships

The following sections address the two specifications for trust relationships. First, we cover WS-Trust and then WS-Privacy.

WS-Trust

Throughout this book, we have described the technical issues around securing Web services. Although these issues can be complex, they are still only technical issues. By far, the most difficult issues arise around the more subtle business and personal issues of trust. Think about your own definition of trust and how you determine whom to trust. Do you trust someone who has been referred by someone else you trust? Do you trust in some people in relatively low-risk situations but not in a high-risk situation? How you determine trust might be called your personal *trust model*. A lot of work and thought has gone into defining, describing, and implementing trust models, and much of the complexity in Public Key Infrastructure technology derives from the complexity of modeling trust.

A major Web services trust problem arises when credentials are issued in one *trust domain* and then presented in another. Say your employer, ABC Supply, is a supplier to

XYZ Truck Company, and XYZ Truck Company has decided to expose its critical business systems to its suppliers. One strategy could be for XYZ Truck Company to directly issue credentials to each individual within every supplier and take on the management of these credentials. This would mean that, even if you do not work for XYZ, you would receive a credential from the company to present to its Web service when using its *Bid for Order* Web service. But how would XYZ Truck Company know if you were to be fired from ABC Supply or change positions? It would be very difficult, if not impossible, for XYZ Truck Company to manage the credentials given to those privileged few employees of ABC Supply allowed to directly order at XYZ.

Another approach that XYZ could choose is to blindly *trust* ABC Supply (and all its employees). From a technical perspective, this strategy might mean that X.509 certificates issued by ABC Supply (probably with certain attributes) could be presented to XYZ Truck Company for access to its Web services. You can probably see the trust issues here immediately. Perhaps these are highly sensitive capabilities that XYZ Truck Company is allowing access to, so much so that even its own employees must show up in person to be granted a credential. Suppose XYZ Truck Company has tight procedures for periodically refreshing credentials and revoking them when they are lost or the employee changes responsibilities. If ABC Supply Company does not have similar rigorous procedures, XYZ Company has seriously degraded its security by opening up the company to ABC's much lower standards. This level of trust becomes the arena of contracts and law because that is the way that companies express their trust, or lack thereof, and the way violations of that trust become enforceable.

Prior to having secure communications, each party needs to determine whether it can "trust" the asserted credentials of the other party. WS-Trust defines extensions to WS-Security that provide

- Methods for issuing and exchanging security tokens
- Ways to establish and access the presence of trust relationships

Similar to SAML, WS-Trust defines a request/response mechanism for obtaining security tokens.

The most important attributes of WS-Trust to understand are

- The relationships between Web service requestor, Web service provider, and the Security Token Service (STS), as shown in Figure 9.3
- These two methods: `<RequestSecurityToken>` and `<RequestSecurityTokenResponse>`

Security Token Services form the basis of trust by issuing security tokens that can be used to broker trust relationships between different trust domains. As Figure 9.3 shows, a Security Token Service is a trust broker ready and willing to provide a Web service with a way to determine whether it will trust an incoming request from a different (possibly unknown) trust domain. A policy statement at the Web service provider notifies the Web service requestor that a security token is required for use of this service. The requestor provides such a token, either having obtained it previously or by the requestor now sending a `<RequestSecurityToken>` to the Security Token Service. The so-obtained WS-Security–compatible security token is then provided when requesting service from the Web service provider. WS-Trust also provides for a challenge-response protocol for the Web service provider to strongly validate the efficacy and timeliness of the requestor's security token.

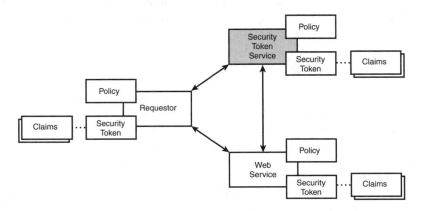

Figure 9.3   The WS-Trust model for providing a Security Token Service trust broker in support of WS-Security.

The Web service security model defined in WS-Trust is based on a process in which a Web service can require that an incoming message prove a set of claims (for example, name, key, permission, capability, and so forth). If a message arrives without having the required proof of claims, the service ignores or rejects the message outright. A service can indicate its required claims and related information in its policy as described by the WS-Policy and WS-PolicyAttachment specifications described in detail in Chapter 8.

A requestor can send messages that demonstrate its ability to prove a required set of claims by associating security tokens with the messages and including message signatures that demonstrate proof of possession of (the contents of) the tokens.

If the requestor does not have the necessary token or tokens to prove the claim, it contacts a Security Token Service and obtains the tokens. These "authorities" may, in turn, require their own set of claims.

The WS-Trust model illustrated in Figure 9.3 shows that any requestor may also be a service and that the Security Token Service is itself a Web service, including expressing policy and requiring security tokens.

This general messaging model—claims, policies, and security tokens—subsumes and supports several more specific models, such as identity-based security, access control lists, and capabilities-based security. It allows use of existing technologies such as X.509 public key certificates, XML-based tokens, Kerberos shared-secret tickets, and even passwords. The general model, in combination with the WS-Security and WS-Policy primitives, is sufficient to construct higher-level key exchange, authentication, policy-based access decisions, auditing, and complex trust relationships.

A quick overview of the WS-Trust model is that a Web service has a policy applied to it, receives a message from a requestor that possibly includes security tokens, and may have some protection applied to it using WS-Security mechanisms. The following steps are performed by the trust engine of a Web service:

1. Verify that the claims in the requestor's security token are sufficient to comply with the provider's policy and that the message conforms to this policy.

2. Verify that the attributes of the claimant are proven by the signatures. In brokered trust models, the signature may not verify the identity of the claimant; it may verify the identity of the intermediary, who may simply assert the identity of the claimant. The claims are either proven or not based on policy.

3. Verify that the issuers of the security tokens (including all related and ancestral security tokens) are trusted to issue the claims they have made. The trust engine may need to send tokens to a Security Token Service to exchange them for other security tokens that it can use directly in its evaluation.

If these conditions are met, and the requestor is authorized to perform the operation, the service can process the service request within the specified trust model just described.

Now that you know how the model is supposed to work and you understand the key relationships between Web service provider, requestor, and Security Token Service, it's time to look at the two key WS-Trust elements needed to perform its prescribed functions: `<RequestSecurityToken>` and `<RequestSecurityTokenResponse>`.

`<RequestSecurityToken>`

Listing 9.1 shows a request to have a security token issued.

Listing 9.1   **The `<RequestSecurityToken>` Element**

```
<RequestSecurityToken>
    <TokenType>...</TokenType>
    <RequestType>...</RequestType>
    <Base>...</Base>
    <Supporting>...</Supporting>
</RequestSecurityToken>
```

Now let's explore each element that makes up a `<RequestSecurityToken>` element.
`<TokenType>`   The optional `<TokenType>` element describes the type of security token requested, specified as a QName (see the following section). That is, it describes the type of token that will be returned in the `<RequestSecurityTokenResponse>` message.
`<RequestType>`   The `<RequestType>` element is used to indicate, using a QName, the action that is being requested. The following QNames are predefined:

QName	Description
wsse:ReqIssue	Issue security token
wsse:ReqValidate	Validate security token
wsse:ReqExchange	Exchange security token

<Base>   The optional <Base> element has the same type as the
<SecurityTokenReference> element and references the base (primary) tokens that are
used to validate the authenticity of a request. In general, this element isn't used because
signatures provided on the request prove the right to make the request.

<Supporting>   The optional <Supporting> element has the same type as the
<SecurityTokenReference> element and references the supporting tokens that are used
to authorize this request. Typically, this element is used to identify tokens in a certificate
authority. It is not required to specify any or all supporting tokens; it is simply a hint or
aid to the recipient service.

The example in Listing 9.2 shows an X.509 security token being requested based on
the security token located in the <Security> header with the ID "myToken". This token
specifies a username, and a signature is placed over the request using a key derived from
the password (or password equivalent), nonce, and time stamp.

Listing 9.2   **Requesting an X.509 Security Token Based on a Key Derived from a
Password**

```
<S:Envelope xmlns:S="..." xmlns=".../secext" xmlns:wsu=".../utility>
    <S:Header>
        ...
        <Security>
            <UsernameToken wsu:Id="myToken">
                <Username>NNK</Username>
                <Nonce>FKJh...</Nonce>
                <wsu:Created>2001-10-13T09:00:00Z </wsu:Created>
            </UsernameToken>
            <ds:Signature xmlns:ds="...">
                ...
            </ds:Signature>
        </Security>
        ...
    </S:Header>
    <S:Body wsu:Id="req">
        <RequestSecurityToken>
            <TokenType>wsse:X509v3</TokenType>
            <RequestType>wsse:ReqIssue</RequestType>
            <Base>
                <Reference URI="#myToken"/>
            </Base>
        </RequestSecurityToken>
    </S:Body>
</S:Envelope>
```

```
<RequestSecurityTokenResponse>
```

The other half of `<RequestSecurityToken>` is `<RequestSecurityTokenResponse>`. The syntax for this element is shown in Listing 9.3.

Listing 9.3   The `<RequestSecurityTokenResponse>` Element

```
<RequestSecurityTokenResponse>
  <TokenType>...</TokenType>
  <KeyType>...</KeyType>
  <KeySize>...</KeySize>
  <wsp:AppliesTo>...</wsp:AppliesTo>
        <RequestedSecurityToken>...</RequestedSecurityToken>
  <RequestedProofToken>...</RequestedProofToken>
</RequestSecurityTokenResponse>
```

Let's look at each element in `<RequestSecurityTokenResponse>` in turn.

`<TokenType>`   The optional `<TokenType>` element specifies the type of security token returned. Either this element or the optional `<AppliesTo>` element should be specified. `<TokenType>` must be provided if a token type other than the requested type is returned.

`<KeyType>`   The optional `<KeyType>` element specifies the type of key used in the token.

`<KeySize>`   The optional `<KeySize>` element specifies the size of the key returned.

`<wsp:AppliesTo>`   The optional `<wsp:AppliesTo>` element specifies the scope to which this security token applies. The WS-PolicyAttachment specification deals with this scope in detail.

`<RequestedSecurityToken>`   The optional `<RequestedSecurityToken>` element is used to return the requested security token. Normally, this element contains the requested security token, but a security token reference may be used instead. For example, if the requested security token is used in securing the message, the security token is placed into the `<Security>` header, and a `<SecurityTokenReference>` element is placed inside the `<RequestedSecurityToken>` element to reference the token in the `<Security>` header. Although this element is optional, at least one of `<RequestedSecurityToken>` or `<RequestedProofToken>` will be returned unless an error occurs.

`<RequestedProofToken>`   The optional `<RequestedProofToken>` element is used to return the proof-of-possession token associated with the requested security token. Proof of possession is needed when the client does not provide the public key to use and signs (authenticates) this using the corresponding private key, thereby proving possession. Normally, this element contains the proof-of-possession token, but a security token reference may be used instead. The token (or reference) is specified as the content of this element. For example, if the proof token is used in securing the message, it is placed in the `<Security>` header, and a `<SecurityTokenReference>` element is used inside the `<RequestedProofToken>` element to reference the token in the `<Security>` header.

Listing 9.4 is a sample response to a request for a security token. In this example, a pre-existing X.509v3 digital certificate, looked up in a directory and encoded into a security token, is returned. As is typical, this example does not return an explicit proof of possession because the client implicitly provided proof of possession by providing the public key to use (and authenticated it using the corresponding private key).

Listing 9.4   `<RequestSecurityTokenResponse>` **Returning a Pre-existing X.509v3 Certificate**

```
<RequestSecurityTokenResponse>
    <RequestedSecurityToken>
        <BinarySecurityToken ValueType="wsse:X509v3"
                             EncodingType="wsse:Base64Binary">
            MIIEZzCCA9CgAwIBAgIQEmtJZc0...
        </BinarySecurityToken>
    </RequestedSecurityToken>
</RequestSecurityTokenResponse>
...
```

WS-Privacy

WS-Privacy is a not-yet-published proposed standard that will use a combination of WS-Policy, WS-Security, and WS-Trust to communicate privacy policies. It is designed to be used by organizations that deploy Web services and require that incoming SOAP requests contain claims that the sender conforms to the service provider's privacy policies. WS-Security encapsulates these claims into security tokens that are verified before accepting any incoming SOAP request.

WS-Privacy will be a standard that allows Web service providers and requestors to state their privacy preferences and organizational privacy practice statements. As of this writing, no public draft of WS-Privacy is available, but from the information that has been published, it will likely be similar to the W3C's Platform for Project Privacy Preferences (P3P).[2] P3P was primarily designed for the Web application world (versus the Web services world). It allows an organization to specify its privacy policy in a structured manner and post it on the Web server that is being accessed. Then a P3P-enabled browser can read this policy and compare it to the browser user's privacy preferences. Thus, a user can express her privacy preferences and be notified when she surfs to a site that has privacy practices that conflict with her stated preferences. In a similar manner, WS-Privacy will allow this type of privacy policy exchange and agreement for Web services.

As an example, an individual would state a set of "privacy preferences" that describe what the individual does or does not want to allow applications acting on his behalf to do with his personal information. A calendaring application, working on the individual's behalf, can now access a calendaring service that uses a set of "privacy practice rules" to

---

2. The P3P specification is available at `http://www.w3.org/TR/P3P/`. One of this book's authors, Dave Remy, was a contributor to this specification.

make statements and decisions about use and disclosure of personal information. The calendar service makes the decision by combining the privacy practice rules with the privacy preferences to determine whether a proposed use or disclosure is permissible.

WS-* Security Specifications for Interoperability

The following sections address the two WS-* security specifications for interoperability. First, we briefly review WS-Policy and then cover WS-SecureConversation.

WS-Policy

WS-Policy was the subject of Chapter 8; we include a brief review of it here for its context within the WS-* family of specifications.

WS-Policy is a family of three specifications. Version 1.1 of the WS-Policy documents include *Web Services Policy Framework (WS-Policy)*, *Web Services Policy Assertions Language (WS-PolicyAssertions)*, and *Web Services Policy Attachment (WS-PolicyAttachment)*.

The top level of these specifications is WS-Policy. It forms the framework by providing a general-purpose model and corresponding syntax to describe and communicate the policies of a Web service. WS-Policy defines a base set of constructs that can be used and extended by other Web services specifications to describe a broad range of service requirements, preferences, and capabilities.

WS-PolicyAssertions specifies a set of common message policy assertions that can be specified within a policy.

WS-PolicyAttachment specifies three specific attachment mechanisms for using policy expressions with existing XML Web service technologies. Specifically, it defines how to associate policy expressions with WSDL-type definitions and UDDI entities. It also defines how to associate implementation-specific policy with all or part of a WSDL portType when exposed from a specific implementation.

Overall, the WS-Policy family describes a language for expressing requirements of Web services senders, receivers, and endpoints. One type of policy requirement that will be placed on senders, receivers, and endpoints is the security of the extended conversation implemented in a Web service. Sounds like a requirement for a "secure conversation," doesn't it? As you will see, WS-SecureConversation does indeed sit on top of WS-Policy, reinforcing the statement that WS-Policy is a framework for richer Web Services Security constructs.

WS-SecureConversation

WS-SecureConversation, developed by IBM, Microsoft, RSA, and VeriSign, is in initial public draft form last published in December 2002. What SSL does at the transport layer in point-to-point communication, WS-SecureConversation does at the SOAP layer. It makes efficient what would otherwise be individual SOAP messages carrying authentication information in tokens that would have to be evaluated and checked against security policy. In contrast, WS-SecureConversation establishes a mutually authenticated security context in which a series of messages are exchanged. Despite being at the top of the stack and therefore initially considered one of the later specifications to be published, a draft of WS-SecureConversation[3] was published fairly early on.

WS-Security secures SOAP and thereby has a message-level security focus. But many Web service conversations span multiple messages and need an efficient way to secure those conversations. Furthermore, WS-Security is subject to certain kinds of attacks that can be thoroughly addressed only by authenticating a series of messages, not just one message at a time. WS-Security focuses on a single message authentication model in which the message itself must contain everything necessary to authenticate itself. This model can be inefficient considering that, if the exact same message comes in again and again, each time it would go through the same authentication/verification process, which is computationally expensive. WS-Security is well suited for coarse-grained messaging in which a single message at a time (or few in number) from the same requestor are received. When multiple messages are to be exchanged, establishing a security context can greatly improve efficiency. This security context, which contains a shared secret used by both parties to encrypt and/or sign, is shared among the communicating parties until the session expires.

Like SSL, WS-SecureConversation uses public key (asymmetric) encryption to establish a shared secret key and from then on uses shared key (symmetric) encryption for efficiency. The same shared key is used to encrypt a series of SOAP messages.

`<SecurityContextToken>`

The structure of a WS-SecureConversation is based on the `<SecurityContextToken>` element. This element is a security token that describes a security context. This is the context that will apply to one or more messages to follow. The structure of `<SecurityContextToken>` is shown in Listing 9.5.

Listing 9.5   **The `<SecurityContextToken>` Element**

```
<wsse:SecurityContextToken wsu:Id="...">
   <wsu:Identifier>...</wsu:Identifier>
   <wsu:Created>...</wsu:Created>
   <wsu:Expires>...</wsu:Expires>
   <wsse:Keys>
       <xenc:EncryptedKey Id="   ">...</xenc:EncryptedKey>
       <wsse:SecurityTokenReference>...</wsse:SecurityTokenReference>
       ...
   </wsse:Keys>
</wsse:SecurityContextToken>
```

The elements and attributes used in a `<wsse:SecurityContextToken>` element are described in the following sections.

---

3. The WS-SecureConversation specification is available at http://msdn.microsoft.com/ webservices/default.aspx?pull=/library/en-us/dnglobspec/html/ WS-secureconversation.asp.

`<wsu:Identifier>`   The required `<wsu:Identifier>` element identifies the security context using a URI. This security context URI must be globally unique to both the sender and recipient.

`<wsu:Created>`   The optional `<wsu:Created>` element indicates the creation time of the security context. It is typically specified only on the first use of the token.

`<wsu:Expires>`   The optional `<wsu:Expires>` element indicates the expiration time of the security context according to the requestor's clock. It is typically specified only on the first use of the token.

`<Keys>`   The optional `<Keys>` element holds the shared secrets of the security context. It is typically specified only on the first use of the token. If no `<Keys>` element is specified, the shared secret is assumed to be already known and associated with the security context identified by the URI specified in the `<Identifier>` element.

`<xenc:EncryptedKey>`   The optional `<xenc:EncryptedKey>` element holds the shared secret of the security context.

`<xenc:EncryptedKey/@Id>`   The optional `<xenc:EncryptedKey/@Id>` attribute specifies an "ID" for the key. Note that this does not use the `wsu:Id` attribute because the schema doesn't allow for attribute extensibility.

`<SecurityTokenReference>`   The optional `<SecurityTokenReference>` element references the shared secret of the security context.

Establishing a Security Context

There are three ways to establish a security context:

- The security context token can be created by an independent third-party token service.

- The security context token can be created by one of the communicating parties and propagated with a message.

- The security context token can be created through negotiation.

Security Context Token Created by a Security Token Service   The initiator can ask a Security Token Service to create a new security context token. The newly created security context token is distributed to the parties through the protocols defined by WS-SecureConversation and WS-Trust. For this scenario, the initiating party sends a `<RequestSecurityToken>` request to the token service, and a `<RequestSecurityTokenResponse>` is returned. The response contains a `<SecurityTokenReference>` pointing to the new security context token and a `<ProofTokenReference>` pointing to the "secret" for the returned context.

Security Context Token Created by One of the Communicating Parties and Propagated with a Message   The initiator can create a security context token and send it to the other parties on a message using the mechanisms described here and in WS-Security. This model works when the sender is trusted to always create a new security context token. For this scenario, the initiating party creates a security context token and issues a signed unsolicited `<RequestSecurityTokenResponse>` to the other party. The message contains a `<SecurityTokenReference>` pointing to the new security context token and a `<ProofTokenReference>` pointing to the "secret" for the security context token. The recipient can then choose whether to accept the security context token.

Security Context Token Created Through Negotiation When participants need to negotiate about the contents of the security context token, such as a shared secret, WS-SecureConversation allows the parties to exchange data to establish the security context. For this scenario, the initiating party sends a `<RequestSecurityToken>` request to the other party, and a `<RequestSecurityTokenResponse>` is returned. It is likely that the negotiation (challenge/response) semantics described in WS-Trust will be used. Ultimately (if successful), a final response contains a `<SecurityTokenReference>` pointing to the new security context and a `<ProofTokenReference>` pointing to the "secret" for the context.

After the shared secret security context token is established for both parties, it is used within WS-Security to secure each message sent as part of a WS-SecureConversation. This scenario is shown in Listing 9.6.

Listing 9.6   Use of a Shared Secret Security Context in WS–Security as Part of WS–SecureConversation

```
<?xml version="1.0" encoding="utf-8"?>
<S:Envelope xmlns:S="..." xmlns:ds="..." xmlns:wsse="...">
  <S:Header>
    ...
    <wsse:Security>
      <wsse:SecurityContextToken wsu:Id="MyID"
        <wsu:Identifier>uuid:...</wsu:Identifier>
      </wsse:SecurityContextToken>
      <ds:Signature>
      ...
        <ds:KeyInfo>
          <wsse:SecurityTokenReference>
            <wsse:Reference URI="#MyID"/>
          </wsse:SecurityTokenReference>
        </ds:KeyInfo>
      </ds:Signature>
    </wsse:Security>
  </S:Header>
  <S:Body wsu:Id="MsgBody">
    <tru:StockSymbol xmlns:tru="http://fabrikam123.com/payloads">
        QQQ
    </tru:StockSymbol>
  </S:Body>
</S:Envelope>
```

Listing 9.6 is a standard SOAP message, so it begins with a SOAP message header followed by the SOAP body. The SOAP header contains the WS-Security `<Security>` header block, which contains the security-related information for the message. Inside the WS-Security block is a security token associated with the message inside a `<SecurityContextToken>` element. A URI within this element specifies the unique ID of the context. The digital signature uses the security context just established—in this case, based on the secret key associated with the context. The contents of the XML Digital signature here are represented with ellipses (. . .) but would reference the body of the message. The `<ds:KeyInfo>` element holds the key used for the signature. Not surprisingly, it will be the security context token included in the message and therefore will just refer to the URI that is the unique ID of the context specified earlier.

The body of the message comes next and is shown here with another ellipsis.

Much, if not all, of what is described here will be handled for you by the application server platforms and the development tools that support them. It is important to know what they are doing and why, but the details are hidden behind your development tools.

WS-* Security Specifications for Integration

Integration, in the context of Web Services Security, is the federation of identities and uniform authorization policies. Federation is the integration of trust domains across organizational boundaries and is addressed by WS-Federation. Authorization is the unification of access control policies across organizational boundaries and is addressed by WS-Authorization.

WS-Federation

WS-Federation enables the establishment of federated trust using WS-Security, WS-Policy, WS-Trust, and WS-SecureConversation as composable building blocks. Federation in this context means that a group of organizations that will have communicating Web services agrees on a uniform set of standards and policies about identification and authentication of entities for the purpose of translating one entity's security tokens into another type of security token. For example, WS-Federation solves the problem of one organization using Kerberos and the other with which it wants to communicate using X.509. WS-Policy and WS-Trust are used to determine which tokens are consumed and how to apply for tokens from an external service.

Figure 9.4 illustrates one way the WS-Trust model may be applied to simple federation scenarios. Here, security tokens (1) from the requestor's trust realm are used to acquire security tokens from the resource's trust realm (2) to access the resource/service (3). That is, a token from one Security Token Service (STS) is exchanged for another at a second STS (or possibly stamped or cross-certified by a second STS).

Next, Figure 9.5 shows the detailed sequence of steps used to exchange security tokens between a requestor Web service and the Web service provider resource.

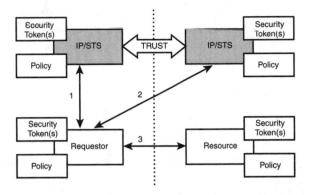

Figure 9.4 Simple federation scenario allowing requestor in one trust domain to interact with a resource in a different trust domain using different security models.

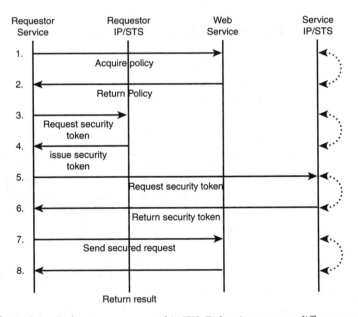

Figure 9.5 Eight-step process used in WS-Federation to cross different trust domains with a security token.

This process is as follows:

1. Acquire policy.

   If the requestor doesn't already have the policy for the service, it can obtain the policy using the mechanisms defined in WS-MetadataExchange. WS-MetadataExchange allows a service to directly obtain information using *WSDL*, or it may choose to use a UDDI service that aggregates this information for multiple target services.

2. Return policy.

   The requested policy is returned using the mechanisms defined in WS-MetadataExchange.

3. Request security token.

   The requestor requests a security token from its IP/STS (assuming short-lived security tokens) using the mechanisms defined in WS-Trust: `<RequestSecurityToken>`.

4. Issue security token.

   The IP/STS returns a security token (and optional proof-of-possession information) using the mechanisms defined in WS-Trust: `<RequestSecurityTokenResponse>` and `<RequestedProofToken>`.

5. Request security token.

   The requestor requests a security token from the Web services IP/STS for the target Web service using the mechanisms defined in WS-Trust: `<RequestSecurityToken>`. Note that this is determined via policy or some out-of-band mechanism.

6. Return security token.

   The Web service's IP/STS returns a token (and optionally proof-of-possession information) using the mechanisms defined in WS-Trust: `<RequestSecurityTokenResponse>`.

7. Send secured request.

   The requestor sends the request to the service attaching and securing the message using the issued tokens as described in WS-Security.

8. Return result.

   The service issues a secured reply using its security token.

WS-Federation, SAML, Liberty, and Passport

WS-Federation deals with identity in a federated Web services context. As of this writing, no specification has been published for WS-Federation, and it is not without controversy due to the Microsoft name on the specification and the questions around the Sun-sponsored Liberty Alliance project and the Microsoft-owned Passport technology.

WS-Federation is working toward compatibility with SAML as SAML tokens become one of the types of federated tokens accepted, along with X.509, Kerberos, and XrML.

That being said, it seems valuable to have a standard approach for federated trust scenarios specific to Web services that is independent of the Liberty Alliance and Passport and generalized enough to fit into both models of identity federation.

At the very least, WS-Federation addresses a really difficult unsolved problem: how to get a Web service based in a domain using Kerberos to work effectively in a trusted fashion with a Web service based in an X.509 domain.

WS-Authorization

WS-Authorization deals with authorization decisions in the context of Web services. It describes how access policies for a Web service will be specified and managed. As of this writing, no specification has been published for WS-Authorization. Its objectives are similar to the eXtensible Access Control Markup Language (XACML) and will undoubtedly be heavily influenced by it.

XML Key Management Specification (XKMS)

The XML Key Management Specification is built on top of and complements the XML standards for Digital Signature and Encryption. XKMS reached version 2.0 W3C working draft in April 2003.

By now, you see that Web services need end-to-end message integrity and confidentiality, which means that they need XML Digital Signature and XML Encryption. Those technologies, in turn, scale best when they use public key cryptography. Public key cryptography needs a supporting infrastructure, PKI, to handle distribution, certification, and life-cycle management (for example, revocation) of keys. PKI has proven to be very difficult and expensive to build and maintain in practice, and many failures have given it a bad reputation as an almost "failed" technology. Web services themselves provide a powerful new approach to PKI that prevents each Web service requestor and provider from having to build their own PKI: accessing a trusted PKI as a service. XKMS aims to do just that.

Origins of XKMS

XKMS specifies protocols for distributing and registering public keys suitable for use in conjunction with the XML Digital Signature standard and the XML Encryption standard. XKMS is composed of two parts:

- XML Key Information Service Specification (X-KISS)
- XML Key Registration Service Specification (X-KRSS)

X-KISS is a protocol to support the creation of a service to which an application delegates the processing of Key Information. Thus, applications needing keys for use with an XML Signature, XML Encryption, or other use of the `<ds:KeyInfo>` element can handle the necessary complex key management by calling a shared service.

X-KRSS is a protocol to support the registration and management of a key pair by a key pair holder, with the intent that the key pair subsequently be usable in conjunction with the XML Key Information Service Specification or a Public Key Infrastructure such as X.509 or PKIX.

Goals of XKMS

XKMS's first goal is to support a simple client's capability to use sophisticated key management functionality. Such a simple client is not concerned with the details of the infrastructure required to support the public key management but may choose to work with X.509 certificates if it is able to manage the details. This ties back to the biggest impediment for PKI, which has been the lack of client support. This goal does not directly impact the discussion of PKI for Web services, but the second goal does.

The second goal is to provide public key management support to XML applications. In particular, it is a goal of XML key management to support the public key management requirements of XML Encryption, XML Digital Signature, and to be consistent with SAML.

One sample use of XKMS is for implementing "transaction accountability." When a Web service embeds trust in electronic transactions using digital signatures, digital receipts, and notary services based on business policies, XKMS can, when needed, transparently link to a *trust* Web service to affix and validate digital signatures, notary stamps, and digital receipts to XML documents.

In this scenario, XKMS represents a strong tangible benefit of XML Signature. The presence of XKMS means that use of XML Signature can be independent of PKI vendor implementations and enables Web services to offer a wider range of options for trust relationships. In particular, access to an XKMS service makes it easier to add attribute-bindings to messages than it would be to add X.509 certificate extensions that require a tight relationship with a PKI vendor.

The XKMS Services

The XKMS protocol follows a request/response mechanism. Each request is followed by a response message. Apart from the Authenticate message, all other messages can be grouped under one of the following message types:

Locate	This message provides name resolution.
Validate	This message provides key validation.
Register	Information is bound to a public key pair through a key binding.
Reissue	A previously registered key binding is reissued.
Recover	A previously registered key binding that may have been lost is recovered.
Revoke	A previously registered key binding is revoked.

The relationship of these messages to the requesting XKMS client and the responding Trust Service is shown in Figure 9.6.

X-KISS

The X-KISS Locate service resolves a `<ds:Keyinfo>` element. It is a name resolution service. The service may resolve the `<ds:Keyinfo>` element using local data or may relay the request to other servers. For example, the XKMS service might resolve a `<ds:RetrievalMethod>` element or act as a gateway to an underlying PKI based on a non-XML syntax.

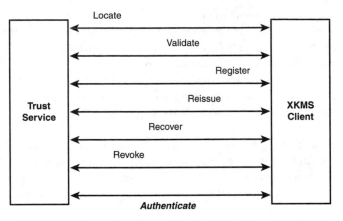

Figure 9.6   XKMS message types and their relationship to the XKMS client
and the Trust Service.

Here's a sample scenario: A Web service receives a signed document that specifies the
sender's X.509v3 certificate but not the key value (which is embedded in the X.509 certificate). The Web service is not capable of processing X.509v3 certificates but can obtain
the key parameters from the XKMS service by means of the Locate service. The Web
service sends the `<ds:Keyinfo>` element to the Locate service and requests that the
`<KeyName>` and `<KeyValue>` elements be returned, as shown in Listing 9.7. When it has
these elements, it has the information needed to decode the XML Digital Signature it
just received.

Listing 9.7   **X-Kiss Request to XKMS Locate Service to Process X.509 Certificates to
Obtain Key Parameters**

```
<?xml version="1.0" encoding="utf-8"?>
<LocateRequest xmlns:ds="http://www.w3.org/2000/09/xmldsig#"
      xmlns:xenc="http://www.w3.org/2001/04/xmlenc#"
      Id="I4593b8d4b6bd9ae7262560b5de1016bc"
      Service="http://test.xmltrustcenter.org/XKMS"
      xmlns="http://www.w3.org/2002/03/xkms#">
  <RespondWith>KeyValue</RespondWith>
  <QueryKeyBinding>
    <ds:KeyInfo>
      <ds:X509Data>
        <ds:X509Certificate>MIICAjCCAW+gAwIBAgIQlzQov
IEbLLhMa8K5MR/juzAJBgUrDgMCHQUAMBIxEDAOBgNVBAMTB1Rlc3QgQ0EwHhcNMDIwNjEzMjEzMzQ
xWhcNMzkxMjMxMjM
1OTU5WjAsMSowKAYDVQQGEyFVUyBPPUFsaWNlIENvcnAgQ049QWxpY2UgQWFyZHZhcmswgZ8wDQYJK
oZIhvcNAQEBBQADg
Y0AMIGJAoGBAMoy4c9+NoNJvJUnV8pqPByGb4FOJcU0VktbGJpO2imiQx+EJsCt27z/pVUDrexTyctC
WbeqR5a40JCQmvN
```

Listing 9.7 **Continued**

```
mRUfg2d81HXyA+iYPl4L6nUlHbkLjrhPPtMDSd5YHjyvnCN454+Hr0paA1MJXKuw8ZMkjGYsr4fSYpP
ELOH5PDJEBAgMBA
AGjRzBFMEMGA1UdAQQ8MDqAEEVr1g8cxzEkdMX4GAlD6TahFDASMRAwDgYDVQQDEwdUZXN0IENBghBy
sVHEiNFiiE2lxWv
mJYeSMAkGBSsOAwIdBQADgYEAKp+RKhDMIVIbooSNcoIeV/wVew1bPVkEDOUwmhAdRXUA94uRifiFfm
p9GoN08Jkurx/gF
18RFB/7oLrVY+cpzRoCipcnAnmh0hGY8FNFmhyKU1tFhVFdFXB5QUglkmkRntNkOmcb8O87xOOXktmv
NzcJDes9PMNxrVt
ChzjaFAE=</ds:X509Certificate>
        </ds:X509Data>
      </ds:KeyInfo>
      <KeyUsage>Signature</KeyUsage>
    </QueryKeyBinding>
</LocateRequest>
```

When the Locate service receives the X.509v3 certificate from the `<LocateRequest>` in Listing 9.7, it extracts the key information from the certificate and constructs the elements it needs to return from the requesting service, as shown in Listing 9.8.

Listing 9.8 **Response from XKMS Locate Service to Preceding Request**

```
<?xml version="1.0" encoding="utf-8"?>
<LocateResult xmlns:ds="http://www.w3.org/2000/09/xmldsig#"
      xmlns:xenc="http://www.w3.org/2001/04/xmlenc#"
      Id="I46ee58f131435361d1e51545de10a9aa"
      Service="http://test.xmltrustcenter.org/XKMS" ResultMajor="Success"
      RequestId="#I4593b8d4b6bd9ae7262560b5de1016bc"
      xmlns="http://www.w3.org/2002/03/xkms#">
  <UnverifiedKeyBinding Id="I36b45b969a9020dbe1da2cb793016117">
    <ds:KeyInfo>
      <ds:KeyValue>
        <ds:RSAKeyValue>

<ds:Modulus>zvbTdKsTprGAKJdgi7ulDR0eQBptLv/SJNIh3uVmPBObZFsLbqPwo5nyLOkzWlEHNbS
hPMRp1qFrAfF13L
MmeohNYfCXTHLqH1MaMOm+BhXABHB9rUKaGoOBjQPHCBtHbfMGQYjznGTpfCdTrUgq8VNlqM2Ph9XWMc
c7qbjNHw8=</ds
:Modulus>
          <ds:Exponent>AQAB</ds:Exponent>
        </ds:RSAKeyValue>
      </ds:KeyValue>
    </ds:KeyInfo>
    <KeyUsage>Signature</KeyUsage>
    <KeyUsage>Encryption</KeyUsage>
    <KeyUsage>Exchange</KeyUsage>
  </UnverifiedKeyBinding>
</LocateResult>
```

The X-KISS Validate service performs this function, and in addition, the client may obtain an assertion from the X-KISS service specifying the status of the binding between the public key and other data—for example, a name or a set of extended attributes. Furthermore, the service represents that the status of each data element returned is valid and that all are bound to the same public key. The client sends to the XKMS service a prototype containing some or all of the elements for which the status of the key binding is required. If the information in the prototype is incomplete, the XKMS service may obtain additional data required from an underlying PKI Service, as depicted in Figure 9.7. After the validity of the Key Binding has been determined, the XKMS service returns the status result to the client.

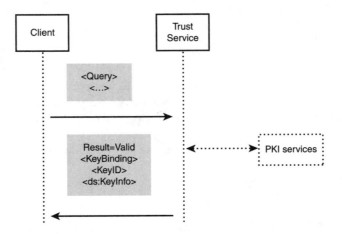

Figure 9.7   The Validate service provides key validation usually sitting on top of a PKI at a trusted third party.

No single set of validation criteria is appropriate to every circumstance. Applications involving financial transactions are likely to require the application of very specific validation criteria that ensure certain contractual and/or regulatory policies are enforced. The Locate service provides a key discovery function that is neutral with respect to the validation criteria that the client application may apply. The Validate service provides a key discovery and validation function that produces results that are specific to a single set of validation criteria.

X-KRSS

From a Web services point of view, Locate and Validate will be the most common form of XKMS service requested. Depending on the nature of the Web service provided and the security policy in place, X-KRSS messages such as Register, Recover, Revoke, and Reissue may be processed only under a much more stringent environment.

In the registration phase, as shown in Figure 9.8, an XML application key pair holder registers its public key with a trusted infrastructure via a registration server. The public key is sent to the registration server using a digitally signed request specified by KRSS using the <Register> tag. The registration server responds with an XML formatted confirmation response using the <RegisterResponse> tag, which indicates status of the registration (accepted, rejected, or pending) and a confirmation of name and attribute information registered with the public key. Except in the case of rejection, a key pair identifier is returned in the <RegisterResponse> tag for subsequent referencing purposes. The registration is typically preceded by generation of the key pair in the key pair holder system.

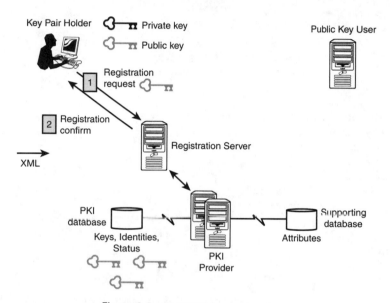

Figure 9.8   X-KRSS key registration.

A sample X-KRSS <Request> is shown in Listing 9.9.

Listing 9.9   **X-KRSS Request to XKMS Registration Service for Key Registration**

```
<?xml version="1.0"?>
 <soap:Envelope xmlns:soap="http://schemas.xmlsoap.org/soap/envelope/"
 xmlns:soapenc="http://schemas.xmlsoap.org/soap/encoding/"
 xmlns:xsi="http://www.w3.org/1999/XMLSchema-instance"
 xmlns:xsd="http://www.w3.org/1999/XMLSchema"
xmlns:ds="http://www.w3.org/2000/09/xmldsig#">
  <soap:Body>
    <Register xmlns="http://www.xkms.org/schema/xkms-2001-01-20">
      <Prototype>
        <Status>Valid</Status>
        <KeyID>mailto:Alice@cryptographer.test</KeyID>
```

Listing 9.9   **Continued**

```
            <ds:KeyInfo>
              <ds:KeyName>mailto:Alice@cryptographer.test</ds:KeyName>
            </ds:KeyInfo>
          <ValidityInterval>
            <NotBefore>2000-09-20T12:00:00</NotBefore>
            <NotAfter>2001-09-20T12:00:00</NotAfter>
          </ValidityInterval>
          <PassPhrase>qfarJIsfcVKLo</PassPhrase>
        </Prototype>
        <AuthInfo>
          <AuthUserInfo>
            <ProofOfPossession>
              <Signature>2PUN8HQlnhf9YI</Signature>
            </ProofOfPossession>
            <AuthKeyBinding>
              <Signature>EfdxSXAidruAszN</Signature>
            </AuthKeyBinding>
          </AuthUserInfo>
        </AuthInfo>
        <Respond>
          <string>KeyName</string>
          <string>KeyValue</string>
        </Respond>
      </Register>
    </soap:Body>
  </soap:Envelope>
```

The X-KRSS `<RegisterResult>` response to this request is shown in Listing 9.10.

Listing 9.10   **X-KRSS Response from the XKMS Registration Service**

```
<?xml version="1.0"?>
 <soap:Envelope xmlns:soap="http://schemas.xmlsoap.org/soap/envelope/"
 xmlns:soapenc="http://schemas.xmlsoap.org/soap/encoding/"
 xmlns:xsi="http://www.w3.org/1999/XMLSchema-instance"
 xmlns:xsd="http://www.w3.org/1999/XMLSchema"
xmlns:ds="http://www.w3.org/2000/09/xmldsig#">
   <soap:Body>
     <RegisterResult xmlns="http://www.xkms.org/schema/xkms-2001-01-20">
       <Result>Success</Result>
       <Answer soapenc:arrayType="KeyBinding[1]">
         <KeyBinding>
           <Status>Valid</Status>
           <KeyID>mailto:Alice@cryptographer.test</KeyID>
             <ds:KeyInfo>
```

Listing 9.10 **Continued**

```
            <ds:KeyValue>
              <ds:RSAKeyValue>
<ds:Modulus>998/T2PUN8HQlnhf9YIKdMHHGM7HkJwA56UD0a1oYq7EfdxSXAidruAszNqBoOqfarJ
IsfcVKLob1hGnQ/16xw==</ds:Modulus>
                <ds:Exponent>AQAB</ds:Exponent>
              </ds:RSAKeyValue>
            </ds:KeyValue>
            <ds:KeyName>mailto:Alice@cryptographer.test</ds:KeyName>
          </ds:KeyInfo>

        <ValidityInterval>
          <NotBefore>2000-09-20T12:00:00</NotBefore>
          <NotAfter>2001-09-20T12:00:00</NotAfter>
        </ValidityInterval>
      </KeyBinding>
    </Answer>
    <Private/>
  </RegisterResult>
 </soap:Body>
</soap:Envelope>
```

Revocation is handled via a similar protocol. The use of desktop (that is, file system) private key storage—as well as more broad XML client encryption applications—mandates some form of *key recovery* provision. Key recovery provides a way to recover a lost private key so that corporate-owned data encrypted with the lost private key is not lost forever. For historical reasons, key recovery is not supported by standardized protocols. In X-KRSS, such support is built in.

eXtensible Access Control Markup Language (XACML) Specification

eXtensible Access Control Markup Language is an XML Schema for representing authorization and entitlement policies. The XACML 1.0 specification was ratified as an OASIS Open Standard by the OASIS eXtensible Access Control Markup Language Technical Committee in February 2003. Version 1.1 was released in August 2003.

XACML represents the rules that specify the who, what, when, and how of information access. Access control, which is often called *rights management*, determines who can look at something, what they can do with it, the type of device they can look at it on, and so on.

A set of access control issues has created the need for XACML. First, computing systems are extremely general. Computing platforms have been made as broad and general as possible for the widest possible set of applications that can be run on those platforms. These computing systems also have the broadest possible set of privileges for accessing data and applications, so they can be used in the widest possible set of applications, including those with very permissive (that is, no) security policies.

Second, access control policy enforcement is handled at many different points. In cases of reasonably strict security policy, systems are access controlled at the point of deployment. Enterprise security policy has many elements and points of enforcement, including HR, Finance, Legal, and others.

The third condition that sets up the need for XACML is the plethora of different access control enforcement mechanisms. Each point of enforcement is typically managed independently to make sure the policy is implemented accurately. This makes it prohibitively expensive to modify security policy. It is impossible to obtain a consolidated view of the overall security situation in an enterprise. Despite this fact, pressures increase to demonstrate and prove best practices when protecting information assets.

On top of these three conditions come the machine-to-machine interactions of Web services, which dramatically exacerbate these issues. Combined, these conditions create the need for a common language for expressing information system security policy.

The target of an XACML specification can be any object that is referenced using XML; this gives XACML very fine-grained control. XACML has three top-level policy elements: Policy, PolicySet, and Rule.

The XACML Data Model

At the root of XACML is a concern with access policies—what XACML refers to as a Policy or a PolicySet. When XACML refers to "policy," it specifically means authorization policy. Each XACML policy document contains exactly one Policy or PolicySet root XML tag. A Policy represents a single access-control policy, expressed through a set of Rules. A *Policy* is intended to form the basis of an authorization decision. A *PolicySet* contains a set of Policy or other PolicySet elements and a specified procedure for combining the results of their evaluation. This is the standard means for combining separate policies into a single combined policy. A *Rule* contains a Boolean expression that can be evaluated in isolation as the basic unit of management; it can be reused in multiple policies.

A few more critical terms used in XACML need to be understood as well. A *Target* defines a set of resources, subjects, and actions to which a Rule is intended to apply. It is the set of decision requests that a Rule, Policy, or PolicySet is intended to evaluate. An *Obligation* is an operation specified in a Policy or PolicySet that should be performed in conjunction with the enforcement of an authorization decision. A *Condition* is an expression that evaluates to True or False or Indeterminate. The *Effect* is the intended consequence of a satisfied Rule—either Permit or Deny.

Figure 9.9 shows these XACML concepts.

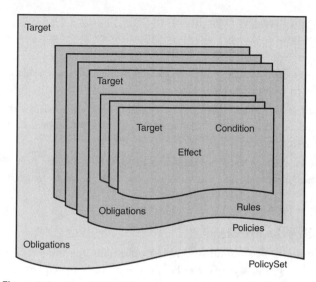

Figure 9.9   Core XACML constructs and their interrelationships.

XACML Operation

XACML defines a very granular set of "layers" to

1. Create policy.
2. Collect the data required for policy evaluation.
3. Evaluate policy.
4. Enforce policy.

This much granularity enables interoperability for a wide variety of access control approaches. It is an architecture that maximizes flexibility.

Because a generic Policy or PolicySet may contain multiple policies or Rules, each of which may evaluate to different access control decisions, XACML needs some way of reconciling the decisions each makes. In XACML, this is done through a collection of *Combining Algorithms*. Each algorithm represents a different way of combining multiple decisions into a single decision to build up increasingly complex policies. XACML utilizes Policy Combining Algorithms (used by PolicySet) and Rule Combining Algorithms (used by Policy). The set of Combining Algorithms takes the form of deny-overrides, permit-overrides, first-applicable, and only-one-applicable. These are just a few examples, but an arbitrary set can be created from basic primitives.

> **XACML Not Really Ready for Prime Time Yet**
>
> XACML is intended primarily to be generated by tools. Its verbose syntax makes it hard to read and tedious to edit for other than very simple policies.
>
> These tools, however, aren't available yet. Nonetheless, a few brave groups have provided a template and sample code for using XACML with Java.
>
> Not many applications will actually require the kind of dynamic discovery provided by XACML. XACML experts suggest that developers think of XACML in relation to wire-formats such as WS-Security just as they do WSDL in relation to SOAP.
>
> The home we expect XACML to find is as the tool to create SAML Policy Decision Points (PDP). PDPs will most likely communicate to back-end policy stores using the XACML access control/policy language.

XACML Policy Example

Following in Listing 9.11 is a simple example to illustrate implementation of an XACML Policy. The Target says that the Policy applies only to requests for the server called `"SampleServer"`. The Policy has a Rule with a Target that requires an action of `"login"` and a Condition that applies only if the Subject is trying to log in between 9 a.m. and 5 p.m.

Listing 9.11   **XACML for SamplePolicy on SampleServer for Login Only Between 9 and 5**

```
<Policy PolicyId="SamplePolicy"
       RuleCombiningAlgId="urn:oasis:names:tc:xacml:1.0:
         rule-combining-algorithm:first-applicable">

  <!-- This Policy only applies to requests on the SampleServer -->
  <Target>
    <Subjects>
      <AnySubject/>
    </Subjects>
    <Resources>
      <ResourceMatch MatchId="urn:oasis:names:tc:xacml:1.0:
        function:string-equal">
        <AttributeValue DataType="http://www.w3.org/2001/XMLSchema#string">
          SampleServer</AttributeValue>
        <ResourceAttributeDesignator DataType="http://www.w3.org/2001/
          XMLSchema#string"
                              AttributeId="urn:oasis:names:tc:xacml:
                                1.0:resource:resource-id"/>
      </ResourceMatch>
    </Resources>
    <Actions>
      <AnyAction/>
```

Listing 9.11 **Continued**

```
    </Actions>
  </Target>

  <!-- Rule to see if we should allow the Subject to login -->
  <Rule RuleId="LoginRule" Effect="Permit">

    <!-- Only use this Rule if the action is login -->
    <Target>
      <Subjects>
        <AnySubject/>
      </Subjects>
      <Resources>
        <AnyResource/>
      </Resources>
      <Actions>
        <ActionMatch MatchId="urn:oasis:names:tc:xacml:1.0:
          function:string-equal">
          <AttributeValue DataType="http://www.w3.org/2001/XMLSchema#string">
           login</AttributeValue>
          <ActionAttributeDesignator DataType="http://www.w3.org/2001/
            XMLSchema#string"
                                      AttributeId="ServerAction"/>
        </ActionMatch>
      </Actions>
    </Target>

    <!-- Only allow logins from 9am to 5pm -->
    <Condition FunctionId="urn:oasis:names:tc:xacml:1.0:function:and">
      <Apply FunctionId="urn:oasis:names:tc:xacml:1.0:
        function:time-greater-than-or-equal">
        <Apply FunctionId="urn:oasis:names:tc:xacml:1.0:function:
          time-one-and-only">
          <EnvironmentAttributeSelector DataType="http://www.w3.org/2001/
            XMLSchema#time"
                                        AttributeId="urn:oasis:names:tc:
                                        xacml:1.0:environment:current-time"/>
        </Apply>
        <AttributeValue DataType="http://www.w3.org/2001/XMLSchema#time">
          09:00:00</AttributeValue>
      </Apply>
      <Apply FunctionId="urn:oasis:names:tc:xacml:1.0:
        function:time-less-than-or-equal">
        <Apply FunctionId="urn:oasis:names:tc:xacml:1.0:
          function:time-one-and-only">
          <EnvironmentAttributeSelector DataType="http://www.w3.org/2001/
```

Listing 9.11   Continued

```
                XMLSchema#time"
                                    AttributeId="urn:oasis:names:tc:
                                    xacml:1.0:environment:current-time"/>
        </Apply>
        <AttributeValue DataType="http://www.w3.org/2001/XMLSchema#time">
          17:00:00</AttributeValue>
      </Apply>
    </Condition>

  </Rule>

  <!-- We could include other Rules for different actions here -->

  <!-- A final, "fall-through" Rule that always Denies -->
  <Rule RuleId="FinalRule" Effect="Deny"/>

</Policy>
```

XACML will probably affect the way security policy is built into applications, making less work for developers. XACML would do that by taking implicit policy that today is often spread across multiple applications in the form of executable code and bringing it to a central point of administration where it can be more easily created, modified, made consistent, and analyzed for effect by individuals other than developers responsible for security policy.

The following are some XACML resources:

http://www.oasis-open.org/committees/tc_home.php?wg_abbrev=xacml

http://sunxacml.sourceforge.net/guide.html#xacml

http://www.idevnews.com/TipsTricks.asp?ID=57

http://www.entrust.com/resources/standards/xacml.htm

eXtensible Rights Markup Language (XrML) Management Specification

The eXtensible Rights Markup Language specifies rights to control access to digital content and services. XrML is part of the effort to create an infrastructure to manage digital rights on copyright and for-fee content that is moved across the public networks.

XrML is a rights language that supports a wide variety of business models from free content that still must control who accesses it (for example, real estate home listings) to valuable content that must be purchased by the end user (for example, digital music). It can specify simple and complex rights. It is designed to handle any type of digital content or service. It gives precise meaning to all components of the system. A couple of its critical early design goals were that it be interoperable with other standards and specifications and that it be platform neutral.

The XrML Data Model

The data model for XrML consists of four entities and the relationship between those entities. The most important relationship is the XrML assertion Grant. A Grant is structured as follows:

- The Principal to whom the Grant is issued
- The Right that the Grant specifies
- The Resource that is the direct object of the "rights" verb
- The Condition that must be met for the right to be exercised

A *Principal* is an individual who must present identification credentials such as an X.509 certificate or a digital signature. If the authentication of this individual is successful, that person may be granted some Rights to the digital content. The *Right* is a verb that a Principal can be granted to exercise agaist some content. For example, the Right might be to read, view, print, forward, or even grant rights to others. The *Resource* is the object to which a Principal can be granted a Right. It might be an e-book, an audio or video file, or an image. It can also be a service such as email or a Web service. A *Condition* specifies the terms, conditions, and obligations under which the Rights can be exercised. This might be a time interval, or it might require that someone else has also granted some Rights first, such as a trusted third party. The relationships of the four key XrML constructs are shown in Figure 9.10.

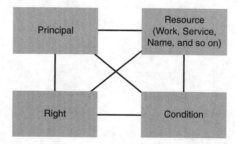

Figure 9.10   Core XrML constructs and their interrelationships.

XrML Use Case Example

The following use case illustrates how to use XrML in a service-centric business model, which focuses on specifying Rights, Conditions, and metadata for services, such as Web services. In this use case, Alice pays $2 each time she uses a Web service to receive stock quotes. Figure 9.11 illustrates this use case.

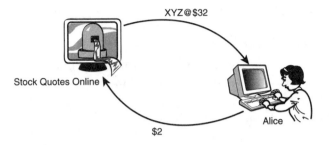

Figure 9.11 Alice may use the content from a Stock Quote Web service if she pays $2 for such use.

To specify this information in XrML, you need to

1. Identify Alice as the person to whom the Rights are granted.
2. Specify the Right that Alice is granted—the right to use the stock service.
3. Identify the Resource (the Web service) to which Alice is being granted rights.
4. Specify the Condition (the fee) that applies when Alice exercises her right to use the stock service.

Figure 9.12 illustrates the structure of Alice's license.

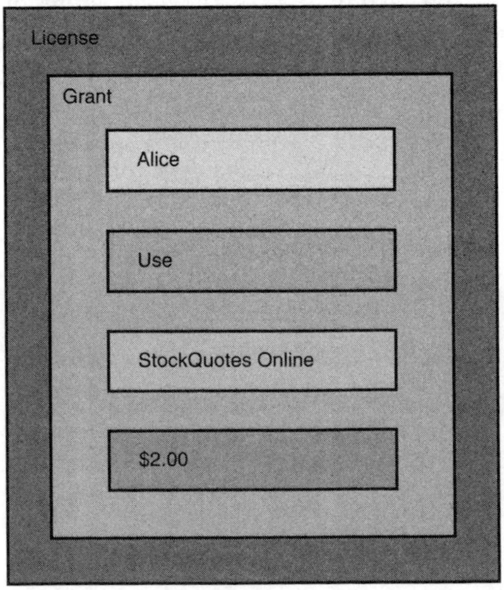

License

Grant

Alice

Use

StockQuotes Online

$2.00

Figure 9.12 The XrML license for Alice's use case.

The license in Listing 9.12 illustrates how Alice's right to use a stock quote service subject to a fee could be expressed in XrML. In this example, the prefix sx: identifies elements from the standard extension. The prefix service: identifies elements from the sample service extension. The prefix stocks: refers to the WSDL definition namespace. The prefix dsig: refers to the namespace that defines XML signatures. All other elements are defined in the XrML core.

Listing 9.12   XrML Specifying Alice's Rights to Use a Fee-Based Stock Quote Service

```
<license>
  <grant>

<!- -
Alice is represented as the holder of a particular key
 - ->
    <keyHolder licensePartId="Alice">
      <info>
        <dsig:KeyValue>
          <dsig:RSAKeyValue>
            <dsig:Modulus>4hre4NP7R...</dsig:Modulus>
            <dsig:Exponent>AQABAA==</dsig:Exponent>
          </dsig:RSAKeyValue>
        </dsig:KeyValue>
      </info>
    </keyHolder>

<!- -
Alice is granted the right to use the stock quote service
 - ->
    <service:use/>

<!- -
The stock quote service is represented with a service reference that contains
  a WSDL file
 - ->
    <serviceReference>
      <wsdl>
        <xml>
          <wsdl:definitions name="StockQuote" targetNamespace="http://
            www.xrml.org/examples/2001/11/wsdl-stocks/stockquote.wsdl">
            <wsdl:types>
              <xsd:schema targetNamespace="http://www.xrml.org/examples/2001/
                11/wsdl-stocks/stockquote.xsd">
              <xsd:element name="TradePriceRequest">
                <xsd:complexType>
                  <xsd:all>
```

Listing 9.12 **Continued**

```
                    <xsd:element name="tickerSymbol" type="xsd:string"/>
                  </xsd:all>
                </xsd:complexType>
              </xsd:element>
              <xsd:element name="TradePrice">
                <xsd:complexType>
                  <xsd:all>
                    <xsd:element name="price" type="xsd:float"/>
                  </xsd:all>
                </xsd:complexType>
              </xsd:element>
            </xsd:schema>
          </wsdl:types>
          <wsdl:message name="GetLastTradePriceInput">
            <wsdl:part name="body" element="stocks-xsd:TradePriceRequest"/>
          </wsdl:message>
          <wsdl:message name="GetLastTradePriceOutput">
            <wsdl:part name="body" element="stocks-xsd:TradePrice"/>
          </wsdl:message>
          <wsdl:portType name="StockQuotePortType">
            <wsdl:operation name="GetLastTradePrice">
              <wsdl:input message="stocks:GetLastTradePriceInput"/>
              <wsdl:output message="stocks:GetLastTradePriceOutput"/>
            </wsdl:operation>
          </wsdl:portType>
          <wsdl:binding name="StockQuoteSoapBinding" type="stocks:
            StockQuotePortType">
            <soap:binding style="document" transport="http://
              schemas.xmlsoap.org/soap/http"/>
            <wsdl:operation name="GetLastTradePrice">
              <soap:operation soapAction="http://example.com/
                GetLastTradePrice"/>
              <wsdl:input>
                <soap:body use="literal"/>
              </wsdl:input>
              <wsdl:output>
                <soap:body use="literal"/>
              </wsdl:output>
            </wsdl:operation>
          </wsdl:binding>
          <wsdl:service name="StockQuoteService">
            <wsdl:documentation>My first service</wsdl:documentation>
            <wsdl:port name="StockQuotePort" binding=
              "stocks:StockQuoteSoapBinding">
              <soap:address location="http://example.com/stockquote"/>
```

Listing 9.12   **Continued**

```
              </wsdl:port>
            </wsdl:service>
          </wsdl:definitions>
        </xml>
      </wsdl>
      <service>stocks:StockQuoteService</service>
      <portType>stocks:StockQuotePortType</portType>
    </serviceReference>

<!- -
  Alice pays $2.00 each time she exercises her right to use the stock
    quote service
  - ->
      <sx:fee>
        <sx:paymentPerUse>
          <sx:rate>
            <sx:amount>2.00</sx:amount>
            <sx:currency>US</sx:currency>
          </sx:rate>
        </sx:paymentPerUse>
        <sx:to>
          <sx:aba>
            <sx:institution>13937151</sx:institution>
            <sx:account>4281938823</sx:account>
          </sx:aba>
        </sx:to>
      </sx:fee>
    </grant>
  </license>
```

The following are some XrML resources:

http://www.oasis-open.org/committees/tc_home.php?wg_abbrev=rights

http://www.xrml.org/

http://xml.coverpages.org/xrml.html

http://www.giantstepsmts.com/DRM%20Watch/xrml20.htm

SAML, XACML, XrML: Overlapping Standards?

XACML and XrML both deal with authorization. They share requirements from many of the same application domains. Both share the same concepts but use different terms. Both are based on XML Schema.

Both SAML and XrML have the concept of attribute assertion. In SAML it's just an Attribute, whereas in XrML it's based on the PossessProperty construct.

Both XACML and XrML deal with an authorization policy. In XACML it's just Policy, whereas in XrML its part of the License construct.

XrML operates in terms of licenses and rights. XACML operates in terms of policies. But attributes can seem like rights.

XACML is consistent with and builds on SAML. XrML may be focused more tightly on the specific issues of Digital Rights Management. In the meantime, however, the overlap is confusing; OASIS knows this and claims to be trying to make sense of it.

Because it is trivial to write an XSLT transform for an SAML:Request into XACML:Context, it follows that the two are closely related.

It is also interesting to note that SAML's PDP is implemented with XACML. Figure 9.13 shows how SAML depends on XACML.

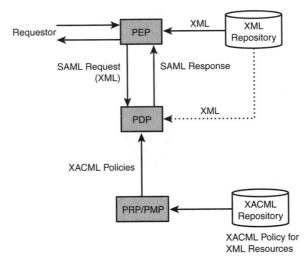

Figure 9.13   How SAML PDPs communicate policy using XACML.

What does all of this overlap portend? It's hard to say, but OASIS is trying to simplify matters. There are always the politics of standards with territories that need to be protected, so expect this situation to take quite some time to settle.

Summary

This chapter augmented the chapters on WS-Security and WS-Policy by covering the rest of the WS-Security family. We presented a conceptual model of a triangle of security; this model is addressed by a set of standards that builds on what we have developed to this point in the book. The apexes of the triangle are trust, interoperability, and integration.

The WS-* security specifications for trust relationships include WS-Trust and WS-Privacy. WS-Trust has a request/response protocol utilizing `<RequestSecurityToken>` and `<RequestSecurityTokenResponse>`, which are designed to allow a Web service requestor to obtain a security token to be used in WS-Security to project trust as it requests service from a Web service provider. WS-Privacy establishes a set of policies that will be enforced on Web service endpoints when dealing with personally identifiable information about human participants.

The WS-* security specifications for interoperability include WS-Policy and WS-SecureConversation. WS-Policy is itself a family of related specifications, which, in addition to WS-Policy, include WS-PolicyAssertions and WS-PolicyAttachments. WS-Policy is a framework to describe and communicate the policies of a Web service. WS-PolicyAssertions describe policy assertions that can be specified within a policy. WS-PolicyAttachment specifies three specific attachment mechanisms for using policy expression within Web services.

The WS-* security specifications for integration include WS-Federation and WS-Authorization. WS-Federation deals with the issues when one entity with one trust model wants to use a Web service to communicate with a different entity with a different trust model. One might be using Kerberos, while the other uses X.509. Understanding federation will be important both because business-to-business Web services will provide a significant source of overall business productivity improvements and because major initiatives such as Passport and Liberty Alliance are based on the concept of federated identity.

Beyond the WS-* family of specification is a small set of vitally important Web services security specifications you need to learn and track. The XML Key Management Specification (XKMS) is one of them. It will be the way PKI is leveraged and becomes truly ubiquitous because it allows PKI to operate as a trusted Web service. XKMS specifies an X-KISS protocol for Locate and Validate operations on keys. It uses the X-KRSS protocol for registration, revocation, and recovery of keys.

The specification for XML Access Control is XACML. XACML is complicated and will probably become buried in development tools but is important because it allows fine-grained control over access to all sorts of resources from Web services.

The XML Rights Management Specification is XrML, which provides a rich digital rights management specification in XML for XML.

10

Building a Secure Web Service Using BEA's WebLogic Workshop

THE WEBLOGIC WORKSHOP INTEGRATED DEVELOPMENT Environment (IDE) bundled with BEA WebLogic Server provides an easy-to-use and powerful tool for developing Web services. In Workshop, a Web service is written as a Java Web service (JWS) file, which is simply a Java file with metadata specified in the form of Javadoc annotations.

WebLogic Workshop security works in concert with the WebLogic Security Framework built into WebLogic Server. The WebLogic Security Framework is a powerful, extensible security framework that can be used standalone or integrated with the security environment at your organization. The WebLogic Security Framework is responsible for accepting credentials, mapping those credentials to a user, and then associating that user to a set of roles. In WebLogic Workshop, the focus you have when developing your JWS programs tends to be on roles, whereas administrators typically focus on the WebLogic Server aspects (credential to user to roles) of security policy.

WebLogic Workshop supports three categories of security: HTTP Transport Security, message security, and role-based security. From the JWS program's perspective, transport- and message-based security are perimeter based. They guard the door to the Web services application. The result of using transport- or message-based security is transparent from the Web service program's perspective; the result is that a user is associated with the running thread, and you can determine the roles the current user has. This leads to role-based security, which allows you to declare roles that a user must be associated with to run Web services operations.

> **Note**
>
> You can download WebLogic Workshop Developer Edition from `http://commerce.bea.com/`
> `index.jsp`. This example uses version 8.1 (Service Pack 2 or later).
>
> Documentation for version 8.1 is available at `http://edocs.bea.com/workshop/docs81/doc/`
> `en/core/index.html`.

Security Layer Walkthrough

Figure 10.1 shows a simplified flow through the WebLogic Server runtime and into the WebLogic Workshop runtime. This diagram shows the three security areas, with WebLogic Server having responsibility for transport security and WebLogic Workshop having responsibility for message-based security and role-based security.

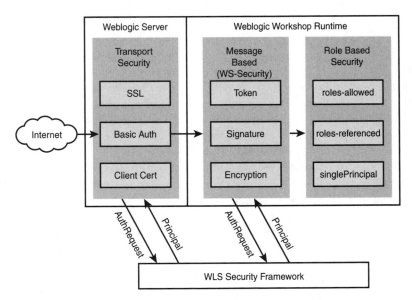

Figure 10.1   Web Services Security layers.

When a message comes into WebLogic Server destined for a Workshop Web service and transport security has been configured, WebLogic Server, taking advantage of the WebLogic Security Framework, does the following:

1. Negotiates the SSL connection.
2. Gathers and validates credentials (username/password, X.509 certificate, and so on).
3. Maps the credentials to a user.
4. Maps the user to roles.

If transport security is not specified, or even if it is, the next layer is message-based security, which is handled by the WebLogic Workshop runtime. You can receive three types of security artifacts in a message security scenario: tokens, XML Encryption, and XML Signature. WebLogic Workshop works with the WebLogic Security Framework to

1. Extract the token (similar to credentials), validate it, and perform the credential-to-user-to-role mapping.

2. Decrypt or encrypt the XML Encryption.

3. Sign and verify XML Signatures.

For both transport- and message-based security, the result in your JWS is that a user (an *authenticated Subject*, to use Java Authentication and Authorization Service, that is JAAS, terms) is bound to your thread, and you are subsequently able to use role-based security. Although Figure 10.1 shows both transport- and message-based security, it is likely that in WebLogic Workshop you will choose one or the other to secure your Web services.

Once you are in your JWS, you can use several annotations to enforce role-based security. Role-based security allows you to specify what *roles* can access functionality within your Web services. Using roles instead of specific users allows administrators to add and remove users from the roles versus having to change code to accomplish this task. The most common way to use roles is to specify the roles that are allowed using the @common:roles-allowed annotation either at the top of the JWS or over a specific operation within a JWS.

The following sections briefly describe how Workshop supports these three security layers.

Transport-Level Security

Three interrelated options are available when you use transport security. One is to use one-way SSL; this accomplishes two tasks:

- The server is authenticated.
- The session is encrypted.

The second option is to use basic authentication. HTTP basic authentication is username/password-based authentication. One point to remember when designating basic authentication is that the password is put in an HTTP header in the clear. To overcome this, you usually combine one-way SSL with basic authentication.

The final, most powerful, but also most complex option is to use two-way SSL, also known as *client authentication*. When you use this option, both the client and server authenticate to each other using X.509 certificates.

The primary approach to configuring transport security *inbound* is to make configuration changes in web.xml within your Web application's WEB-INF directory. You can consult the WebLogic Workshop documentation for specific setup information. In the case of client authentication, you also must tell WebLogic Server to request the client certificate by selecting this option on the console.

For *outbound* transport security, for example, when you call a Web service that requires transport security, WebLogic Workshop provides an API for setting the username/password or client certificate information.

Message-Level Security

WebLogic Workshop supports all three types of security artifacts that can be contained in a WS-Security security header: tokens, an XML Encryption element, and/or an XML Signature element.

The WebLogic Workshop implementation supports two token types: `UserNameToken`, which represents a username and a password, and `BinarySecurityToken` with a type of `X509` (we call this `X509Token`), which represents an X.509 certificate. You can include a `UserNameToken` by itself; however, in Workshop, `X509Token` must be accompanied by an XML Signature. This makes sense because an X.509 certificate is a public piece of information that, by itself, does not prove anything about the identity of the sender. A corresponding XML Signature is needed to prove that the sender had control of the associated private key associated with `X509Token`.

In WebLogic Workshop, if you designate encryption, the SOAP body is encrypted along with the conversation header if you are participating in a conversation.

XML Signature is used for two purposes:

- To authenticate the identity of the sender, which is accomplished via the `X509Token`.

- To ensure the integrity of the message. If even a single bit of the message has changed, the XML Signature validation will fail.

In WebLogic Workshop, if you designate a signature, the SOAP body is digitally signed along with the conversation header if you are participating in a conversation.

To configure WS-Security in WebLogic Workshop, you create a WS-Security policy file and associate it with your Web service by using the following annotation:

```
@jws:ws-security-policy-service file="yourPolicy.xml"
```

Putting this annotation at the top of your JWS configures the WS-Security policy for messages coming into your Web service. Putting this annotation at the top of a Web service control configures the WS-Security policy for a Web service you are calling.

The WS-Security annotation points to an XML file containing the WS-Security policy you want to apply. Corresponding to the request and response message in a typical synchronous Web service call are two sections in a WS-Security policy: `wsSecurityIn` and `wsSecurityOut`.

In `wsSecurityIn`, you declare what security you expect in your Web service. This policy answers the following questions:

- Does this Web service require a token, and if so, which type?

- Does it require encryption?

- If the Web service requires encryption, where is the private key to decrypt with?

- Is a signature required?

On the other hand, `wsSecurityOut` answers these questions:

- Does a token need to be added to this message on the way out, and if so, which type?
- Does this message need to be encrypted?
- If so, what public key should be used to encrypt the message?
- Does the message need to be signed, and if so, what private key should be used to create the XML Signature?

Role-Based Security

The result of transport- or message-based security is an authenticated subject that has a corresponding set of roles associated. These roles are your primary mechanism for security within your JWS. The annotation `@common:security` is used for role-based security, and the possible attributes are `roles-allowed`, `roles-referenced`, and `run-as`. You can also use the API `context.isCallerInRole("role")`, where `context` is an instance of the `weblogic.jws.JwsContext` class within your code to test for a specific role.

The most commonly used annotation is `roles-allowed`. As you might expect, if you use `roles-allowed`, only users belonging to the specified roles can execute the requested operation. The `roles-allowed` annotation can be used at the class level (above the class declaration) or above an operation. When an operation is invoked, `roles-allowed` at the class level and `roles-allowed` at the operation level are unioned. Thus, adding `roles-allowed` at the operation level *expands* the number of roles able to access a particular application.

The `@common:security roles-referenced` attribute enables you to surface the roles that you have accessed in your JWS code using `context.isCallerInRole("role")`. The objective is to allow the roles that you have used in your code to be mapped to the roles that are appropriate for the target environment. Thus, you can choose roles that make sense in the scope of your application but are named differently in the deployment environment.

The `@common:security run-as` attribute enables you to change your identity within your JWS so that when you call out, you assume this new identity. For example, if you have a database or Enterprise JavaBean (EJB) that requires you to have the role of system, you can use `run-as` to change the outbound identity of your JWS.

Now let's walk through an example of using these security types in WebLogic Workshop.

WebLogic Workshop Web Service Walkthrough

For this example, you will create two Web services, `POClient.jws` and `POService.jws`, where `PO` is the acronym for a purchase order. As the name suggests, `POClient.jws` will pass data to `POService.jws`, which will create the purchase order and return a purchase order number. You will first secure the `POService.jws` Web service by applying transport security using one-way SSL and HTTP basic authentication and then check how to use two-way SSL. Next, you will apply message-level security by using WebLogic Workshop's implementation of WS-Security, tweak its features, and analyze the output. Finally, you will authorize access to `POService.jws` by using role-based security. Figure 10.2 depicts the security architecture used in this example.

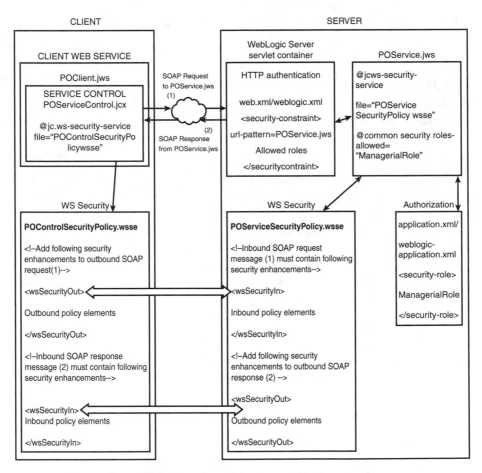

Figure 10.2   Security architecture used in the example.

Here are the steps in detail:

1. Create a new application in Workshop by choosing File, New, Application from the main menu. A Workshop application is just an exploded Java 2 Enterprise Edition (J2EE) application—that is, an Enterprise Archive (EAR) file.

2. Choose the Default Application option. Click the Browse button to browse to the directory in which you want to create the application—for example, `c:\apps`. You can also type the path yourself in the Directory text box. Then type a name for the application in the Name text box—for example, `SecureApp` (see Figure 10.3).

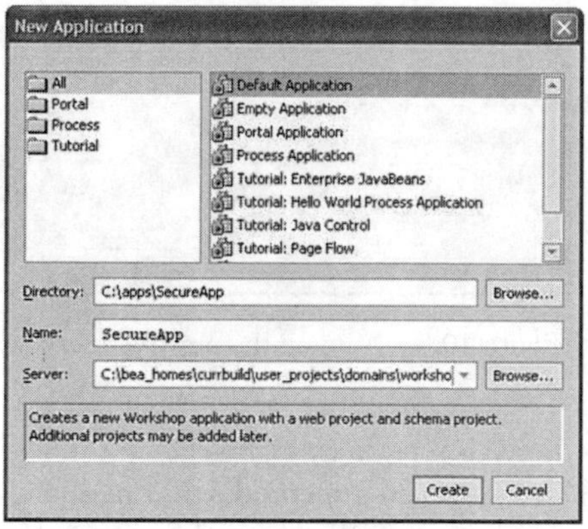

Figure 10.3 Naming the new application.

A Web project named SecureAppWeb is created by default in the application. A Web project in WebLogic Workshop is a J2EE Web application.

3. Create a new folder in the SecureAppWeb project by right-clicking the project and choosing New, Folder. Name the folder `securePackage` (see Figure 10.4).

Figure 10.4 Naming the folder.

4. Create a new Web service in the `securePackage` folder by right-clicking the folder and choosing New, Web Service. Name the Web service `POService.jws` (see Figure 10.5).

5. A Web service in Workshop has two views: Design View and Source View. Design View provides a graphical representation of the Web service, and Source View enables you to view the source. You can move between these two views by choosing the appropriate tab at the bottom of the central window in the Workshop IDE or by using the options in the View menu.

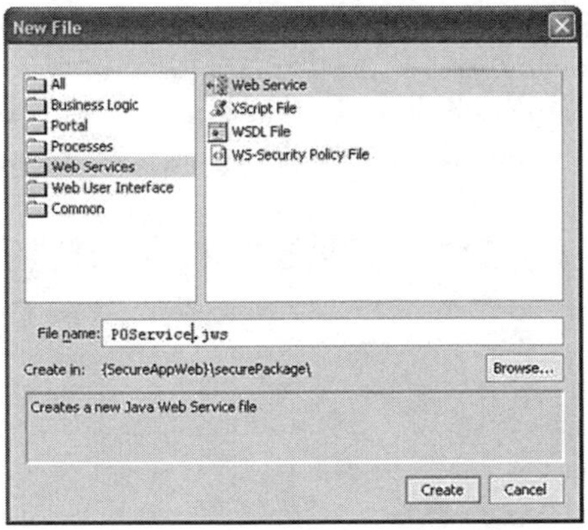

Figure 10.5   Naming the new Web service.

Add a method to the Web service by right-clicking the service in the Design View, as shown in Figure 10.6. To add a method, you can also choose Insert, Method or drag the Method icon from the Palette window in the lower-left corner of the IDE to the Web service's Design View. Rename the method **submitPO** (see Figure 10.7).

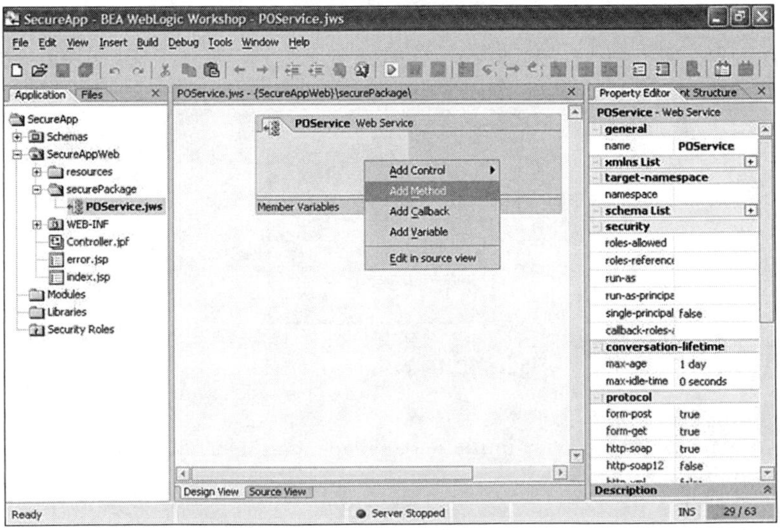

Figure 10.6   Adding a method to POService.jws.

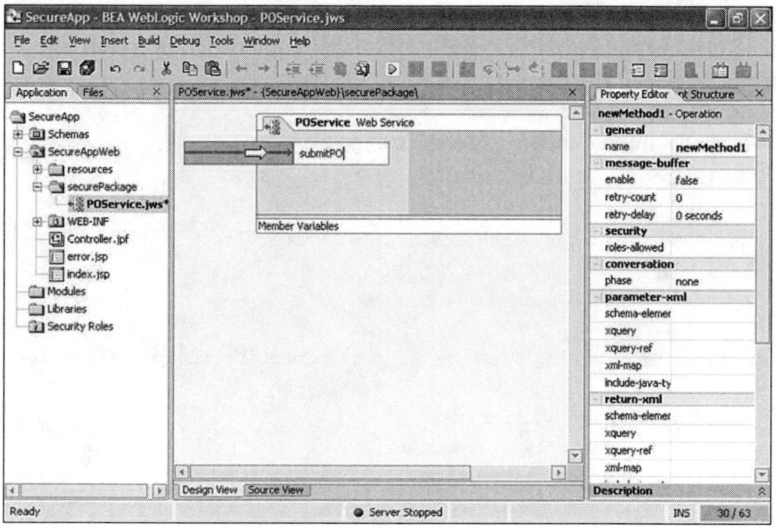

Figure 10.7   Renaming the method.

6. Switch to the Source View. There, you see the source shown in Listing 10.1.

Listing 10.1   POService.jws **Created by Default**

```
package securePackage;

public class POService implements com.bea.jws.WebService
{
    /**
     * @common:operation
     */
    public int submitPO()
    {
    }
}
```

> **Note**
>
> The Workshop runtime uses the Javadoc annotation at the top of the submitPO method to generate the underlying support for Web services, such as SOAP-to-Java marshalling. As you can see, these annotations are automatically generated when you add a method in the service's Design View. The same holds true for any property you change in the service's Design View.

7. Create a static inner class called POBean in POService.jws and provide an implementation for the submitPO method. You can copy the source code shown in Listing 10.2 into the file.

Listing 10.2 **Fully Implemented** POService.jws

```
package securePackage;

public class POService implements com.bea.jws.WebService
{
    public static class POBean
    {
        public POBean(String itemName, int itemQuantity, double itemPrice)
        {
            this.itemName = itemName;
            this.itemQuantity = itemQuantity;
            this.itemPrice = itemPrice;
        }

        public POBean(){};

        public String itemName;
        public int itemQuantity;
        public double itemPrice;
    }

    /**
     * This is an exposed method that users will be able to invoke.
     * @common:operation
     */
    public int submitPO(POBean poBean)
    {
        // Code for entering the purchase order in the database
        return 1;
    }
}
```

Transport Security

Now you're ready to implement transport-level security and basic HTTP authentication for the Web service:

1. Locate the deployment descriptors named web.xml and weblogic.xml, which are present in the WEB-INF directory within the SecureAppWeb project (see Figure 10.8). In a J2EE-compliant Web application, such as the SecureAppWeb project, the web.xml and weblogic.xml deployment descriptors are used to specify

deployment-specific properties, which are read and interpreted by the underlying WebLogic Server at deployment time. These descriptors include security-related properties such as use of SSL and HTTP authentication, which you will use in this example.

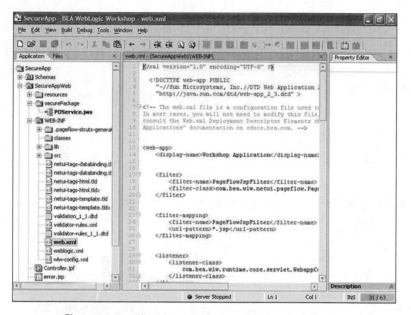

Figure 10.8   The web.xml deployment descriptor in the SecureAppWeb/WEB-INF directory.

2. Double-click the web.xml file so that it shows up in the central window. Add security constraints to it by pasting the code shown in Listing 10.3 just above the last </web-app> element.

Listing 10.3   **Security-Related Elements in the** SecureAppWeb/WEB-INF/web.xml **Deployment Descriptor**

```
<security-constraint>
    <display-name>Security Constraints</display-name>
    <web-resource-collection>
        <web-resource-name>
            Secure Resources
        </web-resource-name>
        <url-pattern>
            /securePackage/POService.jws
        </url-pattern>
        <http-method>GET</http-method>
        <http-method>POST</http-method>
```

Listing 10.3   **Continued**

```
    </web-resource-collection>
    <auth-constraint>
        <role-name>GoodRole</role-name>
    </auth-constraint>
    <user-data-constraint>
        <transport-guarantee>
            CONFIDENTIAL
        </transport-guarantee>
    </user-data-constraint>
</security-constraint>

<security-role>
    <description>Role description</description>
    <role-name>GoodRole</role-name>
</security-role>
```

You add the following four important properties here:

- The `<url-pattern>` element identifies the service(s) to be secured based on the URL pattern.
- The `<auth-constraint>` element specifies the security role to which the access is restricted. You need to add users to this role to provide them access to the secured services.
- The `<transport-guarantee>` element restricts access to the HTTPS protocol by specifying a value of `CONFIDENTIAL` or `INTEGRAL`.
- The `<security-role>` element defines the security role.

3. Map the role named `GoodRole` to a user in `weblogic.xml` by adding the following elements just after the start of the `<weblogic-web-app>` element. At this time, the user may or may not be an existing user in the realm used by the underlying WebLogic Server instance:

```
<security-role-assignment>
    <role-name>GoodRole</role-name>
<principal-name>GoodUser</principal-name>
</security-role-assignment>
```

4. If the user named `GoodUser` does not exist in the current realm of the server on which this application will be deployed, you must create one.

To add a user, start the server that the Workshop IDE is pointing to. By default, the IDE points to the *BEA-HOME*/weblogic81/samples/domains/workshop domain, where *BEA-HOME* is the directory you chose as BEA Home Directory while installing WebLogic Platform. Choose Tools, WebLogic Server, Start WebLogic Server to start the server.

A pop-up window, as shown in Figure 10.9, indicates the progress in the server startup process. After the server starts, open the WebLogic Server console by clicking Tools, WebLogic Server, WebLogic Console. The default username and password are both `weblogic`.

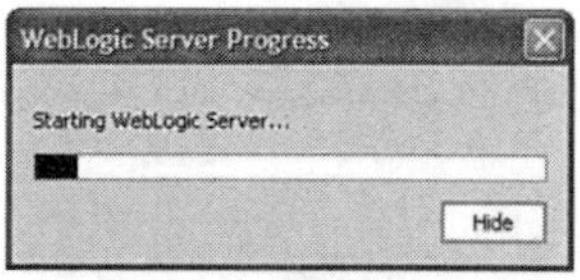

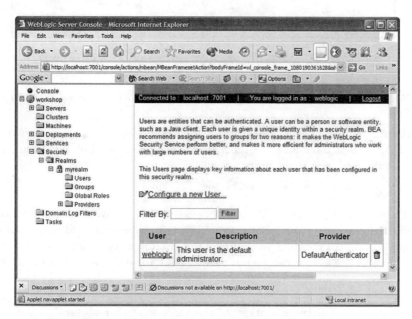

Figure 10.9 WebLogic Server startup progress window.

Add a user to the out-of-the-box default realm `myrealm` by clicking the Configure a New User link in the Security, Realms, myrealm, Users screen on the WebLogic Server console, as shown in Figure 10.10.

Figure 10.10 Adding a user using the WebLogic Server console.

Name the user `GoodUser` and enter any password—for example, `weblogic`. The default minimum length required of a password is eight characters (see Figure 10.11).

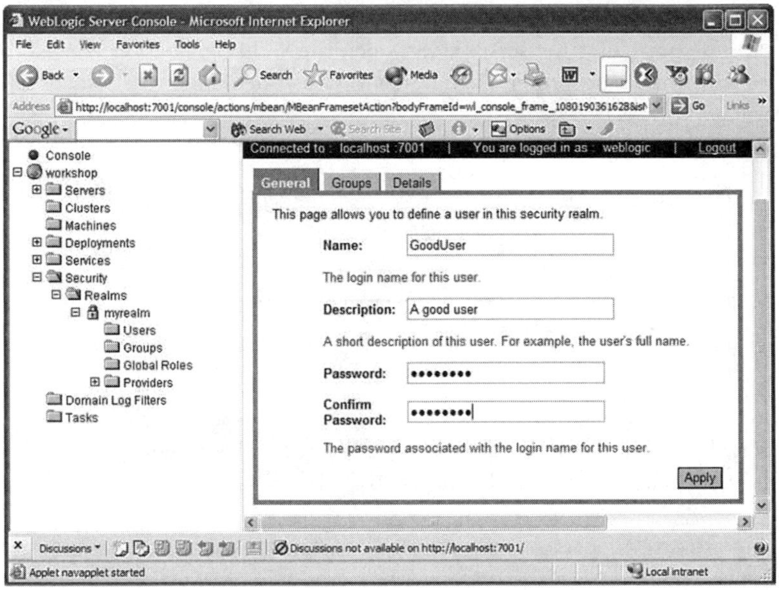

Figure 10.11   Adding the username and password for the new user.

5. Right-click the `POService.jws` Web service and generate a service control (JCX) file.

A control file is a client-side proxy for a Workshop Web service. The default name of the generated file is `POServiceControl.jcx`. The control file, by default, contains the following annotation:

```
@jc:location http-url="POService.jws"
```

The value is the endpoint URL of `POService.jws`, relative to the service control file. Because the service is in the same directory as the control file, the relative URL is just the filename. To configure this control proxy to send an HTTPS request to the service, change this relative URL to an absolute HTTPS URL as follows:

```
/**
@jc:location http-url="https://localhost:7002/SecureAppWeb/
securePackage/POService.jws"
*/
```

When you try to modify the file the first time, Workshop pops up the warning shown in Figure 10.12.

Click OK to proceed. Accepting this message just means that the next time you modify and save your JWS file, the JCX file will not be automatically updated. You can regenerate the control file by right-clicking the JWS at any time. The control file then looks like Listing 10.4, followed by the WSDL at the bottom.

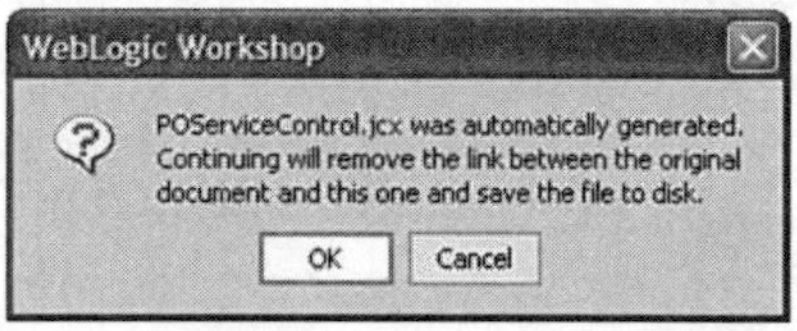

Figure 10.12   Warning on modifying auto-generated service control file.

Listing 10.4   `POServiceControl.jcx`

```
package securePackage;

/**
  @jc:location http-url="https://localhost:7002/SecureAppWeb/securePackage
  /POService.jws" jms-url="POService.jws"
 * @jc:wsdl file="#POServiceWsdl"
 */
public interface POServiceControl extends com.bea.control.ControlExtension,
com.bea.control.ServiceControl
{
    public static class POBean
        implements java.io.Serializable
    {
        public java.lang.String itemName;
        public int itemQuantity;
        public double itemPrice;
    }


    /**
     * This is an exposed method that users will be able to invoke.
     * @jc:protocol form-post="false" form-get="false"
     */
    public int submitPO (POBean poBean);

    static final long serialVersionUID = 1L;
}
```

6. Look at the service endpoint URL in the WSDL, at the bottom of the `POServiceControl.jcx` file, which is the value of the location attribute in the `<soap:address>` element. Notice that it specifies the HTTP protocol by default:

```
<service name="POService">
    <port name="POServiceSoap" binding="s0:POServiceSoap">
    <soap:address
     location="http://localhost:7001/securePackage/POService.jws"/>
    </port>
</service>
```

To ensure that the endpoint URL for the POService specifies the HTTPS protocol in its WSDL file, copy the following text in the `wlw-config.xml` file in the `WEB-INF` directory:

```
<wlw-config xmlns="http://www.bea.com/wlw/runtime/core/config">
    <protocol>http</protocol>
        <hostname>localhost</hostname>
        <http-port>7001</http-port>
        <https-port>7002</https-port>
        <jws>
            <class-name>securePackage.POService</class-name>
            <protocol>https</protocol>
        </jws>
</wlw-config>
```

Note that this step is not mandatory to run the example, because you have changed the service endpoint URL in the previous step by modifying the value of the **jc:location http-url** annotation in the `POServiceControl.jcx` file.

7. Create another Web service named `POClient.jws` to call the first service. Right-click the `securePackage` folder and choose New, Web Service to create the service. Then rename it **POClient.jws**. Drag and drop `POServiceControl.jcx` into the Design View of the `POClient.jws` file (see Figure 10.13).

   In the Data Palette window, which is at the bottom right of the IDE screen by default, you can see the methods and callbacks exposed by the control. Drag and drop the `submitPO()` method to the Design View window at the center of the screen.

8. Switch to the Source View and check that Workshop has automatically generated the source shown in Listing 10.5.

Listing 10.5 `POClient.jws` **Created by Default**

```
package securePackage;

public class POClient implements com.bea.jws.WebService
{
    /**
     * @common:control
     */
    private securePackage.POServiceControl pOServiceControl;
```

Listing 10.5 **Continued**

```
static final long serialVersionUID = 1L;

/**
 * @common:operation
 */
public int submitPO(securePackage.POServiceControl.POBean poBean)
{
    return pOServiceControl.submitPO(poBean);
}
}
```

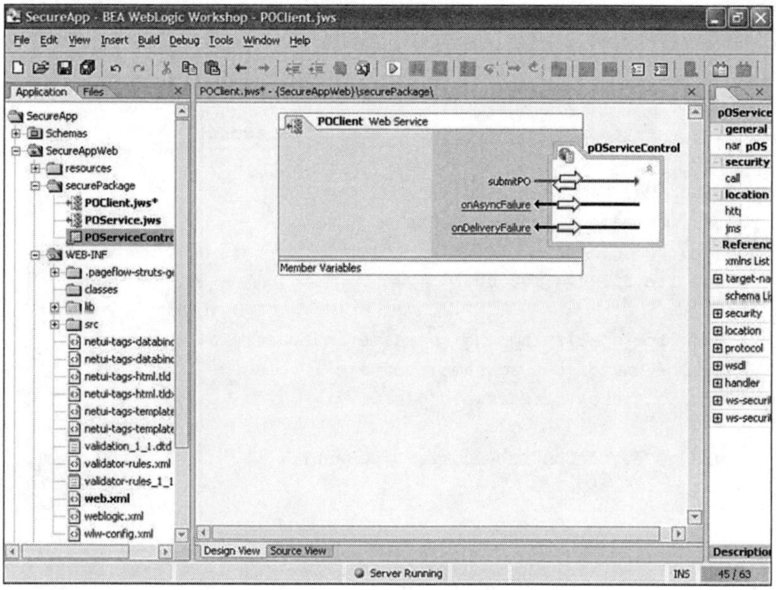

Figure 10.13   `POClient.jws`.

9. Make the following changes in the Control file:

   - Create an instance of `POBean` to pass to the control's `submitPO` method.
   - Change the signature of the `submitPO` method to accept the username and password.
   - Set the username and password on the control. This username and password are encoded and passed as HTTP headers to the service. The HTTP basic authentication method is used here.

   The code for the service is shown in Listing 10.6.

Listing 10.6 **Fully Implemented** POClient.jws

```
package securePackage;

import securePackage.POServiceControl.POBean;

public class POClient implements com.bea.jws.WebService
{
    /**
     * @common:control
     */
    private securePackage.POServiceControl pOServiceControl;

    static final long serialVersionUID = 1L;

    /**
     * @common:operation
     */
    public int submitPO(String username, String password)
    {
        POBean poBean = new POBean();
        poBean.itemName = "Metal sheets";
        poBean.itemQuantity = 1;
        poBean.itemPrice = 100.00;

        // Code for specifying the username and password
        pOServiceControl.setUsername(username);
        pOServiceControl.setPassword(password);

        return pOServiceControl.submitPO(poBean);
    }
}
```

10. Build and run the Web service by clicking the Start button on the IDE, which is a small blue triangle in the icon tray at the top, or by choosing Debug, Start from the menu. Workshop's built-in browser pops up. On the Test Form tab, you can enter the username and password in text boxes.

11. Enter an incorrect username and password and click the submitPO button to invoke the method (see Figure 10.14). The authentication fails and a SOAP fault is returned, which you can see in the logs (see Figure 10.15).

    The Message Log tab has two sub-tabs. Click the submitPO tab and scroll to the bottom to see a message containing the following string:

    ```
    "String:Response: '401: Unauthorized xxx' for url:
    'https://GoodUser:weblogic1@localhost:7002/
    SecureAppWeb/securePackage/POService.jws'"
    ```

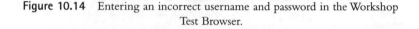

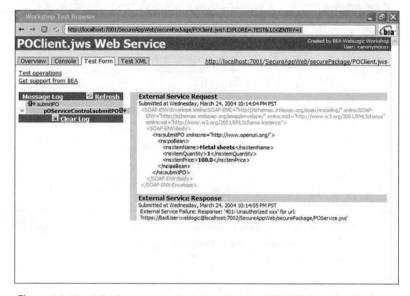

Figure 10.14   Entering an incorrect username and password in the Workshop Test Browser.

Figure 10.15   SOAP request and response logs in the Workshop Test Browser on passing an incorrect username and password.

12. Enter **GoodUser** as the username and its corresponding password. Now the service can be accessed successfully, and the log containing the SOAP request and response appears as shown in Figure 10.16.

This example showed the use of one-way SSL with basic authentication. Similar to the API for setting the username and password on a Control file, Workshop also provides an API for setting a certificate for using two-way SSL, in which the client authenticates itself using a certificate. The following sample shows how to set the client-side certificate on the control:

```
pOServiceControl.useClientKeySSL( true );
pOServiceControl.setClientKeyAlias( "mykey" );
pOServiceControl.setClientKeyPassword( "password" );
pOServiceControl.setClientKeyStoreLocation
                ("c:/bea/weblogi81/server/lib/mycacerts");
pOServiceControl.setClientKeyStorePassword( "password" );
```

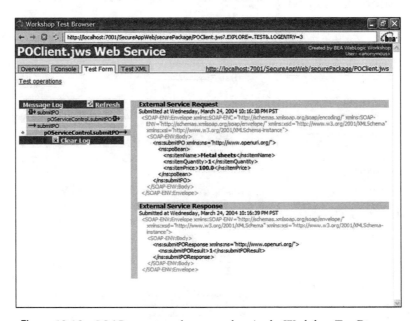

Figure 10.16 SOAP request and response logs in the Workshop Test Browser
on passing the correct username and password.

Message-Based Security

As mentioned previously, WebLogic Workshop supports all three security artifacts provided by WS-Security: tokens, XML Encryption, and XML Signature.

Both the client side (that is, the service control) and the server side (that is, the Web
service) should reference a WS-Security policy file (*.wsse) to use WS-Security. For this
next example, you will add two WS-Security policy files to the securePackage folder:
one for POService.jws and the other for POServiceControl.jcx. Let's walk through
the steps required:

1. Create a WS-Security policy file in the securePackage folder by right-clicking
   the folder and choosing the Other File Types option. Then choose the Web
   Services, WS-Security Policy file option. Name the file
   POServiceSecurityPolicy.wsse (see Figure 10.17).

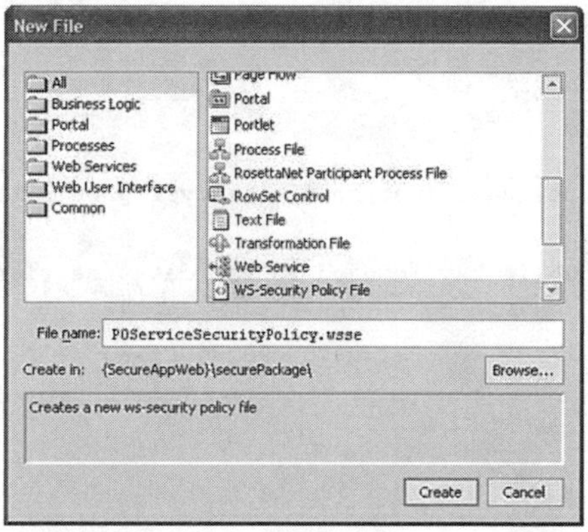

Figure 10.17   Naming the WS-Security policy file.

The following code is generated by default in the file:

```
<?xml version="1.0" ?>
<wsSecurityPolicy xsi:schemaLocation="WSSecurity-policy.xsd"
    xmlns="http://www.bea.com/2003/03/wsse/config"
    xmlns:xsi="http://www.w3.org/2001/XMLSchema-instance">
</wsSecurityPolicy>
```

2. Paste the code shown in Listing 10.7 into the file.

Listing 10.7   `POServiceSecurityPolicy.wsse`

```
<wsSecurityPolicy xsi:schemaLocation="WSSecurity-policy.xsd"
xmlns="http://www.bea.com/2003/03/wsse/config"
xmlns:xsi="http://www.w3.org/2001/XMLSchema-instance"
xmlns:xsd="http://www.w3.org/2001/XMLSchema">

    <wsSecurityIn>
        <!--
        Incoming SOAP message must be accompanied by a valid username
        and password.
        -->
        <token tokenType="username"/>
        <!--
        Incoming SOAP messages must be encrypted with POService.jws's
        public key. The alias and password to access the POService.jws's
        decrypting private key in the keystore are provided by
        the <decryptionKey> element below.
        -->
        <encryptionRequired>
            <decryptionKey>
                <alias>mycompany</alias>
                <password>password</password>
```

Listing 10.7   **Continued**

```
            </decryptionKey>
        </encryptionRequired>
        <!--
        Incoming SOAP messages must be digitally signed with the sender's
        private key.
        The sender's public key is used to validate the signature.
        -->
        <signatureRequired>true</signatureRequired>
    </wsSecurityIn>

    <wsSecurityOut>
        <!--
        Accompany the SOAP message with a valid username and password
        -->
        <userNameToken>
                <userName>GoodUser</userName>
                <password type="TEXT">weblogic</password>
        </userNameToken>
        <!--
        Encrypt the SOAP message with the recipient's (POClient.jws) public key.
        Only the recipient's private key can decrypt it.
        Ensures the confidentiality of the SOAP message.
        (This process requires that the sender's keystore already contains
        a digital certificate containing the recipient's public key.)
        -->
        <encryption>
            <encryptionKey>
                <alias>client1</alias>
            </encryptionKey>
        </encryption>
         <!--
        Sign the SOAP message with the sender's (POService.jws) private key.
        Only the sender's public key can validate the signature.
        Ensures the authenticity of the sender, i.e., that the sender is
        in fact the source of the SOAP message.
        -->
        <signatureKey>
            <alias>mycompany</alias>
            <password>password</password>
        </signatureKey>
    </wsSecurityOut>

    <!--
    Look for the samples_mycompany.jks keystore in the default location,
    the server domain root, in this case,
    BEA_HOME\weblogic81\samples\domains\workshop.
    -->
```

Listing 10.7   **Continued**

```
<keyStore>
    <keyStoreLocation>samples_mycompany.jks</keyStoreLocation>
    <keyStorePassword>password</keyStorePassword>
</keyStore>
</wsSecurityPolicy>
```

In addition to the bold comments in the policy file, here is a brief explanation of the various elements:

- `<wsSecurityIn>` specifies what security enhancements you expect in the incoming SOAP. For the service `POService.jws`, it indicates the security credentials/encryption/signature expected in the SOAP request from the client control.

- `<token>` means that the incoming message should have a token. The two possible token types are `UsernameToken` and `X509Token`. Use `UsernameToken` in this example.

- `<decryptionKey>` contains the alias and password of the private key that will be used to decrypt the incoming message.

- `<signatureRequired>` states whether the incoming message should be signed.

- `<wsSecurityOut>` specifies how you want to secure the messages being sent out on the wire from your Web service.

- `<usernameToken>` contains the username and password that should be sent with the outgoing message.

- `<encryption>` specifies the alias of the public key used to encrypt the message.

- `<signatureKey>` is the private key used to sign the outgoing message.

- `<keystore>` points to a keystore, which stores all the public/private keys and certificates referred to in that policy file. The location and password of the keystore are specified as subelements of the `<keystore>` element.

The use of tokens, Encryption, and Signature are independent of each other. You can use one, some, or all of them simultaneously.

3. Reference the `POServiceSecurityPolicy.wsse` file from the `POService.jws` file by adding the filename to the `ws-security-service` property in the Property Editor (see Figure 10.18).

Click the ellipses ... button on the right end of the `ws-security-file` property text box to open the window shown in Figure 10.19. Type the name of the WSSE file and click OK.

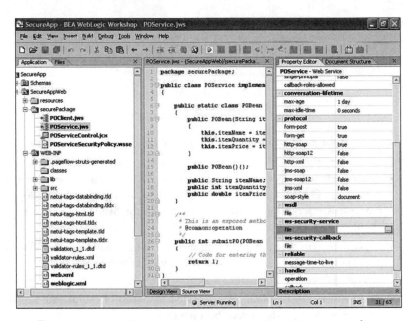

Figure 10.18   Referencing `POServiceSecurityPolicy.wsse` from `POService.jws`.

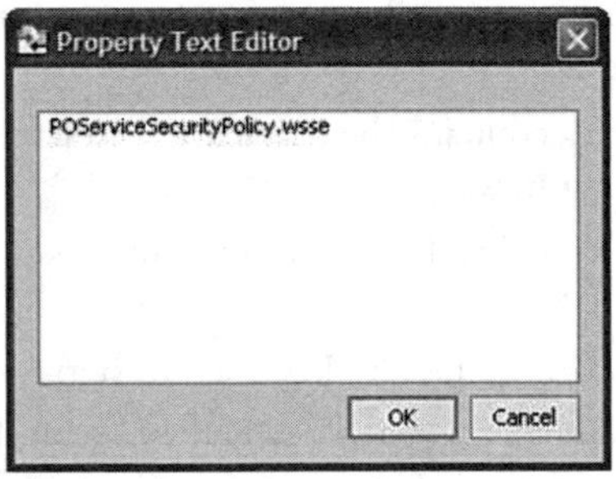

Figure 10.19   Naming the referenced WS–Security policy file.

This step adds the following annotation to the top of the JWS file:

```
/**
 * @jws:ws-security-service file="POSecuritySecurityPolicy.wsse"
 */
```

A green squiggly line appears below the WSSE filename. Pointing the mouse to this filename shows the following warning message:

```
WARNING: Passwords in the ws-security-policy file are in clear text format
(i.e. unencrypted).
```

SUGGESTION: See Topic "Securing WS-Security passwords" in help for
strategies for securing passwords in policy files

You can refer to the documentation as mentioned for help in encrypting the passwords in the WSSE file.

4. You have already created a server-side WS-Security policy file that defines the
security enhancements expected by `POService.jws` in the incoming SOAP
request and the security enhancements added to the outgoing SOAP response.
Now you need to make sure that the client sends a SOAP request with corresponding security additions and can decipher the secure response sent by the server.
Hence, you must create a corresponding WS-Security policy file for
`POServiceControl.jcx` on the client side. Name it
POControlSecurityPolicy.wsse. The `<wsSecurityOut>` element of this file states
the security enhancement for the outgoing SOAP request to `POService.jws` and,
hence, corresponds to the `<wsSecurityIn>` element in the server side's policy file
named `POServiceSecurity.wsse`. Similarly, the `<wsSecurityIn>` element of this
file corresponds to the `<wsSecurityOut>` element of the
`POServiceSecurity.wsse` file. Now paste the code shown in Listing 10.8 into the
file.

Listing 10.8   POControlSecurityPolicy.wsse

```
<wsSecurityPolicy xsi:schemaLocation="WSSecurity-policy.xsd"
xmlns="http://www.bea.com/2003/03/wsse/config"
xmlns:xsi="http://www.w3.org/2001/XMLSchema-instance">
    <wsSecurityOut>
        <!--
        Accompany the SOAP message with a valid username and password
        -->
        <userNameToken>
                <userName>GoodUser</userName>
                <password type="TEXT">weblogic</password>
        </userNameToken>
        <!--
        Encrypt the SOAP message with the recipient's (POService.jws) public key.
        Only the recipient's private key can decrypt it.
        Ensures the confidentiality of the SOAP message.
        (This process requires that the sender's keystore already contains
        a digital certificate containing the recipient's public key.)
        -->
        <encryption>
            <encryptionKey>
                <alias>mycompany</alias>
            </encryptionKey>
        </encryption>
        <!--
```

Listing 10.8 **Continued**

```
            Sign the SOAP message with the sender's (POClient.jws) private key.
            Only the sender's public key can validate the signature.
            Ensures the authenticity of the sender, i.e., that the sender is
            in fact the source of the SOAP message.
            -->
            <signatureKey>
                <alias>client1</alias>
                <password>password</password>
            </signatureKey>
        </wsSecurityOut>

        <wsSecurityIn>
            <!--
            Incoming SOAP message must be accompanied by a valid username
            and password.
            -->
            <token tokenType="username"/>
            <!--
            Incoming SOAP messages must be encrypted with POClient.jws's
            public key. The alias and password to access the POClient.jws's
            decrypting private key in the keystore are provided by
            the <decryptionKey> element below.
            -->
            <encryptionRequired>
                <decryptionKey>
                    <alias>client1</alias>
                    <password>password</password>
                </decryptionKey>
            </encryptionRequired>
            <!--
            Incoming SOAP messages must be digitally signed with the sender's
            private key.
            The sender's public key is used to validate the signature.
            -->
            <signatureRequired>true</signatureRequired>
        </wsSecurityIn>

    <!--
    Look for the samples_client.jks keystore in the default location, the server
    domain root, in this case, BEA_HOME\weblogic81\samples\domains\workshop.
    -->
      <keyStore>
          <keyStoreLocation>samples_client.jks</keyStoreLocation>
          <keyStorePassword>password</keyStorePassword>
      </keyStore>
</wsSecurityPolicy>
```

5. Run the `POClient.jws` Web service, which will in turn call `POService.jws`, by providing a valid username and password. The service will run successfully, and you will see the same SOAP messages in the log that you saw before applying WS-Security. However, this does not mean that these were the messages sent over the wire! This simplified message is shown just to prevent the underlying complex message from showing up in the Message log every time the service is run. For analysis purposes or just for curiosity, if you would like to view the actual message payload, you need to restart the underlying WebLogic Server from the command line and provide the `verbose` parameter as in

```
C:\bea\weblogic81\samples\domains\workshop> startWebLogic verbose
```

assuming that your BEA home directory, where the WebLogic Server is installed, is `C:\bea`. Now when you run the `POClient.jws` service, it will output debug messages to a file called `workshop_debug.log`, which is present in the WebLogic Server domain directory, `C:\bea\weblogic81\samples\domains\workshop`, for the Workshop samples domain.

6. The SOAP request message I found in my `workshop_debug` file is shown in Listing 10.9. I have added comments to help you understand the details. Elements in the message use URI reference IDs to point to other elements within the message.

> **Note**
>
> Notice the three pairs of reference IDs in Listing 10.9. The first pair is shaded. The second pair is boxed. The third pair is indicated with white text on a black background. These typographical conventions are intended to help you quickly spot these ID pairs and have no other purpose.

Listing 10.9   **WS-Security–Enabled SOAP Request Message**

```
<SOAP-ENV:Envelope xmlns:SOAP-ENC="http://schemas.xmlsoap.org/soap/encoding/"
xmlns:xsi="http://www.w3.org/2001/XMLSchema-instance"
xmlns:xsd="http://www.w3.org/2001/XMLSchema" xmlns:SOAP-
ENV="http://schemas.xmlsoap.org/soap/envelope/">
  <SOAP-ENV:Header>
    <wsse:Security xmlns:wsse
     ="http://schemas.xmlsoap.org/ws/2002/07/secext" SOAP-ENV:mustUnderstand="1">
    <!--Presence of EncryptedKey element means that the symmetric key used for
    encryption of this message has been encrypted using the public key
    of the recipient -->
    <xenc:EncryptedKey xmlns:xenc="http://www.w3.org/2001/04/xmlenc#">
    <!--The algorithm used for encrypting the symmetric key is the asymmetric rsa-1
5 algorithm -->
      <xenc:EncryptionMethod Algorithm="http://www.w3.org/2001/04/xmlenc#rsa-1_5"/>
      <!--KeyInfo element defines the public key of the recipient -->
```

Listing 10.9 **Continued**

```
<dsig:KeyInfo xmlns:dsig="http://www.w3.org/2000/09/xmldsig#">
  <dsig:KeyName>
    CN=MyCompany, OU=Development, O=MyDevTeam, L=Sealand, ST=WA,
    C=US
  </dsig:KeyName>
</dsig:KeyInfo>

<!--CipherValue element in CipherData element contains the encrypted symmetric
encryption key -->
  <xenc:CipherData>
    <xenc:CipherValue>T7XFvXJuVC9E7QcpRrxFOEcpEEr9BY5FaRkfFegZpdbmpf+
      GbyZQKF+mmQfwoFVXjiAXEmPWxfrhH9ePURAKHPoJTEWOx9lvl5vgD+f5heXAM/SpDIAv4y
      mwQd+za4ngZXif8JwWwyvuyASsoCHhnG+KMsBog+n5hnOrwteviT8=
    </xenc:CipherValue>
  </xenc:CipherData>

  <!--The ReferenceList points to the SOAP-ENV:Body which is being encrypted -->
  <xenc:ReferenceList>
    <xenc:DataReference URI="#Id-+FglEUcUjcIRrOwvJ3BuBw/e"/>
  </xenc:ReferenceList>
</xenc:EncryptedKey>

<!-- The wsse:BinarySecurityToken element represents the public key of the client
which can be used to validate the digital signature stored in the
dsig:SignatureValue element. We can see that it is being referenced by the
dsig:Reference element in dsig:KeyInfo within dsig:Signature -->
<wsse:BinarySecurityToken
xmlns:wsu="http://schemas.xmlsoap.org/ws/2002/07/utility" ValueType="wsse:X509v3"
EncodingType="wsse:Base64Binary" wsu:Id="Id-zPMylqRFyhQ948HEXkvYl4Cx">
MIICRTCCAa6gAwIBAAIEPrBeaTANBgkqhkiG9w0BAQUFADBnMQswCSqGSIb3DQEBBQUAA4
GBAKgcU99Prrz37UgiTp5NTX4oLDPM+HBmETQB9EnQPDPZ829tsHsPymM42Pe2Qk4TNM/+
ZIdbrFRSft64WWHYjr8K8uBR9F7/a1WyJmiNPE3wkiZlM140HjV8l0fAfwR2d+cdB0RvJpwLx/
onTxFcnMlCzJfUUp5mFHzebkw19/WD</wsse:BinarySecurityToken>
<!-- Presence of dsig:Signature element shows that this message is digitally
signed. -->
<dsig:Signature xmlns:dsig="http://www.w3.org/2000/09/xmldsig#">
  <dsig:SignedInfo>
    <dsig:CanonicalizationMethod
      Algorithm="http://www.w3.org/2001/10/xml-exc-c14n#"/>
    <dsig:SignatureMethod Algorithm="http://www.w3.org/2000/09/
      xmldsig#rsa-sha1"/>
<!-- The dsig:Reference element refers to the SOAP-ENV:Body element, indicating
that the SOAP-ENV"Body element (which is already encrypted in this case) has
been signed -->
    <dsig:Reference URI="#Id-TbcdlduqOVja2Z7ijsb0CgYB">
```

Listing 10.9   **Continued**

```
        <dsig:Transforms>
          <dsig:Transform Algorithm="http://www.w3.org/2001/10/xml-exc-c14n#"/>
          </dsig:Transforms>
          <dsig:DigestMethod Algorithm="http://www.w3.org/2000/09/xmldsig#sha1"/>
          <dsig:DigestValue>VZ8Wd+Mw2wuXVjWW/sXrF4zW+yE=</dsig:DigestValue>
      </dsig:Reference>
    </dsig:SignedInfo>
    <dsig:SignatureValue>cG9hUTE4dUSnjCH287TbDbwM1pJq1gmQexd8lu6Ktx2tNBwZfI
    vscgJkFk0Ly7nf9CGXWd5W4ng5UcTwjY00U2Bxgh37YvXzCjmfb+l5DzxZSiOxRvCFmAeHi0Oy
    j+bb8yXVMIQjPBb1lemnHXVXdqDkL5aYtWMCCP85Eyc+O7M=</dsig:SignatureValue>
    <!--The KeyInfo points to the public key of the client that can be used
    to validate the signature. In this case, the public key is the
    wsse:BinarySecurityToken above in the page -->
    <dsig:KeyInfo>
      <wsse:SecurityTokenReference>
        <wsse:Reference URI="#Id-zPMylqRFyhQ948HEXkvYl4Cx"/>
      </wsse:SecurityTokenReference>
    </dsig:KeyInfo>
</dsig:Signature>

<!-- UsernameToken contains the username and password sent over the wire
 for authentication. Note this is different from the HTTP BASIC authentication
 credentials, which if used, is part of the HTTP header not the SOAP:Header -->
<wsse:UsernameToken xmlns:wsu=http://schemas.xmlsoap.org/ws/2002/07/utility
 wsu:Id="Id-mov1HAgSeynOrd4SpjaBKdFS">
  <wsse:Username>GoodUser</wsse:Username>
    <wsse:Password Type="wsse:PasswordText">weblogic</wsse:Password>
  </wsse:UsernameToken>
</wsse:Security>

</SOAP-ENV:Header>
<SOAP-ENV:Body Id="Id-Tbcd1duqOVja2Z7ijsb0CgYB">
<!-- The SOAP body is encrypted using a symmetric algorithm "aes128-cbc" -->
    <xenc:EncryptedData xmlns:xenc="http://www.w3.org/2001/04/xmlenc#"
    Id="Id-+FglEUcUjcIRrOwvJ3BuBw/e"
    Type="http://www.w3.org/2001/04/xmlenc#Element">
    <xenc:EncryptionMethod
    Algorithm="http://www.w3.org/2001/04/xmlenc#aes128-cbc"/>
<!-- CipherValue element within CipherData element contains the
encrypted SOAP body content -->
  <xenc:CipherData>
  <xenc:CipherValue>p1hd0mhmmkPJALDACivYd7LFvDDtN1xxp3HGexiIDtPrj+jAWxn7vrAj
   +uhDeGwoZzx+waGBNhggXCzl6g0VrWPXEMepzwEY5YBzs8+pLJtdlk73yKGeNmmdyXHU1+i7ufCh
   r0Rh9XMcLfnOqPx9aFcaOL0v4bYrE3psFB+fgwnt2ujO+StVK/yCRefH76Hhep0CLJq/zE0M4zPD
   0w2KNfG+C9X2hf8a2dND216GHuHI6ZT7vEXUXMDdsIrEgqSKWegK19S6p3FCUwjuUlaXI5FF4Gom
```

Listing 10.9 **Continued**

```
  SwG8JmdBzHjfmq8=</xenc:CipherValue>
  </xenc:CipherData>
 </xenc:EncryptedData>
</SOAP-ENV:Body>
</SOAP-ENV:Envelope>
```

Now let's tweak some features in WS-Security and analyze the results. First, change the username specified in POControlSecurityPolicy.wsse to BadUser as follows:

```
<userNameToken>
        <userName>BadUser</userName>
        <password type="TEXT">weblogic</password>
</userNameToken>
```

This means that POServiceControl.jcx will pass in the user BadUser in its outgoing SOAP request to POService.jws (see Figure 10.20). Now pass the username GoodUser and its password to POClient.jws and run the submitPO method.

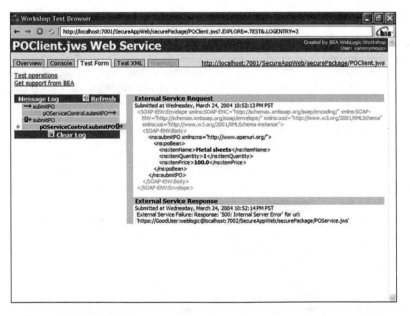

Figure 10.20   Error log on setting an incorrect username and password in POControlSecurityPolicy.wsse.

POClient.jws sets the valid username and password in the POControlSecurity.jcx control. The HTTP basic authentication then succeeds on the server side. However, the WSSE user authentication fails because POControlSecurityPolicy.wsse does not have a valid user in the <userToken> element.

Next, remove the `<signature>` element from the `POControlSecurityPolicy.wsse` file. This means that the SOAP request sent by the control will not be signed. Now run the method and provide the valid username (`GoodUser`) and password. Note that the server requires the message to be signed, due to the presence of the following line in the `<wsSecurityIn>` element in the `POServiceSecurityPolicy.wsse` file:

```
<signatureRequired>true</signatureRequired>
```

Because the client request is not signed, the service returns an HTTP 500 error.

You can see the error stack trace containing the string

```
String:Response: '500: Internal Server Error' for url:
'https://GoodUser:weblogic@localhost:7002/SecureAppWeb/securePackage/
POService.jws'
```

by clicking the `submitPO` link in the Message log (see Figure 10.21).

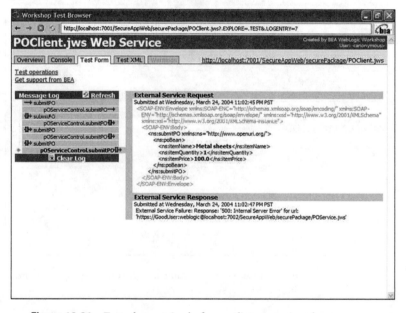

Figure 10.21   Error log received after sending an unsigned message to `POService.jws`.

You can see that multiple layers of security are at work here. Although the request cleared the first layer of HTTP basic authentication due to the valid username and password, the request could not be processed because it was not signed. Therefore, the method execution fails.

Now change the value of the `<signatureRequired>` element in the `POServiceSecurityPolicy.wsse` file to `false`. This means that the `POService` no longer requires the message to be signed. The method now runs successfully.

Change the `<password>` element value in the `POControlSecurityPolicy.wsse`
`<signature>` element to any value other than the original `password` value—for example, `badpassword`:

```
<signatureKey>
    <alias>client1</alias>
    <password>badpassword</password>
</signatureKey>
```

When you run the service, a `java.security.UnrecoverableKeyException` error shows
up because the control is now unable to recover its private key from the keystore to sign
the outgoing message (see Figure 10.22).

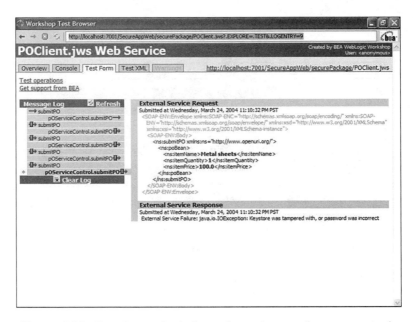

Figure 10.22   Error log received after setting an incorrect keystore password
in `POServiceSecurityPolicy.wsse`.

You can see an error stack trace containing the following by clicking the submitPO tab
under the Message Log tab:

```
<error>
<faultcode>JWSError</faultcode>
<faultstring>SERVICE FAULT:
Code:com.bea.wlw.runtime.jws.wssecurity.exception.WLWWSSEException
String:java.security.UnrecoverableKeyException: Cannot recover key
Detail:
END SERVICE FAULT</faultstring>
</error>
```

Now test how message-based security helps ensure the integrity of the message. You can test this security by modifying the message during transport and checking whether the server side can detect that the message has been corrupted. For this example, you will use a TCP sniffer tool, Apache's TCPMON, to intercept and modify the message. TCP-MON is bundled with Apache's AXIS, which you can download from `http://ws.apache.org/axis/`. Because TCPMON cannot intercept SSL-encrypted messages, you can disable HTTPS to perform this test:

1. Configure TCPMON to listen on port 8000, for example, and act as a listener to the hostname and port where your WebLogic Server instance is listening; in this case, they are localhost (127.0.0.1) and 7001, respectively (see Figure 10.23).

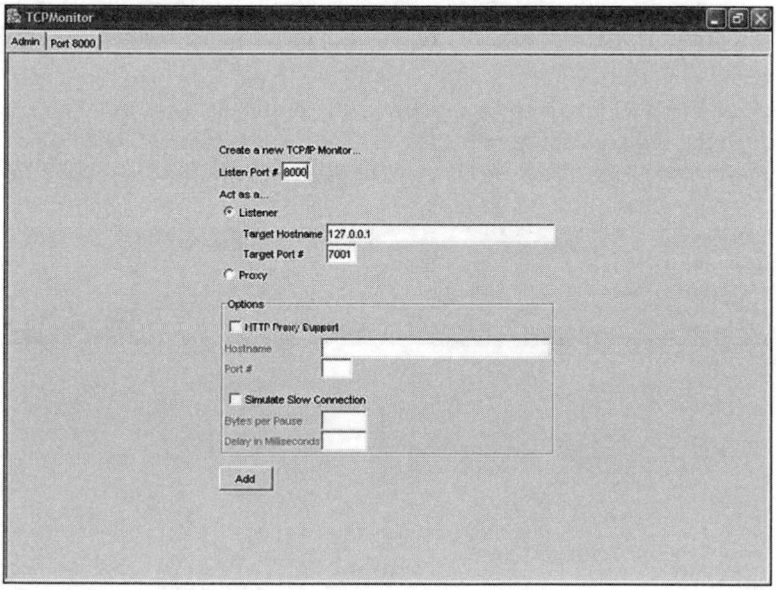

Figure 10.23   The TCPMON Admin window.

2. To disable HTTPS communication to POService.jws, change the `<transport-guarantee>` element value in the `WEB-INF/web.xml` file from `CONFIDENTIAL` to `NONE`:

   `<transport-guarantee>NONE</transport-guarantee>`

3. To route the HTTP request from `POServiceControl.jcx` to port 8000, where TCPMON is listening, change the `jc:location` annotation in `POServiceControl.jcx` from

```
/**
 * @jc:location http-
url="https://localhost:7002/SecureAppWeb/securePackage/PO
Service.jws" jms-url="POService.jws"
```

to

```
/**
 * @jc:location http-
url="http://localhost:8000/SecureAppWeb/securePackage/PO
Service.jws" jms-url="POService.jws"
```

4. Run the `POClient.jws` Web service by passing a valid username and password. The service will run successfully, and you will see the message shown in Figure 10.24 in the TCPMON logs. As you can see, the response received has an HTTP status of 200, which means it's a valid response.

5. Change the HTTP request by modifying any of the elements in it; for example, change the first element in the `<xenc:CipherValue>` element. Then send this request to `POService.jws` by clicking the Resend button (see Figure 10.24).

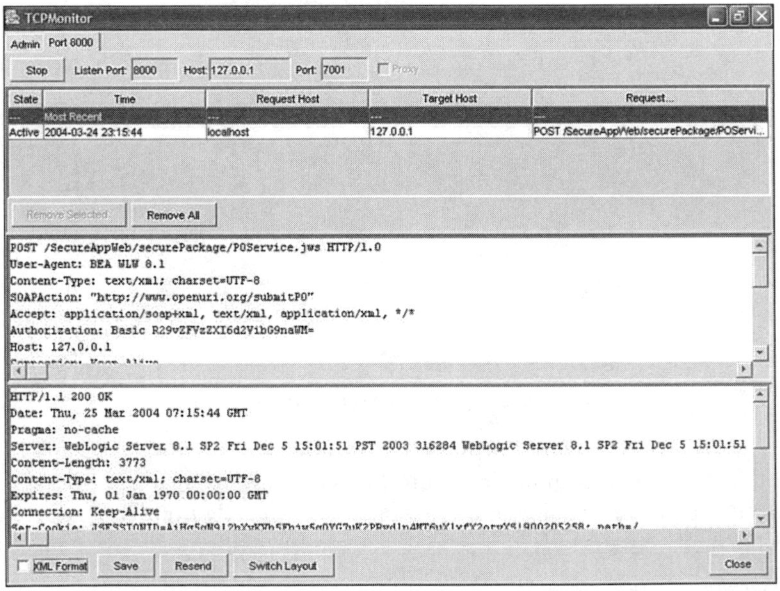

Figure 10.24 SOAP request and response logs in TCPMON.

6. The server detects that the message has been corrupted and returns an HTTP 500 error showing the underlying `com.bea.wlw.runtime.jws.wssecurity.exception.WLWWSSEException`. A sample HTTP response that can be seen in TCPMON's response window is shown in Listing 10.10.

Listing 10.10   SOAP Response Message in TCPMON Logs

```
HTTP/1.1 500 Internal Server
ErrorDate: Tue, 27 Jan 2004 03:28:41
GMTPragma: no-cache
Server: WebLogic Server 8.1 SP2 Fri Dec 5 15:01:51 PST 2003 316284
Content-Type: text/xml; charset=UTF-8
Expires: Thu, 01 Jan 1970 00:00:00 GMT
Set-Cookie: JSESSIONID=AVap4tbLVQpswtd1wEiXwmG1nrSxIJxgsy6F
OJzsQP3nk9JnxqbI!-842907816; path=/
Cache-Control: no-cacheConnection: Close
<?xml version="1.0" encoding="UTF-8"?>
<SOAP-ENV:Envelope
SOAP-ENV:encodingStyle=http://schemas.xmlsoap.org/soap/encoding/
   xmlns:SOAP-ENV="http://schemas.xmlsoap.org/soap/envelope/" xmlns:xsi=http://
www.w3.org/2001/XMLSchema-instance
   xmlns:SOAP-ENC="http://schemas.xmlsoap.org/soap/encoding/">
<SOAP-ENV:Body><SOAP-ENV:Fault>
   <faultcode>    SOAP-ENV:Client </faultcode>
   <faultstring>    EJB Exception: ;
nested exception is:
    com.bea.wlw.runtime.jws.wssecurity.exception.WLWWSSEException:
   weblogic.xml.security.encryption.EncryptionException:
Invalid key data length - with nested exception:
[com.rsa.jsafe.JSAFE_InvalidKeyException: Invalid key data length]
   </faultstring>    <detail><![CDATA[
java.rmi.RemoteException: EJB Exception: ; nested exception is:
    com.bea.wlw.runtime.jws.wssecurity.exception.WLWWSSEException:
   weblogic.xml.security.encryption.EncryptionException: Invalid key
data length - with nested exception:[com.rsa.jsafe.JSAFE_InvalidKeyException:
   Invalid key data length]
```

Role-based security can be used to provide authorization either for the Web service as a whole or for a specific Web service method. A Web service (JWS) file in Workshop compiles to an Enterprise JavaBean (EJB). Hence, the roles referred to within a JWS to provide authorization, using the role-based security annotations, such as `roles-allowed` and `run-as`, are the roles defined at the EJB or application tier. In this next example, you will create them in the `application.xml` file, which is in the `SecureApp/META-INF` directory. Because these roles are defined for authorization at the application tier, they are different from the roles defined in the `web.xml` and `weblogic.xml` deployment descriptors, which are used for authentication at the HTTP tier. To authorize access to `POService.jws` based on role-based security, you will define another role named `ManagerialRole`, with a corresponding user named `Manager`, in the EJB tier and restrict access to the `submitPO()` method to this role. You will also add this role to the allowed roles in the HTTP tier. Therefore, `Manager` will have access at both the HTTP tier and

EJB tier, but `GoodUser` will have access only at the HTTP tier and hence will fail the authentication check at the EJB tier. Here are the steps in detail:

1. To define a Security role called `ManagerialRole` at the application level with the principal name `Manager`, right-click Security Roles and then select Create a New Role.

   Type **ManagerialRole** in the Name text box and enter a description. Check the Use Custom Principal Name check box and type **Manager** as the user—that is, principal name (see Figure 10.25). Then click OK.

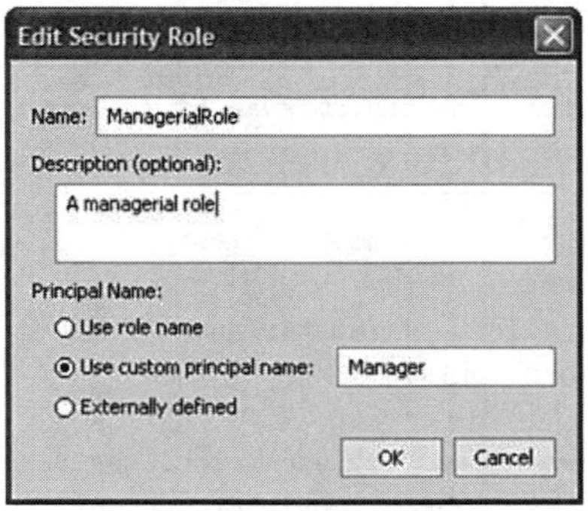

Figure 10.25   Naming the role.

The following entries are automatically generated in the `application.xml` and `weblogic-application.xml` file part of the `META-INF` directory of the `SecureApp` application:

```
application.xml
--------------------
    <security-role>
      <description>Managerial role</description>
      <role-name>ManagerialRole</role-name>
    </security-role>


weblogic-application.xml
-------------------------------
    <security>
      <security-role-assignment>
        <role-name>ManagerialRole</role-name>
        <principal-name>Manager</principal-name>
      </security-role-assignment>
    </security>
```

2. Click the `roles-allowed` property within the security group in the Property Editor while in the Design View of `POService.jws` and add the name **ManagerialRole** (see Figure 10.26).

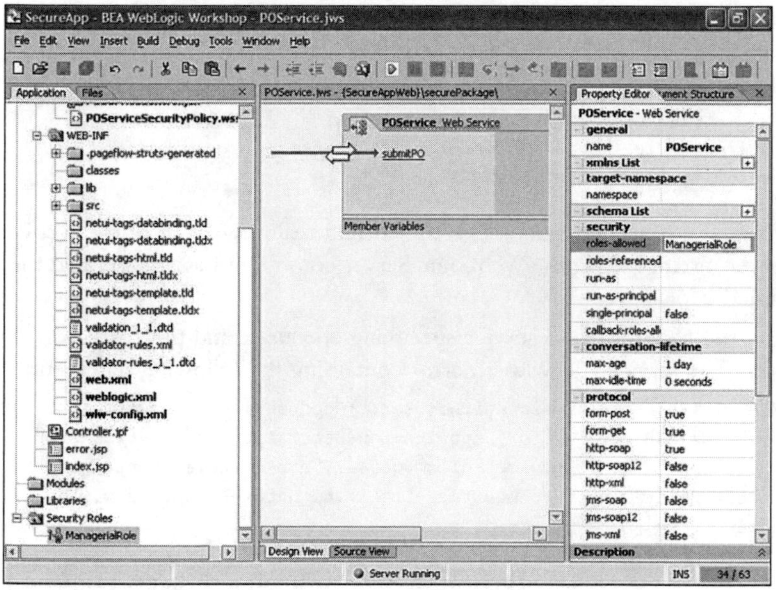

Figure 10.26   Specifying `roles-allowed` for `POService.jws`.

This step restricts access to methods in `POService.jws` at the EJB tier. The annotation generated in the file looks like this:

```
/**
    * @common:security roles-allowed="ManagerialRole"
    */
```

Similarly, you can specify the other role-based properties provided by Workshop: `roles-referenced` and `run-as`.

3. Allow access to `Manager` at the HTTP tier by defining a role named `ManagerialRole` in the `web.xml` deployment descriptor:

```
<security-role>
        <description>Managerial role</description>
            <role-name>ManagerialRole</role-name>
</security-role>
```

4. Add `ManagerialRole` to the `<auth-constraint>` element along with `GoodRole`. This allows any user in `ManagerialRole` to access `POService.jws`:

```
<auth-constraint>
    <role-name>GoodRole</role-name>
    <role-name>ManagerialRole</role-name>
</auth-constraint>
```

5. Add the user named `Manager` to the role named `ManagerialRole` in the `weblogic.xml` deployment descriptor:

```
<security-role-assignment>
        <role-name>ManagerialRole</role-name>
        <principal-name>Manager</principal-name>
</security-role-assignment>
```

6. Define a user named `Manager` in the current realm `myrealm` of the WebLogic Server instance using the WebLogic Server console just as you defined the user named `GoodUser`.

7. Run the `POClient.jws` service specifying `GoodUser` and the corresponding password. The service fails with an error containing the following statement:

```
[EJB:010160]Security Violation: User: 'GoodUser' has insufficient permission
to access EJB: type=<ejb>, application=SecureApp, module=.workshop/
SecureAppWeb/EJB/POService_-u11c40qoq4e1, ejb=StatelessContainer,
method=submitPO, methodInterface=Local, signature={com.bea.wlw.
runtime.core.request.Request}.
```

You receive this message because access to methods in `POService.jws` is restricted to the role `ManagerialRole`.

8. Run the service again, this time passing `Manager` and the corresponding password, and check that it runs fine.

Summary

This chapter walked you through examples depicting all the salient aspects of Web Services Security supported by WebLogic Workshop as of release 8.1. WebLogic Workshop does a good job of providing ease of use to the customer, in an area such as security, which has been traditionally difficult for developers to use. For instance, the use of a WS-Security policy file (`*.wsse`) allows the configuration of WS-Security without any additional coding effort. At the same time, the Workshop runtime environment is J2EE compliant and runs on top of WebLogic Server, which is the leading J2EE application server in the market. However, note that this is not the only way of implementing J2EE-based Web Services Security. Because most of the relevant standards discussed in this book have not been finalized at the time of publication, the implementations across various J2EE products may vary significantly.

A

Security, Cryptography, and Protocol Background Material

THIS APPENDIX IS A COLLECTION of detailed reference information covering algorithms, protocols, and mathematics to support the core material in the book. We kept this detail out of the core chapters to make them easier to read but felt this material is useful for you to gain a deeper understanding of the protocols and algorithms used throughout Web Services Security. In particular, we believe an understanding of the computational complexity of these algorithms will lend a deeper appreciation of the way your deployed secure Web services applications will perform.

The SSL Protocol

In this section, we explain how the Secure Socket Layer (SSL) protocol works using an example in which the client is a Web service requestor and the server is the Web service provider. The steps outlined in Figure A.1 are as follows:

1. The client opens a connection to the server and sends a `ClientHello` message. This message lists the capabilities of the client, including the version of SSL it is using and the cipher suites it supports.

2. The server responds with a `ServerHello` message. The server returns the cipher suite it has chosen and a session ID that identifies this connection.

3. The server sends its certificate. This is an X.509 site certificate signed by a certificate authority. The certificate contains the server's public key.

4. The server (optionally) sends the client a request for its certificate. Client authentication is necessary for almost all Web services, but if the Web service is a thin veneer directly to a human user, username/password authentication may be used.

5. The client (optionally, if requested in step 4) sends its certificate. Some trust authority will have signed this certificate, indicating that the server must have policies in place to assign trust levels to. The server may or may not choose to trust that this is really the entity it claims to be.

6. The client sends a `ClientKeyExchange` message. The client has created a pre-master shared key and is sending it to the server with this message. The full session key is not created directly because different symmetric ciphers use different key lengths. The browser encrypts this shared key using the server's public key and sends it back to the server.

7. The client (optionally, if requested in step 4) sends a `CertificateVerify` message. This is the authentication step in client-authenticated, or "two-way," SSL. The client has to prove it knows the correct private key. The shared key from step 6 is signed using the client's private key (which only it has and which it guarantees it has kept secret) and sent to the server, which verifies this key using the client public key forwarded earlier in the certificate.

8. Both client and server send a `ChangeCipherSpec` message, which indicates that both sides are ready to communicate in encrypted form only using the shared secret session key.

9. Both client and server send a `Finished` message. This is an MD5 or SHA hash of the entire conversation up to this point to confirm that this entire conversation was received by the other party intact and not tampered with en route.

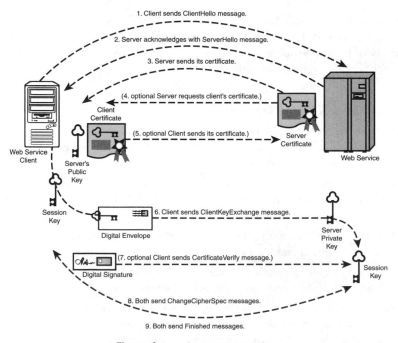

Figure A.1   The SSL protocol.

Testing for Primality

This section on testing for whether two numbers are relatively prime relates to the computational complexity of manufacturing key pairs used in asymmetric public key cryptography. Private and public keys are generated as a pair with the private key always kept secret and the public key accessible for broad consumption. We have said many times in this book that public key cryptography is a computationally expensive process but is essential for digital signatures and shared key transport because of the difficulty of securely transporting shared symmetric keys. Key pair generation is computationally expensive because it is based on the mathematics of factoring large numbers.

How hard is factoring large numbers? The best-known algorithm, the number field sieve (NFS), factored a 428-bit number by having 600 people use 1,600 computers that took about 5,000 mips-years to compute.

Fermat's theorem from the year 1640 says that if m is prime and a is not a multiple of m, then

$$a^{m-1} = 1 \ (mod \ m)$$

This is the inverse modulo problem. In general, $a^{-1} = x \ (mod \ n)$ has a unique solution if a and n are relatively prime. Determining when m is *not* a prime because this relationship fails is relatively fast, requiring only $O(log \ n)$ operations. Unfortunately for cryptography algorithms, the critical issue is determining whether something *is* a prime, not whether it *isn't*—and this is a lot more difficult to determine.

For this reason, we do not take the approach of creating a random number and then factoring it to determine whether it is prime. This also explains why cracking crypto-algorithms that are based on prime factors is so intractable.

In practice, what we do is generate suspect prime numbers and test to see whether they indeed are prime *without* complete factoring. The simplest and most common algorithm for doing this is the Rabin–Miller algorithm. This probability algorithm creates a number that with a certain probability is prime. Performing this algorithm multiple times reduces the probability of it reporting a non-prime as prime to near zero. Here is how it works:

1. Choose a random number p to test. Calculate b, where b is the number of times 2 divides $b - 1$ (that is, $2b$ is the largest power of 2 that divides $p - 1$). Then calculate m, such that $p = 1 + 2b \star m$.

2. Choose a random number a, such that a is less than p.

3. Set $j = 0$ and set $z = am \ mod \ p$.

4. If $(z = 1)$ or if $(z = p - 1)$, then p passes the test and may be prime.

5. If $(j > 0)$ and $(z = 1)$, then p is not prime.

6. Set $j = j + 1$. If $(j < b)$ and $(z \star p - 1)$, set $z = z^2 \ mod \ p$ and go back to step 4. If $z = p - 1$, then p passes the test and may be prime.

7. If $j = b$ and $z \star p - 1$, then p is not prime.

A composite (non-prime) will slip through t tests no more than $1/4^t$ times. The real-world implementation of this is as follows:

1. Generate a random n-bit number candidate, p.

2. Set high- and low-order bits to 1 to make sure this is of the correct bit length and is odd.

3. Check to make sure p is not divisible by any small primes such as 3, 5, and 7. Best implementations check all primes less than 2,000.

4. Perform the Rabin-Miller test for some random a, as shown previously. If p passes, generate another small a and repeat this test five times. If p fails any of the five tests, go back to step 1 and try all over again.

One saving grace for computational complexity considerations of asymmetric cryptography key generation is that the operation is performed only once, and then the private-public key pair is used over and over again for numerous encryption operations. In contrast, symmetric encryption is much more efficient in the key creation and in the encryption operations themselves, but a new session key must be created for each distinct session. Also, you should note that expensive public key pair generation is typically performed on client machines, not centrally at servers, both to offload centralized resources and to ensure that the private key never leaves the machine on which it is created.

RSA Cryptography

An important reason that public key encryption is so much slower than shared key encryption is that RSA public key asymmetric encryption/decryption is based on the mathematics of *modular exponentiation*. In simple terms, this means that this algorithm takes each input value, raises it to a power (requiring a large number of multiplications), and then performs the modulo operation (a form of division). On the other hand, shared key symmetric algorithms are based on much faster logical operations on bit arrays. On average, public-private key operations are 13 times slower than symmetric key operations. Furthermore, the private key has a much larger exponent than the public key, so private key operations take substantially longer in asymmetric encryption than do public key operations. In confidentiality applications (that is, message encryption) where the public key is used for encryption, decryption takes substantially longer than encryption. In integrity applications (that is, integrity as in digital signature) where the private key is used for encryption, it is the other way around. This imbalance would be a problem when applied to large messages, but it is not an issue when applied only to small messages such as the 200-bit symmetric encryption key when this algorithm is used for key transport.

Choosing RSA Key Pairs

The RSA algorithm for choosing key pairs is as follows:

1. Choose two large prime numbers, p and q, of equal length. Now compute the product:

   $n = p \star q$

   n will be the modulus used later.

2. Choose two more numbers: the public exponent e and the private exponent d.

   Choose e to be less than n and relatively prime to $(p - 1) \star (q - 1)$. This means that $(p - 1)$ and $(q - 1)$ and e have no common factors other than 1.

   Choose d such that $(e \star d - 1)$ is divisible by $(p - 1)(q - 1)$. In other words,

   $e \star d = 1 \bmod (p - 1) \star (q - 1)$

   which means after you choose e, you know d to be

   $d = e^{-1} \bmod ((p - 1) \star (q - 1))$

The two key values so produced are actually each a pair of values:

public key $= (n, e)$

private key $= (n, d)$

Padding

The input to RSA encryption operations is interpreted as a number, so special padding is required to make the input totally consistent. The total length of the data must be a multiple of the modulus size, and the data must be numerically less than the modulus. A 1,024-bit RSA key has a 128-byte modulus. Therefore, data must be encrypted in blocks of 128 bytes. Each input number must be padded with zeros until its numerical value is less than that of the modulus. XML Encryption specifies the use of PKCS#1 Block 02 padding. This padding places a critical restriction on the size of data that RSA can encrypt. This is why RSA is never used to encrypt the entire plaintext message but encrypts only the shared key being exchanged between communicating parties or the fixed-size message digest in digital signature.

RSA Encryption

The intended recipient's public key is used for message encryption. As stated previously, you must divide the message m into numerical blocks smaller than the modulus n. So if p and q are 100-digit primes, then n will be less than 200 digits, which will be the upper limit for message blocks to be encrypted. This upper limit works well for sending encrypted shared keys because they will fit into this block size limitation. The encryption formula to take an input plaintext message block m and create an output ciphertext message block c is then as follows:

$c = m^e \bmod n$

RSA Decryption

The recipient uses his or her private key for decryption. Decryption takes each encrypted block c and computes

$m = c^d \bmod n$

to create a plaintext message block m.

The number theory behind this algorithm proves that it does not matter which key you use first; its pair used in the corresponding formula will reverse the initial operation. This is great because it means you can use the sender's private key to encrypt when you want to prove identity and non-repudiation to anyone with the sender's public key, and you can use the recipient's public key to encrypt when you want to prove confidentiality to the only one recipient who possesses the matching private key.

DSA Digital Signature Algorithms

DSA Signature is required by the XML Signature specification: DSA is only for signatures; it is not defined for encryption the way RSA is. Even though DSA is required, RSA is still officially the recommended approach[1].

The DSA algorithm is composed of three phases: parameter generation, key generation, signing and verifying. Like RSA, the private key is used for signing and the public key for verifying a signature.

Private and public keys, x and y respectively, are generated from parameters called p, q, and g. p is the prime, q is the subprime, and g is the base. Parameter generation uses primality testing and modular exponentiation. After the parameters have been generated, computation of the keys is relatively fast. Key generation chooses a random private key x that is related to q, and then the public key y is generated from x.

DSA Key Generation

In the following sections, we will show how the DSA algorithm works. Used in the algorithm are a series of terms we define here:

- p = a prime number L bits long, where L ranges from 512 to 1,024 and is a multiple of 64.
- q = a 160-bit prime factor of $p - 1$.
- $g = h^{(p - 1)/q} \bmod p$, where h is any number less than $p - 1$ such that $h^{(p - 1)/q} \bmod p$ is greater than 1.
- x = a number less than q.
- $y = g \star x \bmod p$.

---

1. The W3C's policy for its specifications is not to require technologies that have patent protection still applied to them. The RSA algorithm still had an active patent on it at the time these drafts were originally being developed. That patent has now expired, so RSA can be fully embraced by the W3C for XML Signature.

DSA message signing and verification make use of the one-way hash function SHA1, which we will refer to as $H(m)$ for an input message m. Given public parameters p, q, and g and the private key x, a message is signed. Signature verification uses the same public parameters and the public key y.

DSA Algorithm Operation

The DSA algorithm operates by first having the sender generate a random number k, less than q.

Next, the sender generates

1. $r = (g^k \bmod p) \bmod q$
2. $s = (k^{-1} (H(m) + x \star r)) \bmod q$

The parameters r and s are the sender's signature; they are sent to the recipient along with the original message m.

The recipient verifies the signature by computing

1. $w = s^{-1} \bmod q$
2. $u_1 = (H(m) \star w) \bmod q$
3. $u_2 = (r \star w) \bmod q$
4. $v = ((g^{u1} \star y^{u2}) \bmod p) \bmod q$

If $v = r$, then the DSA signature is verified.

Block Cipher Processing

XML Encryption uses only block ciphers.[2] This means that XML Encryption works by taking the plaintext message and breaking it into fixed-size blocks before encrypting each block. Two algorithms are part of the XML Encryption draft: the Triple Data Encryption Standard (3DES) and Advanced Encryption Standard (AES). They both require fixed size input blocks and so require a block cipher padding algorithm.

Block Cipher Padding (PKCS#5)

This section describes the block cipher padding algorithm specified in the standard PKCS#5 and used in block ciphers DES and AES.

---

2. Block ciphers are the only required or recommended algorithms, but you can extend XML Encryption with stream ciphers. They are mentioned in the specification at http://www.w3.org/TR/xmlenc-core/#sec-Alg-Stream.

Given an n-byte plaintext block and a b-byte block size where $n <= b$, the block cipher padding algorithm is as follows:

If $n < b$ {

      let $k = b - n - 1$ arbitrary pad bytes and append these bytes to n

} else if ($n == b$) {

      let $k = b - 1$ arbitrary pad bytes and append these bytes to n

}

in both cases if ($n < b$ and $n == b$) {

      append a final byte whose value is $k + 1$

}

Block Cipher Feedback

Another critical concept you need to understand is feedback between blocks in a message. You don't want blocks completely independent of each other because an attacker could subtract them from a message at will. Additionally, you want to combat pattern-based and frequency attacks, too. If the previous block affects the encryption of the next block, common words or patterns cannot be detected in the cipher. This concept is important for XML-based documents because XML has such a strong common structure. Therefore, you need some way to create a relationship between blocks. A technique called *cipher block chaining (CBC)* is the most common mechanism for creating such a relationship.

In CBC, you simply combine the current block with the previous block using XOR as you move through the plaintext blocks in order. Now each successive block is tied to and related in the ciphertext to the preceding block, making it impossible to remove a single block and replace it.

DES Encryption Algorithm

The DES encryption algorithm is called for in the XML Encryption standard. It is the basis for 3DES, which is the recommended way to use DES. In both cases, it is best performed in hardware and was designed with that use in mind.

The DES algorithm begins with an initial permutation performed to accommodate DES hardware limitations. The incoming message block is then broken into a right half and a left half, each 32 bits long.

On that message block, the algorithm performs the following function that combines the data with the key for 16 rounds:

1. The key bits are shifted.
2. Then 48 bits are selected from 56 bits of the key.
3. The right half is expanded to 48 bits via an expansion transformation.

4. These bits are combined with 48 bits of a shifted and permuted key via XOR.

5. This output is sent through a substitution box, producing 32 new bits, and is permuted again.

6. This output is then combined with the left half using another XOR.

7. The left and right halves are combined.

8. The final permutation produces the ciphertext.

As you can see, several substitutions, permutations, XORs, and shifts are necessary to get the DES encrypted ciphertext. The design of DES is so clever that decryption uses exactly the same algorithm as encryption. The only difference is that the order the key parts are used is exactly reversed.

AES Encryption Algorithm

AES is a newer encryption standard and is now the preferred one to use for XML Encryption. AES is a substitution-linear transformation network with 10, 12, or 14 rounds, depending on the key sizes, which are currently set at 128, 192, or 256 bits. The block size used in AES is 16 bytes.

The data block to be processed is partitioned into an array of bytes forming a matrix with rows and columns. Each cipher operation is byte-oriented.

The next step has four layers:

1. An 8-by-8 substitution box is applied to each byte.

2. Two layers of linear mixing are performed in which the rows of the byte array are shifted and the columns are mixed.

3. Subkey bytes are combined into each byte of the array using XOR.

4. The column mixing is omitted in the last round.

The algorithm was designed to be very fast and suitable to hardware.

Hashing Details and Requirements

Encrypting large byte arrays is computationally expensive. You therefore have a strong need for a small and consistent size byte array created out of any arbitrary plaintext input. This way, you can limit the computation time spent performing the encryption, and many simplifications ensue downstream when the encrypted message is always of a fixed small size. However, it would be disastrous if two different messages mapped to the same exact byte array. This would mean that someone could substitute a new message for the original and fool the recipient into thinking the new fraudulent message is the correct one. It must be impossible to reverse the function, take the small output byte array, and regenerate the original message. Small fixed size, collision avoidance, and non-reversibility are characteristics of good hash functions.

Motivation for Using Hash Functions

Integrity (proof that a message has not been altered in any way) requires the use of a hash function. But functions that avoid duplicate values are exceedingly rare. The birthday paradox demonstrates this: With any random 23 people in a room, the chance that two have the same birthday is 50%. This example says that mapping a set of 365 possible input values (possible birthdays in the year) into 23 output values or keys (the people in the room) has a 50% chance of a collision into the same key.

A very common, easy-to-understand hash function is the modulo operation that gives the remainder after a division operation:

$h(K) = K \bmod M$

For example, the hash function $f(x) = x \bmod 7$ takes as input the infinite domain of integers and produces as output only the range of values 0, 1, 2, 3, 4, 5, and 6. If x were an entire message represented as an integer, this hash function would still produce only a value in the range 0..6. Unfortunately, several messages would end up producing the same output value; in other words, there would be many collisions.

Requirements for Digital Signature

Hash functions used in digital signatures must be highly collision resistant. The goal is to make finding two different inputs that produce the same output be intractable. If this were easy, an intruder would make that substitution, and the hash function would fail to provide the basic message integrity you require.

The requirements can be stated as follows for a hash function $H(M)$ operating on an arbitrary-length message M that returns a fixed-length hash value h:

$h = H(M)$, where h is of length m

What you require is an efficient, one-way algorithm that always generates unique results.

The idea is to hash the entire plaintext message and then to protect that hash value from being modified in any way. If the sender and receiver input the exact same message to the exact same hash algorithm and the original hash code is carefully protected during transmission, the recipient can check and verify the integrity of the message without the huge expense of trying to encrypt the entire message. That, in fact, is the basic outline of a digital signature, which is the basis for XML Signature, as you saw in Chapter 4, "Safeguarding the Identity and Integrity of XML Messages."

SHA1

SHA stands for Secure Hash Algorithm, and the 1 refers to it being the first (implying there may be a need for variants in the future). SHA1 creates a fixed-size 20-byte hash output value sometimes called the *message digest*. It meets all the requirements for a secure one-way hash algorithm for cryptography: It is collision resistant, secure, and efficient.

Collision Resistance

Guessing a second message that maps to the same value as the original message for a 20-byte or 160-bit hash value requires 2^{160} random hashes, making it computationally infeasible to find two messages that hash to the same value. There is no attack that is more efficient than brute force.

Guessing a 20-byte hash has a 1 in 2^{160} chance of coming up with the original message. By way of scaling this,

2^{61} sec is the total lifetime of the universe.

2^{170} is the total number of atoms in the earth.

On a 1 billion hashes per second computer (still beyond computing capacity today), brute-force guessing of a 20-byte hash would take 10^{22} billion years to accomplish, which is more than the lifetime of the universe.

Security

SHA1 is not based on any assumption like the difficulty of factoring. Therefore, there is no assumption to be proven wrong that will compromise its security.

Simplicity and Efficiency

No large data structures are required in SHA1, and the program to implement it is not complicated (it needs to run identically on client machines as well as server machines). It is suitable for high-speed software implementations and is based on simple bit manipulations on 32-bit operands.

SHA is called secure because it is designed to be computationally infeasible to recover a message corresponding to a given message digest, or to find two different messages that produce the same message digest. Any change to a message in transit will, with a very high probability, result in a different message digest, and the signature will fail to verify. SHA is based on principles similar to those used by Professor Ronald L. Rivest of MIT when designing the MD4 message digest algorithm, and is closely modeled after that algorithm.

Silvio Micali's Fast Validation/Revocation

A certificate authority (CA) must keep an up-to-date list of all certificates revoked in a certificate revocation list (CRL). It goes without saying that the CA must make it easy for registration authorities to revoke any given certificate (but prove that they have the right to do so). With CRLs, relying parties have the burden of checking this list each time a certificate is presented. Best practices call for a certificate deployment point (CDP) URL to be embedded in each certificate. A CDP is a pointer to the location of the CRL on the Internet, accessible programmatically by any relying party's applications. CRLs are usually updated once per day because the process of generating them is non-trivial. When an organization is dealing with a compromised key or a rogue employee, once-per-day updates can mean a huge loss during that day of compromise. Currently, almost no one checks revocation lists at all. Although the sponsoring CAs obediently create CRLs, and numerous tools can and do process them, there are so many unsolved problems with them that, in our view, CRLs on the Internet are a technological failure.

Online Certificate Status Protocol (OCSP) was an attempt to create a much finer granularity protocol for essentially real-time revocation checking. But like CRLs, the information provided must be signed by the originating CA, which is an expensive operation to perform in real time. The best case on an unloaded system of moderate speed is 26ms response time for a single OCSP request in our tests. In our view, this makes OCSP so limited in scope that it will continue to be only a bit player in revocation solutions. We expect to see very little deployment of OCSP in the future.

Web Services Security must have a workable revocation, and the existing technologies are not strong enough. In our opinion, there is much promise in emerging revocation techniques that are scalable and respond in microseconds, such as Silvio Micali's technique based on chains of hashed secret codes.

The CA generates a secret random 20-byte value X_0. Using X_0 as input to hash function H, you generate $X_1 = H(X_0)$. Then you use the output of the previous hash computation as input to the next until you achieve X_{365}. Finally, you insert the value X_{365} into the certificate before it is signed by the CA:

$$C = \text{SIG}_{CA}(serial\ no., \text{PK}_U, \text{U}, issue\ date, expiration\ date, X_{365})$$

This process is shown in Figure A.2.

Validation

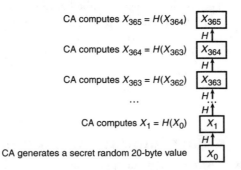

Figure A.2 Silvio Micali's fast certification validation scheme.

This certificate is valid on the day it is signed by virtue of the fact that X_{365} indicates this is a valid certificate. On the next day, the CA reveals X_{364}.

Validity Check

To check the validity of this certificate on the next day, you take the revealed X_{364} and compute one hash computation using $X'_{365} = H(X_{364})$, and if the new $X'_{365} = X_{365}$

stored in the certificate, this certificate is still valid. In general, on day D before expiration, the CA reveals X_D, from which the correct number of hashes is performed to reach X_{365}. If the value matches what is in the certificate, it is still a valid certificate. Only the CA knows the starting point; nowhere along the chain can you compute backwards because these are one-way non-reversible hash functions. Furthermore, the intermediate values can always be openly revealed and published. The cost to the CA is a table lookup. The cost to the relying party is a few hashes.

Revocation

Revocation will be a binary check; either the certificate is revoked, or it is not. Initially, the CA generates a random 20-byte value Y_0 and from this computes $Y_1 = H(Y_0)$. Y_1 is stored in the certificate before it is signed:

$$C = SIG_{CA}(\textit{serial no.}, PK_U, U, \textit{issue date, expiration date}, X_{365}, Y_1)$$

Although the certificate is valid, the revocation sentinel revealed by the CA is 0 because $H(0) \neq Y_1$ for any Y_1. But as soon as this certificate is revoked, the CA reveals Y_0 as the revocation sentinel.

The beauty of this scheme is that the proofs do not need to be signed, so they can be posted on insecure sites all over the Internet or even published in the *Wall Street Journal*. We believe this scheme or something like it will be essential to broad-based secure Web services.

This information has been used with permission from Silvio Micali: U.S. Patent nos. 6,292,893; 5,960,083; 5,793,868; 5,666,416; and others.

Canonicalization of Messages for Digital Signature Manifests

In Chapter 4 on XML Signature, we briefly discussed a complex concept called *canonicalization*. As you recall, canonicalization of message text prior to applying a digital signature is critical because signature verification will fail if any changes occur to the message through "normal" XML processing as it moves from one node in a Web service network to another. The following sections discuss some of the detailed steps used in canonicalization. You can find even more details in the definitive reference for Canonical XML version 1.0 at `http://www.w3.org/TR/2001/REC-xml-c14n-20010315`.

Canonicalization V1 Transform Steps

The following is a list of the transformations that occur to an XML document when it goes through a Canonical XML version 1.0 transform:

- The document is encoded in UTF-8.
- Line breaks are normalized to #xA on input, before parsing.
- Attribute values are normalized, as if by a validating processor.

- Character and parsed entity references are replaced.
- CDATA sections are replaced with their character content.
- The XML declaration and Document Type Definition (DTD) are removed.
- Empty elements are converted to start-end tag pairs.
- Whitespace outside the document element and within start and end tags is normalized.
- All whitespace in character content is retained (excluding characters removed during line-feed normalization).
- Attribute value delimiters are set to quotation marks (double quotes).
- Special characters in attribute values and character content are replaced by character references.
- Superfluous namespace declarations are removed from each element.
- Default attributes are added to each element.
- Lexicographic order is imposed on the namespace declarations and attributes of each element.

Canonicalization Subtleties: Exclusive Canonicalization

Although the concept of standardizing the XML before digesting and before verifying is reasonably simple, complex subtleties arise in some specific situations. One of the subtleties became a significant issue upon the creation of practical implementations of XML Signing. It came up when applying XML Signing to fragments of XML within a larger XML document, which is the predominant scenario in Web services using SOAP. The issue was primarily related to namespaces. Per the XML Canonicalization version 1.0 specification, namespaces are to be propagated down to all their descendents. This makes sense because, in the context of a document, these namespaces are implicit, so making them explicit seems to be a reasonable strategy. However, removing an XML fragment from the context of a document—as in the case of SOAP when you have an XML payload within the overall document—can cause significant problems.

This issue resulted in the creation of a new canonicalization algorithm called *Exclusive Canonicalization* (http://www.w3.org/TR/2002/REC-xml-exc-c14n-20020718/). This canonicalization method strives to "exclude ancestor context" as much as is practical. It primarily does so by not propagating the ancestor namespaces down to the children nodes. It turns out that this canonicalization approach is the most practical in most circumstances and the one that you should use. As Donald Eastlake points out in his book *Secure XML* (Addison-Wesley, 2003, p. 218), "Almost all CanonicalizationMethod elements should specify Exclusive XML Canonicalization."

The extensibility of the canonicalization method is a tribute to the XML Signature working group and is what made the advent of the Exclusive canonicalization method possible. Custom canonicalization methods are also possible; however, you should be extremely careful about using one because the canonicalization algorithm modifies the XML to be signed and is verified in a way that is difficult to see. It would not be difficult for a canonicalization algorithm to modify the XML, for example, to have all signatures verify correctly.

Base-64 Encoding

Transmitting binary data such as keys or digital certificates in printable textual form is the goal of Base-64 encoding. This type of encoding is necessary if these objects are sent in the body of an email message, through a Web page, or as part of an XML message.

A 65-character subset of US-ASCII is used, enabling 6 bits to be represented per printable character. (The extra 65th character, =, is used to signify a special processing function. See Table A.1.)

The encoding process represents 24-bit groups of input bits as output strings of four encoded characters. Proceeding from left to right, a 24-bit input group is formed by concatenating three 8-bit input groups. These 24 bits are then treated as four concatenated 6-bit groups, each of which is translated into a single digit in the Base-64 alphabet.

Each 6-bit group is used as an index into an array of 64 printable characters. The character referenced by the index is placed in the output string.

Table A.1   **The 65-Character Subset of US-ASCII**

Value	Code	Value	Code	Value	Code	Value	Code
0	A	17	R	34	I	51	z
1	B	18	S	35	j	52	0
2	C	19	T	36	k	53	1
3	D	20	U	37	l	54	2
4	E	21	V	38	m	55	3
5	F	22	W	39	n	56	4
6	G	23	X	40	o	57	5
7	H	24	Y	41	p	58	6
8	I	25	Z	42	q	59	7
9	J	26	a	43	r	60	8
10	K	27	b	44	s	61	9
11	L	28	c	45	t	62	+
12	M	29	d	46	u	63	/
13	N	30	e	47	v		
14	O	31	f	48	w	(pad)	=
15	P	32	g	49	x		
16	Q	33	h	50	y		

PGP

We include Pretty Good Privacy (PGP) here because it is supported as one of the token types in WS-Security headers. This approach, invented by Philip Zimmerman, is very different from the idea of there being a small number of trusted third parties as in Public Key Infrastructure (PKI). PGP is the most widely used email encryption and signing mechanism in use today. The second most widely used email encryption does not even register as a sliver on a pie chart of market share. Many people think that S/MIME certificates for signed and/or encrypted emails are prevalent. Not so. Even though tools such as Outlook, Eudora, and Lotus support S/MIME certificates, if measured by number of encrypted or signed emails sent, PGP has more than a 95% share. And one version of PGP is free with no overriding central authority.[3]

Strong freeware versions of PGP have always been available. Its deployment was always a grass-roots effort with a goal of free distribution to anyone and everyone worldwide, regardless of U.S. State Department restrictions about export because these types of crypto-systems were classified as "munitions." The PGP leaders struck back by publishing the complete source code in MIT Press books that were optimized for optical character recognition. Because books were not controlled as munitions, overseas groups were able to scan the books and obtain the source code easily.

PGP uses the IDEA algorithm for symmetric key encryption and the RSA algorithm with keys up to 2047 for key management and digital signatures. Its one-way hash algorithm is MD5.

Random public keys are seeded from keyboard latency while the subscriber is typing and uses probabilistic primality testing.

PGP encrypts a user's private key using a hashed passphrase instead of a password. A passphrase is just a longer password than the normal eight or so characters. The user is encouraged to think of a complete phrase instead of just a word.

PGP's security is based on a layered approach. The only thing an attacker can tell about an encrypted message is who the recipient is. Only after the recipient decrypts the message does anyone know who the sender is if it was signed as well as encrypted.

PGP uses a distributed key management scheme with no certification authorities. The concept is instead a "Web of Trust"; this is symbiotic with the fundamental nature of the Internet. Users generate and distribute their own public keys, and users sign each others' public keys.

---

3. See http://www.pgpi.org/products/pgp/versions/freeware/.

Glossary

AES   Advanced Encryption Standard. AES replaces DES as the newest government-sponsored symmetric block cipher encryption standard. AES is also known as Rijndael after its developer. In addition to 3DES, AES is the encryption method of choice specified in the XML Encryption specification.

ASN.1   Abstract Syntax Notation 1, published jointly by the International Standards Organization, the International Electrotechnical Commission, and the International Telecommunications Union. This structured data language allows well-defined data structures to be passed among differing applications and platforms. Unlike XML, it is a binary format. It is older than XML and is more compact. It is also the underlying format in all the PKCS key and certificate interchange specifications and is therefore important for current Web Services Security implementations.

Asymmetric encryption   Non-matching but mathematically related keys are used for encryption and decryption. One key (it does not matter which) is used for encryption. That key is useless for decryption. Only the matching key can be used for decryption. This process is referred to throughout this text as *public key encryption*. This concept will be used by XML Signature for key exchange to establish and transport a symmetric key for use in XML Encryption.

Attribute assertion   In SAML, once an identity (a subject) is established, an attribute-issuing authority receives the credentials for a subject with the intent of attaching certain attributes to these credentials. Examples of attributes that might be attached include the subject's current account paid status, credit limit, and so forth.

Authentication   The process of an individual proving he really is someone who has already had his identity established. The receiver of a message needs to be able to ascertain its origin and not have an intruder masquerade as someone else. A message sender authenticates himself by providing a shared secret of some sort that the receiver has and that he also either *has* (a token or key), *knows* (a password, passphrase, or PIN) or *is* (biometric). Authentication in Web services will use the same mechanisms the Web has been using for some time, including username/password, X.509 digital certificates, and biometric devices. The form this will take in Web services is most often SAML.

Authentication assertion   An SAML authentication authority receives a subject's credentials. It processes those credentials according to its established policy. If the authentication process is successful, the authority asserts that subject S was identified and that it has authentically represented itself by method M at time T so that its digital identity can be trusted to represent its physical identity.

Authorization The process of establishing what someone who has been authenticated is allowed to do. The entity receiving the request for service will grant permissions for each identity to access certain items. In Web services, SAML is used for authorization—specifying what they can do—as well as for authentication—specifying who they are.

Authorization assertion An SAML authorization authority receives credentials for subject S along with a request for authorization. This authority asserts that subject S can be granted access of type A to resource R given evidence E. The subject could be a human or a computer (Web service) and the requested resource could be another Web service.

Availability Timely, reliable access to data and information services for authorized users. Availability is a security requirement for Web services not only because it speaks to authorization of users, but also because security is compromised or meaningless in the face of unreliable services.

Base-64 Transmitting binary data such as keys or digital certificates in printable textual form is the goal of BASE-64 encoding. Transmitting data this way is necessary if these objects are sent in the body of an email message, through a Web page, or as part of an XML message. Base-64 is used extensively in the Web Services Security specifications when cipher text is placed inline within the XML message itself (for example, CipherValue in XML Encryption).

Basic authentication An authentication protocol supported by most browsers. It is a method of authentication that encodes username and password data transmissions. Basic authentication is sometimes called "clear text" authentication because the Base-64 encoding can be decoded by anyone with a freely available decoding utility. Note that encoding is not the same as encryption.

Binding One of three things a WSDL must specify in addition to operations and services. Binding defines how the operations will be performed. The two most common bindings are RPC/encoded and Document/literal. The first specifies a fine-grained request-response synchronous mode of communication. The second specifies a mode in which a document is contained within the message and the style of communication is asynchronous.

Binding also refers to the way SAML itself is made secure. A binding is a way to transport SAML requests and responses to and from SAML authorities. A binding is the mapping of SAML request/response message exchanges into standard communication protocols. The SAML specification requires SOAP over HTTP as one binding.

Biometrics Aids in authentication by providing *something you are*. These aids include palm scan, hand geometry scan, retina scan, iris scan, signature dynamics analysis (how you move the pen), keyboard dynamics (your typing pattern), voice print, facial scan, and hand topology; others are being developed and perfected. Today in extensive experimentation, the most effective biometric (leading to the fewest false positives) is a palm scan, followed by hand geometry and iris scan.

Block cipher   A plaintext message first broken into fixed-size blocks before each block is encrypted. 3DES and AES are block encryption ciphers. XML Encryption uses only block ciphers.

Canonicalization   Often abbreviated to C14N, a strategy for standardizing XML structures so that they compare identically across multiple platforms. C14N is critical because if even a single bit changes in a document that is being signed, the digest (hash) will not be the same and signature validation will fail. With XML in particular because it is text-based, certain differences may exist between an XML document and XML fragment that has nothing to do with the underlying meaning of the XML. Therefore, XML is always canonicalized before being hashed or signed, and both sides of the communication must agree on the canonicalization method used.

Certificate authority (CA)   The signer of certificates. Primary tasks include issuing, renewing, and revoking certificates. A CA will receive a Certificate Signing Request (CSR) that contains the just-generated public key along with some identifying information about the associated individual or entity. The certificate authority's job is to bind that identity to the public key so that all possible parties who rely on that public key can be sure it remains valid and associated with the entity. Examples of public CAs include VeriSign, GeoTrust, Entrust, RSA, and Comodo.

Certificate path validation   A digital certificate from one CA can be linked or "chained" to one from another CA for the purposes of increasing the trustworthiness of the certificate. Through a process called *certificate path validation,* an attempt is made to create a "path" of valid, non-revoked certificates to one of the defined trusted certificate issuers in the trust list accessible to the recipient of the initial certificate.

CGI   Common Gateway Interface is a way for a browser to execute any server function through script executed on behalf of the browser by the Web server. Early attempts to create the functionality of Web services were accomplished by having one server (acting like a browser) issue HTTP POST calls to cause CGI scripts to execute remote procedures on the Web server.

Cipher block chaining   Because the most common encryption ciphers encrypt fixed-size blocks separately, you don't want blocks completely independent of each other because blocks could be subtracted from a message at will. If the previous block affects the encryption of the next block, common words or patterns cannot be detected in the cipher. This is important for XML-based documents because XML has such a strong common structure. So you need some way to create a relationship between blocks. CBC is the most common mechanism for this.

Ciphertext   The process of taking plaintext (or cleartext) and disguising it in such a way as to make it indecipherable is called encryption. The output of this process is called ciphertext. Ciphertext is the input to the decryption process that, if successful, results in the starting plaintext.

Confidentiality   The goal of cryptography is to keep messages secret. You want to prevent an attacker from eavesdropping and being able to either intercept or modify your messages. The way you accomplish this in general is through encryption, and for Web services, in particular, this is the domain of XML Encryption.

CORBA   Common Object Request Broker Architecture. CORBA was a huge middleware project led by the Object Management Group. The underlying communications protocol used by CORBA was called Internet Inter-ORB Protocol (IIOP). Much of what was learned from the experiences with CORBA has shown up in simpler, better, cleaner standards for the Web services form of middleware.

CPS   Certificate Practice Statement. A CPS is a formal statement by a certificate authority (CA) about its processes such that a relying party can determine what level of trust to place in certificates signed by this CA. The CA can be thought of as a digital notary. A user's identity is based on the assurance (honesty) of the notary. A certificate policy specifies the levels of assurance the PKI has to provide, and the Certificate Practice Statement (CPS) specifies the mechanisms and procedures to be used to achieve a level of assurance.

CRL   Certificate revocation list. Authentication of clients and servers requires a way to verify each certificate within the chain, as well as a way to determine whether a certificate is valid or revoked. A certificate could be revoked if a key is compromised or lost

or because of modification of privileges, misuse, or termination. The most commonly used method of certificate revocation is through a CRL that a CA publishes in a well-known place.

Cross certification   CAs certify each other to establish lateral trust relationships and also issue cross-certificates to represent these trust relationships. The idea is that another CA has performed the identification procedure on an individual who is otherwise a total stranger to your CA and all organizations yours serves. But the two CAs have agreed that their processes are in lock-step and agree to cross-certify each other's certificates. Because Web services will cross many trust domain boundaries and therefore cross between CA domains as well, cross certification will be critical for Web services trust.

Cryptanalysis   The art and science of breaking ciphertext—that is, seeing through the disguise placed on plaintext to make it indecipherable. Cryptanalysis is part of a branch of mathematics called cryptology.

Cryptography   The art and science of keeping messages secure and secret. It is practiced by cryptographers. Like cryptanalysis, cryptography is part of the branch of mathematics called cryptology. Algorithms such as 3DES, AES, and RSA all came out of this branch of mathematics.

DCE   Distributed Computing Environment. An effort to standardize various competing RPC technologies. DCE was driven by the Open Group—a consortium of otherwise competing companies. The goal was distributed applications across heterogeneous systems. DCE was implemented as a set of software services that reside on top of the operating system. It was middleware that used lower-level OS and network resources. DCE broke ground on major distributed applications and formed the knowledge base from which Web services evolved.

DCOM   Distributed Component Object Model. Microsoft took its COM and extended it to allow applications to be built from COM objects that resided in different networked machines. This was Win32 platform specific. DCOM was complex, fine-grained, and proprietary, but not scalable; however, it provided a critical foundation that went directly into Microsoft's .NET Web services.

Decryption   The process of turning ciphertext back into plaintext. The algorithms for encryption and decryption require a key, which is a special numeric value that is required as a parameter for the algorithm to perform its task. The wrong key will get garbage out, not the correct output. Algorithms for encryption and decryption do not need to be and normally are not kept secret. It is the key that is kept secret.

Denial of Service   Also known as DoS, an attack that disrupts the availability of systems and transmissions. If a system is made unavailable because it is so busy responding to a threat, a complete disruption of its intended purpose occurs. Intrusion detection systems and firewall configurations help stop DoS at the Web service endpoints.

Deployment descriptor   Specific to J2EE, necessary to deploy J2EE applications. All information about deployment of the application is contained in one XML deployment descriptor. The deployment descriptor specifies all EJB components, Web components, and client components, and it is the place where security roles are defined. The deployment descriptor is created and modified during the life cycle of a J2EE Web service's development.

DES and 3DES   Data Encryption Standard and Triple-DES. DES is 25 years old; it was designed (and adapted over the years) to work really well in hardware. DES uses a 64-bit key, 56 effective bits, and 8 for parity; plus, it operates on an 8-byte fixed-size block. Due to the fact that 2^{56} possible keys made plain DES susceptible to a brute-force attack, the DES algorithm is run three times with a much longer key in 3DES. Triple-DES (3DES) uses a 192-bit key, of which 168 bits is the effective key length. The idea is to use DES three times: Encrypt-Decrypt-Encrypt. This makes 3DES very secure and, on hardware, very fast.

Detached Signature   In XML Signature, a Detached Signature points to an XML element or binary file outside the `<Signature>` element hierarchy. The item being pointed to is neither parent nor child. This allows XML Signature to provide for integrity of completely external objects such as Web pages or binary files.

Digital certificate   X.509 digital certificates are containers for public keys. Distribution of public keys is so important they needed containers; public authorities (certificate authorities) verify they are accurate; and a substantial infrastructure called Public Key Infrastructure creates, maintains, and administers them.

Digital enveloping   Also known as *key transport*. It combines digital signature concepts and XML Encryption to encrypt the encryption key with the public key of a specific recipient and put it into the `KeyInfo/EncryptedKey` block. The idea is to take advantage of the speed and unlimited plaintext size that can be encrypted with the key management capability of public key techology.

Digital signature   An electronic signature that can be used to authenticate the identity of a message's sender or of a document's signer. It delivers the core security principle of integrity by ensuring that the original content of the message or document that has been conveyed is unchanged. Digital signature involves a one-way mathematical function called hashing and uses public key (asymmetric) encryption. The basic idea is to create a hashed message digest and then to encrypt that.

DIME   Direct Internet Message Encapsulation, an IETF draft specification in progress. A format that enables binary encapsulation of messages. DIME is used to combine entries and data packages of different types and sizes that originate from applications into a single message construction. DIME is meant to address issues that MIME has with speed and efficiency, especially for large attachments.

Distributed computing   An approach to computer-to-computer communication that separates an application into units that are executed on different computers and communicate through a network. The means of communication— frequently euphemistically referred to as *plumbing*—is called middleware. Web services are distributed computing based on Web technologies.

Document/literal   One of the two modes of interaction SOAP supports, the other being RPC/encoded. Document/literal supports a more loosely coupled approach. Document communications tend to be asynchronous and coarse-grained, making them suitable for inter-organization (for example, B2B) integrations.

DOM   Document Object Model. A standardized XML API that allows XML documents to be created and modified as if they were program objects. DOM makes the elements of these documents available to a program as data structures and supplies methods that may be invoked to perform common operations upon the document's structure and data. DOM is both platform- and language-neutral and is a standard of the World Wide Web Consortium (W3C).

DSA   Digital Signature Algorithm. A public key algorithm used as part of the Digital Signature Standard (DSS). DSA cannot be used for encryption, only for digital signatures. It is part of the required set of supported algorithms for XML Signature and therefore for WS-Security.

DTD   Document Type Definition. The Schema specification method for SGML and XML documents. DTDs are either contained in the document or belong to its external subset and are then referenced from within the document's document type declaration per URI. For XML, DTDs have now been replaced by the newer XML Schema specification method.

EAI   Enterprise Application Integration. A comprehensive framework for integrating multiple application systems. The merging of applications and data from various new and legacy systems within a business. Various means are employed to accomplish this, including middleware, to unify IT resources, maximize new IT investments, diminish errors, and more. XML and Web services are now added to the set of tools used to accomplish EAI.

EbXML   Electronic Business using Extensible Markup Language. A standard XML-based Web services framework designed to support B2B integration. It greatly expands the power of electronic data interchange (EDI) on which it was based. It was a joint effort of OASIS and UN/CEFACT.

EDI   Electronic Data Interchange. A standard format for exchanging business data and documents (purchase orders, invoices, payments, inventory analyses, and others). EDI is an older version of electronic commerce between buyers and suppliers that is more cumbersome and costly than Internet-based commerce and therefore feasible only for large companies and their most significant trading partners.

Encryption   The conversion (scrambling) of data, using a mathematical algorithm, into a form that cannot be read by unauthorized users. Encryption ensures message confidentiality. Authorized users need a decryption key to unscramble the information. There are different strengths of data encryption, determined by the algorithm used and the length (in bits) of the key used.

Enveloped Signature   An Enveloped Signature in XML Signature is one where the <Signature> element is a descendent of the resource being signed. In other words, the reference points to a parent XML element.

Federal Bridge   A non-hierarchical "hub" that is designed to permit disparate agency public key infrastructures to interoperate seamlessly. In essence, the Federal Bridge allows one recipient to accept with confidence the sender's electronic credential even when identification was done by another member of the Federal Bridge system.

Federated identity   A single identity credential that can map to identity information on different systems within a circle of trust. This enables single sign-on across security domains. Partners in a federated identity network depend on each other to authenticate their respective users and vouch for their access to services. This is the basic premise of the Liberty Alliance.

Federated trust   Related to federated identity, federated trust involves the federation of security credentials (SAML) to allow businesses to securely integrate their networks with those of their customers, partners, employees, and suppliers.

Hash   A one-way mathematical function that creates a unique fixed-size message digest from an arbitrary size text message. One-way means that you can never take the hash value and re-create the original message. Hash functions are designed to be very fast and are good at never creating the same result value from two different messages (they avoid collisions). A digital signature is the encryption of the hashed message digest of the document to be signed.

HMAC   Hashed Message Authentication Code. A key-dependent one-way hash function. Only someone with the identical key can verify the hash. Hashing is a very fast operation, so HMAC is a fast way to guarantee message integrity when secrecy and non-repudiation are not important but speed is.

HTTP   Hypertext Transfer Protocol. An IETF standard protocol for distributed, collaborative, hypermedia information systems. HTTP is the protocol that Web browsers use to communicate with Web servers, and it is the first and most common protocol used by Web services.

Identification   A process through which a user ascertains the identity of a person or entity; a process that results in stored shared secrets that later are used in the authentication process in the form of a challenge that must be met correctly for successful authentication.

Identity   An individual or an entity that might be an organization or a machine that is part of an organization. Establishing identity is a critical prerequisite to determining the legitimate actions this identity may perform. Identity is initially established and verified in some trust domain by some third party resulting in credentials. A core concept for SAML.

IDL   Interface Description Language. A machine-readable language for defining interfaces enabling communication between computing systems independent of implementation language. Used in one form or another in all types of middleware such as DCE and CORBA. The Web services replacement for IDL is WSDL.

IETF   Internet Engineering Task Force. The IETF is a large, open international community of network designers, operators, vendors, and researchers concerned with the evolution of the Internet architecture and the smooth operation of the Internet. Responsible for TCP/IP, DNS, SSL/TLS, HTTP, SMTP, and FTP. Collaborates with NIST on security.

IIOP   Internet Inter-ORB (Object Request Broker) Protocol. An object-oriented protocol that allows distributed programs written in different programming languages to communicate over the Internet. IIOP is a critical part of CORBA and formed part of the backdrop for how Web services standards and protocols evolved.

Integrity   The ability to detect any modification to a message from when it was initially sent to when it is received. One of the core message-level security foundational elements that is addressed through digital signatures which encrypt a message and attach its hashed message digest to the original plaintext message before it is sent.

Intermediary   A Web services component that lies between the service requester and the service provider. It intercepts the request from the requester, provides the service (functionality), and forwards the request to the service provider. Similarly, it intercepts the response from the service provider and forwards it to the requester.

JAX-RPC   Java APIs for XML-based RPC. A WSDL-aware RPC-style Java API for SOAP. JAX-RPC makes SOAP look and feel like RMI. JAX-RPC is the J2EE standard way to insert a message-observing component into the J2EE server sending and receiving XML that is critical to Web service and XML communication monitoring and analysis.

J2EE   Java 2 Enterprise Edition. A Java-based, runtime platform created by Sun used for developing, deploying, and managing multi-tier server-centric applications on an enterprisewide scale. J2EE is the Java framework to use when building Web services in Java much as .NET is the Microsoft framework to use when building Web services for Windows.

Kerberos   An authentication protocol first developed at MIT and standardized by OSF. It is the primary authentication mechanism used in Windows. A Kerberos authentication token is called a ticket. Kerberos is an alternative approach to shared keys useful only in a closed environment. Its importance to Web Services Security is that when services cross organization boundaries and therefore cross trust domains, provisions have to be made to map between Kerberos and other trust environments.

Key escrow   Key escrow is a very important and controversial aspect of PKI. Key escrow is about storage and retrieval of private keys to recover data in the absence of the private key owner. Key escrow goes against the idea of a private key. Requirements for key escrow/recovery systems may come from customer support, or legal or policy requirements. International PKI implementations may require key escrow to comply with government and law enforcement restrictions.

Key transport   See **digital enveloping**.

Key wrapping   The digital enveloping strategy used in WS-Security whereby the shared (symmetric) key to be used for XML Encryption is wrapped by the public key of the recipient and is placed in the WS-Security header.

Liberty Alliance   A project developing a set of standards that allow you to use an SAML authentication assertion across multiple security domains. The Liberty federated identity infrastructure allows you to create a circle of trust with your affiliates. Although each member of this circle maintains and protects his or her unique user information, a single federated identity credential can be used as proof of authentication with all members of the circle.

Man-in-the-middle   A dangerous type of attack in which an attacker intercepts all the communications between two parties, making each think that it is communicating with the other. The SSL/TLS protocol was specifically designed to protect against this attack and is the reason SSL should always be used in point-to-point Web services connections.

MD5 Message Digest 5 (after MD1–4 were improved upon). A one-way message-digest hash function. It processes input text and creates a 128-bit message digest that is unique to the message and can be used to verify data integrity. MD5, developed by Ron Rivest, is intended to be used in digital signature applications. Earlier message digest algorithms include MD2 and MD4. SHA1 is stronger than MD5 and is now the recommended choice for digital signature applications.

Message digest Another word for a hash value. The result of running a hash function. It is the message digest that is encrypted to form the basis of a digital signature.

Middleware Software systems that sit between application code and its underlying platform, providing easy access to core system facilities such as the network, storage, and processors. Web services add a set of core standards and protocols to the existing Web technologies to create middleware for the Internet.

MIME Multipurpose Internet Mail Extensions. A specification defined in 1992 by the Internet Engineering Task Force (IETF) for formatting and attaching non-ASCII messages so that they can be sent over the Internet. Broadly used in email systems, enabling them to send and receive graphics, audio, and video attachments. Web browsers also support various MIME types. SOAP Messages with Attachments propose MIME as an approach for handling attachments to SOAP messages.

.NET A huge initiative and set of technologies from Microsoft that the company considers its "platform for the digital future." The most important aspect of .NET for the subject of this book is XML Web services. .NET includes the .NET Framework, Visual Studio .NET, .NET My Services, and a set of .NET Enterprise Servers. Microsoft has developed new languages to support these efforts (C# and J#) and has fully endorsed XML to the extent that even the Office Suite tools generate and consume XML.

Nonce An arbitrary set of random bytes generated on the client side that helps prevent replay attacks as well as adding entropy to the resulting password digest. It is used to deal with the issue of a password being passed in the clear.

Non-repudiation The assurance that the sender is provided with proof of delivery and that the recipient is provided with proof of the sender's identity so that neither can later deny having processed the data. Digital signature supports non-repudiation.

OASIS Organization for the Advancement of Structured Information Standards. A consortium that develops standards for Web services and e-business including SAML, WS-Security, ebXML and XACML. At http://www. oasis-open.org.

OCSP Online Certificate Status Protocol. Used to provide real-time validation of a digital certificate's status. An OCSP responder is used to respond to certificate status requests on the basis of CRLs (Certificate Revocation Lists) provided to it by certification authorities. XKMS provides a means to do revocation and status checks on certificates as a Web service.

P3P   Platform for Privacy Preferences Project. A project of the World Wide Web Consortium (W3C) that provides an easy way to learn about and react to the way Web sites may be using personal information. P3P is forming the framework on which WS-Privacy is being developed.

Passport   Microsoft's approach to single sign-on. Consumers are asked to store commonly used personal information in a Passport profile stored at a Microsoft data center. This information can be transmitted after authentication to any participating site. One clear benefit it has is the elimination of the proliferation of dozens of passwords that just causes password security to degrade. Detractors are concerned about concentrating more power over consumers in the hands of a central dominating company.

Payload   Information contained in the SOAP body. This information is being sent from one application to another. It might be a full document such as a purchase order or contract. Or it might be a description of remote procedure call information, including the methods to call and the parameters to those method calls.

PGP   Pretty Good Privacy. Invented by Philip Zimmerman, PGP uses symmetric key encryption and the RSA algorithm with keys up to 2047 for key management and digital signatures. Its one-way hash algorithm is MD5. PGP encrypts a user's private key using a hashed passphrase instead of a password. PGP uses a distributed key management scheme with no certification authorities. The concept is instead a "Web of Trust";

this is symbiotic with the fundamental nature of the Internet. PGP is one of the authentication methods supported by SAML.

PKCS   Public Key Cryptography Standards. A set of inter-vendor standard protocols for making possible secure information exchange on the Internet using a Public Key Infrastructure (PKI). Interactions with certificate authorities are among the most common usage of PKCS standards. For example, PKCS#10 is the certification request standard. PKCS#12 is the way private key information is stored.

PKI   Public Key Infrastructure. A security infrastructure for the Internet designed by the IETF to ensure that, for an online transaction, the person is who she says she is and that no one else has access to the information. Under PKI, a digital certificate is generated by a trusted third party certificate authority (CA) and verified by a registration authority (RA). This digital certificate is a unique electronic credential used to generate personalized encryption keys.

Plaintext   A message that is completely readable and is in no way scrambled or disguised. It is the input to an encryption algorithm that produces ciphertext and is the output from a decryption algorithm that operates on ciphertext.

Policy Decision Point   A PDP is the part of the SAML infrastructure responsible for making decisions about access control based on one or more parameters. Simple types of access can be granted, or complex conditional access such as a specific group on a specific day at a specific time can be granted access. PDPs can be implemented using XACML.

Policy Enforcement Point   A PEP is part of the SAML infrastructure responsible for policy enforcement. A PEP makes a connection to the appropriate PDP for the decision. The policy function is evaluated with data supplied from the PEP to the PDP.

Policy Retrieval Point   A PRP is an optional part of the SAML infrastructure. One is required if the PDP is external to the system, in which case the PDP uses the PRP to retrieve policies for the decisions it is required to make.

Port   The WSDL *where* part. A WSDL element that defines the endpoint of a Web service implementation. The Web service implements a specific binding of a portType.

Portable identity   The identity of valid users must move around when information moves from one trust domain to another, so portable trust was an early requirement for Web Services Security.

Portal   An integrated and personalized Web-based interface to information, applications, and collaborative services. Access to most portals is limited to corporate employees (an intracompany portal) or corporate employees and certain qualified vendors, contractors, customers, and other parties within the extended enterprise (an intercompany portal).

POST/GET   The normal mode of operation for HTTP when interacting with Web sites. The almost desperate use of HTTP POST as an integration scheme for Web-based applications foretold the need

for Web services. Using this approach, one site that had a Web application accessed by humans through browsers could be integrated into another site's Web application by posting all the interactions necessary to "fool" the service-provider site into thinking a browser was interacting with it. When bound to HTTP as the transport protocol, SOAP uses POST/GET as its communication mechanism.

Private key   Public key systems work with paired keys, one of which (the private key) is kept strictly private and the other (the public key) is freely distributed. It is vital for trust in signed or encrypted communications that the *private* key never leaves the possession of its creator.

Proof of possession   For authentication, public key technology depends on the notion of *something you have,* which is the private key. In the case of an X.509 certificate, proof of possession means a digital signature, and in the case of WS-Security, it means an XML Signature. This proves that the sender has possession of the private key matching the public key you rely on.

Protocol   A set of standardized rules for exchanging information among computers. Different protocols are used for different kinds of communication. HTTP is a transport protocol used by SOAP. SOAP is a message-level protocol used by Web services. SAML includes protocols to communicate with SAML authorities. XKMS includes protocols to communicate with security token services.

Proxy   An intermediary application that acts as a liaison between a client and a server. In Web services, a client proxy is a communications routine, generated from a WSDL file that a client application uses to invoke a service. Proxies are also used to intercept Web services messages to perform various security or management functions.

Public key   Public key encryption is the way you deliver integrity, non-repudiation, and authentication to XML messages and to Web services. Public key encryption is also referred to as *asymmetric encryption* because there are two different but matched keys: Whichever one is used to encrypt requires the other be used to decrypt.

Registration authority   An entity that is responsible for identification and authentication of certificate subjects but that does not sign or issue certificates (that is, an RA is delegated certain tasks on behalf of a CA).

Relying party   A person or agency that has received information including a certificate and a digital signature verifiable with reference to a public key listed in the certificate, and is in a position to rely on them. The relying party relies on the validity of the binding of the subscriber's name to a public key. The relying party is responsible for deciding whether or how to check the validity of the certificate by checking the appropriate certificate status information. The relying party can use the certificate to verify the integrity of a digitally signed message to identify the creator of the message or to establish confidential

communications with the holder of the certificate. A relying party may use information in the certificate to determine the suitability of the certificate for a particular use. The relying party is the owner of the application.

Replay attack   When an attacker gains access to authentication information of an authorized entity that is then used to falsely gain access to a network or application. WS-Security includes facilities designed to help thwart replay attacks such as the inclusion of a time stamp in a `UserNameToken`.

Revocation   The process of changing the status of a certificate from valid or suspended to revoked. The status of a certificate as revoked means that it should no longer be relied upon by any entity for whatever purpose. Revocation checking has been problematic in PKI systems. XKMS provides facilities for revocation checking.

Rights management   Access control, which is often called *rights management*, determines who can look at something, what they can do with it, the type of device they can use to look at it, the conditions of their access, and the time frame in which it will be allowed. XACML and XrML are two XML standards that deal with rights management.

RMI   Remote Method Invocation. Java-based technology that allows Java programs to access the objects of another Java program running on a different computer.

Root CA   A CA must be trusted or vouched for by someone who is trusted. A root CA is trusted by everyone. Root CAs have their public key embedded in common tools (such as servers and browsers) that other CAs link to in certificate chains.

RPC   Remote procedure call. A middleware system that uses a synchronous, client/server-based style of communication. A client uses RPC to invoke a procedure to be executed on a remote, networked system. RPC makes the remote procedure appear as if it were local.

RPC/encoded   A constrained way to structure SOAP messages to simulate an RPC request. The request message contains a method name and the parameters needed to execute the method call. The response message contains the result of the remotely executed method.

RSA   Rivest, Shamir, and Adelman are the inventors of a public key cipher that can be used both for encrypting messages and making digital signatures. The company the inventors founded—RSA Data Security Inc.—takes its name from this algorithm.

SAML   Security Assertion Markup Language. An XML framework for exchanging authentication and authorization information. The basis for portable identity. One of the WS-Security recognized security token types.

SAML authorities   SAML defines a set of assertions, a protocol, and a set of bindings. The SAML protocol describes a request/response interaction with SAML authorities for policy decisions and enforcement. They are trusted third parties such as certificate authorities.

SAML profile   An SAML profile describes how SAML assertions are embedded into and extracted from a framework or protocol. SAML profiles are like documented processes that define patterns of SAML usage needed to secure a resource. Profiles have been defined for browsers, for securing SOAP, for WS-Security as part of the WS-Security specification, and for Liberty Alliance.

SAX   Simple API for XML. An event-driven interface in which the parser invokes one of several methods supplied by the caller when a parsing event occurs, such as recognizing an XML tag, finding an error, encountering a reference to an external entity, or processing a DTD specification.

Security token   Pieces of information used for authentication or authorization added to a SOAP header. WS-Security starts with XML security and combines it with pre-existing security technologies (such as X.509, Kerberos, and others), which it then binds to SOAP using constructs called security tokens. Examples of security tokens are usernames/passwords, X.509 digital certificates, SAML assertions, and Kerberos tickets.

Security Token Service   An STS forms the basis of trust by issuing security tokens that can be used to broker trust relationships between different trust domains. An STS provides a Web service with a way to determine whether it will trust an incoming request from a different (possibly unknown) trust domain. WS-Trust defines how an STS works. WS-Policy allows a Web service to specify what it requires from an STS for incoming requests.

Serialization   In RPC mode, an important function of SOAP is a set of encoding rules that define a serialization mechanism that creates a standard way of capturing programming language data elements such as integers, strings, and complex structures in a language-neutral, interoperable format. The result is a remote procedure call expressed in XML and serialized by SOAP over HTTP.

Service-oriented architecture   An architectural approach for linking resources on demand. In an SOA, resources are made available to other participants in the network as independent services that are accessed in a standardized way. This provides for more flexible loose coupling of resources. An SOA defines mechanisms for describing services, advertising and discovering services, and communicating with services. Most RPC-based middleware—including Web services—uses SOA.

Servlet   A server-based Java applet that operates in conjunction with a Web server and offers an alternative to using Common Gateway Interface (CGI) to communicate with Web server processes. A WSDL file describes *where* a service resides through a specific URL address that in many cases will be a servlet that processes incoming Web Service requests.

SGML   Standard Generalized Markup Language. SGML is a 1986 ISO standard indicating how to specify a document markup language or tag set. SGML is not in itself a document language, but a metalanguage for how to specify one. HTML and XML are examples of SGML-based languages.

SHA1   Secure Hash Algorithm 1 (1 because of an understanding that there will someday be a 2). Developed by NIST and NSA, it has superceded MD5 (which had weaknesses) as the preferred hash algorithm used in digital signatures.

Shared key   Also known as symmetric key or secret key. The sender and recipient both have the same key used for encrypting and decrypting a confidential message. It is the basis for XML Encryption and SSL.

Shared secret   Information representing *something you know* communicated between two parties at identification time. The shared secret is later used for authentication to prove that a digital identity maps to a known physical identity. Checking shared secrets is typically done in a challenge-response mode, as in "what is your mother's maiden name" and is best combined with another authentication factor such as *something you have* or *something you are*.

Signature transform   A signature transform provides the essential capability of being selective about the data within a message that is being signed while still including mutable information in the signature itself. Signature transforms work like a waterfall with one's input being the output of the previous transform. Types of signature transforms that can be applied include canonicalization, Base-64 decoding, XPATH filtering, XSLT transform, and enveloped transform. An important practical use of signature transform is in a legal document that needs multiple digital signatures.

Signature verification   An important procedure a signed message recipient must perform to confirm that the `<SignedInfo>` element in an XML Signature has not been changed, can prove integrity, and that the appropriate key has signed this information, which proves non-repudiation.

Single sign-on   Allows a user to log in once with a recognized security authority and use the returned login credentials to access multiple resources. Microsoft's Passport and the Liberty Alliance were motivated by the need for SSO, especially with Web services. The Web services security standard for SSO is SAML.

SOA   See **Service-oriented architecture**.

SOAP   The standard for Web services messages. Based on XML, SOAP defines an envelope format and various rules for describing its contents. Seen (with WSDL and UDDI) as one of the three foundation standards of Web services, it is the preferred protocol for exchanging Web services messages.

SSL   Secure Socket Layer. Invented by Netscape and then renamed Transaction Layer Security (TLS) when it was turned over to IETF. Most commonly used for browser-to-server security for e-commerce. SSL is effective at maintaining confidentiality of transactions and will be broadly useful for Web services point-to-point security.

Super encryption   In XML Encryption, using an `<EncryptedData>` element to encrypt other `<EncryptedData>` elements is called *super*

encryption. This capability is useful when you have a confidential document with multiple recipients involved.

Symmetric encryption   When the same key is used to both encrypt and decrypt the message. This key must be kept secret from all non-intended parties to keep the encrypted message secret.

Symmetric key   See **shared key**.

Time stamp   When WS-Security is used with a username/password security token, a time stamp is added to create "freshness" constraints on messages to defend against replay attacks.

Transport Layer Security (TLS)   See **SSL**.

Trust assertions   In SAML, a claim, statement or declaration of fact (according to someone) specifying authentication, authorization, or attributes.

Trust domain   One organization or entity that operates with a consistent set of policies and certification practice statements used to establish identity and what those identities are allowed to do.

Two-factor authentication Combining two of the three authentication schemes—*something you have, something you are*, and *something you know*—to increase the level of trust in the result.

UDDI   Universal Description, Discovery, and Integration. An OASIS standard for a registry of Web services. A UDDI registry is a Web service that manages information about service types and service providers.

URI   Uniform resource identifier. The address of an Internet resource. A URI is the unique name used to access the resource. It is not necessarily a specific file location (it may be a call to an application or a database, for example), which is why it is preferred over the similar acronym URL.

URL   Uniform resource locator. The global address of resources on the Internet. Relating it to URI, URL substitutes *locator* for *identifier* and is a URI that is bound to a physical network address.

URN   Uniform resource name. A URI that is simply a name. It cannot be dereferenced. Used for namespaces in XML documents. A URI with a DNS registered hostname is guaranteed to be unique across the entire Internet.

W3C   World Wide Web Consortium. A consortium that develops standards for the World Wide Web, including HTML, XML, SOAP, and many other technologies.

Web service   An application that provides a Web API. A Web service is a software application identified by a URI, whose interfaces and bindings are capable of being defined, described, and discovered as XML artifacts. A Web service supports direct interactions with other software agents using XML-based messages exchanged via Internet-based protocols.

WebTrust   WebTrust for CAs is an audit process defined by the Association of Independent Certified Public Accountants (AICPA) that independently audits each CA to assess whether it meets a minimum standard for disclosures, policies, practices, and monitoring procedures.

WS-Authorization   A to-be-published specification that will define how authorization decisions are made in the context of Web services. Very similar in objectives to XACML, it will be heavily influenced by it.

WSDL   Web Services Description Language. An XML format to describe the various network services and associated parameters and data types hosted by a system. A WSDL file tells a client what SOAP services are available and how to use them.

WS-Federation   A to-be-published specification that will describe how to manage and broker the trust relationships in a heterogeneous federated Web services environment. It is built out of WS-Security plus WS-Policy plus WS-Trust plus WS-SecureConversation.

WS-Policy   Provides a general-purpose model and syntax to describe and communicate the policies of a Web service. It defines a base set of constructs that can be used and extended by other Web services specifications to describe a broad range of service requirements, preferences, and capabilities. The goal is a common language for describing the rules for interacting with a Web service, or what a client requires of a Web service, regardless of whether the domain is security, privacy, transactions, or any other category.

WS–PolicyAssertions Defines a set of common policy assertions that are applicable across all Web services. Included are what character sets are supported, what languages are supported, what specification versions are supported, and required message predicates.

WS–PolicyAttachments Defines how policies are attached to a resource. One way is through additions to WSDL (but Web service clients do not have WSDLs), and the other way is to have the policy stand alone and point to the Web service with which it is associated.

WS–Privacy A to-be-published specification that will establish a set of policies to be enforced on Web service endpoints with rules for dealing with personally identifiable information about human participants. It is built on WS-Policy plus WS-Trust plus WS-Security.

WS–SecureConversation Establishes a mutually authenticated security context in which a series of messages are exchanged. WS-SecureConversation does at the SOAP layer what SSL does at the transport layer. WS-SecureConversation uses asymmetric encryption to establish a shared secret key and from then on uses symmetric encryption for efficiency.

WS–Security The Web Services Security extension is a set of optional SOAP features. It includes XML Signature, which is used to sign XML data to provide integrity and origin. It also includes XML Encryption, which is used to encrypt XML data to provide confidentiality. Numerous security tokens are supported in WS-Security, allowing portable identity (SAML), public key

transport (X.509), rights management information (XrML), and others.

WS–SecurityPolicy Provides a set of WS-Security–specific policy assertions used to publish information about all aspects of WS-Security. It is built out of WS-Policy plus WS-PolicyAssertions plus WS-PolicyAttachments.

WS–Trust Defines extensions to WS-Security that provide methods for issuing and exchanging security tokens, and ways to establish and access the presence of trust relationships. Most importantly, WS-Trust defines a request/response mechanism for obtaining security tokens from a Security Token Service.

X.509 Part of International Telecommunications Union-T X.500 specification that defines a framework to provide and support data origin authentication and peer entity authentication services, including formats for X.509 public key certificates, X.509 attribute certificates, and X.509 certificate revocation lists. One of WS-Security's supported security token types.

XACML eXtensible Access Control Markup Language. An OASIS specification for representing authorization and entitlement policies. XACML represents the rules that specify the who, what, when, and how of information access control for *rights management*.

XCBF XML Common Biometric Format. An OASIS specification that defines an XML vocabulary for representing and exchanging biometric information in XML. XCBF tokens are a type of security token supported by WS-Security.

X-KISS   XML Key Information Service Specification. This is the part of the XKMS specification that defines a protocol for *Locate* and *Validate* operations. These operations support the delegation of the processing of key information to a service. Such key information processing might be associated with an XML Signature, XML Encryption, or any other PKI situation.

XKMS   XML Key Management Specification. Allows PKI to operate as a trusted Web service. Consists of two protocols: X-KISS for key validation and X-KRSS for key registration.

X-KRSS   XML Key Registration Service Specification. Part of the XKMS specification that defines a protocol for *Register*, *Recover*, *Revoke*, and *Reissue* operations that support the registration and management of a key pair for use in XML Signature, XML Encryption, or any other PKI situation.

XML   eXtensible Markup Language. A W3C standard data format for electronic documents and messages. It is a self-describing meta-markup language that provides a universal data format that can be interpreted, processed, and transformed by any application running on any platform.

XML Encryption   A W3C standard that defines a process for encrypting and decrypting all or part of an XML document. Uses shared key cryptography to deliver the core security principle of confidentiality. XML Encryption is a fundamental building block for WS-Security.

XML Namespace   A collection of element and attribute names identified by a

URI reference. An XML Namespace prevents collisions between semantically different elements that happen to have the same name in different documents in much the same way a class in C++ or Java keeps the names of local data or methods from colliding with those in other classes.

XML Schema   A W3C standard, XML Schemas are created to define and validate an XML document. Unlike DTD, XML Schema is an XML format itself. XML Schemas describe data types and specify any required ordering of elements. Web services use XML Schema to define the format of communicating XML messages.

XML Signature   A W3C standard that defines a process digitally signing all or part of an XML document. Uses public key cryptography to deliver the core security principles of integrity and non-repudiation. XML Signature is a fundamental building block for WS-Security.

XML-RPC   An XML-based protocol for performing remote procedure calls over HTTP. A precursor to SOAP. XML-RPC is SOAP without the Envelope or Header elements, and restricted to RPC over HTTP.

XPATH   XML Path Language. A standard naming convention for accessing XML elements within a document. Allows for consistent addressing and naming of document elements. XPATH is the result of an effort to provide a common syntax and semantics for functionality shared between XSLT and XPOINTER. XPATH is used in XML Signature to determine exactly what is being signed.

XPOINTER   XML Pointer Language
is a W3C Working Draft. It builds on
XPATH to provide a framework for
addressing the internal structures of XML
documents, such as elements, attributes,
and content.

XQUERY   An SQL-like language covering much the same functionality as
XSLT with a data-centric transformation
as opposed to a document-centric transformation. Relies on XPATH.

XrML   eXtensible Rights Markup
Language. A universal method for securely specifying and managing rights and
conditions associated with all kinds of
resources, including digital content and
services. Part of the effort to create an
infrastructure to manage digital rights on
copyright and for-fee content that is
moved across the public networks. One
of the supported WS-Security tokens.

XSLT   eXtensible Stylesheet Language
Transformations. XSL is the language
used to define how XML elements are to
be displayed and presented, and XSLT is
the use of the XSL language to transform
XML data into specific output, such as
HTML.

Index

F–G–H

I

Your Guide to Computer Technology

www.informit.com

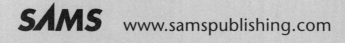

Related Titles from Sams Publishing

J2EE Developer's Handbook

Paul Perrone, et al
ISBN: 0-672-32348-6
$59.99 US
Build enterprise Java systems with J2EE 1.4

Covert Java

Alex Kalinovsky
ISBN: 0-672-32638-8
$34.99 US
Decompile and reverse-engineer to solve unsurpassable problems

ASP.NET Unleashed, Second Edition

Stephen Walther
ISBN: 0-672-32542-X
$54.99 US
Take full advantage of the next generation of Active Server Pages

---

Building Web Services with Java, Second Edition
Steve Graham, et al
ISBN: 0-672-32641-8 • $49.99 US

BEA WebLogic Server 8.1 Unleashed
Mark Artiges, et al
ISBN: 0-672-32487-3 • $59.99 US

Struts Kick Start
James Turner and Kevin Bedell
ISBN: 0-672-32472-5 • $34.99 US

Extreme Programming with Ant
Jeremy Poteet and Glenn Niemeyer
ISBN: 0-672-32562-4 • $34.99 US

Microsoft Visual Basic .NET 2003 Kick Start
Duncan Mackenzie, et al
ISBN: 0-672-32549-7 • $34.99 US

XQuery Kick Start
James McGovern, et al
ISBN: 0-672-32479-2 • $34.99 US

XPath Kick Start: Navigating XML with XPath 1.0 and 2.0
Steven Holzner
ISBN: 0-672-32441-3 • $34.99 US

JavaServer Pages Developer's Handbook
Nick Todd and Mark Szolkowski
ISBN: 0-672-32438-5 • $49.99 US

Microsoft .NET Kick Start
Hitesh Seth
ISBN: 0-672-32574-8 • $34.99 US

BEA WebLogic Workshop 8.1 Kick Start
Al Saganich, et al
ISBN: 0-672-32622-1 • $34.99 US

Microsoft Visual C++ .NET 2003 Kick Start
Kate Gregory
ISBN: 0-672-32600-0 • $34.99 US

All prices are subject to change.

www.samspublishing.com